T5-ARW-407

CRIMINAL JUSTICE 95/96

Nineteenth Edition

Editor

John J. Sullivan
Mercy College, Dobbs Ferry, New York

John J. Sullivan, professor and former chair of the
Department of Law, Criminal Justice, and Safety
Administration at Mercy College, received his B.S. in 1949
from Manhattan College and his J.D. in 1956 from St. John's
Law School. He was formerly captain and director of the
Legal Division of the New York City Police Department.

Editor

Joseph L. Victor
Mercy College, Dobbs Ferry, New York

Joseph L. Victor is professor and chairman of the
Department of Law, Criminal Justice, and Safety
Administration at Mercy College. Professor Victor has
extensive field experience in criminal justice agencies,
counseling, and administering human service programs. He
earned his B.A. and M.A. at Seton Hall University, and his
Doctorate of Education at Fairleigh Dickinson University.

Annual Editions
A Library of Information from the Public Press

Cover illustration by Mike Eagle

**Dushkin Publishing Group/
Brown & Benchmark Publishers**
Sluice Dock, Guilford, Connecticut 06437

The Annual Editions Series

Annual Editions is a series of over 65 volumes designed to provide the reader with convenient, low-cost access to a wide range of current, carefully selected articles from some of the most important magazines, newspapers, and journals published today. Annual Editions are updated on an annual basis through a continuous monitoring of over 300 periodical sources. All Annual Editions have a number of features designed to make them particularly useful, including topic guides, annotated tables of contents, unit overviews, and indexes. For the teacher using Annual Editions in the classroom, an Instructor's Resource Guide with test questions is available for each volume.

Printed on Recycled Paper

VOLUMES AVAILABLE

Africa
Aging
American Foreign Policy
American Government
American History, Pre-Civil War
American History, Post-Civil War
Anthropology
Archaeology
Biology
Biopsychology
Business Ethics
Canadian Politics
Child Growth and Development
China
Comparative Politics
Computers in Education
Computers in Business
Computers in Society
Criminal Justice
Developing World
Drugs, Society, and Behavior
Dying, Death, and Bereavement
Early Childhood Education
Economics
Educating Exceptional Children
Education
Educational Psychology
Environment
Geography
Global Issues
Health
Human Development
Human Resources
Human Sexuality
India and South Asia

International Business
Japan and the Pacific Rim
Latin America
Life Management
Macroeconomics
Management
Marketing
Marriage and Family
Mass Media
Microeconomics
Middle East and the Islamic World
Money and Banking
Multicultural Education
Nutrition
Personal Growth and Behavior
Physical Anthropology
Psychology
Public Administration
Race and Ethnic Relations
Russia, the Eurasian Republics, and
   Central/Eastern Europe
Social Problems
Sociology
State and Local Government
Urban Society
Violence and Terrorism
Western Civilization,
   Pre-Reformation
Western Civilization,
   Post-Reformation
Western Europe
World History, Pre-Modern
World History, Modern
World Politics

Cataloging in Publication Data
Main entry under title: Annual editions: Criminal justice. 1995/96.
   1. Criminal Justice, Administration of—United States—Periodicals.
I. Sullivan, John J., *comp.* II. Victor, Joseph L., *comp.* III. Title: Criminal justice.
HV 8138.A67   364.973.05   77–640116
ISBN: 1–56134–349–8

© 1995 by Dushkin Publishing Group/Brown & Benchmark Publishers, Guilford, CT 06437

Copyright law prohibits the reproduction, storage, or transmission in any form by any means of any portion of this publication without the express written permission of Dushkin Publishing Group/Brown & Benchmark Publishers, and of the copyright holder (if different) of the part of the publication to be reproduced. The Guidelines for Classroom Copying endorsed by Congress explicitly state that unauthorized copying may not be used to create, to replace, or to substitute for anthologies, compilations, or collective works.

Annual Editions® is a Registered Trademark of Dushkin Publishing Group/Brown & Benchmark Publishers, a division of Times Mirror Higher Education Group, Inc.

NineteenthEdition

Printed in the United States of America

Editors/ Advisory Board

EDITORS

John J. Sullivan
Mercy College, Dobbs Ferry

Joseph L. Victor
Mercy College, Dobbs Ferry

ADVISORY BOARD

Harry Babb
SUNY College, Farmingdale

Peter Chimbos
University of Western Ontario

Joseph DeSanto
Iona College

Helen Taylor Greene
Old Dominion University

R. A. Helgemoe
University of New Hampshire

K. C. Hollington
Mount Royal College

Patrick J. Hopkins
Harrisburg Area Community
College

Paul Lang, Jr.
Radford University

Michael Langer
Loyola University

Moses Leon
Pima Community College

Matthew C. Leone
University of Nevada
Reno

Robert J. McCormack
Trenton State College

John J. McGrath
Mercy College, Dobbs Ferry

Stephen O'Brien
Macomb Community College

Barbara Raffel Price
John Jay College
of Criminal Justice

Sue Titus Reid
Florida State University

Dinah Robinson
Auburn University

George Rush
California State University
Long Beach

Leslie Samuelson
University of Saskatchewan

Linda Stabile
Prince George's
Community College

David Struckhoff
Loyola University

Ken Venters
University of Tennessee

STAFF

Ian A. Nielsen, Publisher
Brenda S. Filley, Production Manager
Roberta Monaco, Editor
Addie Raucci, Administrative Editor
Cheryl Greenleaf, Permissions Editor
Deanna Herrschaft, Permissions Assistant
Diane Barker, Proofreader
Lisa Holmes-Doebrick, Administrative Coordinator
Charles Vitelli, Designer
Shawn Callahan, Graphics
Steve Shumaker, Graphics
Lara M. Johnson, Graphics
Laura Levine, Graphics
Libra A. Cusack, Typesetting Supervisor
Juliana Arbo, Typesetter

To the Reader

In publishing ANNUAL EDITIONS we recognize the enormous role played by the magazines, newspapers, and journals of the *public press* in providing current, first-rate educational information in a broad spectrum of interest areas. Within the articles, the best scientists, practitioners, researchers, and commentators draw issues into new perspective as accepted theories and viewpoints are called into account by new events, recent discoveries change old facts, and fresh debate breaks out over important controversies.

Many of the articles resulting from this enormous editorial effort are appropriate for students, researchers, and professionals seeking accurate, current material to help bridge the gap between principles and theories and the real world. These articles, however, become more useful for study when those of lasting value are carefully *collected, organized, indexed,* and *reproduced* in a *low-cost format,* which provides easy and permanent access when the material is needed. That is the role played by *Annual Editions.* Under the direction of each volume's *Editor,* who is an expert in the subject area, and with the guidance of an *Advisory Board,* we seek each year to provide in each *ANNUAL EDITION* a current, well-balanced, carefully selected collection of the best of the public press for your study and enjoyment. We think you'll find this volume useful, and we hope you'll take a moment to let us know what you think.

During the 1970s, criminal justice emerged as an appealing, vital, and unique academic discipline. It emphasizes the professional development of students who plan careers in the field and attracts those who want to know more about a complex social problem and how this country deals with it. Criminal justice incorporates a vast range of knowledge from a number of specialties, including law, history, and the behavioral and social sciences. Each specialty contributes to our fuller understanding of criminal behavior and of society's attitudes toward deviance.

In view of the fact that the criminal justice system is in a constant state of flux, and because the study of criminal justice covers such a broad spectrum, today's students must be aware of a variety of subjects and topics. Standard textbooks and traditional anthologies cannot keep pace with the changes as quickly as they occur. In fact, many such sources are already out of date the day they are published. *Annual Editions: Criminal Justice 95/96* strives to maintain currency in matters of concern by providing up-to-date commentaries, articles, reports, and statistics from the most recent literature in the criminal justice field.

This volume contains units concerning crime and justice in America, victimology, the police, the judicial system, juvenile justice, and punishment and corrections. The articles in these units were selected because they are informative as well as provocative. The selections are timely and useful in their treatment of ethics, punishment, juveniles, courts, and other related topics.

Included in this volume are a number of features designed to be useful to students, researchers, and professionals in the criminal justice field. These include a *topic guide* for locating articles on specific subjects; the *table of contents abstracts,* which summarize each article and feature key concepts in bold italics; and a comprehensive *bibliography, glossary,* and *index.* In addition, each unit is preceded by an *overview* that provides a background for informed reading of the articles, emphasizes critical issues, and presents challenge questions.

We would like to know what you think of the selections contained in this edition. Please fill out the article rating form on the last page and let us know your opinions. We change or retain many of the articles based on the comments we receive from you, the user. Help us to improve this anthology—annually.

John J. Sullivan

Joseph L. Victor
Editors

Contents

Unit 1

Crime and Justice in America

Seven selections focus on the overall structure of the criminal justice system in the United States. The current scope of crime in America is reviewed, and topics such as criminal behavior, drugs, and organized crime are discussed.

The concepts in bold italics are developed in the article. For further expansion please refer to the Topic Guide, the Index, and the Glossary.

Unit

Victimology

Seven articles discuss the impact of crime on the victim. Topics include the rights of crime victims and the consequences of family violence, rape, and incest.

The concepts in bold italics are developed in the article. For further expansion please refer to the Topic Guide, the Index, and the Glossary.

Unit 3

Police

Five selections examine the role of the police officer. Some of the topics discussed include the stress of police work, utilization of policewomen, and ethical policing.

The concepts in bold italics are developed in the article. For further expansion please refer to the Topic Guide, the Index, and the Glossary.

Unit 4

The Judicial System

Seven selections discuss the process by which the accused are moved through the judicial system. Prosecutors, courts, the jury process, and judicial ethics are reviewed.

The concepts in bold italics are developed in the article. For further expansion please refer to the Topic Guide, the Index, and the Glossary.

Unit 5

Juvenile Justice

Eight selections review the juvenile justice system. The topics include effective ways to respond to violent juvenile crime, juvenile detention, and children in gangs.

The concepts in bold italics are developed in the article. For further expansion please refer to the Topic Guide, the Index, and the Glossary.

Unit 6

Punishment and Corrections

Eight selections focus on the current state of America's penal system and the effects of sentencing, probation, overcrowding, and capital punishment on criminals.

The concepts in bold italics are developed in the article. For further expansion please refer to the Topic Guide, the Index, and the Glossary.

Charts and Graphs

Topic Guide

This topic guide suggests how the selections in this book relate to topics of traditional concern to students and professionals involved with the study of criminal justice. It is useful for locating articles that relate to each other for reading and research. The guide is arranged alphabetically according to topic. Articles may, of course, treat topics that do not appear in the topic guide. In turn, entries in the topic guide do not necessarily constitute a comprehensive listing of all the contents of each selection.

TOPIC AREA	TREATED IN:	TOPIC AREA	TREATED IN:
Alcohol	7. Drugs, Alcohol and Violence: Joined at the Hip	Criminal Behavior	4. Violence in America 7. Drugs, Alcohol, and Violence: Joined at the Hip
Attitudes	34. American Killers Are Getting Younger	Criminal Justice	1. Overview of the Criminal Justice System 14. Battered Women 20. Abuse of Power in the Prosecutor's Office 21. Trials of the Public Defender
Attorneys	20. Abuse of Power in the Prosecutor's Office 21. Trials of the Public Defender 22. Why Lawyers Lie 26. Jury Consultants: Boon or Bane?		
		Date Rape	7. Drugs, Alcohol, and Violence: Joined at the Hip
Battered Families	10. 'Til Death Do Us Part 11. When Men Hit Women 12. Incest: A Chilling Report 13. Murder Next Door 14. Battered Women	Death Penalty	23. Inside the Mind of the Juror 42. 'This Man Has Expired'
		Defense Counsel	21. Trials of the Public Defender 22. Why Lawyers Lie
Bias	24. Racial, Ethnic, and Gender Bias in the Courts	Delinquency	See Juveniles
Bobbitt, Lorena	25. Fault Lines	Discrimination	16. Police Work from a Woman's Perspective 24. Racial, Ethnic, and Gender Bias in the Courts
Brutality	19. Pepper Spray and In-Custody Deaths		
Child Abuse	7. Drugs, Alcohol and Violence: Joined at the Hip 12. Incest: A Chilling Report	Drugs	7. Drugs, Alcohol, and Violence: Joined at the Hip
Children	See Juveniles	Ethics	20. Abuse of Power in the Prosecutor's Office 22. Why Lawyers Lie
Civilian Review Boards	18. Prof. Carl Klockers		
		Ethnic Considerations	24. Racial, Ethnic, and Gender Bias in the Courts
Community Policing	2. What to Do About Crime 18. Prof Carl Klockers	Family Violence	10. 'Til Death Do Us Part 11. When Men Hit Women 12. Incest: A Chilling Report 14. Battered Women
Constitutional Rights	21. Trials of the Public Defender 22. Why Lawyers Lie		
Consultants	26. Jury Consultants: Boon or Bane?	Force	18. Prof. Carl Klockers 19. Pepper Spray and In-Custody Deaths
Corrections	36. Doing Soft Time 37. Punishment and Prevention 38. . . . And Throw Away the Key 39. Privatizing America's Prisons	Gangs	6. Russian Gangsters
		Gender	24. Racial, Ethnic, and Gender Bias in the Courts
Courts	20. Abuse of Power in the Prosecutor's Office 21. Trials of the Public Defender 23. Inside the Mind of the Juror 24. Racial, Ethnic, and Gender Bias in the Courts 25. Fault Lines 26. Jury Consultants: Boon or Bane? 27. Delinquency Cases in Juvenile Court 33. On the Front Lines	IACP	19. Pepper Spray and In-Custody Deaths
		Incest	12. Incest: A Chilling Report
		Infant Mortality	31. Throw Away the Key
		Judges	30. Juvenile Judges Say: Time to Get Tough 33. On the Front Lines
Crime	1. Overview of the Criminal Justice System 2. What to Do About Crime 9. Crime's Toll on the U.S.	Jury	23. Inside the Mind of the Juror 26. Jury Consultants: Boon or Bane?
Crime Victims	See Victimology	Justice Department	19. Pepper Spray and In-Custody Deaths

Crime and Justice in America

Crime and violence are still major concerns in America. The year 1994 saw real violence brought home to Americans in the celebrated cases involving O. J. Simpson, the Menendez brothers, Lorena Bobbitt, and the tragic deaths of two infants at the hand of their mother in North Carolina. Some of the issues surrounding these cases are discussed in subsequent units of this reader.

In this section, "An Overview of the Criminal Justice System" charts the flow of events in the administration of the criminal justice system. Calls for action to help stem the flow of crime are discussed in "What to Do About Crime" and "Violence in America."

In the second unit article, James Wilson offers some new approaches to dealing with crime (such as expanding police powers to stop and frisk suspects). On the other hand, the last unit article takes a more cautious approach. In "Drugs, Alcohol, and Violence: Joined at the Hip," Joseph Califano discusses the interrelationship of drugs and alcohol with violence. In "The Economics of Crime" the stunning high cost of crime is analyzed.

Organized crime is still an issue to be dealt with. There have been several successful local and federal prosecutions of major organized crime figures in the past, and in "Mob Tightens Secretive Style in Retreat from Prosecutors," we see that, as a result of this relentless pursuit, some mob leaders have sought a more secluded existence. While there might be some reduction of the influence of the traditional Mafia, a new group has arisen to cause concern. A fallout of the Soviet Union breakup is the emergence of a Russian Mafia in this country. There is evidence that crime gangs from Russia are now establishing bases in émigré communities, and "Russian Gangsters in the United States" traces the problem in one New York community.

Looking Ahead: Challenge Questions

Do you agree or disagree with the suggestion that the police be given more power to stop and search people on the streets? Defend your answer.

How do you think members of the Mafia may influence life within your community? Are there any indications of gangs from foreign countries operating in your community?

Describe what you think could be done to control violence in your community, throughout the United States, and throughout the world.

Unit 1

An Overview of the Criminal Justice System

The response to crime is a complex process that involves citizens as well as many agencies, levels, and branches of government

The private sector initiates the response to crime

This first response may come from any part of the private sector: individuals, families, neighborhood associations, business, industry, agriculture, educational institutions, the news media, or any other private service to the public.

It involves crime prevention as well as participation in the criminal justice process once a crime has been committed. Private crime prevention is more than providing private security or burglar alarms or participating in neighborhood watch. It also includes a commitment to stop criminal behavior by not engaging in it or condoning it when it is committed by others.

Citizens take part directly in the criminal justice process by reporting crime to the police, by being a reliable participant (for example, witness, juror) in a criminal proceeding, and by accepting the disposition of the system as just or reasonable. As voters and taxpayers, citizens also participate in criminal justice through the policymaking process that affects how the criminal justice process operates, the resources available to it, and its goals and objectives. At every stage of the process, from the original formulation of objectives to the decision about where to locate jails and prisons and to the reintegration of inmates into society, the private sector has a role to play. Without such involvement, the criminal justice process cannot serve the citizens it is intended to protect.

The government responds to crime through the criminal justice system

We apprehend, try, and punish offenders by means of a loose confederation of agencies at all levels of government. Our American system of justice has evolved from the English

common law into a complex series of procedures and decisions. There is no single criminal justice system in this country. We have many systems that are similar, but individually unique.

Criminal cases may be handled differently in different jurisdictions, but court

decisions based on the due process guarantees of the U.S. Constitution require that specific steps be taken in the administration of criminal justice.

The description of the criminal and juvenile justice systems that follows portrays the most common sequence of events

What is the sequence of events in the criminal justice system?

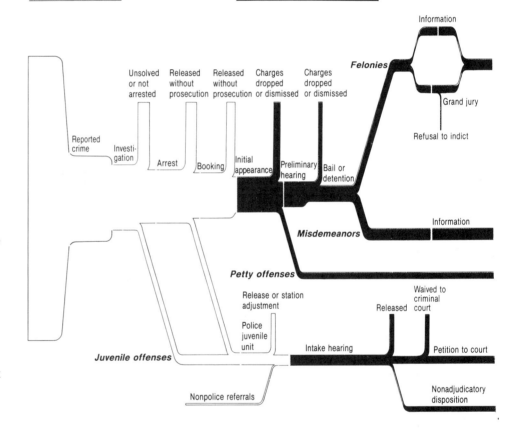

Entry into the system

Prosecution and pretrial services

Note: This chart gives a simplified view of caseflow through the criminal justice system. Procedures vary among jurisdictions. The weights of the lines are not intended to show the actual size of caseloads.

From *Report to the Nation on Crime and Justice,* Bureau of Justice Statistics, U.S. Department of Justice, March 1988, pp. 56-60.

in the response to serious criminal behavior.

Entry into the system

The justice system does not respond to most crime because so much crime is not discovered or reported to the police. Law enforcement agencies learn about crime from the reports of citizens, from discovery by a police officer in the field, or from investigative and intelligence work.

Once a law enforcement agency has established that a crime has been com-

Prosecution and pretrial services

After an arrest, law enforcement agencies present information about the case and about the accused to the prosecutor, who will decide if formal charges will be filed with the court. If no charges are filed, the accused must be released. The prosecutor can also drop charges after making efforts to prosecute (nolle prosequi).

A suspect charged with a crime must be taken before a judge or magistrate

nation of guilt and assessment of a penalty may also occur at this stage.

In some jurisdictions, a pretrial-release decision is made at the initial appearance, but this decision may occur at other hearings or may be changed at another time during the process. Pretrial release and bail were traditionally intended to ensure appearance at trial. However, many jurisdictions permit pretrial detention of defendants accused of serious offenses and deemed to be dangerous to prevent them from committing crimes in the pretrial period. The court may decide to release the accused on his/her own recognizance, into the custody of a third party, on the promise of satisfying certain conditions, or after the posting of a financial bond.

In many jurisdictions, the initial appearance may be followed by a preliminary hearing. The main function of this hearing is to discover if there is probable cause to believe that the accused committed a known crime within the jurisdiction of the court. If the judge does not find probable cause, the case is dismissed; however, if the judge or magistrate finds probable cause for such a belief, or the accused waives his or her right to a preliminary hearing, the case may be bound over to a grand jury.

A grand jury hears evidence against the accused presented by the prosecutor and decides if there is sufficient evidence to cause the accused to be brought to trial. If the grand jury finds sufficient evidence, it submits to the court an indictment (a written statement of the essential facts of the offense charged against the accused). Where the grand jury system is used, the grand jury may also investigate criminal activity generally and issue indictments called grand jury originals that initiate criminal cases.

Misdemeanor cases and some felony cases proceed by the issuance of an information (a formal, written accusation submitted to the court by a prosecutor). In some jurisdictions, indictments may be required in felony cases. However, the accused may choose to waive a grand jury indictment and, instead, accept service of an information for the crime.

Source: Adapted from *The challenge of crime in a free society.*
President's Commission on Law Enforcement and Administration of Justice, 1967.

Adjudication

Once an indictment or information has been filed with the trial court, the accused is scheduled for arraignment. At the arraignment, the accused is informed of the charges, advised of the

mitted, a suspect must be identified and apprehended for the case to proceed through the system. Sometimes, a suspect is apprehended at the scene; however, identification of a suspect sometimes requires an extensive investigation. Often, no one is identified or apprehended.

without unnecessary delay. At the initial appearance, the judge or magistrate informs the accused of the charges and decides whether there is probable cause to detain the accused person. Often, the defense counsel is also assigned at the initial appearance. If the offense is not very serious, the determi-

rights of criminal defendants, and asked to enter a plea to the charges. Sometimes, a plea of guilty is the result of negotiations between the prosecutor and the defendant, with the defendant entering a guilty plea in expectation of reduced charges or a lenient sentence.

If the accused pleads guilty or pleads *nolo contendere* (accepts penalty without admitting guilt), the judge may accept or reject the plea. If the plea is accepted, no trial is held and the offender is sentenced at this proceeding or at a later date. The plea may be rejected if, for example, the judge believes that the accused may have been coerced. If this occurs, the case may proceed to trial.

If the accused pleads not guilty or not guilty by reason of insanity, a date is set for the trial. A person accused of a serious crime is guaranteed a trial by jury. However, the accused may ask for a bench trial where the judge, rather than a jury, serves as the finder of fact. In both instances the prosecution and defense present evidence by questioning witnesses while the judge decides on issues of law. The trial results in acquittal or conviction on the original charges or on lesser included offenses.

After the trial a defendant may request appellate review of the conviction or sentence. In many criminal cases, appeals of a conviction are a matter of right; all States with the death penalty provide for automatic appeal of cases involving a death sentence. However, under some circumstances and in some jurisdictions, appeals may be subject to the discretion of the appellate court and may be granted only on acceptance of a defendant's petition for a *writ of certiorari*. Prisoners may also appeal their sentences through civil rights petitions and writs of habeas corpus where they claim unlawful detention.

Sentencing and sanctions

After a guilty verdict or guilty plea, sentence is imposed. In most cases the judge decides on the sentence, but in some States, the sentence is decided by the jury, particularly for capital offenses such as murder.

In arriving at an appropriate sentence, a sentencing hearing may be held at which evidence of aggravating or mitigating circumstances will be considered. In assessing the circumstances surrounding a convicted person's criminal behavior, courts often rely on presentence investigations by probation

agencies or other designated authorities. Courts may also consider victim impact statements.

The sentencing choices that may be available to judges and juries include one or more of the following:
• the death penalty
• incarceration in a prison, jail, or other confinement facility
• probation—allowing the convicted person to remain at liberty but subject to certain conditions and restrictions
• fines—primarily applied as penalties in minor offenses
• restitution—which requires the offender to provide financial compensation to the victim.

In many States, State law mandates that persons convicted of certain types of offenses serve a prison term.

Most States permit the judge to set the sentence length within certain limits, but some States have determinate sentencing laws that stipulate a specific sentence length, which must be served and cannot be altered by a parole board.

Corrections

Offenders sentenced to incarceration usually serve time in a local jail or a State prison. Offenders sentenced to less than 1 year generally go to jail; those sentenced to more than 1 year go to prison. Persons admitted to a State prison system may be held in prisons with varying levels of custody or in a community correctional facility.

A prisoner may become eligible for parole after serving a specific part of his or her sentence. Parole is the conditional release of a prisoner before the prisoner's full sentence has been served. The decision to grant parole is made by an authority such as a parole board, which has power to grant or revoke parole or to discharge a parolee altogether. The way parole decisions are made varies widely among jurisdictions.

Offenders may also be required to serve out their full sentences prior to release (expiration of term). Those sentenced under determinate sentencing laws can be released only after they have served their full sentence (mandatory release) less any "goodtime" received while in prison. Inmates get such credits against their sentences automatically or by earning it through participation in programs.

If an offender has an outstanding charge or sentence in another State, a

detainer is used to ensure that when released from prison he or she will be transferred to the other State.

If released by a parole board decision or by mandatory release, the releasee will be under the supervision of a parole officer in the community for the balance of his or her unexpired sentence. This supervision is governed by specific conditions of release, and the releasee may be returned to prison for violations of such conditions.

The juvenile justice system

The processing of juvenile offenders is not entirely dissimilar to adult criminal processing, but there are crucial differences in the procedures. Many juveniles are referred to juvenile courts by law enforcement officers, but many others are referred by school officials, social services agencies, neighbors, and even parents, for behavior or conditions that are determined to require intervention by the formal system for social control.

When juveniles are referred to the juvenile courts, their *intake* departments, or prosecuting attorneys, determine whether sufficient grounds exist to warrant filing a petition that requests an *adjudicatory hearing* or a request to transfer jurisdiction to criminal court. In some States and at the Federal level prosecutors under certain circumstances may file criminal charges against juveniles directly in criminal courts.

The court with jurisdiction over juvenile matters may reject the petition or the juveniles may be diverted to other agencies or programs in lieu of further court processing. Examples of diversion programs include individual or group counseling or referral to educational and recreational programs.

If a petition for an adjudicatory hearing is accepted, the juvenile may be brought before a court quite unlike the court with jurisdiction over adult offenders. In disposing of cases juvenile courts usually have far more discretion than adult courts. In addition to such options as probation, commitment to correctional institutions, restitution, or fines, State laws grant juvenile courts the power to order removal of children from their homes to foster homes or treatment facilities. Juvenile courts also may order participation in special programs aimed at shoplifting prevention, drug counseling, or driver education. They also may order referral to criminal court for trial as adults.

Despite the considerable discretion associated with juvenile court proceedings, juveniles are afforded many of the due-process safeguards associated with adult criminal trials. Sixteen States permit the use of juries in juvenile courts; however, in light of the U.S. Supreme Court's holding that juries are not essential to juvenile hearings, most States do not make provisions for juries in juvenile courts.

The response to crime is founded in the intergovernmental structure of the United States

Under our form of government, each State and the Federal Government has its own criminal justice system. All systems must respect the rights of individuals set forth in court interpretation of the U.S. Constitution and defined in case law.

State constitutions and laws define the criminal justice system within each State and delegate the authority and responsibility for criminal justice to various jurisdictions, officials, and institutions. State laws also define criminal behavior and groups of children or acts under jurisdiction of the juvenile courts.

Municipalities and counties further define their criminal justice systems through local ordinances that proscribe additional illegal behavior and establish the local agencies responsible for criminal justice processing that were not established by the State.

Congress also has established a criminal justice system at the Federal level to respond to Federal crimes such as bank robbery, kidnaping, and transporting stolen goods across State lines.

The response to crime is mainly a State and local function

Very few crimes are under exclusive Federal jurisdiction. The responsibility to respond to most crime rests with the State and local governments. Police protection is primarily a function of cities and towns. Corrections is primarily a function of State governments. More than three-fifths of all justice personnel are employed at the local level.

	Percent of criminal justice employment by level of government		
	Local	State	Federal
Police	77%	15%	8%
Judicial (courts only)	60	32	8
Prosecution and legal services	58	26	17
Public defense	47	50	3
Corrections	35	61	4
Total	62%	31%	8%

Source: *Justice expenditure and employment, 1985,* BJS Bulletin, March 1987.

Discretion is exercised throughout the criminal justice system

Discretion is "an authority conferred by law to act in certain conditions or situations in accordance with an official's or an official agency's own considered judgment and conscience."[1] Discretion is exercised throughout the government. It is a part of decisionmaking in all government systems from mental health to education, as well as criminal justice.

Concerning crime and justice, legislative bodies have recognized that they cannot anticipate the range of circumstances surrounding each crime, anticipate local mores, and enact laws that clearly encompass all conduct that is criminal and all that is not.[2] Therefore, persons charged with the day-to-day response to crime are expected to exercise their own judgment within *limits* set by law. Basically, they must decide—
• whether to take action

• where the situation fits in the scheme of law, rules, and precedent
• which official response is appropriate.

To ensure that discretion is exercised responsibly, government authority is often delegated to professionals. Professionalism requires a minimum level of training and orientation, which guides officials in making decisions. The professionalism of policing discussed later in this chapter is due largely to the desire to ensure the proper exercise of police discretion.

The limits of discretion vary from State to State and locality to locality. For example, some State judges have wide discretion in the type of sentence they may impose. In recent years other States have sought to limit the judges' discretion in sentencing by passing mandatory sentencing laws that require prison sentences for certain offenses.

Who exercises discretion?

These criminal justice officials. . .	. . .must often decide whether or not or how to—
Police	Enforce specific laws Investigate specific crimes Search people, vicinities, buildings Arrest or detain people
Prosecutors	File charges or petitions for adjudication Seek indictments Drop cases Reduce charges
Judges or magistrates	Set bail or conditions for release Accept pleas Determine delinquency Dismiss charges Impose sentence Revoke probation
Correctional officials	Assign to type of correctional facility Award privileges Punish for disciplinary infractions
Paroling authority	Determine date and conditions of parole Revoke parole

1. CRIME AND JUSTICE IN AMERICA

More than one agency has jurisdiction over some criminal events

The response to most criminal actions is usually begun by local police who react to violation of State law. If a suspect is apprehended, he or she is prosecuted locally and may be confined in a local jail or State prison. In such cases, only one agency has jurisdiction at each stage in the process.

However, some criminal events because of their characteristics and location may come under the jurisdiction of more than one agency. For example, such overlapping occurs within States when local police, county sheriffs, and State police are all empowered to enforce State laws on State highways.

Congress has provided for Federal jurisdiction over crimes that—
• materially affect interstate commerce
• occur on Federal land
• involve large and probably interstate criminal organizations or conspiracies
• are offenses of national importance, such as the assassination of the President.[3]

Bank robbery and many drug offenses are examples of crimes for which the States and the Federal Government both have jurisdiction. In cases of dual jurisdiction, an investigation and a prosecution may be undertaken by all authorized agencies, but only one level of government usually pursues a case. For example, a study of FBI bank robbery investigations during 1978 and 1979 found that of those cases cleared—

• 36% were solved by the FBI alone
• 25% were solved by a joint effort of the FBI and State and local police
• 40% were solved by the State and local police acting alone.

In response to dual jurisdiction and to promote more effective coordination, Law Enforcement Coordinating Committees have been established throughout the country and include all relevant Federal and local agencies.

Within States the response to crime also varies from one locality to another

The response differs because of statutory and structural differences and differences in how discretion is exercised. Local criminal justice policies and programs change in response to local attitudes and needs. For example, the prosecutor in one locality may concentrate on particular types of offenses that plague the local community while the prosecutor in another locality may concentrate on career criminals.

The response to crime also varies on a case-by-case basis

No two cases are exactly alike. At each stage of the criminal justice process officials must make decisions that take into account the varying factors of each case. Two similar cases may have very different results because of various factors, including differences in witness cooperation and physical evidence, the availability of resources to investigate

and prosecute the case, the quality of the lawyers involved, and the age and prior criminal history of the suspects.

Differences in local laws, agencies, resources, standards, and procedures result in varying responses in each jurisdiction

The outcomes of arrests for serious cases vary among the States as shown by Offender-based Transaction Statistics from nine States:

	% of arrests for serious crimes that result in . . .		
	Prose-cution	Convic-tion	Incarcer-ation
Virginia	100%	61%	55%
Nebraska	99	68	39
New York	97	67	31
Utah	97	79	9
Virgin Islands	95	55	35
Minnesota	89	69	48
Pennsylvania	85	56	24
California	78	61	45
Ohio	77	50	21

Source: Disaggregated data used in *Tracking offenders: White-collar crime,* BJS Special Report, November 1986.

Some of this variation can be explained by differences among States. For example, the degree of discretion in deciding whether to prosecute differs from State to State; some States do not allow any police or prosecutor discretion; others allow police discretion but not prosecutor discretion and vice versa.

What To Do About Crime

James Q. Wilson

Few of the major problems facing American society today are entirely new, but in recent years most of them have either taken new forms or reached new levels of urgency. To make matters more difficult, in many cases the solutions formerly relied upon have proved to be ineffective, leaving us so frustrated that we seize desperately on proposals which promise much but deliver little.

In the hope of bringing greater clarity to the understanding of these problems, and of framing workable solutions and policies, we are inaugurating this new series of articles. Like James Q. Wilson's below, each subsequent piece in the series will begin with a reexamination of a particular issue by a writer who has lived with and studied it for a long time and who will then proceed to suggest "What To Do About" it. Among those already scheduled for publication in the coming months are Charles Murray and Richard J. Herrnstein on welfare; Gertrude Himmelfarb on the universities; William J. Bennett on our children; Robert H. Bork on the First Amendment; and Richard Pipes on Russia.

JAMES Q. WILSON, *professor of management and public policy at UCLA, is the author of many books and articles on crime, including* Thinking about Crime; Varieties of Police Behavior; *and* Crime and Human Nature *(written with Richard J. Herrnstein). He is also the editor of* Crime and Public Policy *and co-editor, with Joan Petersilia, of* Crime *(forthcoming from ICS Press).*

WHEN the United States experienced the great increase in crime that began in the early 1960's and continued through the 1970's, most Americans were inclined to attribute it to conditions unique to this country. Many conservatives blamed it on judicial restraints on the police, the abandonment of capital punishment, and the mollycoddling of offenders; many liberals blamed it on poverty, racism, and the rise of violent television programs. Europeans, to the extent they noticed at all, referred to it, sadly or patronizingly, as the "American" problem, a product of our disorderly society, weak state, corrupt police, or imperfect welfare system.

Now, 30 years later, any serious discussion of crime must begin with the fact that, except for homicide, most industrialized nations have crime rates that resemble those in the United States. All the world is coming to look like America. In 1981, the burglary rate in Great Britain was much less than that in the United States; within six years the two rates were the same; today, British homes are more likely to be burgled than American ones. In 1980, the rate at which automobiles were stolen was lower in France than in the United States; today, the reverse is true. By 1984, the burglary rate in the Netherlands was nearly twice that in the United States. In Australia and Sweden certain forms of theft are more common than they are here. While property-crime rates were

declining during most of the 1980's in the United States, they were rising elsewhere.[1]

America, it is true, continues to lead the industrialized world in murders. There can be little doubt that part of this lead is to be explained by the greater availability of handguns here. Arguments that once might have been settled with insults or punches are today more likely to be settled by shootings. But guns are not the whole story. Big American cities have had more homicides than comparable European ones for almost as long as anyone can find records. New York and Philadelphia have been more murderous than London since the early part of the 19th century. This country has had a violent history; with respect to murder, that seems likely to remain the case.

But except for homicide, things have been getting better in the United States for over a decade. Since 1980, robbery rates (as reported in victim surveys) have declined by 15 percent. And even with regard to homicide, there is relatively good news: in 1990, the rate at which adults killed one another was no higher than it was in 1980, and in many cities it was considerably lower.

This is as it was supposed to be. Starting

---

[1] These comparisons depend on official police statistics. There are of course errors in such data. But essentially the same pattern emerges from comparing nations on the basis of victimization surveys.

From *Commentary*, September 1994, pp. 25-34. © 1994 by the American Jewish Committee. All rights reserved. Reprinted by permission.

around 1980, two things happened that ought to have reduced most forms of crime. The first was the passing into middle age of the postwar baby boom. By 1990, there were 1.5 million fewer boys between the ages of fifteen and nineteen than there had been in 1980, a drop that meant that this youthful fraction of the population fell from 9.3 percent to 7.2 percent of the total.

In addition, the great increase in the size of the prison population, caused in part by the growing willingness of judges to send offenders to jail, meant that the dramatic reductions in the costs of crime to the criminal that occurred in the 1960's and 1970's were slowly (and very partially) being reversed. Until around 1985, this reversal involved almost exclusively real criminals and parole violators; it was not until after 1985 that more than a small part of the growth in prison populations was made up of drug offenders.

Because of the combined effect of fewer young people on the street and more offenders in prison, many scholars, myself included, predicted a continuing drop in crime rates throughout the 1980's and into the early 1990's. We were almost right: crime rates did decline. But suddenly, starting around 1985, even as adult homicide rates were remaining stable or dropping, *youthful* homicide rates shot up.

Alfred Blumstein of Carnegie-Mellon University has estimated that the rate at which young males, ages fourteen to seventeen, kill people has gone up significantly for whites and incredibly for blacks. Between 1985 and 1992, the homicide rate for young white males went up by about 50 percent but for young black males it *tripled*.

The public perception that today's crime problem is different from and more serious than that of earlier decades is thus quite correct. Youngsters are shooting at people at a far higher rate than at any time in recent history. Since young people are more likely than adults to kill strangers (as opposed to lovers or spouses), the risk to innocent bystanders has gone up. There may be some comfort to be had in the fact that youthful homicides are only a small fraction of all killings, but given their randomness, it is not much solace.

THE United States, then, does not have *a* crime problem, it has at least two. Our high (though now slightly declining) rates of property crime reflect a profound, worldwide cultural change: prosperity, freedom, and mobility have emancipated people almost everywhere from those ancient bonds of custom, family, and village that once held in check both some of our better and many of our worst impulses. The power of the state has been weakened, the status of children elevated, and the opportunity for adventure expanded; as a consequence, we have experienced an explosion of artistic creativity, entrepreneurial zeal, political experimentation—

and criminal activity. A global economy has integrated the markets for clothes, music, automobiles—and drugs.

There are only two restraints on behavior—morality, enforced by individual conscience or social rebuke, and law, enforced by the police and the courts. If society is to maintain a behavioral equilibrium, any decline in the former must be matched by a rise in the latter (or vice versa). If familial and traditional restraints on wrongful behavior are eroded, it becomes necessary to increase the legal restraints. But the enlarged spirit of freedom and the heightened suspicion of the state have made it difficult or impossible to use the criminal-justice system to achieve what custom and morality once produced.

This is the modern dilemma, and it may be an insoluble one, at least for the West. The Islamic cultures of the Middle East and the Confucian cultures of the Far East believe that they have a solution. It involves allowing enough liberty for economic progress (albeit under general state direction) while reserving to the state, and its allied religion, nearly unfettered power over personal conduct. It is too soon to tell whether this formula—best exemplified by the prosperous but puritanical city-state of Singapore—will, in the long run, be able to achieve both reproducible affluence and intense social control.

Our other crime problem has to do with the kind of felonies we have: high levels of violence, especially youthful violence, often occurring as part of urban gang life, produced disproportionately by a large, alienated, and self-destructive underclass. This part of the crime problem, though not uniquely American, is more important here than in any other industrialized nation. Britons, Germans, and Swedes are upset about the insecurity of their property and uncertain about what response to make to its theft, but if Americans only had to worry about their homes being burgled and their autos stolen, I doubt that crime would be the national obsession it has now become.

Crime, we should recall, was not a major issue in the 1984 presidential election and had only begun to be one in the 1988 contest; by 1992, it was challenging the economy as a popular concern and today it dominates all other matters. The reason, I think, is that Americans believe something fundamental has changed in our patterns of crime. They are right. Though we were unhappy about having our property put at risk, we adapted with the aid of locks, alarms, and security guards. But we are terrified by the prospect of innocent people being gunned down at random, without warning and almost without motive, by youngsters who afterward show us the blank, unremorseful faces of seemingly feral, presocial beings.

CRIMINOLOGY has learned a great deal about who these people are. In studies both here and abroad it has been established that about 6 percent of the boys of a given age will commit half or more of all the serious crime produced by all boys of that age. Allowing for measurement errors, it is remarkable how consistent this formula is—6 percent causes 50 percent. It is roughly true in places as different as Philadelphia, London, Copenhagen, and Orange County, California.

We also have learned a lot about the characteristics of the 6 percent. They tend to have criminal parents, to live in cold or discordant families (or pseudo-families), to have a low verbal-intelligence quotient and to do poorly in school, to be emotionally cold and temperamentally impulsive, to abuse alcohol and drugs at the earliest opportunity, and to reside in poor, disorderly communities. They begin their misconduct at an early age, often by the time they are in the third grade.

These characteristics tend to be found not only among the criminals who get caught (and who might, owing to bad luck, be an unrepresentative sample of all high-rate offenders), but among those who do not get caught but reveal their behavior on questionnaires. And the same traits can be identified in advance among groups of randomly selected youngsters, long before they commit any serious crimes—not with enough precision to predict which individuals will commit crimes, but with enough accuracy to be a fair depiction of the group as a whole.[2]

Here a puzzle arises: if 6 percent of the males causes so large a fraction of our collective misery, and if young males are less numerous than once was the case, why are crime rates high and rising? The answer, I conjecture, is that the traits of the 6 percent put them at high risk for whatever criminogenic forces operate in society. As the costs of crime decline or the benefits increase; as drugs and guns become more available; as the glorification of violence becomes more commonplace; as families and neighborhoods lose some of their restraining power—as all these things happen, almost all of us will change our ways to some degree. For the most law-abiding among us, the change will be quite modest: a few more tools stolen from our employer, a few more traffic lights run when no police officer is watching, a few more experiments with fashionable drugs, and a few more business deals on which we cheat. But for the least law-abiding among us, the change will be dramatic: they will get drunk daily instead of just on Saturday night, try PCP or crack instead of marijuana, join gangs instead of marauding in pairs, and buy automatic weapons instead of making zip guns.

A metaphor: when children play the schoolyard game of crack-the-whip, the child at the head of the line scarcely moves but the child at the far end, racing to keep his footing, often stumbles and falls, hurled to the ground by the cumulative force of many smaller movements back along the line. When a changing culture escalates criminality, the at-risk boys are at the end of the line, and the conditions of American urban life—guns, drugs, automobiles, disorganized neighborhoods—make the line very long and the ground underfoot rough and treacherous.

MUCH is said these days about preventing or deterring crime, but it is important to understand exactly what we are up against when we try. Prevention, if it can be made to work at all, must start very early in life, perhaps as early as the first two or three years, and given the odds it faces—childhood impulsivity, low verbal facility, incompetent parenting, disorderly neighborhoods—it must also be massive in scope. Deterrence, if it can be made to work better (for surely it already works to some degree), must be applied close to the moment of the wrongful act or else the present-orientedness of the youthful would-be offender will discount the threat so much that the promise of even a small gain will outweigh its large but deferred costs.

In this country, however, and in most Western nations, we have profound misgivings about doing anything that would give prevention or deterrence a chance to make a large difference. The family is sacrosanct; the family-preservation movement is strong; the state is a clumsy alternative. "Crime-prevention" programs, therefore, usually take the form of creating summer jobs for adolescents, worrying about the unemployment rate, or (as in the proposed 1994 crime bill) funding midnight basketball leagues. There may be something to be said for all these efforts, but crime prevention is not one of them. The typical high-rate offender is well launched on his career before he becomes a teenager or has ever encountered the labor market; he may like basketball, but who pays for the lights and the ball is a matter of supreme indifference to him.

Prompt deterrence has much to recommend it: the folk wisdom that swift and certain punishment is more effective than severe penalties is almost surely correct. But the greater the swiftness and certainty, the less attention paid to the procedural safeguards essential to establishing guilt. As a result, despite their good instincts for the right answers, most Americans, frustrated by the restraints (many wise, some foolish) on swiftness and certainty, vote for proposals to increase severity: if the penalty is 10 years, let us make it 20 or 30; if the penalty is life imprisonment, let us make it death; if the penalty is jail, let us make it caning.

---

[2] Female high-rate offenders are *much* less common than male ones. But to the extent they exist, they display most of these traits.

Yet the more draconian the sentence, the less (on the average) the chance of its being imposed; plea bargains see to that. And the most draconian sentences will, of necessity, tend to fall on adult offenders nearing the end of their criminal careers and not on the young ones who are in their criminally most productive years. (The peak ages of criminality are between sixteen and eighteen; the average age of prison inmates is ten years older.) I say "of necessity" because almost every judge will give first-, second-, or even third-time offenders a break, reserving the heaviest sentences for those men who have finally exhausted judicial patience or optimism.

Laws that say "three strikes and you're out" are an effort to change this, but they suffer from an inherent contradiction. If they are carefully drawn so as to target only the most serious offenders, they will probably have a minimal impact on the crime rate; but if they are broadly drawn so as to make a big impact on the crime rate, they will catch many petty repeat offenders who few of us think really deserve life imprisonment.

Prevention and deterrence, albeit hard to augment, at least are plausible strategies. Not so with many of the other favorite nostrums, like reducing the amount of violence on television. Televised violence may have some impact on criminality, but I know of few scholars who think the effect is very large. And to achieve even a small difference we might have to turn the clock back to the kind of programming we had around 1945, because the few studies that correlate programming with the rise in violent crime find the biggest changes occurred between that year and 1974. Another favorite, boot camp, makes good copy, but so far no one has shown that it reduces the rate at which the former inmates commit crimes.

Then, of course, there is gun control. Guns are almost certainly contributors to the lethality of American violence, but there is no politically or legally feasible way to reduce the stock of guns now in private possession to the point where their availability to criminals would be much affected. And even if there were, law-abiding people would lose a means of protecting themselves long before criminals lost a means of attacking them.

As for rehabilitating juvenile offenders, it has some merit, but there are rather few success stories. Individually, the best (and best-evaluated) programs have minimal, if any, effects; collectively, the best estimate of the crime-reduction value of these programs is quite modest, something on the order of 5 or 10 percent.[3]

W HAT, then, is to be done? Let us begin with policing, since law-enforcement officers are that part of the criminal-justice system which is closest to the situations where criminal activity is likely to occur.

It is now widely accepted that, however important it is for officers to drive around waiting for 911 calls summoning their help, doing that is not enough. As a supplement to such a reactive strategy—comprised of random preventive patrol and the investigation of crimes that have already occurred—many leaders and students of law enforcement now urge the police to be "proactive": to identify, with the aid of citizen groups, problems that can be solved so as to prevent criminality, and not only to respond to it. This is often called community-based policing; it seems to entail something more than feel-good meetings with honest citizens, but something less than allowing neighborhoods to assume control of the police function.

The new strategy might better be called problem-oriented policing. It requires the police to engage in *directed*, not random, patrol. The goal of that direction should be to reduce, in a manner consistent with fundamental liberties, the opportunity for high-risk persons to do those things that increase the likelihood of their victimizing others.

For example, the police might stop and pat down persons whom they reasonably suspect may be carrying illegal guns.[4] The Supreme Court has upheld such frisks when an officer observes "unusual conduct" leading him to conclude that "criminal activity may be afoot" on the part of a person who may be "armed and dangerous." This is all rather vague, but it can be clarified in two ways.

First, statutes can be enacted that make certain persons, on the basis of their past conduct and present legal status, subject to pat-downs for weapons. The statutes can, as is now the case in several states, make all probationers and parolees subject to nonconsensual searches for weapons as a condition of their remaining on probation or parole. Since three-fourths of all convicted offenders (and a large fraction of all felons) are in the community rather than in prison, there are on any given day over three million criminals on the streets under correctional supervision. Many are likely to become recidivists. Keeping them from carrying weapons will materially reduce the chances that they will rob or kill. The courts might also declare certain dangerous street gangs to be continuing criminal enterprises, membership in which constitutes grounds for police frisks.

---

[3] Many individual programs involve so few subjects that a good evaluation will reveal no positive effect even if one occurs. By a technique called meta-analysis, scores of individual studies can be pooled into one mega-evaluation; because there are now hundreds or thousands of subjects, even small gains can be identified. The best of these meta-analyses, such as the one by Mark Lipsey, suggest modest positive effects.

[4] I made a fuller argument along these lines in "Just Take Away Their Guns," in the *New York Times Magazine*, March 20, 1994.

Second, since I first proposed such a strategy, I have learned that there are efforts under way in public and private research laboratories to develop technologies that will permit the police to detect from a distance persons who are carrying concealed weapons on the streets. Should these efforts bear fruit, they will provide the police with the grounds for stopping, questioning, and patting down even persons not on probation or parole or obviously in gangs.

Whether or not the technology works, the police can also offer immediate cash rewards to people who provide information about individuals illegally carrying weapons. Spending $100 on each good tip will have a bigger impact on dangerous gun use than will the same amount spent on another popular nostrum—buying back guns from law-abiding people.[5]

Getting illegal firearms off the streets will require that the police be motivated to do all of these things. But if the legal, technological, and motivational issues can be resolved, our streets can be made safer even without sending many more people to prison.

T HE same directed-patrol strategy might help keep known offenders drug-free. Most persons jailed in big cities are found to have been using illegal drugs within the day or two preceding their arrest. When convicted, some are given probation on condition that they enter drug-treatment programs; others are sent to prisons where (if they are lucky) drug-treatment programs operate. But in many cities the enforcement of such probation conditions is casual or nonexistent; in many states, parolees are released back into drug-infested communities with little effort to ensure that they participate in whatever treatment programs are to be found there.

Almost everyone agrees that more treatment programs should exist. But what many advocates overlook is that the key to success is steadfast participation and many, probably most, offenders have no incentive to be steadfast. To cope with this, patrol officers could enforce random drug tests on probationers and parolees on their beats; failing to take a test when ordered, or failing the test when taken, should be grounds for immediate revocation of probation or parole, at least for a brief period of confinement.

The goal of this tactic is not simply to keep offenders drug-free (and thereby lessen their incentive to steal the money needed to buy drugs and reduce their likelihood of committing crimes because they are on a drug high); it is also to diminish the demand for drugs generally and thus the size of the drug market.

Lest the reader embrace this idea too quickly, let me add that as yet we have no good reason to think that it will reduce the crime rate by very much. Something akin to this strategy, albeit one using probation instead of police officers, has been tried under the name of "intensive-supervision programs" (ISP), involving a panoply of drug tests, house arrests, frequent surveillance, and careful records. By means of a set of randomized experiments carried out in fourteen cities, Joan Petersilia and Susan Turner, both then at RAND, compared the rearrest rates of offenders assigned to ISP with those of offenders in ordinary probation. There was no difference.

Still, this study does not settle the matter. For one thing, since the ISP participants were under much closer surveillance than the regular probationers, the former were bound to be caught breaking the law more frequently than the latter. It is thus possible that a higher fraction of the crimes committed by the ISP than of the control group were detected and resulted in a return to prison, which would mean, if true, a net gain in public safety. For another thing, "intensive" supervision was in many cases not all that intensive—in five cities, contacts with the probationers only took place about once a week, and for all cities drug tests occurred, on average, about once a month. Finally, there is some indication that participation in treatment programs was associated with lower recidivism rates.

Both anti-gun and anti-drug police patrols will, if performed systematically, require big changes in police and court procedures and a significant increase in the resources devoted to both, at least in the short run. (ISP is not cheap, and it will become even more expensive if it is done in a truly intensive fashion.) Most officers have at present no incentive to search for guns or enforce drug tests; many jurisdictions, owing to crowded dockets or overcrowded jails, are lax about enforcing the conditions of probation or parole. The result is that the one group of high-risk people over which society already has the legal right to exercise substantial control is often out of control, "supervised," if at all, by means of brief monthly interviews with overworked probation or parole officers.

Another promising tactic is to enforce truancy and curfew laws. This arises from the fact that much crime is opportunistic: idle boys, usually in small groups, sometimes find irresistible the opportunity to steal or the challenge to fight. Deterring present-oriented youngsters who want to appear fearless in the eyes of their comrades while indulging their thrill-seeking natures is a tall order. While it is possible to deter the crimes they commit by a credible threat of prompt sanctions, it is easier to reduce the chances for risky group idleness in the first place.

---

[5] In Charleston, South Carolina, the police pay a reward to anyone identifying a student carrying a weapon to school or to some school event. Because many boys carry guns to school in order to display or brag about them, the motive to carry disappears once any display alerts a potential informer.

In Charleston, South Carolina, for example, Chief Reuben Greenberg instructed his officers to return all school-age children to the schools from which they were truant and to return all youngsters violating an evening-curfew agreement to their parents. As a result, groups of school-age children were no longer to be found hanging out in the shopping malls or wandering the streets late at night.

There has been no careful evaluation of these efforts in Charleston (or, so far as I am aware, in any other big city), but the rough figures are impressive—the Charleston crime rate in 1991 was about 25 percent lower than the rate in South Carolina's other principal cities and, for most offenses (including burglaries and larcenies), lower than what that city reported twenty years earlier.

All these tactics have in common putting the police, as the criminologist Lawrence Sherman of the University of Maryland phrases it, where the "hot spots" are. Most people need no police attention except for a response to their calls for help. A small fraction of people (and places) need constant attention. Thus, in Minneapolis, *all* of the robberies during one year occurred at just 2 percent of the city's addresses. To capitalize on this fact, the Minneapolis police began devoting extra patrol attention, in brief but frequent bursts of activity, to those locations known to be trouble spots. Robbery rates evidently fell by as much as 20 percent and public disturbances by even more.

Some of the worst hot spots are outdoor drug markets. Because of either limited resources, a fear of potential corruption, or a desire to catch only the drug kingpins, the police in some cities (including, from time to time, New York) neglect street-corner dealing. By doing so, they get the worst of all worlds.

The public, seeing the police ignore drug dealing that is in plain view, assumes that they are corrupt whether or not they are. The drug kingpins, who are hard to catch and are easily replaced by rival smugglers, find that their essential retail distribution system remains intact. Casual or first-time drug users, who might not use at all if access to supplies were difficult, find access to be effortless and so increase their consumption. People who might remain in treatment programs if drugs were hard to get drop out upon learning that they are easy to get. Interdicting without merely displacing drug markets is difficult but not impossible, though it requires motivation which some departments lack and resources which many do not have.

The sheer number of police on the streets of a city probably has only a weak, if any, relationship with the crime rate; what the police do is more important than how many there are, at least above some minimum level. Nevertheless, patrols directed at hot spots, loitering truants, late-night wanderers, probationers, parolees, and possible gun carriers, all in addition to routine investigative activities, will require more officers in many cities. Between 1977 and 1987, the number of police officers declined in a third of the 50 largest cities and fell relative to population in many more. Just how far behind police resources have lagged can be gauged from this fact: in 1950 there was one violent crime reported for every police officer; in 1980 there were three violent crimes reported for every officer.

I HAVE said little so far about penal policy, in part because I wish to focus attention on those things that are likely to have the largest and most immediate impact on the quality of urban life. But given the vast gulf between what the public believes and what many experts argue should be our penal policy, a few comments are essential.

The public wants more people sent away for longer sentences; many (probably most) criminologists think we use prison too much and at too great a cost and that this excessive use has had little beneficial effect on the crime rate. My views are much closer to those of the public, though I think the average person exaggerates the faults of the present system and the gains of some alternative (such as "three strikes and you're out").

The expert view, as it is expressed in countless op-ed essays, often goes like this: "We have been arresting more and more people and giving them longer and longer sentences, producing no decrease in crime but huge increases in prison populations. As a result, we have become the most punitive nation on earth."

Scarcely a phrase in those sentences is accurate. The probability of being arrested for a given crime is lower today than it was in 1974. The amount of time served in state prison has been declining more or less steadily since the 1940's. Taking all crimes together, time served fell from 25 months in 1945 to 13 months in 1984. Only for rape are prisoners serving as much time today as they did in the 40's.

The net effect of lower arrest rates and shorter effective sentences is that the cost to the adult perpetrator of the average burglary fell from 50 days in 1960 to 15 days in 1980. That is to say, the chances of being caught and convicted, multiplied by the median time served if imprisoned, was in 1980 less than a third of what it had been in 1960.[6]

---

[6] I take these cost calculations from Mark Kleiman, *et al.*, "Imprisonment-to-Offense Ratios," Working Paper 89-06-02 of the Program in Criminal Justice Policy and Management at the Kennedy School of Government, Harvard University (August 5, 1988).

Beginning around 1980, the costs of crime to the criminal began to inch up again—the result, chiefly, of an increase in the proportion of convicted persons who were given prison terms. By 1986, the "price" of a given burglary had risen to 21 days. Also beginning around 1980, as I noted at the outset, the crime rate began to decline.

It would be foolhardy to explain this drop in crime by the rise in imprisonment rates; many other factors, such as the aging of the population and the self-protective measures of potential victims, were also at work. Only a controlled experiment (for example, randomly allocating prison terms for a given crime among the states) could hope to untangle the causal patterns, and happily the Constitution makes such experiments unlikely.

Yet it is worth noting that nations with different penal policies have experienced different crime rates. According to David Farrington of Cambridge University, property-crime rates rose in England and Sweden at a time when both the imprisonment rate and time served fell substantially, while property-crime rates declined in the United States at a time when the imprisonment rate (but not time served) was increasing.

Though one cannot measure the effect of prison on crime with any accuracy, it certainly has some effects. By 1986, there were 55,000 more robbers in prison than there had been in 1974. Assume that each imprisoned robber would commit five such offenses per year if free on the street. This means that in 1986 there were 275,000 fewer robberies in America than there would have been had these 55,000 men been left on the street.

Nor, finally, does America use prison to a degree that vastly exceeds what is found in any other civilized nation. Compare the chance of going to prison in England and the United States if one is convicted of a given crime. According to Farrington, your chances were higher in England if you were found guilty of a rape, higher in America if you were convicted of an assault or a burglary, and about the same if you were convicted of a homicide or a robbery. Once in prison, you would serve a longer time in this country than in England for almost all offenses save murder.

James Lynch of American University has reached similar conclusions from his comparative study of criminal-justice policies. His data show that the chances of going to prison and the time served for homicide and robbery are roughly the same in the United States, Canada, and England.

OF LATE, drugs have changed American penal practice. In 1982, only about 8 percent of state-prison inmates were serving time on drug convictions. In 1987, that started to increase sharply; by 1994, over 60 percent of all federal and about 25 percent of all state prisoners were there on drug charges. In some states, such as New York, the percentage was even higher.

This change can be attributed largely to the advent of crack cocaine. Whereas snorted cocaine powder was expensive, crack was cheap; whereas the former was distributed through networks catering to elite tastes, the latter was mass-marketed on street corners. People were rightly fearful of what crack was doing to their children and demanded action; as a result, crack dealers started going to prison in record numbers.

Unfortunately, these penalties do not have the same incapacitative effect as sentences for robbery. A robber taken off the street is not replaced by a new robber who has suddenly found a market niche, but a drug dealer sent away is replaced by a new one because an opportunity has opened up.

We are left, then, with the problem of reducing the demand for drugs, and that in turn requires either prevention programs on a scale heretofore unimagined or treatment programs with a level of effectiveness heretofore unachieved. Any big gains in prevention and treatment will probably have to await further basic research into the biochemistry of addiction and the development of effective and attractive drug antagonists that reduce the appeal of cocaine and similar substances.[7]

In the meantime, it is necessary either to build much more prison space, find some other way of disciplining drug offenders, or both. There is very little to be gained, I think, from shortening the terms of existing non-drug inmates in order to free up more prison space. Except for a few elderly, nonviolent offenders serving very long terms, there are real risks associated with shortening the terms of the typical inmate.

Scholars disagree about the magnitude of those risks, but the best studies, such as the one of Wisconsin inmates done by John DiIulio of Princeton, suggest that the annual costs to society in crime committed by an offender on the street are probably twice the costs of putting him in a cell. That ratio will vary from state to state because states differ in what proportion of convicted persons is imprisoned—some states dip deeper down into the pool of convictees, thereby imprisoning some with minor criminal habits.

But I caution the reader to understand that there are no easy prison solutions to crime, even if we build the additional space. The state-prison population more than doubled between 1980 and 1990, yet the victimization rate for robbery fell by only 23 percent. Even if we assign all of that gain

---

[7] I anticipate that at this point some readers will call for legalizing or decriminalizing drugs as the "solution" to the problem. Before telling me this, I hope they will read what I wrote on that subject in the February 1990 issue of COMMENTARY. I have not changed my mind.

to the increased deterrent and incapacitative effect of prison, which is implausible, the improvement is not vast. Of course, it is possible that the victimization rate would have risen, perhaps by a large amount, instead of falling if we had not increased the number of inmates. But we shall never know.

Recall my discussion of the decline in the costs of crime to the criminal, measured by the number of days in prison that result, on average, from the commission of a given crime. That cost is vastly lower today than in the 1950's. But much of the decline (and since 1974, nearly all of it) is the result of a drop in the probability of being arrested for a crime, not in the probability of being imprisoned once arrested.

Anyone who has followed my writings on crime knows that I have defended the use of prison both to deter crime and incapacitate criminals. I continue to defend it. But we must recognize two facts. First, even modest additional reductions in crime, comparable to the ones achieved in the early 1980's, will require vast increases in correctional costs and encounter bitter judicial resistance to mandatory sentencing laws. Second, America's most troubling crime problem—the increasingly violent behavior of disaffected and impulsive youth—may be especially hard to control by means of marginal and delayed increases in the probability of punishment.

Possibly one can make larger gains by turning our attention to the unexplored area of juvenile justice. Juvenile (or family) courts deal with young people just starting their criminal careers and with chronic offenders when they are often at their peak years of offending. We know rather little about how these courts work or with what effect. There are few, if any, careful studies of what happens, a result in part of scholarly neglect and in part of the practice in some states of shrouding juvenile records and proceedings in secrecy. Some studies, such as one by the *Los Angeles Times* of juvenile justice in California, suggest that young people found guilty of a serious crime are given sentences tougher than those meted out to adults.[8] This finding is so counter to popular beliefs and the testimony of many big-city juvenile-court judges that some caution is required in interpreting it.

There are two problems. The first lies in defining the universe of people to whom sanctions are applied. In some states, such as California, it may well be the case that a juvenile *found guilty of a serious offense* is punished with greater rigor than an adult, but many juveniles whose behavior ought to be taken seriously (because they show signs of being part of the 6 percent) are released by the police or probation officers before ever seeing a judge. And in some states, such as New York, juveniles charged with having committed certain crimes, including serious ones like illegally carrying a loaded gun or committing an assault, may not be fingerprinted. Since persons with a prior record are usually given longer sentences than those without one, the failure to fingerprint can mean that the court has no way of knowing whether the John Smith standing before it is the same John Smith who was arrested four times for assault and so ought to be sent away, or a different John Smith whose clean record entitles him to probation.

The second problem arises from the definition of a "severe" penalty. In California, a juvenile found guilty of murder does indeed serve a longer sentence than an adult convicted of the same offense—60 months for the former, 41 months for the latter. Many people will be puzzled by a newspaper account that defines five years in prison for murder as a "severe" sentence, and angered to learn that an adult serves less than four years for such a crime.

The key, unanswered question is whether prompt and more effective early intervention would stop high-rate delinquents from becoming high-rate criminals at a time when their offenses were not yet too serious. Perhaps early and swift, though not necessarily severe, sanctions could deter some budding hoodlums, but we have no evidence of that as yet.

For as long as I can remember, the debate over crime has been between those who wished to rely on the criminal-justice system and those who wished to attack the root causes of crime. I have always been in the former group because what its opponents depicted as "root causes"—unemployment, racism, poor housing, too little schooling, a lack of self-esteem—turned out, on close examination, not to be major causes of crime at all.

Of late, however, there has been a shift in the debate. Increasingly those who want to attack root causes have begun to point to real ones—temperament, early family experiences, and neighborhood effects. The sketch I gave earlier of the typical high-rate young offender suggests that these factors are indeed at the root of crime. The problem now is to decide whether any can be changed by plan and at an acceptable price in money and personal freedom.

If we are to do this, we must confront the fact that the critical years of a child's life are ages one to ten, with perhaps the most important being the earliest years. During those years, some children are put gravely at risk by some combination of heritable traits, prenatal insults (maternal drug and alcohol abuse or poor diet), weak parent-child attachment, poor supervision, and disorderly family environment.

---

8 "A Nation's Children in Lock-up," *Los Angeles Times,* August 22, 1993.

If we knew with reasonable confidence which children were most seriously at risk, we might intervene with some precision to supply either medical therapy or parent training or (in extreme cases) to remove the child to a better home. But given our present knowledge, precision is impossible, and so we must proceed carefully, relying, except in the most extreme cases, on persuasion and incentives.

We do, however, know enough about the early causes of conduct disorder and later delinquency to know that the more risk factors exist (such as parental criminality and poor supervision), the greater the peril to the child. It follows that programs aimed at just one or a few factors are not likely to be successful; the children most at risk are those who require the most wide-ranging and fundamental changes in their life circumstances. The goal of these changes is, as Travis Hirschi of the University of Arizona has put it, to teach self-control.

Hirokazu Yoshikawa of New York University has recently summarized what we have learned about programs that attempt to make large and lasting changes in a child's prospects for improved conduct, better school behavior, and lessened delinquency. Four such programs in particular seemed valuable—the Perry Preschool Project in Ypsilanti, Michigan; the Parent-Child Development Center in Houston, Texas; the Family Development Research Project in Syracuse, New York; and the Yale Child Welfare Project in New Haven, Connecticut.

All these programs had certain features in common. They dealt with low-income, often minority, families; they intervened during the first five years of a child's life and continued for between two and five years; they combined parent training with preschool education for the child; and they involved extensive home visits. All were evaluated fairly carefully, with the follow-ups lasting for at least five years, in two cases for at least ten, and in one case for fourteen. The programs produced (depending on the project) less fighting, impulsivity, disobedience, restlessness, cheating, and delinquency. In short, they improved self-control.

They were experimental programs, which means that it is hard to be confident that trying the same thing on a bigger scale in many places will produce the same effects. A large number of well-trained and highly motivated caseworkers dealt with a relatively small number of families, with the workers knowing that their efforts were being evaluated. Moreover, the programs operated in the late 1970's or early 1980's before the advent of crack cocaine or the rise of the more lethal neighborhood gangs. A national program mounted under current conditions might or might not have the same result as the experimental efforts.

Try telling that to lawmakers. What happens when politicians encounter experimental successes is amply revealed by the history of Head Start: they expanded the program quickly without assuring quality, and stripped it down to the part that was the most popular, least expensive, and easiest to run, namely, preschool education. Absent from much of Head Start are the high teacher-to-child case loads, the extensive home visits, and the elaborate parent training—the very things that probably account for much of the success of the four experimental programs.

IN THIS country we tend to separate programs designed to help children from those that benefit their parents. The former are called "child development," the latter "welfare reform." This is a great mistake. Everything we know about long-term welfare recipients indicates that their children are at risk for the very problems that child-helping programs later try to correct.

The evidence from a variety of studies is quite clear: even if we hold income and ethnicity constant, children (and especially boys) raised by a single mother are more likely than those raised by two parents to have difficulty in school, get in trouble with the law, and experience emotional and physical problems.[9] Producing illegitimate children is not an "alternative life-style" or simply an imprudent action; it is a curse. Making mothers work will not end the curse; under current proposals, it will not even save money.

The absurdity of divorcing the welfare problem from the child-development problem becomes evident as soon as we think seriously about what we want to achieve. Smaller welfare expenditures? Well, yes, but not if it hurts children. More young mothers working? Probably not; young mothers ought to raise their young children, and work interferes with that unless *two* parents can solve some difficult and expensive problems.

What we really want is *fewer illegitimate children*, because such children, by being born out of wedlock are, except in unusual cases, being given early admission to the underclass. And failing that, we want the children born to single (and typically young and poor) mothers to have a chance at a decent life.

Letting teenage girls set up their own households at public expense neither discourages illegitimacy nor serves the child's best interests. If they do set up their own homes, then to reach those with the fewest parenting skills and the most difficult children will require the kind of expensive and intensive home visits and family-support programs characteristic of the four successful experiments mentioned earlier.

---

[9] I summarize this evidence in "The Family-Values Debate," COMMENTARY, April 1993.

One alternative is to tell a girl who applies for welfare that she can only receive it on condition that she live either in the home of *two* competent parents (her own if she comes from an intact family) or in a group home where competent supervision and parent training will be provided by adults unrelated to her. Such homes would be privately managed but publicly funded by pooling welfare checks, food stamps, and housing allowances.

A model for such a group home (albeit one run without public funds) is the St. Martin de Porres House of Hope on the south side of Chicago, founded by two nuns for homeless young women, especially those with drug-abuse problems. The goals of the home are clear: accept personal responsibility for your lives and learn to care for your children. And these goals, in turn, require the girls to follow rules, stay in school, obey a curfew, and avoid alcohol and drugs. Those are the rules that ought to govern a group home for young welfare mothers.

Group homes funded by pooled welfare benefits would make the task of parent training much easier and provide the kind of structured, consistent, and nurturant environment that children need. A few cases might be too difficult for these homes, and for such children, boarding schools—once common in American cities for disadvantaged children, but now almost extinct—might be revived.

Group homes also make it easier to supply quality medical care to young mothers and their children. Such care has taken on added importance in recent years with discovery of the lasting damage that can be done to a child's prospects from being born prematurely and with a very low birth weight, having a mother who has abused drugs or alcohol, or being exposed to certain dangerous metals. Lead poisoning is now widely acknowledged to be a source of cognitive and behavioral impairment; of late, elevated levels of manganese have been linked to high levels of violence.[10] These are all treatable conditions; in the case of a manganese imbalance, easily treatable.

My focus on changing behavior will annoy some readers. For them the problem is poverty and the worst feature of single-parent families is that they are inordinately poor. Even to refer to a behavioral or cultural problem is to "stigmatize" people.

Indeed it is. Wrong behavior—neglectful, immature, or incompetent parenting; the production of out-of-wedlock babies—*ought* to be stigmatized. There are many poor men of all races who do not abandon the women they have impregnated, and many poor women of all races who avoid drugs and do a good job of raising their children. If we fail to stigmatize those who give way to temptation, we withdraw the rewards from those who resist them. This becomes all the

more important when entire communities, and not just isolated households, are dominated by a culture of fatherless boys preying on innocent persons and exploiting immature girls.

We need not merely stigmatize, however. We can try harder to move children out of those communities, either by drawing them into safe group homes or facilitating (through rent supplements and housing vouchers) the relocation of them and their parents to neighborhoods with intact social structures and an ethos of family values.

Much of our uniquely American crime problem (as opposed to the worldwide problem of general thievery) arises, not from the failings of individuals but from the concentration in disorderly neighborhoods of people at risk of failing. That concentration is partly the result of prosperity and freedom (functioning families long ago seized the opportunity to move out to the periphery), partly the result of racism (it is harder for some groups to move than for others), and partly the result of politics (elected officials do not wish to see settled constituencies broken up).

I seriously doubt that this country has the will to address either of its two crime problems, save by acts of individual self-protection. We could in theory make justice swifter and more certain, but we will not accept the restrictions on liberty and the weakening of procedural safeguards that this would entail. We could vastly improve the way in which our streets are policed, but some of us will not pay for it and the rest of us will not tolerate it. We could alter the way in which at-risk children experience the first few years of life, but the opponents of this—welfare-rights activists, family preservationists, budget cutters, and assorted ideologues—are numerous and the bureaucratic problems enormous.

Unable or unwilling to do such things, we take refuge in substitutes: we debate the death penalty, we wring our hands over television, we lobby to keep prisons from being built in our neighborhoods, and we fall briefly in love with trendy nostrums that seem to cost little and promise much.

Much of our ambivalence is on display in the 1994 federal crime bill. To satisfy the tough-minded, the list of federal offenses for which the death penalty can be imposed has been greatly enlarged, but there is little reason to think that executions, as they work in this country (which is to say, after much delay and only on a few offenders), have any effect on the crime rate and no reason to think that executing more federal prisoners (who account, at best, for a tiny fraction of all homicides) will reduce the murder rate. To

---

[10] It is not clear why manganese has this effect, but we know that it diminishes the availability of a precursor of serotonin, a neurotransmitter, and low levels of serotonin are now strongly linked to violent and impulsive behavior.

satisfy the tender-minded, several billion dollars are earmarked for prevention programs, but there is as yet very little hard evidence that any of these will actually prevent crime.

In adding more police officers, the bill may make some difference—but only if the additional personnel are imaginatively deployed. And Washington will pay only part of the cost initially and none of it after six years, which means that any city getting new officers will either have to raise its own taxes to keep them on the force or accept the political heat that will arise from turning down "free" cops. Many states also desperately need additional prison space; the federal funds

allocated by the bill for their construction will be welcomed, provided that states are willing to meet the conditions set for access to such funds.

Meanwhile, just beyond the horizon, there lurks a cloud that the winds will soon bring over us. The population will start getting younger again. By the end of this decade there will be a million more people between the ages of fourteen and seventeen than there are now. Half of this extra million will be male. Six percent of them will become high-rate, repeat offenders— 30,000 more muggers, killers, and thieves than we have now.

Get ready.

THE ECONOMICS OF CRIME

The toll is frightening. Can anything be done?

Americans are scared. The fear of crime permeates their lives. They worry about being mugged or raped in a parking lot or while walking home from work. They're afraid of being robbed at a highway rest stop or having their children kidnapped at a suburban mall. They put bars on their windows, alarms in their cars, and cans of tear gas in their pockets. And they should be frightened. All told, some 14 million serious crimes were reported to the police last year, a number that surely understates the actual magnitude of America's No. 1 problem.

But the daily reality of muggings and murders that make the headlines and TV news shows is hurting the public in a far different, yet no less destructive, way. Crime in America is exacting an enormous economic toll on the nation—far bigger than anyone realizes.

New estimates by BUSINESS WEEK show that crime costs Americans a stunning $425 billion each year. That figure comes from a detailed analysis of all of the direct and indirect costs of both property and violent crimes, from emergency-room care for a mugging victim to the price of a new alarm system for a home to the income lost to the family of a murdered cab driver.

Human misery aside, from a purely dollars-and-sense perspective, the U.S. isn't devoting enough resources to the fight against crime—and is frittering away many of the resources it is using.

The U.S. spends some $90 billion a year on the entire criminal-justice system. That includes $35 billion for police protection, less than the country is spending on toiletries each year. Indeed, anticrime policy over the years has been a series of quick, cheap fixes: New prisons are being built, but the number of police has barely kept pace with the growing population. Meanwhile, economic and social programs that could quickly bring down crime have been largely ignored.

Even the spate of crime-fighting legislation going through Congress falls far short of what is needed. The Brady Bill, just signed into law, simply requires a five-day waiting period for the purchase of handguns. And the highly acclaimed anticrime bill recently passed by the Senate would add a meager $4.5 billion a year to total criminal-justice spending.

TV VIOLENCE. Why is the nation underspending on crime-fighting? The public may well believe that there's little more money can do short of putting the Army on every street corner. Some have blamed crime and violence on the decline of "family values" or the loss of inner-city manufacturing jobs, neither of which can be solved by government action. Most recently, excessive violence on TV has been fingered as a key culprit by Attorney General Janet Reno and Surgeon-General M. Joycelyn Elders.

Economists, on the other hand, view crime as a choice that can be affected by changes in punishments and rewards. Recent research by economists shows that higher levels of anticrime spending, if well-directed, can make a big dent in crime. Crime can be reduced by increasing what economists call the "expected punishment"—the

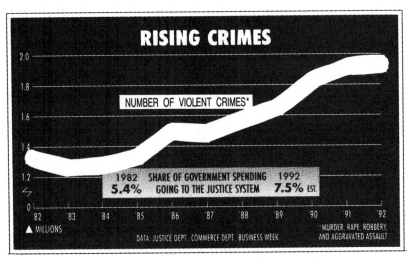

RISING CRIMES

NUMBER OF VIOLENT CRIMES*

| 1982 | SHARE OF GOVERNMENT SPENDING | 1992 |
| 5.4% | GOING TO THE JUSTICE SYSTEM | 7.5% EST. |

▲ MILLIONS

'82 '83 '84 '85 '86 '87 '88 '89 '90 '91 '92

DATA: JUSTICE DEPT. COMMERCE DEPT. BUSINESS WEEK

*MURDER, RAPE, ROBBERY, AND AGGRAVATED ASSAULT

From *Business Week*, December 13, 1993, pp. 72-75, 78-80, 85. © 1993 by McGraw-Hill, Inc. Reprinted by special permission.

average prison time served for a crime, adjusted for the chances of being caught and convicted. Today, the expected punishment for committing a serious crime is only about 11 days—half what it was in the 1950s. At the same time, job prospects for young adults and teenagers have soured, lowering the economic rewards for staying straight. "Criminals are sensitive to incentives," says Morgan O. Reynolds, a Texas A&M University economist who studies the economics of crime. Adds Ann Witte, a Wellesley economist: "The carrot can work, and the stick can work."

What's needed is a cost-effective way of raising the punishment that potential criminals can expect, argue these economists. That means the U. S. needs to devote many more resources to every aspect of law enforcement, not just prisons. That means more police on the streets, tougher sentences for young criminals, and closer monitoring of criminals on probation.

At the same time, it's crucial that the U. S. boost spending for job training and other programs in order to give teenagers and young adults better alternatives to crime. Typically, these programs are cheaper than the $20,000-to-$30,000-a-year cost of imprisonment. "We will never be able to afford enough prisons if that's our only approach to the criminal-justice problem," says Stephen Goldsmith, the Republican mayor of Indianapolis and a district attorney for 12 years. "You have to give people some hope for jobs and housing."

Such sentiments are far more common today than they were just a few years ago. In the 1980s, politicians were quick to call for longer, harsher sentences for all types of crimes. And one of the most damaging labels for a local politician in those years was "soft on crime." Yet for all the harsh rhetoric, few additional resources were devoted to fighting crime on the streets. Spending on prisons and the judicial system soared in the 1980s, but the number of police per 10,000 people barely rose. Indeed, in the second half of the decade, the total number of state and local police increased by only

16%, while the number of violent crimes jumped by 37%.

Now, fiscally strapped local officials find themselves begging for federal help and admitting defeat. District of Columbia Mayor Sharon Pratt Kelly unsuccessfully sought to deploy National Guard troops on the capital's streets, saying: "We're dealing with a war, yet people don't seem to want to win this war." After 300 stores were robbed and 52 people killed during holdups this year, Kelly's police chief recently suggested that a good way to cut crime was to close stores earlier.

The best deterrent is the simple presence of police

The analogy to war is a good one. By BUSINESS WEEK's calculation, the real cost of violent and property crime—when properly toted up—far exceeds the $300 billion defense budget. Spending by businesses and consumers on private security alone—including alarms, guards, and locks—comes to some $65 billion, according to William Cunningham, president of Hallcrest Systems Inc., a McLean (Va.) security-industry consulting firm. "People are more fearful, and they're taking a greater stake in their own protection." This has turned into a bonanza for companies such as Winner International Corp. in Sharon, Pa., which engineers and markets The Club, a steering-wheel lock to discourage auto theft. From 1990 to 1992, Club sales grew from $22 million to $107.3 million.

But Winner's bonanza is just another burden for business and consumers. "I call this the 'security tax' that business now has to pay because government hasn't been able to make us feel safe at home, work, or play," says Frank J. Portillo Jr., chief executive of Brown's Chicken & Pasta Inc., a 100-store fast-food chain based in Oak Brook, Ill. He had to install security cameras and hire guards for some of his stores in rougher neighborhoods after seven employees were massacred on Jan. 8 at a

Brown's Chicken outlet in Palatine, Ill.

The security tax hits urban areas particularly hard. According to BUSINESS WEEK's analysis of FBI crime statistics, most large cities have violent crime rates from two to seven times higher than their suburbs. As a result, many businesses and residents of crime-prone areas move to safer surroundings. That can quickly become a self-perpetuating cycle, since as jobs move out, the area becomes even more hopeless for the people who remain. BUSINESS WEEK estimates that annual damage to large urban economies from high crime rates is about $50 billion.

MIAMI VISE. Because of Miami's dependence on tourism, it is probably the urban area facing the clearest threat from crime. The city "has two problems," says Joseph P. Lacher, president of Miami-based Southern Bell-Florida and chairman of the Greater Miami Chamber of Commerce. "We have a serious crime problem to deal with and an even worse perception of crime." Dade County, where Miami is located, has one of the highest crime rates in the country. "People are scared to come to Florida," says Roberto Willimann, owner of Specialized Travel Systems, a Miami travel agency that caters to Germans. His business fell to about half of last year's after the Sept. 8 murder of a German tourist.

But crime's most devastating impact is measured in more than lost jobs and added security costs. The victim of a mugging or a rape carries the physical and emotional scars for years. Moreover, the damage to friends, family, and society from every murder is enormous.

Economists are able to measure the economic value of such intangible damages of violent crime using techniques originally developed for the cost-benefit analysis of safety regulations. According to newly published estimates by Ted R. Miller, a health-and-safety economist at National Public Services Research Institute in Landover, Md., and two colleagues, the value of a human life cut short by murder is about $2.4 million. They estimate the economic damage of a rape

ARREST AND PRISON: WHAT COPING WITH CRIMINALS COSTS

NUMBER OF VIOLENT CRIMES

PRISONERS HELD FOR VIOLENT CRIMES

ARRESTS FOR VIOLENT CRIMES

DATA: JUSTICE DEPARTMENT, BUSINESS WEEK

ALL ARRESTS

AVERAGE COST PER ARREST*

*POLICE AND COURT SYSTEM

ALL PRISONERS

AVERAGE ANNUAL COST PER PRISONER $27,000

to average about $60,000, while the typical robbery or assault costs more than $20,000. With more than 20,000 murders committed each year plus 2 million other crimes of violence, the so-called intangible damages come to a mind-numbing $170 billion, says Miller and his co-authors.

If America really wants to bring down violent crime, there's simply no way of dealing cheaply with a problem of this magnitude. "If you are going to have an effect, you have to spend a lot of money," says Wellesley economist Witte. But in a time of belt-tightening, it's essential to make every dollar as effective as possible. The ultimate goal is to reduce the incentives for criminal behavior. "We need the positives from participating in the legitimate economy to go up and the negatives from participating in the criminal economy to go up," says Goldsmith. "We've got the mix exactly backward."

DIMINISHING RETURNS. Spending on corrections has quadrupled over the past decade, rising far faster than spending on police or the courts. In part, that has been because of court-ordered up-grades of existing prisons, but actual incarcerations in state and federal prisons have tripled since 1980. And some economists, like Texas A&M'S Reynolds, believe that this prison boom has helped boost expected punishment a bit, keeping the crime problem from getting even worse than it already is.

But now the law of diminishing returns is setting in. Building and staffing prisons is extremely expensive, especially as sentences get longer and older inmates require increased medical care. Imprisoning a 25-year-old for life costs a total of $600,000 to $1,000,000. So putting someone in prison for life puts a huge financial

burden on the next generation—just as a big budget deficit does.

For that reason, much of the additional spending on law enforcement should go toward beefing up police forces rather than building new prisons. Indeed, evidence from economic studies shows that putting more police on the front lines has more of a deterrent effect than longer prison sentences. Explains Judge Richard Fitzgerald of Jefferson District Family Court in Louisville: "Most cops I know think that what really deters is the certainty of apprehension, not the sanction that would be imposed."

Even so, any concerted attempt to raise expected punishment will necessarily mean spending more on prisons. Every year, more than 60,000 violent criminals receive probation, largely because of overcrowding, according to Michael Block, a University of Arizona economist who was a member of

---

A COST-EFFECTIVE PLAN FOR REDUCING CRIME

Removing the incentives for criminal behavior can make Americans safer. Here's how:

1 IMPROVE ENFORCEMENT
Boost spending on police and courts by one-third, or $15 billion, to make apprehension and conviction much more certain. Increase spending on prisons and jails by 20%, or $5 billion

2 FOCUS PUNISHMENT
Release juvenile records at the first adult felony conviction so that longtime offenders can be quickly identified. In-

crease use of boot camps for youthful offenders.

3 CONTROL DRUG-RELATED CRIME
Test convicted criminals on probation for drug use on a regular basis, which could cut down on repeat offenders. Boost spending on drug rehabilitation.

4 EXPAND JOB TRAINING
Give teenagers an alternative to crime by doubling the size of the Job Corps, which has a proven crime-reducing record. Expand funding for privately run remedial

education and socialization programs.

5 SUPPORT NEIGHBORHOOD SAFETY
Encourage a shift to community policing, which puts more cops on the street instead of behind desks. Use police to prevent problems, not just respond to emergencies.

6 LESSEN LEVELS OF VIOLENCE
Expand violence-prevention and conflict-reduction programs in the schools. Toughen federal gun control, and buy back illegally owned handguns in cities.

the U. S. Sentencing Commission. That means one of the cheapest solutions to the crime problem, he says, is to "punish those people who are already captured."

FEW WORRIES. But the largest holes are in the juvenile-justice system. Violent-crime rates among young people have been rising far faster the among adults. "We are seeing juveniles committing more of the violent crimes at a younger age and with more destructive force and impact," says Judge Fitzgerald.

Part of the problem is that expected punishment for juveniles is very low. Young people often get little punishment for the first three or four felonies. "Juveniles have been getting the message that they can get away with anything," says Marvin Wolfgang, a criminologist at the University of Pennsylvania. Adds Mark A. Kleiman, an expert in the economics of crime at Harvard University:"It trains people to be criminals."

In addition, teenagers have little worry that crimes committed as juveniles will hurt them as adults. In most states, juvenile criminal records are permanently sealed. So a cost-effective way of identifying multiple offenders would be to unseal juvenile criminal records at the first adult felony conviction.

America's solution for dealing with illegal drug use has cost it dearly, too. In the 1980s, draconian sentencing laws were used to combat the drug problem, putting tens of thousands of people—and not necessarily the most violent ones—in prison. Currently, 60% of inmates in federal prisons and 20% of inmates in state prisons are there on drug charges. That helped drive up spending on prisons without doing much to deter violent crime.

One alternative strategy to keep down drug use and related crime without filling up scarce prison cells is to monitor more closely the nearly 3 million convicts on probation. Kleiman argues that regular drug-testing of criminals on probation could dramatically reduce drug use, at a cost of perhaps $5 billion annually. That can be combined with increased funding

for drug-rehab programs like the one at DC General Hospital in Washington, which treats 900 people each year at a cost of about $1,800 per person. "Most people who are heavy users can and will quit if they are under heavy pressure," says Kleiman, "and you'll reduce the criminal activities of the people you're testing."

But by itself, increased enforcement will not be enough to stem the tide of violence. "Short term, we need more cops and more aggressiveness in enforcement and prosecution," says Louisville Mayor Jerry Abramson, chairman of the U. S. Conference of Mayors. "But when a police officer gets involved that's too late. The focus has to be not just on catching criminals but on preventing criminals."

Moreover, giving young people alternatives to crime can multiply the effectiveness of the existing criminal-justice system. For every person not committing crimes, police can concentrate more resources on hard-core criminals. For example, if job training and education programs lowered the crime rate by 25%, that could mean an increase of as much as one-third in the expected punishment for lawbreakers.

Unlike many social programs, intensive training and education have already provided good evidence that they can reduce the crime rate. "Crime is a young man's game," says Witte. "Keep them busy and doing things that are not illegal, and they don't get in trouble."

For example, studies of the federal Job Corps, which is a residential program for basic education and hands-on vocational training, show a big drop in arrests for program participants. "There are few programs for young men that we can document as working well," says David Long, a senior research associate at Manpower Demonstration Research Corp., a nonprofit research organization in New York. "The Job Corps stands out as strikingly effective."

A NEW WORLD. The key to the success of the Job Corps and similar private programs is providing kids with a whole new environment. That

makes such programs expensive to run: A year in the Job Corps costs about $22,000. Adding enough slots in these programs to make a difference could cost billions. About 650,000 juveniles were arrested in 1992 for violent and property crimes. To provide programs for half of them would cost about $7 billion annually.

These programs are cheaper than the prisons they could replace, though. Average per-inmate cost for all juvenile facilities nationwide runs at about $30,000 annually. That's far more than the yearly cost of a slot in the Job Corps. In some cases, the difference can be even bigger. Take City Lights School in Washington, with 100 inner-city adolescents, many of them violent juvenile offenders. According to Stephen E. Klingelhofer, development director at City Lights, the $53-a-day cost is a bargain compared with the $147 daily tab at Lorton Reformatory Youth Center in Lorton, Va. Treatment at City Lights can be as simple as setting a good example. "A lot of these kids have never seen anyone getting up in the morning and going to a job," says Klingelhofer. "A lot of them come here not knowing any other way to settle disputes than by violence."

More and more police departments are focusing on prevention as well. This new philosophy goes under the name of "community policing," which means reorganizing police departments to put more officers in the field and focusing on helping neighborhoods prevent crime rather than just reacting to emergencies. That approach may include having more police out walking beats, working with social service and community agencies, and generally getting to know the residents. "We want to improve the quality of life in the neighborhoods," says Jerry Galvin, police chief of Vallejo, Calif., which has used community policing for six years and seen violent crime drop by 33%.

If combined with organizational reforms, a shift to community policing need not mean a huge expenditure of new resources, advocates say. "Community policing has nothing to do with new officers or more money," says Galvin. "But you have to remake the

AN ANGUISHED CRY OF 'ENOUGH' IN AMERICA'S KILLING FIELDS

Crime is an American tragedy, especially for blacks. African Americans are disproportionately both perpetrators and victims of criminal violence. Blacks make up almost half the country's prison admissions, and nearly one in four black men between the ages of 20 and 29 is in prison, on parole, or on probation. And homicide is the leading cause of death among black youths. Says Marian Wright Edelman, president of the Children's Defense Fund: "We lose more black men to guns in our cities in one year than we lost to all the lynchings after the Civil War."

Fear stalks inner-city streets. And in recent months, political leaders, ministers, and academics have all begun a crusade against crime, crying out to young black men to stop the violence. The Reverend Jesse Jackson rails against the lethal combination of guns and drugs in inner-city high schools. President Bill Clinton invokes the legacy of Dr. Martin Luther King Jr. in a plea to stop killing "each other with reckless abandonment." Increasingly, both liberals and conservatives are crossing racial and ideological divides to find common ground on policies that nurture families, support communities, create jobs, and provide more police protection in America's ghettos.

What's so discouraging is that black crime has become pervasive in many cities even as black politicians have gained power throughout the land, as the ranks of the black middle class have expanded, and as black high school graduation rates have risen.

CRIME PAYS. The reasons for the increase in violent crime are multifaceted, but the starting point is economic: The rewards for honest work for the less-educated have fallen, while the payoff for crime has risen. Urban jobs declined sharply beginning in the early 1970s, as foreign competition heated up. Inner cities began a downward spiral as work disappeared.

At the same time, explosive growth in the drug trade and other illegal pursuits

offered jobs and good money. A 1989 survey of youth crime in Boston shows that average hourly pay from crime ranged from $9.75 to $19 an hour (and no taxes), vs. the $5.60 an hour that youths earned after taxes from legitimate work, according to Richard B. Freeman, an economist at Harvard University. "Essentially, what is happening is that wage and employment opportunities have declined dramatically, and opportunities in the criminal sector have grown," says Harry J. Holzer, an economist at Michigan State University.

The sharp decline of the two-parent family is also part of the crime problem.

BLACKS AND CRIME — Blacks make up 12% of the nation's population but have high arrest rates...

SHARE OF ALL ARRESTS, 1992
MURDER AND NONNEGLIGENT MANSLAUGHTER 55.1%
ROBBERY 60.9%
AGGRAVATED ASSAULT 38.8%
BURGLARY 30.4%

...make up an increasing share of prison admissions...
WHITE '86 40% '91 35%
BLACK '86 45% '91 49%

MEN, AGES 20 TO 29, IN JAIL, OR ON PAROLE OR PROBATION
...with nearly one in four under correctional supervision...
WHITE 6.2% HISPANIC 10.4% BLACK 23.0%

VICTIMS (1991)
...and are more likely to be crime victims
HOMICIDE PER 100,000 — WHITE 4.9 BLACK 34.0
VIOLENT CRIME PER 1,000 — WHITE 29.6 BLACK 44.4

DATA: FEDERAL BUREAU OF INVESTIGATION, THE SENTENCING PROJECT, JUSTICE DEPT., NATIONAL CENTER ON INSTITUTIONS AND ALTERNATIVES

These days, 56% of black families are headed by women, and the figure increases significantly in inner-city neighborhoods. A large part of the decline in marriage rates is traceable to male joblessness and extraordinary poverty levels. The welfare system encourages female-headed households by providing financial support to unmarried mothers. The upshot: Juveniles from single-parent families have a greater chance of being involved in crime—especially murder and robbery.

Young criminals are devastating many inner-city communities, and throwing them into jail for short periods only seems to make things worse in the long run. When they return to their communities, they bring back the violent ethics of the cell block. Drugs, violent crime, and prisons are a part of everyday life. "If you haven't been arrested, you haven't gone through a rite of passage," says Marvin Dunn, a psychology professor at Florida International University.

FEW ROLE MODELS. The ecology of crime isolates inner-city communities in other ways. Few entrepreneurs open businesses in high-crime districts, where they can easily become murder or robbery victims. Middle-class blacks have fled for safer streets, too. In racially segregated, poverty-stricken neighborhoods, young people are less exposed to the work ethic, and informal networks of church and community groups are being drained of their most prominent middle-class members.

To make even a dent in the violence will require policies ranging from family support networks to more police. Most important, there must be jobs to compete with the lure of crime. Without jobs, high levels of violence in America's cities will continue, along with disproportionate black incarceration—and unimaginable suffering.

By Christopher Farrell in New York, with bureau reports

department to make community policing work." In Vallejo, 80% of police officers are in the field vs. the national average of about 60%.

New Haven, Conn., has had the same experience. In early 1993, New Haven shifted to community policing rather than just having officers answer 911 calls. That required more police on the street. The solution: substitute civilian staff for cops who used to pump gas into police cruisers and hand out billy clubs and clip boards. It's cost-effective as well. An officer costs about twice as much as a clerical worker and is much more expensive to train.

VICIOUS CYCLE. Part of what's scary about the latest wave of crime is not just the numbers but the brutality involved, especially the rampant use of firearms. From 1986 to 1991, robberies increased by 27%, but the use of a firearm during a robbery increased by 49%. And in a vicious cycle, crime is escalating the number of guns in private hands, as frightened Americans search for protection. At Colt Manufacturing Co. in Hartford, Conn., commercial handgun sales are running about 25% higher in 1993 than they were in 1992. "A whole gamut of industries are supplying the services that are being created by the crime statistics," says Colt Chairman R. C. Whitaker.

The job corps works—and it costs a lot less than prison

Can this spiral of violence be broken? Certainly a federal law making handguns illegal would sharply decrease the number of guns being sold and make their street price much higher, though, like Prohibition in the 1920s or the war against drugs in the 1980s, it might be very expensive to enforce. But with 60 million handguns already in private hands, even an effective ban on guns might not be enough. One intriguing possibility is to return to an approach that has been tried successfully in the past—buying back handguns. In 1974, the City of Baltimore decided to offer $50 per gun. In three months, 13,792 guns were turned in. A similar program today could help get illegally owned guns off the street, especially if combined with national gun control.

Some groups are trying to stamp out juvenile crime before it starts by teaching kids that violence simply is not the only way to settle disputes. That approach can be cost-effective, experts say, if it is started early. For example, Howard University's Violence Prevention Project is trying to teach 40 troubled 4th, 5th, and 6th graders to cope with boredom, frustration, and anger without reaching for a weapon. "Is it working? It's too early to tell," admits Hope Hill, director of the program. "It appears to be, but it will take several years to know."

In the end, no one solution will work, and no cheap and easy cure is possible. But the tremendous cost of crime to Americans demands that we not give up. The country's great wealth can surely be harnessed in an effective way to provide the remedies that will allow people to walk the streets without fear again.

By Michael J. Mandel in New York and Paul Magnussan in Washington, with James E. Ellis in Chicago, Gail DeGeorge in Miami, Keith L. Alexander in Pittsburgh, and bureau reports

Violence in America

A scary orgy of violent crime is fueling another public call to action. But before a binge of new lawmaking takes place, citizens ought to understand what the real problems are and what the limits of any new programs are likely to be.

It hardly made a ripple in the deluge of violence news now gripping the nation, but it was enough to frighten relatively placid Indianapolis. Members of a drug-trafficking gang called the Getto Boys opened fire with a rifle and 9-mm handguns one evening last fall outside the Blackburn Terrace housing project. More than 60 shots failed to hit their intended target, a figure in a narcotics-sales dispute. Instead, they killed a 16-year-old girl visiting friends at the project and critically wounded a 7-year-old boy lying in bed watching "Monday Night Football." All Mayor Stephen Goldsmith can hope is that the shoot-'em-up in an area not usually known for blood and gore will help galvanize public opinion to expand his programs to combat gangs.

That scenario of violence against innocent bystanders has been repeated across the nation. The drumbeat of news coverage has made it seem that America is in the midst of its worst epidemic of violence ever. That sense is not supported by the numbers. The latest evidence is that crime levels actually fell last year. But that does not mean that last year wasn't the scariest in American history. Overriding the statistics is the chilling realization that the big crime stories of recent months have invaded virtually every sanctuary where Americans thought they were safe: their cars (James Jordan's murder); their public transit (the Long Island Rail Road murders); even their bedrooms (the kidnap and murder of young Polly Klaas in Petaluma, Calif.). Gangs have taken root in small towns and suburbs. In addition, a holiday-season burst of multiple killings showed how potent modern weapons are and how random the slaughter can be.

The nation has been through any number of anticrime seasons in the past generation. In many of them, the public's preoccupation with crime rose as citizens' concerns about the economy subsided—and then waned as economic issues regained center stage. Public attitudes also are driven by periodic media orgies of crime coverage. Yet, there are some who believe that the forces gathering behind this season's efforts are different because the threat seems so much graver. There is some hope, too, that a much more serious and comprehensive national attack on violence will emerge—and maybe even show real results. "This is not just a blip on the chart," says Barry Krisberg of the National Council on Crime and Delinquency, who has not seen such sustained public interest in violence since Lyndon Johnson created a crime commission in 1965. Krisberg pre-

· ·

The toll of violence

Violence in modern America began its upward climb in 1960. Violent-crime reports dipped only in the early 1980s, coincident with a decline in the number of teenagers. A survey of victims that includes unreported crimes puts the total above 6 million a year.

■ **PER CAPITA CRIME.** Violent crime grew from 161 reported crimes per 100,000 persons in 1960 to 758 in 1992 —a 371 percent jump.

■ **MURDERS.** The annual homicide total topped 20,000 in the mid-1970s. After a one-year drop, it grew to 23,040 in 1980 before declining for several years. The total began rising again in 1985, hitting 23,760 in 1992. Final figures are not in, but a new record may have been set last year.

■ **PROPERTY CRIMES.** These have risen from 1,726 reported crimes

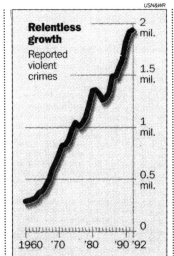

USN&WR

Relentless growth
Reported violent crimes

2 mil.
1.5 mil.
1 mil.
0.5 mil.
0

1960 '70 '80 '90 '92

per 100,000 persons in 1960 to 4,903 in 1992—but the worst jumps occurred before 1980.

■ **GUN SUPPLY.** The number of guns in America increased from 54 million in 1950 to 201 million in 1990.

■ **OUT-OF-WEDLOCK BIRTHS.** The growth of illegitimacy—especially in the inner cities—has been linked to escalating violence. In 1970, about 11 percent of births were out of wedlock. By 1991, nearly 30 percent were.

USN&WR – Basic data: FBI, Bureau of Alcohol, Tobacco and Firearms, National Center for Health Statistics

 From *U.S. New & World Report*, January 17, 1994, pp. 22-24, 26-27, 30, 32-33. © 1994 by U.S. News & World Report. Reprinted by permission.

dicts a new "barrage of punitive, get-tough measures."

A prime element of the new anticrime upswelling is the degree to which the public is furious at the failure of previous efforts to solve the problem. Nothing has stemmed the upward spiral of reported violent incidents: not massive spending on social programs for the poor; not a massive buildup of prison cells; not sweeping changes to impose mandatory minimum sentences; not innovative new policing techniques. That anger-fed cynicism will doubtless play a big role in many elections this year. In response, President Clinton will plug new anticrime programs in his State of the Union address on January 25. Members of Congress will soon begin final bargaining on a massive anticrime bill that, regardless of its provisions, they will label the toughest-ever attack. And governors nationwide have their own plans—ranging from California's Republican Pete Wilson's call for longer prison terms to New York's Democratic Mario Cuomo's call for prosecuting more juvenile criminals in adult courts.

Two other new forces are at play that give the current interest a different shape. One is the rising anger of African-American leaders like Jesse Jackson about black-on-black crime; Jackson complained last week that more American blacks are killed by each other each year than died during the entire history of lynching. Then there's the heightened anticrime fervor of many officials in middle-sized and small towns, which

now are experiencing some of the same trends in the violence contagion that cities have faced for a generation. Typical is the view of Claire McCaskill, chief state prosecutor in the Kansas City area, on violent juvenile repeat offenders who have terrorized her community: "We've got to lock them up for as long as we can."

As the debate shapes up, several points help put it in perspective:

■ The startling string of heinous killings does not represent a sudden new wave of crime. Violent crime levels have been extraordinarily high for many years. The nature of some of the crime is changing, though, making some people more vulnerable and bringing the worst kinds of problems into communities that many thought were safe.

■ Some of the most frightening trends in crime—like the increasing prevalence of stranger-on-stranger robberies and drive-by shootings—might be susceptible to new crime-prevention techniques, but only in the long term. "We are not going to come up with the magic solution to a genuine national crisis," admits Peter Edelman, a senior official of the Department of Health and Human Services who cochairs a Clinton antiviolence team. The group is examining nine basic elements of the problem, including family strife, hate crimes and the role of the media. It could lead to the creation of an unofficial "Department of Violence" to coordinate disjointed federal aid programs.

■ The most likely governmental actions against crime in the short term—expanding police forces and prisons—tend to be costly and yet might only reduce crime marginally. For instance, the prison-building boom of the 1980s had little effect on violent-crime rates.

■ The most promising lines of attack start at the local level, where authorities and residents are mounting block-by-block campaigns to reclaim cities.

The biggest mystery. The true level of violence in America is a mystery. Reports to police compiled by the Federal Bureau of Investigation steadily increased for years after 1960 but leveled off in 1992 and actually declined in the first six months of 1993. Last year's total probably will exceed 1.9 million incidents when the final count is in. Yet a Justice Department survey that asks Americans if they have been victimized, thus including crimes not reported to authorities, estimates the figure at closer to 6.6 million. Even that understates the total, because some victims refuse to disclose even anonymously what happened to them.

What infuriates a growing number of city dwellers is the knowledge that local police do not or cannot bother with petty crimes like thefts from autos. Such crimes (classified as "personal larceny without contact" to distinguish them from purse snatchings and pocket pickings) take place about 12 million times each year—twice the violence total. Insurance agents often pick up the burden of dealing with these crimes. "We're

Killer teens

Teenagers always have been responsible for a disproportionate share of violent crime, but the problem has worsened  *since the mid-1980s. Experts cite a racial disparity: The arrest rate of white males has doubled in recent years, but that of blacks has multiplied 3.5 times.*

■ **OVERALL VIOLENCE.** Arrests for violent crimes by youths under 18, mostly boys, jumped from 54,596 in 1970 to 104,137 in 1992—a 91 percent hike.

■ **POPULATION MYSTERY.** For many years, the violent-crime rate seemed to rise and fall in tandem with the number of teens in the population. But teen violence exploded—murder arrests of youths under 18 have jumped 92 percent since 1985—during a period when the teen population remained steady or declined. A projected 23 percent increase by 2005 in youths ages 15 to 19 may make things worse.

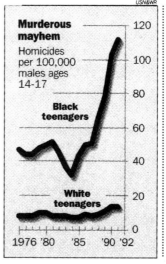

Murderous mayhem
Homicides per 100,000 males ages 14-17
Black teenagers
White teenagers
1976 '80 '85 '90 '92

USN&WR

■ **CASE CLOSED?** Disposition of violence cases in juvenile courts:

Corrections program	**30%**
Probation	**34%**
Case dismissed	**27%**
Sent for trial as adult	**3%**
Other	**6%**

■ **YOUNGER THUGS.** Youths are being arrested for violent crimes at younger ages. In 1982, for example, 390 teens ages 13 to 15 were arrested for murder. A decade later, this total had jumped to 740.

USN&WR—Basic data: FBI, U.S. Office of Juvenile Justice and Delinquency Prevention, Profs. James Alan Fox and Glenn Pierce of Northeastern University

WHAT YOU CAN DO

Thinking through the dangers

No safety rules can protect the law abiding from being hit by random fire from crazed gunmen, but there are ways to reduce the odds in other kinds of attack. "People are picked as crime victims because they are attractive" in some way, says criminologist Terance Miethe of the University of Nevada. That usually means the victim is alone or has what a criminal wants. Most street criminals are interested in getting their booty and leaving undetected, says Jean O'Neil of the National Crime Prevention Council. Some basic strategies:

■ **Act smart.** The council recommends walking with confidence, staying in well-lit, busy areas, walking in groups at night, being aware of your surroundings, wearing shoes and clothes that allow freedom of movement and trusting your instincts. It is most often wise to give up your valuables if that's what the thug is after.

■ **Lock up.** Carjacking has received a lot of attention, but a more common crime is car theft; some 1.6 million were reported in 1992. More than 200,000 vehicles are stolen each year in the United States because drivers leave keys in the ignition, says analyst Louis Mizell.

■ **Be prepared.** People intent on fighting back should be prepared mentally and physically. Assume that the criminal is already prepared to use force. The smartest preventive measure against an assault is a self-defense course, says associate professor Greg Connor of the University of Illinois Police Training Institute. Self-defense instructors point to new studies showing that women who fight back are less likely to be raped. But Connor says potential students should be choosy, seeking well-respected, nonexorbitant programs that teach more than just physical defenses, in case the physical techniques fail. Examples include being firm and repetitious in explaining what you want the assailant to do.

■ **Use defensive weapons.** If you plan to use defensive weapons like tear gas or pepper spray, seek training to reduce the risk that they can be turned against you. Some states and the District of Colum-

---

often the first person at a crime scene—we're part agent and part social worker," says Steve Goldstein of the Insurance Information Institute.

Whatever the bottom line, the violence now is just the latest of the historic peaks the nation has experienced. America has been hit with surges of violence that begin roughly 50 years apart, in 1850, 1900 and 1960, says Ted Robert Gurr, a political scientist at the University of Maryland. Ethnic strife played a large part in all three periods, and crime totals within each era have fluctuated. After murder, robbery and assault reached record levels in 1980, for instance, rates in almost every major category dropped for half a decade. Then, fueled by the crack cocaine epidemic, violent crime climbed back up: A new murder record was set in 1992, even though the total number of youths—the cohort most associated with crime—was dropping. (The shrinking of the teen population did seem, however, to help reduce the number of property crimes.)

Among the basic crime patterns policy makers must confront:

■ **Murder.** While the absolute numbers fluctuated in the past decade, an increase in random murder was especially ominous. Decades ago, most murders were committed by relatives or acquaintances of the victim. Now, the proportion committed by strangers may have risen to one third, fueling the growing fear that there's no place where anyone is really safe. Criminologist Alfred Blumstein of Carnegie Mellon University blames a "large growth in crimes committed by young people who appear not to have absorbed much concern about the value of human life." A new book by Marc Riedel of Southern Illinois University, *Stranger Violence,* concludes that such cases are "pervasively underreported."

■ **Robbery.** Stickups, from simple street muggings to heists at automated teller machines, remain the most prevalent crime that Americans should fear from strangers. The latest victimization survey estimates that robbers strike 1.2 million times each year, injuring their prey a third of the time. Unlike most other

---

Breakdown of the justice system

After a lull in prison sentences in the late 1960s and early 1970s, a get-tough drive has increased stays behind bars ever since.

The inmate count has soared from 218,466 to 925,247 since 1974. But many prisoners are released after serving only a third of their stated terms.

■ **THE FUNNEL EFFECT IN 1990:**

Estimated number of violent crimes	**6.0 mil.**
Number of crimes reported to law enforcement	**1.8 mil.**
Arrests	**580,006**
Felony convictions	**130,226**
Number incarcerated	**107,302**

■ **CRIME ON TOP OF CRIME.** Of persons arrested for violent crimes, about 17 percent have charges pending for other crimes; 13 percent more are on probation, on parole or otherwise already tied up in the justice system.

■ **FEWER CASES SOLVED.** The

USN&WR

Arrests and imprisonment
Convicts sent to prison per 1,000 arrests for serious crimes

400 — 300 — 200 — 100 — 0

1960 '64 '70 '74 '78 '81 '85 '90 '91

share of violent crimes solved by police departments has declined from 47.6 percent in 1970 to 44.6 percent in 1992. The drop has been steepest in homicide cases, from 86.5 to 64.6 percent.

■ **HARDLY HARD TIME.** Violent offenders' median prison time grew from 23 months to just over two years from 1983 to 1991. Murderers usually served under seven years.

USN&WR – Basic data: FBI, U.S. Bureau of Justice Statistics

bia have outlawed some of the sprays.

■ **Don't go.** Avoid getting into an assailant's car if at all possible. O'Neil says victims rarely survive attacks after being forced into a car.

■ **Don't blame yourself.** Finally, John Stein of the National Organization for Victim Assistance tells victims not to blame themselves when they don't react the way that they would have preferred. When attacked, people revert to primitive behavior fueled by a rush of adrenalin. If your attackers have an assault weapon pointed at your head, "it's not the ideal time to duke it out with them unless you're convinced they're going to kill you anyway," says Stein. "It's your decision whether or not you want to go down fighting."

BY KATIA HETTER

violent crimes like murder, rape and assault, in which the assailant more often than not knows the victim, an estimated 84 percent of robberies are committed by strangers. Still, the national robbery rate has declined since a peak in 1981, and most encounters do not end in violence: One in 20 cases results in both serious injury and lost property.

■ **Random crimes.** A common error of citizens and policy makers is to mistake big news stories for big trends and to demand action on a new "crime wave" that really isn't that big. For instance, contrary to conventional wisdom, random slaughters like last month's Long Island Rail Road massacre and recent shooting sprees at postal facilities are not

increasing sharply. The annual count of cases in which more than four persons were killed in a single incident varied from 10 to 30 each year between 1976 and 1991, reports criminologist James Alan Fox of Northeastern University, who still is compiling totals for the past two years but does not expect a marked change. "Most mass murderers do not kill at random in public places," Fox concludes.

■ **Workplace killings.** Murderous episodes at job sites are growing, and a cottage industry of high-priced consultants is arising to exploit it. But like mass killings, they are relatively rare. A Labor Department count for 1992 found 45 revenge-type murders by workers or former employees. A preliminary compilation for 1993 by the Chicago-based National Safe Workplace Institute that included killings in personal or family feuds tallied 70 cases. Although that toll is up from fewer than 20 per year during the 1980s, institute Director Joseph Kinney says it "is hardly at epidemic proportions."

■ **Child snatchings.** Though the nation was sickened by the abduction and murder of 12-year-old Polly Klaas in California and the killing of two elementary school students in St. Louis, the best evidence is that between 50 and 150 such episodes have occurred each year since the late 1970s; the 1993 total probably will be on the low end. Parents need not be so frightened that they keep children indoors excessively, says Ernest Allen of the National Center for Missing and Exploited Children, but they "need to recognize that teenagers are the single most victimized segment of society."

■ **Carjackings and drive-bys.** These are clearly on the rise. Each year, criminals attack nearly 30,000 drivers to rob or rape them or steal their vehicles. While the figure is alarming, it pales when compared with the 1.6 million auto thefts. As for bystander shootings, a survey of news reports by Maryland criminologist Lawrence Sherman found a fourfold increase of such cases in New York City in the late 1980s compared with a decade earlier.

■ **Family strife.** This is one problem that doesn't get the attention it deserves. There are 800,000 or more violent incidents within families each year, but the terror of living in many homes is largely overlooked with the exception of sensational cases like Lorena Bobbitt's slashing of her husband John's penis, the subject of a trial in Virginia this week.

■ **Justice system.** The escalating crime numbers also have an impact on the beleaguered criminal justice system, which gets much of the blame for not controlling violence. So many violent criminals are repeat offenders—estimates range from 50 percent up—it is inevitable that many former prisoners as well as defendants awaiting trial and convicts on probation will be arrested for new crimes. Critics charge that the system remains unaccountably lax; justice professionals respond that their record of singling out career criminals for longer incarceration has improved.

■ **More cops.** For the fifth time since 1984, Congress probably will pass major crime legislation this spring. The most important item likely to emerge from tough bargaining between the House and Senate is money for between 50,000 and

The victims' profiles

Violence affects Americans unevenly. High-risk groups include youths 16 to 19, who are victimized 20 times as much as the elderly; unmarried men; divorced women, and families with incomes under $7,500, who are victimized three times as much as those with incomes over $50,000.

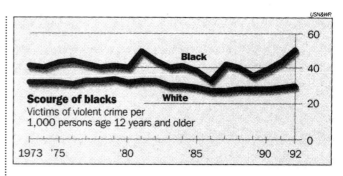

Scourge of blacks Victims of violent crime per 1,000 persons age 12 years and older

1973 '75   '80   '85   '90 '92

■ **THE PLIGHT OF BLACK MALES.** In every age group, black men are significantly more likely to be victims of violent crime than are white men or women of either race. Among youths ages 14 to 17, the black male victimization rate is 65.9 per 100,000 in the population; the white male rate is 8.5.

■ **MEAN CITIES.** The rate of violence against household members in cities has been stable for two decades, hitting 43.2 incidents for every 1,000 households in 1992. The suburban rate is much lower at 28.2 incidents per 1,000 households. It has declined since the 1970s. The rural rate—25.2—

has increased slightly in recent years.

■ **INTERRACIAL CRIME.** About 80 percent of violence occurs among persons of the same race. Of the 20 percent of incidents that are interra-

cial, 15 percent involve white victims and black offenders, 2 percent involve black victims and white offenders and 3 percent involve white victims and offenders of other races.

USN&WR – Basic data: U.S. Bureau of Justice Statistics

100,000 more police officers. Cities will have to pay one fourth to one half the cost of each cop initially and provide full funding after three years, but for now, no one's complaining. "After a great buildup in federal law enforcement, we're finally going to be putting bodies where they're most useful—on city streets," says Patrick Murphy, a former New York City police commissioner now at the U.S. Conference of Mayors.

Yet it will take a year or more for those cops to appear in large numbers, and there is no guarantee that they will lower the crime rate. In a survey of eight large cities, *U.S. News* found that more police does not necessarily mean lower crime rates. For example, Washington, D.C., has the highest police-population ratio of any big city—757 per 100,000 residents in 1992—but that year had one of the highest violent-crime rates, 2,832 per 100,000 residents. After Boston added 54 officers between 1987 and 1992, the overall crime rate dropped, but the number of murders rose sharply before declining to its original level. One city claiming success is Houston, which reports a 22 percent crime drop in the two years since it established a major police-over-time program, adding the equivalent of several hundred officers to a 4,500-member force.

The bill also will probably fund "boot camps" for nonviolent offenders, prisons for violent juveniles, school security, antigang enforcement and "drug courts" that funnel low-level drug offenders to treatment rather than to jail. More debatable are various provisions to "federalize" state crimes. One, for example, would make murders with guns a federal crime punishable by death. But there is no evidence that such efforts in recent years to get federal authorities into basic street-level law enforcement have had much impact.

For their part, Clinton forces promise to mount a balanced attack on violence.

"The president thinks the debate between prevention and punishment is a false one," says domestic-policy adviser Bruce Reed. "We have to do both. We have to try everything." Clinton's eight-agency violence working group soon will send him a plan to short-circuit violence, particularly among the young.

The panel has identified effective local programs and wants to create a clearinghouse where localities can cut through federal red tape and learn quickly about solutions that have worked elsewhere. For instance, Deputy Attorney General Philip Heymann, who cochairs the campaign with HHS's Edelman, marveled at the educational performance of an elementary school he recently visited in "the very worst neighborhood" of New Orleans: "When [we] asked how many in a group of fifth graders had seen a gun in the last 24 hours, it was everybody. How many of you have seen somebody killed? Half of them. It was the hardest possible situation for education and safety. But that school was safe, and the students were learning."

The Clinton group will urge more federal backing for providing mentors to troubled youth and parenting help to mothers. It also will call for putting more pressure on the entertainment media to deglamorize violence; major television networks already have decided to devote large blocs of time in late January to examining the violence problem. Federal housing officials soon will initiate Project Crackdown to clamp down on crime in public housing, including expansion of the federal witness protection program to tenants who observe crime. The group will push for more emphasis on school safety, including expansion of a "safe haven" program to keep schools open into the evening.

State legislators also will consider crime-prevention ideas, but they will focus on parts of the justice process that seem most broken, particularly the sen-

tencing system. Some states will surely adopt "three strikes and you're out" laws requiring life sentences with no parole for third-time felons. But proponents will have to come up with billions of dollars to expand prison space to put such programs into effect. And critics like Vincent Schiraldi of the private Center on Juvenile and Criminal Justice in San Francisco complain that some of the proposed laws are so broad that someone writing a bad check 25 years after committing two juvenile crimes could be put away for life.

With resources scarce at all levels of government, the best hope for progress against violence is at the local level, where grass-roots organizations from San Antonio to Boston are rising up to mount more sophisticated campaigns against street crime. Such drives are hardly new, but anticrime activists report a new, aggressive spirit. Instead of merely reporting crimes to police, some groups, like Washington's Metro Orange Hat Coalition, videotape street-corner drug transactions. Members of the Ivar Hawks Neighborhood Watch in Los Angeles make citizens' arrests of dealers who offer to sell them drugs.

"There is no magic trick or secret formula," says Alvin Wright of the Houston Police Department. "Crime went down here when the citizens of our town decided they were not going to just sit back and watch things." That's just the attitude that seems to be catching on elsewhere.

By Ted Gest with Gorden Witkin,
Katia Hetter and Andrea Wright

Readers can discuss the issues raised by this story in a special, interactive forum on U.S. News Online, beginning January 10 [1994]. U.S. News Online is available on CompuServe; for a free sign-up kit, call (800) 510-4247.

Mob Tightens Secretive Style in Retreat from Prosecutors

Selwyn Raab

Not so long ago, when the Mafia was an expanding industry, mobsters in the New York area were so indifferent to law-enforcement surveillance that they talked freely in their clubhouses, exchanged traditional kisses on the cheek at street meetings and often mocked investigators who trailed them.

But buffeted by convictions, electronic spying by investigators, top-level defections and deadly internal feuds, many leaders and soldiers in New York's five Mafia families are altering their underworld life styles. Law-enforcement officials assert that a widespread fear among Mafiosi of being infiltrated by informers or even observed talking with each other has compelled Mafia members in New York and New Jersey to take extraordinary defensive measures.

The difficulties for New York's five entrenched families and two smaller ones in New Jersey stem largely from the successes of campaigns begun 10 years ago by Federal and state law-enforcement agencies. In the last five years, more than 300 top- and middle-echelon leaders in the seven families have been convicted or are awaiting trial, prosecutors say.

As examples of the mob's new defensive tactics, officials cited these recent developments:

• The Ravenite Social Club, the Gambino crime family's favorite gathering spot in Little Italy for over 30 years, is shuttered six days a week. The storefront club on Mulberry Street was the daily headquarters for John Gotti, who prosecutors charged was the family's boss before his conviction and imprisonment in 1992 on racketeering and murder charges. It is occasionally open on Wednesday nights when Mr. Gotti's brother, Peter, meets with a few loyalists.

• Genovese crime family members sometimes travel to meetings curled up on a car floor or in the trunk to avoid being tracked by investigators.

• Members in several families have been ordered never to utter the real names of leaders and to refer to them in conversations through code names or by hand signals.

• In some families, soldiers are rejecting promotions to capos, the captains of crews or units, apparently for fear it will make them automatic targets of law-enforcement agencies.

Signs have blossomed in many mob clubs warning, "Don't talk. This place is bugged." At the Ravenite, a picture of an insect was pinned to the wall above a telephone.

"They've become so paranoid about being bugged that I wouldn't be surprised this summer if they hold meetings on the beach in swimsuits," says Joseph J. Coffey, the head of intelligence for New York State's Organized Crime Task Force.

Since 1990 most of the Mafia's roster of bosses, underbosses and acting bosses in New York and New Jersey have been sentenced to long prison terms on racketeering charges or have defected to testify against their former underworld colleagues. In addition to Mr. Gotti, the head of the Gambino family since 1986, the bosses and top lieutenants in three other families, the Lucchese, Colombo, and Bonanno groups from New York and the Bruno-Scarfo and DeCavalcante families from New Jersey have been convicted on racketeering charges or are awaiting trials.

Additionally, authorities say that prosecutions and civil suits brought by Federal prosecutors and especially by the Manhattan District Attorney's office have uprooted the Mafia's control of major unions in the New York region. The lawsuits disclosed that through secret influence in the teamsters, carpenters, painters, plumbers and newspaper drivers unions, mob families for decades reaped millions of dollars in illicit profits. The payoffs, according to testimony, came from extortions from employers for labor peace, and from frauds and ghost jobs in the construction, airfreight, waste-hauling, gasoline-distribution, garment-manufacturing and food-supply industries.

Authorities of the Federal Bureau of

Who's Who in the Mob

Law-enforcement officials say these are the major organized crime families in New York and New Jersey. In addition to inducted members, the families rely upon hundreds of associates who assist or act as fronts in criminal activities.

NEW YORK

Genovese 250 TO 300 MEMBERS

BOSS Vincent Gigante, 66. The F.B.I. says he controls the family, although psychiatrists have found him mentally unfit for trial. Relatives say he lives with his mother in Greenwich Village.

RANKING MEMBERS Liborio (Big Barney) Bellomo, 37, of Pelham Manor, acting street boss, is viewed by authorities as possible successor to Mr. Gigante. Other powerful figures are James (Little Jimmy) Ida, 54, of Staten Island, the consigliere, or counsellor, and Rosario (Ross) Gangi, 54, of Brooklyn, a capo who is influential in the Fulton Fish Market. Joseph (Pepe) Lascala, 63, of Bayonne, handles activities in New Jersey.

ACTIVITIES Gambling, loan sharking, narcotics and construction in New York and New Jersey. Also has secret interests in private sanitation companies in New Jersey and is suspected of extortion on New Jersey waterfront.

Gambino 300 MEMBERS

BOSS John Gotti, 53. Federal officials say he runs the family while in Federal prison. Uses his son, John Gotti Jr., 30, of Massapequa, L.I., and brother Peter, 54, of Ozone Park, Queens, to deliver orders. Officials say civil war might erupt in family if Mr. Gotti tries to anoint his son as successor.

RANKING MEMBERS Several law-enforcement experts say that Nicholas Corozzo, a capo from Canarsie, may be the acting street boss. Another important capo and Gotti loyalist is Jack D'Amico, 59, from lower Manhattan.

ACTIVITIES Rackets include private carting in New York City, extortion and bid rigging in construction and in the garment district. Also gambling and loan

sharking in the city, New York suburbs and Connecticut and on Long Island.

Lucchese 75 MEMBERS

BOSS Vittorio Amuso, 59, serving life term in Federal prison

RANKING MEMBERS Family has been disrupted by defections of underboss, Anthony Casso, 53; acting boss, Alphonse D'Arco, 61, and Anthony Accetturo, 55, former head of crew in New Jersey. It is believed to be run by a panel of three capos, Steven Crea, 46, of Pelham Manor, Domenico Cutaia, 57, of Brooklyn, and Joseph DeFede, 60, of Queens. Mr. Crea, who maintains an office and pigeon coops in a construction company in the Bronx, is said to be family's dominant figure.

ACTIVITIES Family's labor racketeering kickbacks damaged by arrests and defections of leaders and corruption charges brought against allies in several unions: teamsters, carpenters, plumbers, painters and newspaper drivers. Rackets in garment district taken over by Gambino family.

Colombo 75 TO 100 MEMBERS

BOSSES Family split into two factions, each led by a boss serving a life sentence. Carmine (the Snake) Persico, 61, who was the boss, and Victor (Little Vic) Orena, 59.

RANKING MEMBERS Internal war since 1991 has resulted in murders of at least 15 members and associates. Persico faction, headed by Joseph (Joe T) Tomasello, 61, of Brooklyn, is believed to be stronger group. More than 100 members and associates arrested or convicted in last three years, and family lost one of its prime rackets, skimming of gasoline taxes. Family also riven by turncoats:

Carmine (Chas) Sessa, 41, a former consigliere, and John (E. T.) Pate, 52, a Persico capo, have become Government witnesses.

ACTIVITIES Narcotics trafficking, gambling, loan sharking, especially in Brooklyn and Queens, and also active in gambling and labor rackets in New Jersey.

Bonanno 50 TO 75 MEMBERS

BOSS Joseph C. Massino, 51, of Howard Beach, Queens, released from Federal prison in 1992. Must confer secretly with associates because parole rules bar him from associating with known criminals.

RANKING MEMBER Anthony Spero, 65, the family consigliere.

ACTIVITIES Considered the weakest of the five New York families and banned for a decade from the Commission, the coordinating and ruling body for the families, because it was vulnerable to infiltration by Government agents and because of its involvement in narcotics.

NEW JERSEY

DeCavalcante 10 MEMBERS

BOSS John M. Riggi, 68, of Linden, N.J., serving life term.

ACTIVITIES Once active in labor rackets and gambling in northern New Jersey, but most of them have been taken over by Gambino family.

Bruno-Scarfo 5 TO 8 MEMBERS

BOSS John Stanfa, 51, of Medford, N.J., awaiting trial in Philadelphia.

ACTIVITIES Family was virtually destroyed by internal wars, turncoats and convictions. A handful of members are still active in gambling, loan sharking and narcotics in Newark.

Investigation and New York State estimate that the families based in New York—the Gambino, Genovese, Lucchese, Colombo and Bonanno groups—have about 850 made, or inducted, members on the streets in New York and New Jersey, compared with more than 1,000 four years ago. Robert T. Buccino, deputy chief of investigations for New Jersey's Organized Crime Bureau, said that the law-enforcement crackdown has reduced the number of made Mafiosi in the state who are not in prison to fewer than 50 from the more than 200 who were operating in the mid-1980's.

RUTHLESS DISCIPLINE IN GENOVESE FAMILY

Law-enforcement officials acknowledge, however, one significant setback: The campaign has failed to dislodge the Genovese family from several lucrative rackets in New York, New Jersey and Connecticut.

"If there is a major trend, it is the consolidation of power by the Genovese family," said William Y. Doran, head of the criminal division in the F.B.I.'s New York office. "The others are wracked, banged up pretty good."

The authorities say that the Genovese family has retained most of its power mainly because of the ruthless discipline and secrecy imposed by Vincent (Chin) Gigante, whom Federal and state prosecutors have identified in indictments as the group's boss since 1980. Under Mr. Gigante's rule the Genovese clan has supplanted the Gambino family as the wealthiest and most powerful crime faction in New York and New Jersey, Federal and state officials say.

Donald V. North, the chief of the organized-crime unit in the F.B.I.'s New York office, said that the Genovese family operated gambling and loan-sharking rackets and thrived on labor racketeering in the construction and waste-hauling industries and at the Fulton Fish Market.

"Nobody will cross Chin Gigante," Mr. North said of Mr. Gigante's role in the family.

STRONG INFLUENCE ON NEW JERSEY PORTS

Mr. Buccino of New Jersey's Organized Crime Bureau said that a Genovese base that has been impregnable for de-

cades is the New Jersey waterfront. A New Jersey Genovese crew, he said, is suspected of extorting payoffs from companies operating at Port Newark and Elizabeth. "We've attempted to infiltrate them over the years and always struck out," Mr. Buccino said of efforts to eradicate the family's influence on the waterfront.

Investigators grudgingly credit Mr. Gigante with exceptional skill in selecting loyal capos who operate crews and funnel illegal profits to him. Unlike the other families in the region, the Genovese group has had no high-level traitors and its hierarchy seems to be intact.

Prospective Genovese members undergo a more rigorous selection process than is required in the other families ad endure a form of probation for about one year before they are formally recognized as soldiers, investigators say.

Dennis J. Marchalonis, the head of an F.B.I. organized-crime squad in New Jersey, said that Genovese leaders conceal the identities of some members to deceive the other families about its actual strength in the event of violent showdowns.

For years Mr. Gigante, 66, has been observed behaving oddly in public, strolling near his home in Greenwich Village in slippers and pajamas and mumbling incoherently. In 1990 he was indicted in Brooklyn on Federal racketeering charges, and last year a charge was added that he conspired to murder Mr. Gotti in retaliation for Mr. Gotti's having engineered the killing of Paul Castellano, his predecessor as Gambino boss, in 1985.

Four psychiatrists have found Mr. Gigante unfit to stand trial, but prosecutors claim that he is feigning mental illness and that former leaders from other families who have defected will testify that his erratic behavior is an act. The question of whether he will stand trial is waiting a ruling by a Federal judge in Brooklyn.

A top Mafia turncoat, Anthony Accetturo, the former head of the Lucchese family's operations in New Jersey, said in an interview in February that "if anybody survives it will be the Genovese." Mr. Accetturo, who was convicted last year in New Jersey on state charges of extortion and racketeering, said the Genovese gang was probably the only family in the region that had not been weakened by a new generation of

leaders whose lust for money and power had created dissension and betrayals.

SOPHISTICATED WEBS OF ILLICIT INTERESTS

Since the 1920's, 24 Mafia families have been organized in cities including Chicago, Philadelphia, Detroit, Boston, Buffalo, Newark, Kansas City, Tampa, New Orleans, Los Angeles, Providence, Milwaukee and Cleveland. These Italian-American gangs outlasted other organized-crime groups, authorities say, because the Mafia organizations had defined autocratic structures and were not dependent on a single leader for their continued existence.

Most criminal organizations rely on one unlawful activity, like narcotics trafficking, bookmaking or extortion. But the American Mafia diversified into sophisticated webs with illicit financial interests in many industries as well as the traditional rackets of gambling and loan sharking.

That is why criminal enterprises that have replaced the mob in specific areas of crime—like Latin American cartels that sell narcotics or Asian groups that extort protection money from merchants—are not considered as formidable a threat by law-enforcement authorities. Investigators who have honed their skills against the mob say they are beginning to use the same techniques against newly emerging crime groups, like Russian, Vietnamese and Chinese gangs. But it is too early to gauge their success against these groups, the officials say.

Until the last decade, the bosses and top leaders in most Mafia families insulated themselves from arrests and convictions through a code of loyalty and secrecy known as omerta and through careful screening of recruits.

Federal officials say that the F.B.I. and state agencies eliminated or reduced the influence of the Mafia in major cities through convictions of mobsters in the 1980's and 1990's for violating the Federal Racketeering Influence Corrupt Organization Act, known as RICO. The law provides for harsh sentences for defendants convicted of belonging to criminal enterprises and is believed to be instrumental in encouraging mobsters to become Government witnesses in return for lenient sentences.

F.B.I. officials said the Mafia in the New York area had been more difficult to overcome because of the existence of seven families in the region, instead of the single groups in other cities. "The New York–New Jersey region is their last stronghold," Mr. Marchalonis said. Based on information from informers and defectors, the officials said the Colombo and Lucchese families are trying to reinvigorate themselves by opening the books—inducting new members.

Mr. Buccino said there are indications that several families may be recruiting recent immigrants from Sicily to bolster their ranks. The Sicilians, he said, are considered more tradition-bound and less likely to become turncoats than American gangsters. But Federal and other law-enforcement officials said that except for the Bonanno family, they had seen no signs of American families recruiting Sicilians.

TURNING ATTENTION TO MOB ASSETS

Mr. Doran conceded that Federal agencies had failed to uncover all the financial ties developed by Mafia families and he said that future investigations and prosecutions may focus on mob assets.

"There is no doubt most of the families have been damaged a great deal," Mr. Doran said. "Have they gone away? No. And it will probably take us another 10 years before we diminish them to the level of street gangs."

Ronald Goldstock, the director of New York State's Organized Crime Task Force, said the five New York families retain fading influence in the construction, waste-hauling and food industries and in drug trafficking.

"They still inflate costs for the general public, hurt union members through payoffs for sweetheart union contracts, and they are always trying to corrupt government and business officials through bid-rigging and other schemes," Mr. Goldstock said. "This is the right time to destroy them and reform the industries where they have power, so that racketeers of the future cannot come in and emulate them."

Russian Gangsters in the United States

Selwyn Raab

PART I: Influx of Russian Gangsters Troubles F.B.I. in Brooklyn

As a Brighton Beach subway train thundered overhead, a hit man pumped one fatal bullet into the back of Oleg Korataev's head. It took four rounds in the face and chest to finish off another suspected gangster, Yanik Magasayev. Alexandre Graber died thousands of miles away in a hail of automatic gunfire.

Near the Brighton Beach boardwalk, a gunman ambushed Naum Raichel, severely wounding him with three bullets in his chest and stomach. That same day in Germany, Mr. Raichel's brother, Simeon, was beaten into unconsciousness and suffered a brain concussion.

Although the five murder and assault cases occurred this year in New York, Moscow and Berlin, Federal and New York City law-enforcement officials say the crimes have a common root cause. According to the officials, a new wave of callous Russian organized-crime figures, with ties to Brighton Beach and the former republics of the Soviet Union, is responsible for the outburst of violence.

The Brighton Beach and Sheepshead Bay sections of Brooklyn have been headquarters for a smattering of émigré Russian crime gangs since the 1970's, when the Soviet Union permitted the first of about 300,000 people to emigrate to the United States. But the disintegration of the

A request from the F.B.I. to Russian-speakers to help fight crime.

Soviet Union in 1991 spawned thousands of powerful crime gangs—collectively known as the Russian mafia—and some of these groups, officials warn, are establishing bases among émigré communities in the United States, particularly in South Brooklyn.

"The ones coming in now are more violent and better organized than the old-timers," says Jim E. Moody, chief of the Federal Bureau of Investigation's organized-crime section. "They are maintaining links to gangs in Moscow and other places in the old Soviet Union with money flowing back and forth."

To combat the latest organized-crime threat, the Justice Department in January elevated the Russian mafia to the highest investigative priority, the same level as the American and Sicilian Mafias, Asian organized-crime groups and Colombian cocaine cartels. Because of the magnitude of the problem in the New York area, the F.B.I. created a Russian squad in its New York office in May, the first F.B.I. unit in the country to deal exclusively with Russian criminals.

"We didn't establish the squad on a whim," said William A. Gavin, the head of the F.B.I. office in New York. "They are dangerous, and our aim is not to allow them to gain a foothold as the Italian-American families did."

A disturbing sign of the Russian mafia's emergence in America, officials acknowledged, is the arrival of Vyacheslav Kirillovich Ivankov, whom Russian police identify as a Vor v Zakone—Russian for a "thief-in-law"—the top criminal category in the old Soviet Union. Law-enforcement officials said they feared that Mr. Ivankov's mission is to oversee and enlarge operations involving émigré racketeers here and gangsters in Russia.

PART II: Top Echelon Of Mobsters Is a Threat

In Russia, they are called Vory v Zakone, "thieves-in-law," the top criminal echelon. For American law-enforcement agencies, they are a new threat.

Jim E. Moody, chief of the Federal Bureau of Investigation's organized-crime section, said an ominous sign in the growth of Russian underworld activities in the United States has been the sightings of four or five Vory v Zakone. The highest-ranking thief-in-law to arrive here is Vyacheslav Kirillovich Ivankov, say F.B.I. and other law-enforcement agencies.

Russian organized-crime experts estimate that there are about 800

From the *New York Times*, August 23, 1994, p. B1. © 1994 by the New York Times Company. Reprinted by permission.

Vory v Zakone in the world, Mr. Moody said.

"They are the closest thing the Russians have to being a made guy in the Cosa Nostra," he said, referring to the full-fledged members of American Mafia families.

Tattoo of an Eagle

The Vory v Zakone are not necessarily members of the same gang but, say Russian law-enforcement officials, belong to an honored category of criminals who are empowered to resolve disputes among gangsters. Mr. Moody said that the existence of the Vory v Zakone was believed to predate the Communist revolution in 1917 and that all members were recruited while in prison and branded with a tattoo of an eagle with talons, usually on their hands.

"They had sort of a coronation ceremony in prison or in the old gulags where they took an oath never to work and never to cooperate with the police or the military," he said.

Mr. Ivankov, 54, was convicted in 1982 in Moscow on charges of robbery, possession of firearms, forgery and drug trafficking. He was sentenced to 14 years in prison but was released in 1991, five years early.

He is believed to have slipped into the United States last year with a false passport. He has been seen strolling on Emmons Avenue in Sheepshead Bay, Brooklyn, and dining at the Rasputin, a nightclub in Brighton Beach, Brooklyn, and at the Russian Samovar, a midtown Manhattan restaurant, said detectives with the New York City Police Department.

Problem of Unfamiliarity

Maj. Aleksander Y. Sirotkin of the Russian Ministry of Interior, who worked on the Ivankov case, said in an interview in Moscow that Mr. Ivankov's emergence in America was "terrifying because his presence in the states will implant a new kind of criminal ideology that will give birth to crimes characteristic of Russian criminals."

Major Sirotkin warned that the F.B.I. would have trouble uprooting the thieves-in-law because the bureau is unfamiliar with the group's ideology and culture. "Ivankov is a smart guy with great life experience," Major Sirotkin said. "He is not likely to be satisfied with a minor role in the criminal world."

Federal agencies are concerned about "reports that Ivankov was sent over to coordinate activities between gangsters in Russia and all of North America," said Joel Campanella, an intelligence agent with the United States Customs Service assigned to Russian organized-crime investigations.

'The First Team' Extends Its Influence

In the 1970's and early 1980's, a wave of Russian-born criminals arrived in New York and lived mainly in South Brooklyn, where they concentrated largely on white-collar crimes, especially frauds involving gasoline taxes, Medicare payments and counterfeit credit cards. Because of the cold war and travel bans, this group had little contact with criminals in the Soviet Union.

The newcomers who have arrived in America in the last three years are labeled "the first team" by detectives and Federal agents. Investigators say they have not only taken over the white-collar crimes established by their predecessors but have expanded into other rackets, including narcotics trafficking, money laundering, extortion of émigré merchants and prostitution.

And Drug Enforcement Administration agents say they have uncovered concrete evidence showing that a Russian gang from Brooklyn imported heroin and for the first time sold it to mobsters working for traditional American Mafia families. Previously, veteran American mobsters imported drugs through their own networks or bought it from non-Russian suppliers.

While many Federal law-enforcement officials portray the Russian groups as a significant problem, some state prosecutors and investigators are dubious about their overall importance in the underworld.

"We don't see any coordination from Russia or the other republics," said Eric Seidel, the chief of the organized-crime bureau in the Brooklyn District Attorney's office. "There is no evidence of large-scale violence or that the Russians are dominant in any specific racket."

Peter Grinenko, an investigator in the Brooklyn District Attorney's office who speaks Russian and has been working on Russian crime cases in the New York area for 13 years, said the émigré racketeers in America have no defined organizational structures like those of the Mafia.

"As individuals, they are into scams and shakedowns to lay their hands on money any way they can," Mr. Grinenko said. "But as organized crime groups go in America, they are a flea on a horse."

F.B.I. Finds Emigrés Reluctant to Inform

The F.B.I. will not disclose the size of its Russian Squad in the city, but Raymond C. Kerr, the head of the unit, said it includes Russian-speaking agents who formerly worked on counterintelligence units. The bureau periodically advertises in Novoye Russkoye Slovo, an American Russian-language newspaper, asking for "all facts and gossip about organized crime rackets, murders, frauds, illegal incomes, narcotics, counterfeiting and all kinds of criminal activities in the United States and abroad."

Alexandre Grant, an editor at the Russian newspaper who reports on organized-crime matters, said Russian émigrés are unlikely to inform or to testify at trials, even if they are placed in the Federal Witness Protection Program. Under that program, participants and their families are given new identities and relocated.

"It won't work because most Russians cannot survive unless they are in a Russian community," Mr. Grant said. "They won't cooperate because even if they feel safe in the U.S. They fear someone will retaliate against their relatives in Russia."

Language and cultural barriers, the authorities concede, have blocked quick solutions to the recent gangland-style murders and shootings linked to Brighton Beach mobsters.

The first victim this year was Oleg Korataev, a former boxer who was convicted in the Soviet Union of robbery and assault and who was identified by Russian authorities as belonging to an organized-crime gang known as the Valiulins. In 1992, Mr. Korataev entered the country on a visitor's visa, married and settled in Trump Village in Brooklyn.

On Jan. 12, Mr. Korataev, 44, was attending a private Russian New Year's Eve party in the Cafe Arbat on Brighton Beach Avenue. At 3 A.M., he stepped outside with another man, who pulled out a .38-caliber pistol and shot Mr. Korataev fatally in the head.

Several passers-by told the police that the killer returned to the restaurant and a few minutes later left with a woman. About 100 people at the party were questioned that night, but none provided a clue to the gunman's identity or motive. Most of the partygoers gave names and addresses in the Boston area that were fictitious, Detective Mackey said.

"Everyone had amnesia," the detective added. "Oleg had a reputation of being a brutal enforcer—a collector of debts—and he had connections to gangs in Russia and in Toronto."

On March 23, the body of Yanik Magasayev, 22, who had been shot four times, was dumped under a mound of plastic garbage bags in a wooded area on Bay 52d Street near Shore Parkway. Detectives said that Mr. Magasayev had been arrested on a burglary charge last year and that

he was under investigation for suspected extortions of émigré merchants in Brooklyn and Queens.

Feeling Secure In Brighton Beach

In the last 20 years, about 200,000 immigrants from the former Soviet Union have settled in the city, Long Island, Westchester County and in New Jersey, with more than 50,000 living in Brooklyn, principally in the Brighton Beach area.

Since 1991, the easing of overseas travel restrictions in Russia and the other 14 former Soviet republics has led more than 140,000 visitors a year to come to America, the United States Customs Service reports. Investigators say that scores of Russian mobsters, often using fake identities, have illegally obtained visitors' visas to enter the United States.

Mr. Moody of the F.B.I. estimated that only a small fraction of Russian immigrants—about 2,000—are hardcore criminals. But, of some 5,000 gangs that sprang up after the collapse of the Soviet regime, members of 29 gangs have been seen recently in America, he noted.

Investigators say that Russian criminals gravitate to Brighton Beach and nearby neighborhoods because they feel secure there and can hatch plots with little danger of being compromised by informers.

"Almost every case involving Russians is somehow linked to Brighton Beach," said Detective Dan Mackey of the 60th Precinct, which covers the neighborhood. "Its the first spot they go to when they arrive in the country."

Favorite meeting places for the Russian mobsters is the row of restaurants on Brighton Beach Avenue, a cacophonous, crowded rialto in the shadow of an elevated subway line. They also favor more sunny cafes on or near the boardwalk.

Gunned Down on a Moscow Street

On June 16, Alexandre Graber and other men were gunned down on a

Moscow sidewalk by two killers who roared off in waiting cars. Mr. Graber, 38, had lived for the last year in the Brighton Beach area, and detectives said he was a secret partner in a Russian nightclub in Brighton Beach.

A Moscow newspaper called Today reported in June that Russian police officials said that Mr. Graber had been associated with several organized-crime groups and that he frequently visited Russia to resolve conflicts among gangsters. F.B.I. agents said that Mr. Graber's murder appeared to be related to his activities in this country.

Shortly before twilight on July 11, Naum Raichel left the Winter Garden Restaurant, which he is constructing on the boardwalk at Brighton Sixth Street. Two men blocked his way and one of them shot him three times in the chest, the police said.

Mr. Raichel was convicted in 1987 in Federal District Court in Brooklyn of extorting $20,000 from two insurance salesmen as protection payoffs. He served four years in prison and was on probation at the time of the shooting.

The same day Mr. Raichel was wounded, his brother, Simeon, who lives in Brooklyn, was severely beaten in Berlin. "We doubt that those two attacks were mere coincidence," said a detective, who spoke on condition of anonymity.

Investigators cite the case of Boris Nayfeld, 46, as an example of the evolution of Russian émigré criminals from local to international status. He immigrated to the country in the late 1970's as a religious refugee. In 1980, Mr. Nayfeld was arrested in Nassau County on a grand larceny charge, pleaded guilty to petty larceny and was placed on probation.

He again attracted attention in May 1985 when Evsei Agron was fatally shot in the vestibule of his Kensington apartment building. The police identified Mr. Agron as the leader of a gang of émigré extortionists and Mr. Nayfeld as his bodyguard and chauffeur. Mr. Nayfeld, detectives said, later worked as a bodyguard for Marat Balagula, a

Russian immigrant who was convicted in 1991 of a $360,000 credit card fraud.

Mr. Nayfeld was arrested in January by narcotics agents as he was about to be driven from his $450,000 home in Egbertville, S.I., to Kennedy International Airport for a flight to Brussels.

A Federal indictment in Manhattan accused him of heading a ring that smuggled hundreds of pounds of heroin from Thailand through Poland into New York. He has pleaded not guilty to narcotics trafficking charges and is to tried in October.

Louis Cardinali and Joseph Massima, Drug Enforcement Administration agents who worked on the case, said in an interview that Mr. Nayfeld's group sold the heroin to three men linked to Mafia crime families in New York. They declined to identify the families.

"The Russians are into narcotics for the long haul," Mr. Massima said. "They don't just have a foot in the door; they are in the house."

Mr. Moody of the F.B.I. conceded that few Russian mobsters had been convicted. "We are still trying to get a handle on them," he added. "And we will before long."

Drugs, Alcohol and Violence: Joined at the Hip

Joseph A. Califano, Jr.

Drugs, alcohol and violence are joined at the hip, three maraud-ing musketeers, marching in lock step through the streets of American cities, towns and villages, leaving in their wake a grisly kaleidoscope of crime, terrified citizens, overcrowded prisons, overwhelmed court systems, and property damage and security systems that raise the price of everything we do from going to the movies to depositing money in the bank and buying groceries at the supermarket.

Murder. Date rape. Vandalism. Child abuse. Wild-west shootouts in urban streets. Devastated neighborhoods. Metal detectors at school entrances and teachers locked in classrooms for their own safety. Forty thousand highway deaths. Hospital emergency rooms chock-a-block with injuries from knife and gunshot wounds, domestic violence and household accidents. City dwellers on an afternoon walk accosted by angry homeless people. Parks shut down at night because they're too dangerous for anyone to walk. Destroyed neighborhood basketball courts and playgrounds.

Look behind any of these symptoms of savagery in our society and more than likely you will find lurking in the shadows alcohol and drug abuse and addiction.

Watch a local television newscast, read a daily newspaper or walk a city street and the anecdotal evidence of the ravages of drug and alcohol abuse is splattered all over it.

► **Twelve-year-old Polly Klaas** was kidnapped at knifepoint during a slumber party and found strangled to death not far from her home in the small, sleepy town of Petaluma, California. The murderer was 39-year-old Richard Allen Davis, an ex-con with a history of alcohol and drug abuse and run-ins with the law since age 12. On parole following a previous kidnapping, Davis was taking a "potpourri" of drugs that night and "still doesn't know why he did it." Raised by an alcoholic father, Davis was first arrested for being drunk and disorderly at age 19. *People Magazine*, December 20, 1993.

► **Thirteen-year-old Joseph Chaney,** held without bail for trial as an adult for robbing a man at gunpoint, was six years old at the time of his first of more than 15 arrests. His home life was

in shambles due to his mother's drug addiction. "Life wasn't like I wanted it to be," says Joseph about those days. He dreamed of living in "a rich house" where the refrigerator was always full. Last year, Joseph missed 120 days of school. *The Wall Street Journal,* November 30, 1993.

► **Ten-year-old Sheriff S. Byrd,** eulogized as a "bright little star" by the firefighter who tried to save him, was playing with friends near his home on a crack-infested block in the Bronx when he was killed by a stray shot from a .357 Magnum during a shootout among four drug dealers. Four years later, 32-year-old Amado Pichardo was charged with second-degree murder and criminal possession of a weapon. A bullet from his gun, police said, hit Sheriff in the back that afternoon when Pichardo shot at three other drug dealers.

► **Two children—a son, 12, and a daughter, 6—**bade their mother a tearful goodbye as she was led away to serve a minimum five-year sentence for killing the man accused of molesting her son. Ellie Nesler shot Mark Driver, 35, five times in the head and neck while he sat in a courtroom during a hearing to determine if he should stand trial. She admitted using methamphetamine on the day of the shooting. *The New York Times,* January 9, 1994.

► **A 28-year-old legal secretary,** Lisa Bongiorno, sits in a cell at Rikers Island facing the possibility of life in prison. Charged with killing two high-ranking Greek Orthodox priests in Queens, New York, she was smoking her weekly ritual—$10 worth of PCP—when her car plowed into theirs. Every weekday morning, Ms. Bongiorno went to her job at a Manhattan law firm; every Sunday morning, she took her 7-year-old daughter to church, and every payday for the last 10 years she "had to get high." The arresting officer reported: "She said she drove into upper Manhattan to purchase two dime bags of PCP. She stated that while driving back she smoked one of the bags of PCP in a pipe and she remembered being in the accident." *New York Newsday,* March 19 and March 26, 1994.

► **A couple living in a shelter** for the homeless in Westchester County, New York, were charged with accidentally smothering their baby to death in a crack-induced stupor. The couple have lengthy criminal records, including drug possession. The

From the *Center on Addiction and Substance Abuse at Columbia University, Annual Report 1993,* pp. 6-10. Reprinted by permission.

mother had fallen asleep and rolled over on her two-month-old infant. She was on probation after conviction of possessing drug paraphernalia. *The New York Times,* December 31, 1993.

► **In Austin, Texas, in CASA's Children at Risk** program for 6th, 7th and 8th graders, parents asked the police to protect safe houses that the parents were willing to establish on each block of a seven-block corridor their children had to walk to school. The parents wanted to give their children a place for escape when drug dealers accosted them or hopped-up teens tried to rape or rob them.

At least two of the three million individuals on probation or parole in the United States have drug or alcohol abuse or addiction problems.

The statistical evidence is overwhelming:

► Alcohol and/or drug abuse is implicated in some three-fourths of all murders, rapes, child molestations and deaths of babies and children from parental neglect.

► In Boston, alcohol and/or drug abuse was involved in 89 percent of the cases of infant abuse.

► In 1993, American taxpayers forked over more than $6 billion in federal, state and local taxes just to incarcerate individuals sentenced for drug offenses.

► At least two of the three million individuals on probation or parole in the United States have drug or alcohol abuse or addiction problems.

► In Arkansas, 95 percent of the children in juvenile court are charged with drug- or alcohol-related crimes.

► The average prisoner downs eight drinks a day during the year before the crime for which he is convicted.

THE COLLAPSE OF THE AMERICAN SYSTEM OF JUSTICE

The pandemic of drug and alcohol abuse is destroying our legal system.

From 1980 until 1993, the number of drug cases prosecuted has tripled. But that is only the tip of the iceberg. Most rape, assault, criminal child abuse and robbery cases involve defendants who were high on alcohol or drugs at the time they committed the offenses for which they are charged.

Prosecutors accept pleas just to get rid of cases. In most cities each prosecutor is handling caseloads more than double the American Bar Association-recommended number of 150 felonies a year.

Judges are demoralized. Corporate lawyers who gave up their practices to become federal judges looked forward to trying high-visibility anti-trust and securities cases. They now find themselves sentencing one drug offender after another, often seeing the same prisoner return two or three times for the same offenses.

The federal and state civil court systems are suffering from the pressure of criminal cases prompted by drug and alcohol abuse. In 1991, the civil jury system was closed down in eight states for at least part of the year to free up judges and other resources to meet the speedy trial requirements of criminal cases.

The collapse of the judicial system poses a threat to our democracy. America is an increasingly bureaucratic society where the individual can easily become a number before big governments, big banks and big private institutions. The courts are the one branch of government where a citizen can go to be treated as an individual. If someone is angry enough to sue, feels abused enough by some action to hire a lawyer and file an action in a civil court and then cannot have his grievance heard on a timely basis, society is clamping a lid on a head of steam that may eventually burst out in a destructive way.

The most vulnerable victims of the overcrowded judicial system are those caught up in the juvenile and family courts. Originally designed to save the children who went astray and repair shattered families, they, too, have been overwhelmed by cases involving alcohol and drug abuse.

The most vulnerable victims of the overcrowded judicial system are those caught up in the juvenile and family courts. Originally designed to save the children who went astray and repair shattered families, they, too, have been overwhelmed by cases involving alcohol and drug abuse.

Eighty percent of juveniles arrested admit to use of illegal drugs, more than half of them before reaching age 13. The murder arrest rate among 10- to 17-year-olds has risen so rapidly—tripling from 1983 to 1993—that states are rushing to treat these youngsters as adult criminals, denying them otherwise available rehabilitation services.

Family courts are awash with the ravages of alcohol and drug abuse. Child abuse and neglect reports have tripled in the past decade, reaching three million in 1993. The National Council of Juvenile and Family Court Judges estimates that substance abuse is a significant factor in up to 90 percent of the cases that get to family court. Most of the battering of some four million women that occurs each year involves drug and alcohol abuse.

THE PRISONS

The United States of America has more prisoners per capita than any other nation in the industrialized world—455 per 100,000, compared to 311 for South Africa, 111 for Canada and 42 for Japan. In 1993, American prisons bulged with more than 900,000 inmates.

Some 80 percent of those incarcerated in state prisons are there for drug- or alcohol-related crimes; more than 60 percent of those in federal prisons are there for violation of federal drug laws.

For the first time in 1990—and in every year since then—the number of individuals sent to prison for drug crimes exceeded the number sent there for property crimes. And most of those convicted of property crimes were under the influence of alcohol or drugs at the time of commission of their offense.

If we do not act across society to attack substance abuse on all fronts—research, prevention and treatment—we will bear witness to the collapse of our individualized system of equal justice for all.

Most prisoners are Dickensian warehouses, crowded with the mentally ill and substance abusers and addicts, with drugs freely available (often sold by guards), and AIDS and tuberculosis rampant. The incidence of AIDS in federal and state prisons was 362 cases per 100,000 inmates in 1992, 20 times the 18 cases per 100,000 in the total U.S. population. More than three-fourths of prisoners are addicted to cigarettes.

PROBATION AND PAROLE

The time when probation and parole officers could handle their caseloads and help their wards is long past. In Los Angeles, a probation officer can have 1,000 cases assigned at any one time. In other large cities, the situation is similar. Since most individuals on probation and parole have drug and alcohol addiction and abuse problems, their need is far greater than the probationer or parolee of 50 years ago.

WHAT WE CAN DO

The sorry state of the entire criminal justice and court system in America has led CASA to embark on a meticulous analysis of the facts. Who is in American prisons? Who sits on the federal and state benches? How are parole and probation officers trained? What happens in prisons? Are treatment programs available—and if so, how effective are they?

It is our intention over 1994 and 1995 to set out before the American people the cost of all substance abuse to our legal system—including criminal, civil, juvenile and family courts; prisons and juvenile homes; probation and parole; health care; quality of judges and lawyers; and taxpayer dollars. No such analysis has been attempted. It is CASA's belief that once presented with the facts and costs, the American people can be moved to take action.

Many of the problems in the legal system lie outside it. Just as American health care is too important to be left to the doctors, and war too important for the generals, so the legal system is too important to our democratic way of life to be left to the lawyers.

One thing is clear: if we do not act across society to attack substance abuse on all fronts—research, prevention and treatment—we will bear witness to the collapse of one of the four pillars of our democracy, an individualized system of equal justice for all. And if the judicial branches cannot function effectively, at the federal level and in the states, the other three pillars—the executive branches, the legislatures and the free press—will lose an essential source of nourishment and protection.

Victimology

For many years, crime victims were not considered an important topic for criminological study. However, criminologists now consider focusing on victims and victimization essential to understanding the phenomenon of crime. The popularity of this area of study can be attributed to the early work of Hans von Hentig and the later work of Stephen Schafer. These writers were the first to assert that crime victims play an integral role in the criminal event, that their actions may actually precipitate crime, and that unless the victim's role is considered, the study of crime is not complete.

In recent years, a growing number of criminologists have devoted increasing attention to the victim's role in the criminal justice process. Generally, areas of particular interest include calculating costs of crime to victims, victim surveys that measure the nature and extent of criminal behavior, establishing probabilities of victimization risks, studying victim precipitation of crime and culpability, and designing services expressly for victims of crime. As more criminologists focus their attention on the victim's role in the criminal process, victimology will take on even greater importance.

Articles in this unit provide sharp focus on key issues. From the lead essay, "Criminal Victimization in the United States, 1992," we learn the extent to which citizens experience crime, characteristics of crime victims, nature of crime incidents, costs of crime, and police response.

The negative impact that crime has on the lives of citizens is clearly evident in "Crime's Toll on the U.S.: Fear, Despair, and Guns."

Should women's unique perspectives be taken into account in areas of legal doctrine? The essay " 'Til Death Do Us Part" explores this controversial issue.

Heidi Vanderbilt's article "Incest: A Chilling Report" provides a revealing look at child abuse victims and offenders.

"Murder Next Door" describes random violence that is happening to our neighbors in Canada. Drive-by shootings and brutal robberies, unheard of a few years ago in Canada, are on the rise.

Returning to the United States, the concluding article, "Battered Women and the Criminal Justice System," challenges traditional concepts about family privacy and presents alternatives for the criminal justice system's response to violence in the home.

Looking Ahead: Challenge Questions

What lifestyle changes might you consider to avoid becoming victimized?

How successful are crime victims when they fight their assailants?

According to "Criminal Victimization in the United States, 1992," how many crime victims are there in the United States? What are the trends and patterns in victimization?

Do young people face a much greater victimization risk than do older people? Why, or why not?

Does marital status influence victimization risk? Defend your answer.

Criminal Victimization in the United States, 1992

A National Crime Victimization Survey Report March 1994, NCJ-145125

Foreword

In this 20th annual report of the National Crime Victimization Survey, the Bureau of Justice Statistics presents over 120 numerical tables describing criminal victimization. The findings include measures of the amount of crime that U.S. residents experience, the characteristics of crime victims, the nature and circumstances of the crime incidents, and costs of crime. There are data on how police responded to reported crimes and on the victims' perception of drug and alcohol use by violent offenders.

Data from the annual Bulletin *Criminal Victimization 1992* have been reprinted to provide the reader with additional information on trends in crime rates.

The Bureau expresses its sincerest gratitude to the nearly 110,000 persons who, by participating in extensive interviews, help to make the National Crime Victimization Survey the second largest ongoing household survey in the Nation. Because of the cooperation by these individuals, criminal justice professionals, lawmakers, researchers, and the public have facts to guide responses to crime and its victims.

Lawrence A. Greenfeld
Acting Director

Preface

This report presents information on criminal victimization in the United States during 1992. This edition is the 20th in a series of annual reports prepared under the National Crime Survey (NCS) program. The survey was recently renamed the National Crime Victimization Survey (NCVS) to more clearly emphasize the measurement of those victimizations experienced by our citizens. The Bureau of the Census has administered the National Crime Victimization Survey for the Bureau of Justice Statistics (formerly the National Criminal Justice Information and Statistics Service of the Law Enforcement Assistance Administration) since the program began in 1972. All of the data presented in this report were derived from a continuing survey of the occupants of a representative sample of housing units in the United States. About 110,000 people age 12 or older living in 66,000 housing units were interviewed. Ninety-six percent of the households selected to participate did so.

Currently, the NCVS focuses on certain criminal offenses, both completed and attempted, which concern the general public and law enforcement authorities. These offenses include the personal crimes of rape, robbery, assault, and larceny and the household crimes of burglary, larceny, and motor vehicle theft.[1] Each report in this series examines the frequency and impact of crimes, characteristics of victims and offenders, circumstances surrounding the crimes, and patterns of reporting to the police. . . .

All rates and percentages in this report are estimates and therefore are subject to errors arising from obtaining data from a sample rather than a complete census. Since these numbers are based on a sample, not a complete census, these estimates are subject to sampling error. In the summary findings presented here, all comparisons were significant at the 90 percent confidence level or more. In fact, most comparisons passed the test at the 95 percent confidence level. Therefore, for most of the comparisons cited, the estimated difference between the values was greater than twice the standard error of this difference. . . .

INTRODUCTION

The National Crime Victimization Survey (NCVS) provides information on crimes which interest the general public and the criminal justice community. Not all crimes are measured; many offenses are difficult to detect through a survey of the general population.

---

[1]Definitions of the measured crimes do not necessarily conform to any Federal or State statutes, which vary considerably. The NCVS offense definitions are generally compatible with conventional usage and with the definitions used by the Federal Bureau of Investigation in its annual publication *Crime in the United States: Uniform Crime Reports.*

Reprinted with permission from the U.S. Department of Justice, Bureau of Justice Statistics, March 1994, pp. iii, 1-4, 8-9, 15, 18-21, 53, 67-68, 100-101.

NCVS-measured crimes

The success of a victimization survey like the NCVS depends on the ability to identify specific crimes. This requires that the victims not only are willing to report the crime but also understand what happened and how it happened. The NCVS measures the crimes most likely to be identified by a general survey, namely, rape, robbery, assault, burglary, personal and household larceny, and motor vehicle theft.

Since crime victims are asked directly about crime, all crimes are measured, whether or not they were reported to the police. No attempt is made to validate reported crimes by checking them against other sources of criminal data, such as police records.

Crimes not measured by the NCVS

The NCVS does not measure murder and kidnaping. Formerly, the survey included commercial burglary and robbery, but these crimes were dropped in 1977, largely for economic reasons. Crimes such as public drunkenness, drug abuse, and prostitution, which are often referred to as victimless crimes, are not measured. The survey also excludes crimes where the victim shows a willingness to participate. Some examples of this type of crime include illegal gambling, con games, and blackmail.

Sometimes people are not aware they have been victims of a crime, making such crimes difficult to measure accurately. Buying stolen property, and certain types of fraud and embezzlement are examples of this type of crime. In addition, many attempted crimes of all types are probably underreported because victims were not aware of the incident.

Classifying the crimes

In any criminal encounter, more than one criminal act may be committed against the same individual. For example, a victim may be both raped and robbed during the same incident.

To record crimes accurately, each criminal incident is counted only once and is classified according to the most serious event that occurred during the crime. Offenses are ranked according to severity by using the system employed by the Federal Bureau of Investigation.

Personal crimes of contact are considered more serious than household crimes. In descending order of severity, the personal crimes are rape, robbery, assault, and personal larceny. The household crimes, in the same order, are burglary, motor vehicle theft, and household larceny. Thus, if a person is both robbed and assaulted, the event is classified as a robbery; if the victim suffers physical harm, the crime is categorized as a robbery with injury.

Victimizations versus incidents

A single crime may victimize one or more individuals. For example, two people may be victimized during a single personal robbery. Thus, a single incident can result in more than one victimization. This distinction is applied to personal crimes, but all household crime incidents are assumed to have only one victim, the household as a unit.

A victimization, the basic measure of the occurrence of crime, is a specific criminal act because it affects a single victim. The number of victimizations is determined by the number of victims of such acts. Victimization counts serve as key elements in computing rates of victimization, as described in the victim characteristics sections of this report. Victimizations also are used in developing a variety of information on crime characteristics and the effects of crime on victims, including injuries and medical care, economic losses, time lost from work, self-protection, and reporting to police. For violent personal crimes, offender characteristics are also measured by victimizations.

An incident is a specific criminal act involving one or more victims. The number of incidents of personal crime is lower than that of victimizations because some crimes are simultaneously committed against more than one individual.

Incident figures are used in describing the settings and circumstances in which crimes occurred, including the time and place of occurrence, number of victims and offenders, and use of weapons.

Series victimizations

A series victimization is defined as three or more similar but separate crimes which the victim is unable to recall individually or describe to the interviewer in detail. Prior to 1979, series victimizations were recorded by the season of occurrence and tabulated according to the quarter of the year in which the data was collected. Because of this procedure, it was not possible to total nonseries and series crimes together.

In January of 1979 the NCVS questionnaire was revised to enable series crimes and regular (nonseries) crimes to be combined. The effects of this change were included in the initial release of the 1980 data.

Locality of residence

Locality of residence, as used in the NCVS, refers to where a person lived when he was interviewed, not to the place where a crime occurred. The country is divided into three locality types: central cities, metropolitan areas not located inside central cities, and non metropolitan places. The areas defined as Metropolitan Statistical Areas are divided into central cities and suburban areas, while the remaining areas are classified as nonmetropolitan. Further distinctions are within the Metropolitan Statistical Areas according to the size of the population. Geographical areas were assigned to the appropriate category on the basis of the 1990 census.

Region

In 1987, the NCVS began presenting crime data according to the region in which the victims lived at the time of the interview. The country has been divided into four regions by the Census

Bureau. These regions [are] the Midwest, Northeast, South, and West.

CRIMINAL VICTIMIZATION 1992— EXCERPT FROM THE BJS BULLETIN

Reproduced over the next [several] pages is an excerpt from the BJS Bulletin *Criminal Victimization 1992*. This document is published annually to provide a first look at final NCVS data for the year under examination, as well as to make comparisons between crime rates for that year and previous ones. This is the third year in which the annual Bulletin has been reproduced in this volume. The addition provides the reader with information on long term trends in crime and comparisons between crime levels and rates for 1992 and 1991, which are not available elsewhere in this volume. Immediately following is a summary of the main findings from the report:

• Persons age 12 or older living in the United States experienced 6.6 million violent victimizations and 12.2 million personal thefts during 1992. In addition, American households were the victims of 14.8 million crimes according to the NCVS. The NCVS measures the violent crimes of rape, robbery, aggravated and simple assault; personal thefts; and the household crimes of burglary, larceny, and motor vehicle theft.

• Just as in 1991, the level of violent crime in 1992 did not differ significantly from the number measured in 1981, the peak year for crime. Approximately 6.6 million violent crimes occurred in both 1981 and 1992.

• Rates of crime either declined or remained stable last year. While violent crime rates did not change significantly compared to figures for 1991, rates of theft, both personal and household, decreased.

• The robbery rate was lower last year than at its highest points in 1981 and 1982, and the rate of household burglary was significantly lower than at any time throughout the 1970's or 1980's.

• Motor vehicle thefts were the most likely to be reported to the police (75%) while larcenies without contact were the least likely (30%).

• Certain demographic groups had higher victimization rates than others: Blacks were more likely than whites to be victims of violent crime; persons under age 25 had higher victimization rates than older persons; and households with the lowest incomes were more likely to be violent crime victims than households with higher incomes.

Crime levels and rates in 1992

The level of theft overall, as well as the level of completed thefts, declined somewhat between 1991 and 1992. However, the number of personal larcenies without contact resulting in losses of $50 or more decreased significantly by 8% in 1992.

The number of household crimes, completed household crimes, and household larcenies, including those with losses under $50, all also decreased, differing measurably over the previous year's levels. Burglaries showed some evidence of a decline in 1992.

Just as in 1991, the level of violent crime did not differ significantly last year from the number measured in 1981, the peak year for crime (table 1 and figure 1). Approximately 6.6 million violent crimes occurred in both 1981 and 1992. Levels in all other general crime categories continued to

decline from the peak. There were 23% fewer thefts and 22% fewer household crimes last year than in 1981. With 12.2 million thefts in 1992, this crime reached its lowest level since the peak year.

Rates of crime—the number of crimes per 1,000 persons for personal crimes or per 1,000 households for household crimes—either declined or remained stable last year. While violent crime rates did not change significantly compared to figures for 1991, rates of theft, both personal and household, decreased.

The rate of personal larceny without contact between the victim and offender dropped significantly in 1992, primarily attributable to a 9% decline in those larcenies that resulted in losses of $50 or more. The total household crime rate also declined about 9% last year, from 166 crimes per 1,000 households in 1991 to 152 per 1,000 in 1992. Much of this decline may be accounted for by an 8% decrease in household larcenies overall, and especially by the sharp 19% drop in the rate of household larcenies resulting in losses under $50. There was some evidence of a decrease in burglaries as well: 54 burglaries per 1,000 households in 1991 compared to 49 per 1,000 in 1992.

Trends in crime rates, 1973–92

In 1992 both the total theft rate and total household crime rate reached all time lows, partly because of significant declines in personal larcenies without

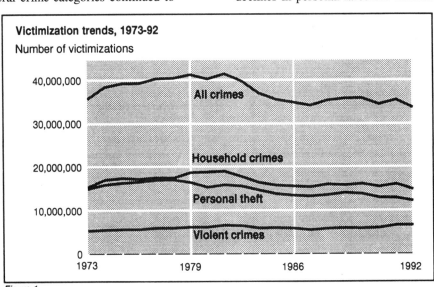

Victimization trends, 1973-92
Number of victimizations

Figure 1

contact and household larcenies. The rate of personal theft was 59 crimes per 1,000 persons in 1992, and for household crime the rate was 152 crimes per 1,000 households. Although the rates of personal crime, theft, and household crime have all generally shown declining trends since the early years of the survey, the violent crime rate has fluctuated. . . .

The rate of violent crime in 1992 was lower than in its peak years during the late 1970's and early 1980's, at 32 crimes per 1,000 persons, but generally higher than at any year between 1985 and 1991.

Although assault rates have also fluctuated, the percent change between 1974 and 1992 was the largest significant *decrease* for aggravated assault (−13.8%). The percent change, 1974–92, represented the largest *increase* for simple assault rates (14.3%).

The robbery rate was lower last year than at its highest points in 1981 and 1982, and the rate of household burglary was significantly lower than at any time throughout the 1970's or 1980's. The burglary rate last year was 49 burglaries per 1,000 households. During the late 1980's the motor vehi-

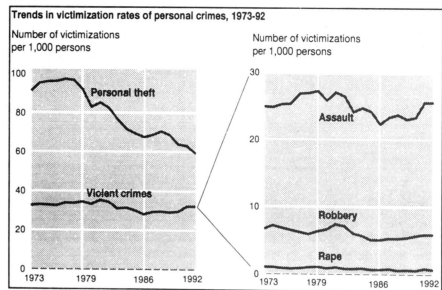

Figure 2

cle theft rate began to increase over its peak years in the early 1970's; the rate has remained stable at these high levels from 1989 to the present.

Reporting of crime remains stable
Of all crimes measured by the NCVS only 39% were reported to law enforcement officials in 1992. The rate at which crimes were reported to the police has not changed significantly since 1990. Fifty percent of all violent crimes were reported to police last

year, as were 30% of all personal thefts and 41% of household crimes.

In specific crime categories, motor vehicle thefts were most likely to be reported to the police (75%), while larcenies without contact were the least likely (30%).

Over time the reporting rate for violent crime has remained stable. However, the rates at which the crimes of theft and household crimes, overall, were reported to the police were generally higher in 1992 than in any year between 1973 and 1980.

Table 1. Victimization levels for selected crimes, 1973-1992

	Number of victimizations (in 1,000's)			
	Total	Violent crimes	Personal theft	Household crimes
1973	35,661	5,350	14,970	15,340
1974	38,411	5,510	15,889	17,012
1975	39,266	5,573	16,294	17,400
1976	39,318	5,599	16,519	17,199
1977	40,314	5,902	16,933	17,480
1978	40,412	5,941	17,050	17,421
1979	41,249	6,159	16,382	18,708
1980	40,252	6,130	15,300	18,821
1981	41,454	6,582	15,863	19,009
1982	39,756	6,459	15,553	17,744
1983	37,001	5,903	14,657	16,440
1984	35,544	6,021	13,789	15,733
1985	34,864	5,823	13,474	15,568
1986	34,118	5,515	13,235	15,368
1987	35,336	5,796	13,575	15,966
1988	35,796	5,910	14,056	15,830
1989	35,818	5,861	13,829	16,128
1990	34,404	6,009	12,975	15,419
1991	35,497	6,587	12,885	16,025
1992	33,649	6,621	12,211	14,817
1981-92*	-18.8%▪	.6%	-23.0%▪	-22.1%▪

*Total victimizations peaked in 1981.
▪The difference is statistically significant at the 95% confidence level.

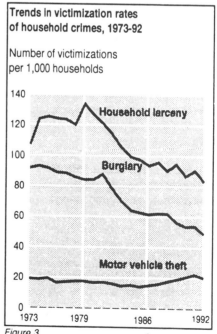

Figure 3

2. VICTIMOLOGY

Differences between estimates based on the 1980- and 1990- decennial censuses

The NCVS employs independent population estimates, derived and updated from decennial censuses, to improve the precision of its statistics on victimization. Use of the latest census counts allows the population controls (which are used in weighting the sample data) to be updated and provides an opportunity for introducing estimation refinements that further enhance the reliability of the estimates.

Table 2 shows that the population counts for 1991 based on the 1980 census compared to those based on the 1990 census varied by only about one-half of one percent for both persons and households. Also, there were no significant differences between estimates of crime rates based on the 1980 census counts compared to rates based on the 1990 census.

Table 2. Estimates based on 1980-decennial and 1990-decennial census population counts, 1991

	Number of victimizations (in 1,000's)			Victimization rates		
	Based on 1980 census	Based on 1990 census	Percent change	Based on 1980 census	Based on 1990 census	Percent change
Personal crimes	19,469	19,472	0%	94.8	95.3	.5%
Crimes of violence	6,567	6,587	.3	32.0	32.2	.8
Rape	173	174	.4	0.8	0.9	.9
Robbery	1,207	1,203	-.4	5.9	5.9	.2
Assault	5,186	5,210	.5	25.3	25.5	1.0
Aggravated	1,623	1,634	.7	7.9	8.0	1.2
Simple	3,563	3,575	.3	17.4	17.5	.9
Crimes of theft	12,902	12,885	-.1	62.8	63.1	.4
Personal larceny						
With contact	501	497	-.8	2.4	2.4	-.2
Without contact	12,402	12,389	-.1	60.4	60.6	.4
Household crimes	16,105	16,025	-.5%	166.3	166.4	.1%
Household burglary	5,213	5,187	-.5	53.8	53.9	.1
Household larceny	8,742	8,702	-.5	90.3	90.4	.1
Motor vehicle theft	2,149	2,136	-.6	22.2	22.2	0

Number of persons		**Number of households**	
1980 based	205,344,340	1980 based	96,839,300
1990 based	204,280,050	1990 based	96,281,890

Note: Detail may not add to totals shown because of rounding. Victimization rates are calculated on the basis of the number of victimizations per 1,000 persons age 12 or older or per 1,000 households. Percent change is based on unrounded numbers.

SUMMARY FINDINGS

The following are statements which illustrate the type of findings that may be obtained from the data in this report.

• The National Crime Victimization Survey (NCVS) estimated that there were 33.6 million crimes committed against individuals or households in the United States in 1992.

• Approximately 36% of all violent crimes reported to NCVS interviewers were completed offenses. Personal thefts were completed at a rate of 94%, and 85% of household crimes were completed.

• The violent crimes of rape, robbery, and assault—which involve a threat or an act of violence in confrontations between victims and offenders—are considered the most serious crimes measured by the NCVS. Twenty percent of all crimes measured by the survey were violent crimes.

• The less serious crimes of personal and household larceny comprised 60% of all offenses committed in 1992. Household burglaries and motor vehicle thefts accounted for another 20% of all crimes.

• In 1992 the rate of violent crime victimization was 32 victimizations per every 1,000 persons age 12 or older; the rate of personal theft was 59 thefts per every 1,000.

CHARACTERISTICS OF PERSONAL CRIME VICTIMS

Victimization rates are measures of the frequency of crime among subgroups of the population. Rates are computed by dividing the number of victimizations occurring in a specific population by the number of persons in that population. The NCVS has consistently shown that criminal victimizations do not occur at the same rate for all subgroups of the population. For example, victimization rates for personal crimes of violence tend to be relatively high for people who are male, black, poor, young, or single. Victimization rates for personal crimes of theft tend to be higher for people who are male, wealthy, young, or single.

Sex, age, race, and ethnicity

• Rates of violent crime and theft victimizations were significantly higher for males than for females.

• Those under 25 years of age had the highest rates of both violent and theft victimizations. For persons over 25, as age increased crime rates decreased.

• Blacks had significantly higher rates of robbery and aggravated assault than either whites or persons of other races, such as Asians or Native Americans. Rates of simple assault and personal theft did not vary significantly between persons of different races.

• Black males had the highest rate of violent crime victimization with 63 victimizations per every 1,000 persons. At 36 per 1,000, white males had a violent victimization rate that was not significantly different from black females (40 per 1,000). White females had the lowest rate (24 per 1,000). There were no significant differences between black and white males or between black and white females in rates of personal theft. However, males continued to have higher theft rates than females of either race.

• Persons of Hispanic origin had higher rates of robbery than did non-Hispanic persons. There were no measurable differences between rates for

The Nation's two crime measures

The National Crime Victimization Survey (NCVS) and the FBI's Uniform Crime Reports (UCR) measure various aspects of crime at the national level. These complementary series each contribute to providing a complete picture about the extent and nature of crime in the United States. Together the NCVS and UCR provide a more comprehensive assessment of crime in the United States than could be obtained from either statistical series alone.

The National Crime Victimization Survey

Using stable data collection methods since 1973, the NCVS has the following strengths:
- It measures both reported and unreported crimes.
- It is not affected by changes in the extent to which people report crime to police or improvements in police record-keeping technology.
- It collects information that is not available when the initial police report is made including contacts the victim has with the criminal justice system after the crime, extent and costs of medical treatment, and recovery of property.
- It collects detailed information about victims and characteristics of the victimization including who the victims are, what their relationship is to the offender, whether the crime was part of a series of crimes occurring over a 6-month period, what self-protective measures were used and how the victims assess their effectiveness, and what the victim was doing when victimized.
- On occasion, it includes special supplements about particular topics such as school crime and the severity of crime.

The Uniform Crime Reports

The UCR program measures police workload and activity. Local police departments voluntarily report information to the Federal Bureau of Investigation (FBI) including the numbers of crimes reported to police, arrests made by police and other administrative information. The UCR program has the following strengths:
- It can provide local data about States, counties, cities and towns.
- It measures crimes affecting children under age 12, a segment of the population that experts agree cannot be reliably interviewed in the NCVS.
- It includes crimes against commercial establishments.
- It collects information about the number of arrests and who was arrested.
- It counts the number of homicides (murders and nonnegligent manslaughters), crimes that cannot be counted in a survey that interviews victims. UCR also collects detailed information about the circumstances surrounding homicides and the characteristics of homicide victims.

NCVS provides information on both reported and unreported crime
Violent crimes measured by NCVS and UCR*

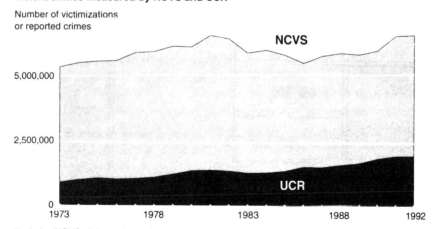

*includes NCVS violent crimes of rape, robbery, aggravated assault, and simple assault; and UCR violent crimes of murder and nonnegligent manslaughter, forcible rape, robbery, and aggravated assault.

Hispanics and non-Hispanics of the crimes of simple and aggravated assault and personal theft.
- Hispanic males had the highest violent crime victimization rates followed by non-Hispanic males. There were no significant differences in violent crime rates for Hispanic and non-Hispanic females.

- Black males age 16 through 19 had a violent crime rate that was significantly higher than that of most other age or racial groups. The rate was nearly double that of white males in the same age range and 3 times the rate for white females between 16 and 19 years of age.

2. VICTIMOLOGY

Marital status

• Those who had never married had the highest rates of both violent crimes and personal thefts; widowed persons had the lowest rates for these crimes.

• Violent victimization rates for widowed and divorced or separated males were not significantly different from violent victimization rates for females of the same marital status. Males who had never married or who were currently married, however, had higher rates than their female counterparts.

Household composition

• In households with a male head and more than a single member, nonrelated members, children of the head under age 18, and other relatives had the highest rates of violent crime victimization.

• Wives of male heads of households, as well as other relatives and male heads living with others, had the lowest theft victimization rates.

• In households headed by females, children of the head who were under 18 years of age and nonrelatives had the highest violent victimization rates. Female heads living alone and husbands of female heads of households had the lowest rates.

• For crimes of theft, nonrelatives and children of a female head of household, who were under 18, had the highest rates.

Income and education

• Persons from families earning less than $7,500 a year had the highest violent crime rates. Members of families with incomes over $50,000 a year generally had the lowest violent crime rates.

• Theft rates were not significantly different for persons from families earning under $7,500 a year compared to persons from families earning $50,000 or more. When compared to all other income categories, individuals from the wealthiest families had higher rates of personal theft.

In findings on education, victimization rates for personal crimes were calculated for persons age 12 or older on the basis of years of school completed:

• Those who had attained only an elementary level education had the highest rates of violent crime, while persons who had attained a college education had the lowest.

• Generally, as educational level increased so did the rate of theft. However, this may be partially explained by an association between educational level and income.

Locality of residence

• Rates of violent crime were not significantly different for residents of suburban and nonmetropolitan areas (28 victimizations per every 1,000 residents versus 25 per every 1,000). Residents of central cities had the highest violent crime victimization rates at 43 victimizations per every 1,000 residents.

• Theft rates were highest for central city residents, followed by suburban residents. Rural residents had the lowest rates of personal theft.

• Black males from central cities experienced violent crime at higher rates than white males who resided in these areas.

• For suburban and non metropolitan area residents, the violent victimization rates of black and white males in each area were not significantly different.

• Only in suburban areas were black females more likely than white females to be violent crime victims (51 victimizations per 1,000 versus 23 per 1,000, respectively); for central city and nonmetropolitan areas there were no significant differences between the two groups.

CHARACTERISTICS OF HOUSEHOLD CRIME VICTIMS

The NCVS regards household crimes as crimes against a household as a whole, rather than a crime directed towards an individual. Thus, rates are computed by dividing the appropriate number of crimes by the number of households, not persons. In general, renters, larger households, and households headed by blacks, Hispanics, and younger persons had higher victimization rates.

Sex, age, race, and ethnicity

• Households headed by blacks had the highest rates of household crimes (199 victimizations per 1,000 households). Rates for households headed by persons of other races (147 victimizations per 1,000) and households headed by whites (146 per 1,000) did not differ significantly. Black households had a higher burglary rate than households headed by whites, and there was some evidence the rate was also higher than that for households headed by persons from other racial groups. There were no significant differences in rates for the crime of household larceny. Households headed by blacks had a higher rate of motor vehicle theft than households headed by whites. There was no significant difference between rates of motor vehicle theft for black households compared to households of persons from other racial groups.

• For each household crime measured by the NCVS, Hispanics had higher rates than non-Hispanics.

• When the rate of motor vehicle theft is calculated on the basis of the number of vehicles owned, households of blacks had a higher theft rate than households of whites, while the rates for blacks and persons of other races were not measurably different from each other. Households that rented their homes had higher theft rates than households that owned or were buying their dwellings.

• Generally, as the age of the household head increased, the rate of each type of household crime decreased.

Annual family income

• Although patterns of household victimization by annual family income were difficult to discern, households with an annual income less than $15,000 were shown to have the highest burglary rates.

• There were no significant differences among any of the income groups in motor vehicle theft rates.

• Rates of burglary were not generally higher for blacks than for whites within specific income categories.

However, black households earning between $10,000 and $14,999 a year had a burglary rate that was significantly higher than that for comparable white households (109 burglaries per 1,000 black households versus 55 per 1,000 white households).

• As with burglary, there were few significant differences in larceny rates for black and white households within specific income groupings; there was some evidence that black households earning between $15,000 and $24,999 a year had a higher larceny rate than white households in the same income category (118 larcenies per 1,000 black households versus 82 per 1,000 white households).

• Black households with annual incomes of $30,000 or more were more likely to experience motor vehicle thefts than white households with similar annual incomes.

Household size and tenure

• Generally, as household size increased, victimization rates in each category of household crime also increased.

• White households that owned their homes were significantly less likely than black households that owned, or households of either race that rented, to be victims of any type of household crime.

• There were no measurable differences in burglary, larceny, or motor vehicle theft rates for black households that owned their homes compared to rates of these crimes for renting households of either race.

• There were no significant differences among renters of either race for any of the household crimes.

Locality of residence

• Households in central cities had the highest victimization rates for household crimes in general, followed by households in suburban areas. Households in nonmetropolitan areas had the lowest rates.

• For each specific category of household crime except burglary, central city households continued to have the highest victimization rates and nonmet-

ropolitan households the lowest. There was no significant difference between burglary rates for suburban and non-metropolitan households.

• Burglary rates for black households were higher than for white households in central cities only. Rates of motor vehicle theft generally followed the same pattern.

• Although central city households had the highest victimization rates, the burglary rate for white households located in central city areas was not significantly different from burglary rates for black households in either suburban or nonmetropolitan areas.

• For white households, motor vehicle theft rates were highest in central cities and lowest in nonmetropolitan areas.

• Auto theft rates were significantly higher for black households in central city areas compared to black households in suburban areas. . . .

VICTIM-OFFENDER RELATIONSHIPS AND CHARACTERISTICS OF OFFENDERS

The NCVS gathers information from victims about their relationship to the offender. Based on this information, victimizations may be classified as having been committed by a stranger or nonstranger, among other categorizations. . . .

• Violent crimes were generally more likely to be committed by strangers than nonstrangers. There were no measurable differences in rates of rapes or simple assaults committed by strangers compared to those committed by nonstrangers.

• Sixty percent of all violent victimizations, 48% of rapes, 81% of robberies, and 56% of all assaults were committed by strangers in 1992.

• Males were more likely than females to be victimized by strangers.

• There was no significant difference between the proportions of violent victimizations committed against blacks and whites by strangers.

• Except for the crime of robbery, women who were divorced or sepa-

rated were less likely than women in any other category of marital status to report that they had been victimized by strangers. For males, however, the likelihood of being victimized by a stranger did not vary with marital status.

Victims were also asked to describe the offenders. The following descriptions of drug use, age, sex, and race are based on the victim's perception of the offender.

• Thirty percent of all violent crime victims perceived the offender or offenders to be under the influence of drugs or alcohol at the time of the offense. Eighteen percent of violent crime victims felt that the offender or offenders were under the influence of alcohol only, and another 4% believed that offenders had been influenced by drugs alone. In 6% of violent victimizations, the victims reported that offenders were under the influence of both drugs and alcohol.

• Males were more likely to be offenders than females in violent victimizations, whether these crimes were committed by a single-offender or by multiple-offenders.

• In nearly one-third of violent victimizations committed by a single-offender, the perpetrator was perceived to be between 21 and 29 years of age; persons age 30 and over were offenders in another third of these victimizations. The offender was perceived to be between the ages of 12 and 20 in 29% of violent single-offender victimizations.

• In multiple-offender victimizations, most frequently the offenders were either all perceived to be between the ages of 12 and 20, or of mixed ages.

• Whites were significantly more likely than blacks to be offenders in single-offender violent crimes, with the exception of robberies.

• In aggravated assaults committed by multiple offenders, victims perceived that similar proportions of blacks and whites had committed the crimes. However, a larger proportion of black offenders than white offenders had committed multiple-offender robberies, while the converse was true for simple assaults.

2. VICTIMOLOGY

• Approximately 73% of all single-of-fender violent crimes against whites were committed by white offenders, and 84% of the single-offender victimizations committed against blacks were by blacks. However, almost all single-offender violent crimes by white offenders were committed against other whites (97%). Forty-eight percent of all single-offender victimizations committed by black offenders were against other blacks.

• Twenty percent of violent victimizations committed by single-offenders involved a victim and offender who were related. In 44% of violent single-offender victimizations the offender was well known but not related to the victim. About 36% of single-offender violent crimes were between casual acquaintances.

• Of multiple-offender violent crimes in which at least one of the offenders was known to the victim, offenders and their victims were casually acquainted with each other in half of these victimizations. Victim and offender were well known but not related to each other in 40%. Approximately 10% of these victimizations involved relatives. . . .

CRIME CHARACTERISTICS

The characteristics of crimes measured by the NCVS may be grouped into two overall categories: (1) the settings and associated circumstances under which the offenses occurred (time and place of occurrence, number of victims and offenders, and weapons used) and (2) the impact of the crimes on the victims, including self-protective measures, physical injury, economic loss, and time lost from work. The first category is based on incidents while the second one is based on victimizations.

Number of victims

• In 1992, 11% more violent crime victimizations than incidents were collected by the survey.

• The vast majority of violent crimes were committed against one individual

only (92%). When a violent incident did involve more than one victim, most commonly two victims were present.

• Violent crimes were more likely to be committed by someone who was a stranger to the victim or victims rather than someone the victim knew. This was especially the case for the crime of robbery.

Time of occurrence

• Personal crimes of theft were significantly more likely to occur during the day, between 6 a.m. and 6 p.m., than at nighttime, while household crimes more frequently occurred at night.

• While violent incidents occurring at night most frequently had been committed between 6 p.m. and midnight, household crimes were more likely to have been committed between midnight and 6 a.m.

• Robberies and assaults in which the offender or offenders were armed were more likely to occur at night than during the day, frequently between 6 p.m. and midnight.

• Violent crimes committed by a stranger were more likely to occur at night than those committed by someone who was known to the victim.

Place of occurrence

• The largest proportion of violent incidents occurred on a street away from the victim's home (24%). As many as 40% of all robberies took place on the street. The victim's home was the next most common site for a violent crime (12%). Almost 9% of violent crimes, overall, occurred in a parking lot or a garage and 12% inside a school building or on school property. Approximately 1% of violent incidents were committed on public transportation or inside the station.

• The most common place for a motor vehicle theft to occur was in a parking lot or garage (35%). Other common areas for these thefts included places near the victim's home, such as a driveway, and the street near the victim's home (21% and 22%, respectively).

• The largest proportions of armed robberies and armed assaults occurred

on a street away from the victim's home, however, nearly 8% of these robberies and 9% of the assaults occurred in the victim's home.

• Violent crimes involving victims and offenders who were strangers to each other were most likely to take place on the street, while violent crimes involving persons who knew each other were most likely to occur in the victim's home.

• About half of all violent incidents occurred five miles or less from the victim's home. Only 4% took place more than 50 miles from home, and another 27% took place inside or near the victim's home or lodging.

Victim activity

• At the time of the violent incident or theft, victims were most likely to have been taking part in some type of leisure activity away from home, such as patronizing a restaurant or nightclub, for example. During the occurrence of a theft, the second most likely activity for a victim to have been participating in was work. In the case of violent crimes, an activity at home (other than sleeping) was next most common.

Number of offenders

• The majority of violent incidents were committed by a lone offender. However, simple assaults were significantly more likely than robberies and aggravated assaults to involve only one offender.

• Violent crimes committed by strangers were more likely to involve multiple-offenders than crimes committed by nonstrangers.

Use of weapons

• Twenty-eight percent of rapes and over 50% of robberies involved an offender with a weapon.

• Violent incidents that had been committed by a stranger were more likely to have involved weapons than violent crimes in which the victim and offender knew each other.

• Firearms (40%), followed by knives (21%) and blunt objects (17%), were the most common weapons used in vi-

olent incidents committed by armed offenders.
• Strangers were more likely to arm themselves with a firearm than non-strangers in violent crimes.

Victim self-protection
• In nearly 72% of all violent victimizations, 80% of rapes, 60% of robberies, and 74% of assaults, victims took some type of measure to protect themselves.
• Victims were no more likely to take self-protective measures when victimized by someone known to them than when victimized by a stranger.
• The likelihood of a victim taking self-protective measures did not vary measurably with sex or race. Persons age 50 and over were generally less likely than younger persons to take self-protective measures.
• Males were more likely than females to protect themselves by attacking an offender without a weapon and by resisting or capturing an offender. Females were more likely to get help or give an alarm, as well as warn or scare the offender as a means of protecting themselves.
• Victims of violent crimes were more likely to report that a protective measure they had taken helped the situation than a measure that had been taken by someone else. The most common way that victims reported their actions helped was by allowing them to avoid injury altogether or to prevent greater injury.
• In those victimizations in which a self-protective measure taken was considered harmful, the most common reason given by victims for this view was that the action made the offender angrier or more aggressive.

Physical injury to victims of personal crimes of violence
• There was some evidence that females were more likely than males to sustain injuries in robberies (45% versus 31%).
• An assault committed by an offender who was known to the victim was significantly more likely to result in

physical injury than an assault that was committed by a stranger.
• Violent crime victims receiving medical care most frequently were treated at a hospital emergency room or emergency clinic (32%) or at their own house, a neighbor's, or a friend's house (30%).
• Victims received hospital care in about 8% of all violent victimizations. In nearly a quarter of the violent victimizations in which injuries were sustained, hospital care was received.
• Black victims were significantly more likely than white victims to receive hospital care, regardless of whether or not injuries had been sustained. There was some evidence that injured male victims received hospital care more frequently than injured female victims.
• In 61% of the victimizations in which those who were injured received hospital care, treatment took place in a hospital emergency room. Victims received inpatient care in 39% of these victimizations, generally remaining at the hospital for less than 1 complete day.

Economic loss
• Seventy-one percent of all personal crimes resulted in economic loss. Ninety-seven percent of all personal crimes of theft, and 23% of all violent crimes involved economic loss. Ninety-one percent of all household crimes resulted in economic loss from theft or damage of property.
• In violent crimes, personal thefts, and household crimes resulting in economic loss, most frequently the value of the loss was under $50. In 13% of the violent crimes, 12% of the thefts and 24% of the household crimes, the value of loss equalled or exceeded $500.

Time lost from work
• Victims lost time from work in approximately 8% of violent victimizations, 4% of personal thefts, and 6% of household crimes.
• Robberies were more likely than simple assaults to result in time lost from work.

• Victims of violent crimes that were completed were more likely than victims of attempted violent crimes to lose time from work.
• Victims were away from work between 1 and 5 days in 55% of the violent victimizations that resulted in loss of time from work. In nearly 13% of the violent victimizations, victims were absent for less than a day, and in 17% they missed work for 11 or more days. . . .

REPORTING CRIMES TO THE POLICE

The majority of crimes measured by the NCVS in 1992 were not reported to the police. The NCVS data examine reasons why crimes were or were not reported, as well as data on who did or did not report crimes.

Rates of reporting
• Only 39% of all victimizations, 50% of violent victimizations, 30% of personal thefts, and 41% of all household crimes were reported to the police. In fact, household crimes and personal thefts were more likely not to be reported to the police than to be reported. There was no significant difference between the proportion of violent crime that was reported to the police and that not reported.
• Of the three major crime categories, violent crimes were most likely to be reported to the police, followed by household crimes. Personal thefts were the least likely crimes to be reported.
• Three out of four motor vehicle thefts were reported to the police, making this the most highly reported crime. Personal larcenies without contact between victim and offender were least likely to be reported (30%).
• Completed robberies, assaults and thefts were more likely to be reported to the police than attempts at these crimes.
• Females were more likely to report violent victimizations to the police than were males, but this was not the case for crimes of theft.
• The reporting rates for both violent crimes and thefts committed against

whites and blacks did not differ measurably.
• Non-Hispanics were significantly more likely than Hispanics to report thefts to the police.
• Violent crimes committed by strangers were no more likely to be reported to the police than violent crimes committed by someone who was known to the victim.
• The youngest victims of violent crimes and thefts—those between 12 and 19 years of age—were less likely than persons in any other age group to report crimes to the police. Generally, reporting rates for persons 20 and over were similar.
• Households that owned their homes were significantly more likely than those that rented to report household crimes to the police (44% versus 38%). White homeowners were also more likely than white renters to report crimes, but this pattern did not hold for black homeowners when compared to black renters.
• There was no consistent pattern in the reporting of crimes to the police based on annual family income.
• Generally, as the value of loss increased, so did the likelihood that a household crime would be reported. Thus, 88% of victimizations involving losses of $1,000 or more were reported to the police.

Reasons for reporting and not reporting
• The most common reason victims

gave for reporting violent crimes to the police was to prevent further crimes from being committed against them by the same offender (20%). For both household crimes and thefts, the most common reason given for reporting was so that the victim could recover property (26% and 29%, respectively).
• Common reasons given for not reporting violent victimizations to the police included: the crime was a private or personal matter (22%), or the offender was unsuccessful (18%).
• The most common reason for not reporting household crimes and thefts was that an object had been recovered (27% and 30%). The next most common reason cited for failing to report a theft was that the crime had been reported to some other official (17%), and in the case of household crime, the next most common reasons were a lack of proof relating to the crime and that the victim thought the police would not want to be bothered.
• The reasons given for not reporting crimes did not vary measurably by race.
• Victims gave different reasons for not reporting victimizations to the police when the offender was a stranger than when a nonstranger. Victims of stranger crimes were more likely not to report the victimization because the offender was unsuccessful, the victim considered the police inefficient, ineffective, or felt that they would not want to be bothered, or because it was not important enough to the victim to

report the crime. Persons who had been victimized by someone they knew chose not to report crimes because they considered them private or personal matters or because they had reported the crime to another official.
• Police response to reported crimes varied by the type of crime that had occurred. Police came to the victim in 75% of violent crimes, 50% of thefts, and 67% of household crimes, for instance. Police were more likely to respond to a violent or household crime than to a theft. In 13% of violent crimes, 35% of thefts, and 25% of household crimes the police did not respond.
• In incidents where the police came to the victim, response time also varied by the type of crime. In 89% of violent crimes, 81% of thefts, and 78% of household crimes, the police came in an hour or less. The police were more likely to respond to a violent crime within 5 minutes than to a theft or household crime. . . .

Editor's Note: In its entirety this 160-page report contains 120 tables, appendixes, and glossary. To obtain a copy (NCJ-14525) call 1-800-732-3277 or write to Bureau of Justice Statistic Clearinghouse, P.O. Box 179, Annapolis Junction, MD 20701-0179.

Crime's Toll on the U.S.: Fear, Despair and Guns

NLJ poll finds self-defense replacing reliance on law enforcement.

Rorie Sherman

National Law Journal Staff Reporter

It is a time of unparalleled desperation about crime. But the mood is decidedly "I'll do it myself" and "Don't get in my way."

Today's citizens believe people must take more responsibility for their own protection. They reject government intrusion on basic civil rights, gun ownership and the media's displays of violence. And there is a pervasive willingness to forgive those who commit serious crimes motivated by the preservation of children or self. Yet for the lawless who lack compelling excuses, little mercy is shown.

The National Law Journal's second comprehensive poll of public attitudes toward crime has found a startling leap in the number of Americans who say they are now "truly desperate" about personal safety. Five years ago, the NLJ's first such poll discovered that 34 percent of the public were "truly desperate" about crime. Today, that figure has soared to 62 percent.

Other significant findings in the wide-ranging, 75-question telephone poll of 800 people nationwide conducted by Penn + Schoen Associated Inc. on March 19–20 included:

■ An overwhelming 75 percent say the police and the justice system alone cannot protect people; people have to take more responsibility for safeguarding themselves. (The poll has a margin of error of 3.5 percent.)

■ A clear majority of Americans (78 percent to 85 percent) are unwilling to give up basic civil liberties even if doing so might enhance their personal safety.

■ Sixty-two percent say the need for guns is increasing, and a majority are unwilling to accept laws that would restrict gun ownership greatly.

■ A majority believes that television encourages crime and violence but no longer wants laws passed to control it.

■ Most Americans are sympathetic to what could be called a "mother lion defense." Eighty-nine percent say they would find it "compelling" if a mother

tried to excuse a serious crime by saying she was trying to protect her children from an abusive father.

■ More than three-quarters favor the "three strikes, you're out" proposal. And that support holds fairly steady even if it means keeping older inmates who've been rendered relatively harmless behind bars at taxpayer expense.

Says Penn + Schoen President Mark J. Penn: "This poll shows the unique

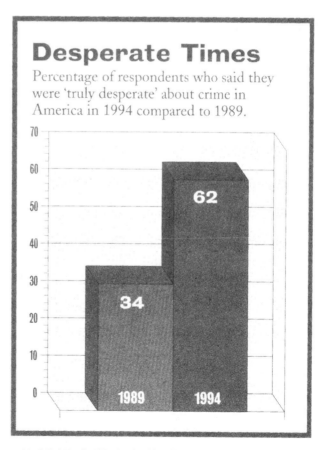

Desperate Times

Percentage of respondents who said they were 'truly desperate' about crime in America in 1994 compared to 1989.

From *The National Law Journal,* April 18, 1994, pp. A1, A19-A20. © 1994 by the New York Law Publishing Company. Reprinted by permission.

American values of individualism and self-preservation."

CRIME EMERGENCY

Significantly more Americans now think crime is a problem requiring emergency action on a national level: 70 percent say so today, as opposed to 60 percent in 1989. In fact, crime, according to a solid 54 percent, is the worst problem facing the country—far outdistancing the economy (18 percent), health care (18 percent) and the environment (6 percent).

And nearly three out of five say racially and ethnically motivated crimes are on the rise.

Direct, personal experience seems to add fuel to the firestorm of desperation.

Today, one quarter of Americans told the NLJ they've been the victim of a crime involving violence or the threat of violence against them. That is up from 17 percent in 1989.

Among blacks, 38 percent today, as opposed to 23 percent in 1989, say they have been victimized in this way.

One out of 10 respondents also say they have been the victim of sexual abuse at some time in their lives.

This rise in the victimization of American citizens is reflected in the most recent U.S. Department of Justice statistics, which found that the number of violent crimes did inch toward an all-time high of 6.62 million in 1992, the last year for which figures are available. That is slightly more than in 1981, when there was a total of 6.58 million violent crimes. But it is significantly greater than the 5.3 million violent crimes experienced during 1973, the lowest recorded year and the first year records were kept.

SPIRIT OF SELF-RELIANCE

As upset as the public is about crime, in the American mind the answers to this escalating national emergency apparently do not lie solely in the government's hands.

Three out of four people say the police and the justice system alone cannot protect people adequately; citizens have to take more responsibility for safeguarding themselves. About the same number of people today are satisfied with President Clinton's crime-fighting efforts (47 percent) as people in 1989 were with President Bush's (54 percent). And 48 percent say they are satisfied with the job Attorney General Janet Reno is doing.

"The interpretation that somebody puts on those statistics is important," says William C. O'Malley, president of the National District Attorneys Association. "I don't think it is vigilantism or hostility to police, prosecutors or the courts. It's more a recognition that the system is powerless without community support and participation."

Instead of more law enforcement, 62 percent of Americans say that the need for guns for personal protection is increasing. Seventy-three percent of blacks, who consistently have the highest victimization rates, think so. And, though 58 percent of the public approves of waiting periods for anyone wishing to buy a gun, there is little support (22 percent) for greatly restricting gun sales.

A majority of Americans believe television encourages crime and violence but few want laws to control it.

Yet ownership of guns has remained consistent during the past five years (40 percent owned guns in 1989, 36 percent in 1994).

For protection, three out of every 10 Americans have a home security system or alarm. Nearly one in five reports moving to a safer neighborhood.

As President Clinton said in his State of the Union address: "Violent crime and the fear it provokes are crippling our society, limiting personal freedom and fraying the ties that bind us."

SAFEGUARD CIVIL LIBERTIES

Despite intense concern about crime, losing basic civil liberties will not be tolerated—even if doing so might enhance safety. A full 85 percent say they are unwilling to allow police to wiretap phones without prior court approval. Eighty-two percent say police should not be allowed to search people randomly, without probable cause. And 78 percent say the practice of reading suspects their *Miranda* rights should be continued.

"I am really pleasantly surprised and heartened," says Nadine Strossen, presi-

Reasons that Excuse Crime

How compelling a reason, by percentage, respondents said it is to excuse a crime in the case of a mother protecting her children from a physically abusive father, or from fury as a result of long-term, institutionalized racism that causes an individual to snap.

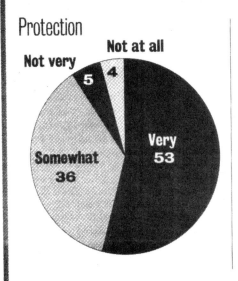

Protection

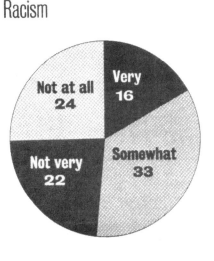

Racism

Perceptions of Crime's Roots

What respondents to polls in 1989 and 1994 said they thought was the greatest cause of crime today, by percentage.

dent of the American Civil Liberties Union.

The tug-of-war between citizens' intense commitment to their civil liberties and their feeling of grave danger is on display right now in Chicago's massive Robert Taylor Homes housing project. Gunfire from a raging gang war has tenants cowering in their apartments. The Chicago Housing Authority is responding by renewing efforts begun in the wake of last summer's violence to have the police, as agents of the city landlord, conduct random gun searches in the projects.

"We're trying to get the guns and drugs out of public housing," Mayor Richard M. Daley explained. "Public housing is owned by the people. They do not want guns, gang-bangers and drugs in their buildings."

As true as that may be, though, many Chicago projects tenants don't want to forfeit their civil liberties. A class action filed on their behalf by the American Civil Liberties Union generated a restraining order from U.S. District Judge Wayne Anderson in February that he transformed into a preliminary injunction this month. Earlier he said a policy of random

searches without probable cause is a "greater evil than the danger of criminal activity." The real answer to safeguarding residents, says the ACLU, is a greater police presence in the projects, not an end run around the Constitution.

PERMIT TELEVISION VIOLENCE

Just as tampering with citizens' civil rights is deemed impermissible, slightly more than half of all Americans now also reject any government interference with the violence shown on television.

Five years ago, in the earlier NLJ poll, 63 percent of Americans said they wanted laws passed that would restrict television violence. Today, only 12 percent say they would agree to such legislation. This despite the fact that there are now pending before Congress no fewer than eight bills proposing to have the federal government in some way control or label violence in television programs.

The leading bill in the batch is the "Children's Protection From Violent Programming Act of 1993," introduced by Sen. Ernest F. Hollings, D-S.C. It would

prohibit violence from being shown on the small screen during hours when children are reasonably likely to comprise a substantial portion of the audience. Also gaining momentum is the "V-Chip" proposal of U.S. Rep. Edward J. Markey, D-Mass., which would combine a rating system with a computer chip enabling television owners to block reception of variously rated programs.

"Hopefully," says Ms. Strossen, "members of Congress will realize that there is little political support for these measures. Many of them [already] realize that it would not be effective, it would not be constitutional," she says. But liberals as well as conservatives think "it would help get them some votes."

Instead of having the government interfere with violence on television, 42 percent of Americans say the networks should adopt a voluntary rating system. And 12 percent say nothing at all should be done about television violence because of the right to free speech.

The public says free expression is to be jealously guarded despite its overwhelming belief that television, pornography, rap music and video games tend to encourage crime and violence. (People in the West describe such media as more influential than people in the Northeast do.)

Three quarters of the public believes that the way television shows depict crime and violence tends to encourage crime. They seem to be listening to reports of many recent studies, including those by the surgeon general, the National Institute of Mental Health and the American Psychological Association purporting to demonstrate a direct link between television violence and aggressive, violent behavior.

Meanwhile, the theory advanced by University of Michigan Law School Prof. Catharine MacKinnon—that pornography's depictions of women and violence tend to encourage violence—also gained considerable support. Seventy-nine percent of women believe pornography encourages violence; 56 percent of men do as well.

Such an attitude is very dangerous, claims Ms. Strossen. The "logical outgrowth of a belief that pornography instigates sexual violence is that it can become a mitigating factor in sentencing or even an outright defense of diminished capacity." Rapists already are beginning to appeal their convictions claiming that "pornography made me do it," she says.

2. VICTIMOLOGY

Fifty-eight percent of Americans also believe rap music tends to encourage crime. And blacks feel the same as whites do.

But the young and the old differ on the impact of violence in video games. Among the youngest group of respondents, 18–34 years old, 42 percent say the way video games depict violence tends to encourage it, as opposed to 63 percent of those in the over-55 group.

Bottom line on the media front, though, is that there is a limit to the liberties Americans want television to take with violence. A majority of Americans say no to televised executions. Only 29 percent believe such broadcasts would deter crime. Many more, 63 percent, think they would become entertainment, "just like wrestling."

SWAYED BY SOME EXCUSES

In theory, Americans are sick of the kind of "excusism" defense lawyers are advancing in courtrooms today. More than half (51 percent) say juries are being "duped" when they take into account all of the circumstances of an accused person's life. Further, 59 percent say the defense of defendants being portrayed as victims has gotten out of hand. (But they fundamentally trust juries. Eighty percent say juries should not be replaced with trial by judges alone.)

By 52 percent to 34 percent, respondents say they would have convicted Lorena Bobbit, with 62 percent of men as opposed to 43 percent of women going for the guilty verdict. (This despite the fact that 61 percent say they find legal insanity either a "very" or a "somewhat" compelling defense.)

Also, in the Menendez brothers' cases, Americans say they would have voted for "murder," the most serious charge, by 68 percent to 15 percent.

Still, as both Ms. Bobbitt's actual acquittal and the Menendez brothers' hung juries suggested, there is in fact a pervasive willingness to be swayed by defendants' self-justifications.

The best excuses apparently come from women who say they committed a serious crime to protect their children or to stop themselves from being battered. A stunning 89 percent of Americans say they would find it a "compelling" defense if a mother said she'd committed a serious crime to protect her children from a physically abusive father. (Fifty-three per-

cent said they would find this defense "very compelling"; 36 percent said "somewhat compelling.")

The public also is deeply sympathetic to the "battered women syndrome" defense. A full 41 percent said it was "very compelling," and 40 percent said it was "somewhat compelling."

Defense lawyers, take note: The jurors who would be most sympathetic to a "mother lion" defense are female, aged 18–34, who did not graduate from high school, earn less than $20,000 and live in the West. Conversely, the tactic will play least well (although they're still very open to it) among Southerners, men and the over-55 crowd, as well as those who earn more than $50,000 a year and those who have been educated beyond college.

But be warned: It seems the mother first must have made an effort to get help from the authorities. Three out of five say that women whose husbands abuse them or their children can reasonably go to the police to get help; taking matters into their own hands is not the only realistic way out.

"Juries are incredibly intelligent, and the fact that they will entertain these defenses reveals the strength of the defenses," says John Henry Hingson III, president of the National Association of Criminal Defense Lawyers Inc. and an Oregon sole practitioner. "The most dangerous place in the world is to be between a bear cub and its mother. And those emotions ring true in Manhattan as much as they do in Madras, Ore."

But, warns Mr. O'Malley, there is terrible danger for women in the increasing acceptance of "Burning Bed"-type defenses. In the end, he says, these kinds of excuses will be used by men, who commit most of the violence in America, to justify their actions against women, just as the Menendez brothers managed to transform the battered women syndrome to make killing their mother and father seem a reasonable act.

'BLACK RAGE'

Nevertheless, sympathy for those who act against their perceived oppressors apparently runs deep in the American psyche.

Nearly one out of every two people also seems open to the "black rage defense" that criminal defense lawyer William M. Kunstler has coined and says he will use for Colin Ferguson, the man

charged with killing six people and wounding 19 in a shooting rampage during rush hour on the Long Island Rail Road Dec. 7, 1993.

Mr. Kunstler says Mr. Ferguson should be found not guilty by reason of insanity and sent to a hospital rather than a prison. The lawyer says he will prove at trial that black rage led a mentally unstable Mr. Ferguson to go off the deep end.

It looks as though Mr. Kunstler may have some luck with such an argument. Forty-nine percent of all Americans say it would be "compelling" for a defendant to argue that fury as a result of long-term, institutionalized racism caused him to snap. (Sixteen percent said it was "very

---

One out of four Americans say they've been a victim of a crime involving violence or the threat of violence

---

compelling"; 33 percent said "somewhat compelling.")

There was a great racial divide in this response. Sixty-eight percent of blacks found the black rage defense compelling. Forty-five percent of whites did.

"Oh my God! That's excellent!" said Mr. Kunstler when he heard the results of the NLJ poll.

"I thought we would get a high degree of resistance from the black community, that they would regard such a defense as somehow demeaning of black people. So I'm glad to find that this high percentage feels [the black rage defense] has some validity. Among whites," Mr. Kunstler added, "it's even more surprising."*

The empathy for black rage may stem from the fact that whites as well as blacks

---

*[Editor's note: Following a competency hearing, county court judge Donald Belfi allowed Colin Ferguson to defend himself in court. The unusual trial (in early 1995) resulted in a guilty verdict for Ferguson.

Failed by Police, Justice...

Percentage of respondents who said people today have to take more responsibility for protecting themselves compared to those who said the police and justice system are able to adequately protect people.

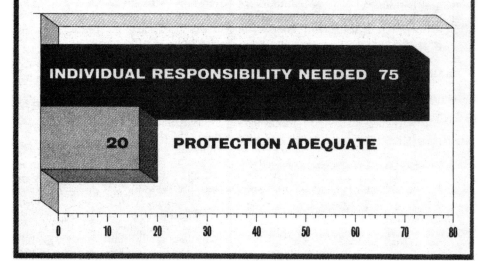

INDIVIDUAL RESPONSIBILITY NEEDED 75

20 PROTECTION ADEQUATE

0 10 20 30 40 50 60 70 80

...People Feel a Need to Arm

How respondents characterize the need to have guns for personal protection.

INCREASING 62

5 DECREASING

STAYING SAME 26

0 10 20 30 40 50 60 70

continue by overwhelming majorities—82 percent and 95 percent, respectively—to see racism in the American criminal justice system. In 1989, 78 percent of whites and 93 percent of blacks thought the American criminal justice system was racist.

No expense should be spared to protect the innocent from being wrongly convicted, say a solid majority of Americans—80 percent. Only 18 percent say that convicting some innocent people is "inevitable and acceptable."

LITTLE FORGIVENESS

For those who do cross the line into lawlessness and have no acceptable excuse, Americans show little forgiveness.

More than three-quarters (77 percent) favor the "three strikes, you're out" measure now being championed in Washington state and California. Washington's law, which took effect in December, sends those convicted of a third qualifying crime to prison for life without the possibility of parole.

When it is explained that such a law would keep more older people in jail at taxpayer cost even though they'd passed the age at which they were likely to commit new crimes, a majority of Americans still support the proposal, even though the number drops somewhat, to 67 percent.

In 1989, 52 percent of Americans said they favored the death penalty for teenage murderers. Today, 75 percent believe execution may be appropriate for those under 20. And overall support for the death penalty holds steady at a high of 77 percent; that number was 73 percent in 1989.

As Sen. Joseph Biden, D-Del., chairman of the Senate Judiciary Committee, recently said about the Senate's passage of the omnibus crime bill, anger at those who break the law has reached a fever pitch in the United States.

The senator adds: "If anyone proposed barbed-wiring the ankles of anyone who jaywalks, I think it would pass."

'Til Death Do Us Part

When a woman kills an abusive partner, is it an act of revenge or of self defense? A growing clemency movement argues for a new legal standard.

Nancy Gibbs

The law has always made room for killers. Soldiers kill the nation's enemies, executioners kill its killers, police officers under fire may fire back. Even a murder is measured in degrees, depending on the mind of the criminal and the character of the crime. And sometime this spring, in a triumph of pity over punishment, the law may just find room for Rita Collins.

"They all cried, didn't they? But not me," she starts out, to distinguish herself from her fellow inmates in a Florida prison, who also have stories to tell. "No one will help me. No one will write about me. I don't have a dirty story. I wasn't abused as a child. I was a respectable government employee, employed by the Navy in a high position in Washington."

"To this day, I don't remember pulling the trigger."

Her husband John was a military recruiter, a solid man who had a way with words. "He said I was old, fat, crazy and had no friends that were real friends. He said I needed him and he would take care of me." She says his care included threats with a knife, punches, a kick to the stomach that caused a hemorrhage. Navy doctors treated her for injuries to her neck and arm. "He'd slam me up against doors. He gave me black eyes, bruises. Winter and summer, I'd go to work like a Puritan, with long sleeves.

Afterward he'd soothe me, and I'd think, He's a good man. What did I do wrong?"

The bravado dissolves, and she starts to cry.

"I was envied by other wives. I felt ashamed because I didn't appreciate him." After each beating came apologies and offerings, gifts, a trip. "It's like blackmail. You think it's going to stop, but it doesn't." Collins never told anyone—not her friends in the church choir, not even a son by her first marriage. "I should have, but it was the humiliation of it all. I'm a professional woman. I didn't want people to think I was crazy." But some of them knew anyway; they had seen the bruises, the black eye behind the dark glasses.

She tried to get out. She filed for divorce, got a restraining order, filed an assault-and-battery charge against him, forced him from the house they had bought with a large chunk of her money when they retired to Florida. But still, she says, he came, night after night, banging on windows and doors, trying to break the locks.

It wasn't her idea to buy a weapon. "The police did all they could, but they had no control. They felt sorry for me. They told me to get a gun." She still doesn't remember firing it. She says she remembers her husband's face, the glassy eyes, a knife in his hands. "To this day, I don't remember pulling the trigger."

The jury couldn't figure it out either. At Collins' first trial, for first-degree murder, her friends, a minister, her doctors and several experts testified about her character and the violence she had suffered. The prosecution played tapes of her threatening her husband over the phone and portrayed her as a bitter,

unstable woman who had bought a gun, lured him to the house and murdered him out of jealousy and anger over the divorce. That trial ended with a hung jury.

"They say I'm a violent person, but I'm not. I didn't want revenge. I just wanted out."

At her second, nine men and three women debated just two hours before finding her guilty of the lesser charge, second-degree murder. Collins' appeals were denied, and the parole board last year recommended against clemency. Orlando prosecutor Dorothy Sedgwick is certain that justice was done. "Rita Collins is a classic example of how a woman can decide to kill her husband and use the battered woman's syndrome as a fake defense," she says. "She lured him to his death. He was trying to escape her." Collins says her lawyers got everything: the $125,000 three-bedroom house with a pool, $98,000 in cash. "I've worked since I was 15, and I have nothing," she says. "The Bible says, 'Thou shalt not kill,' and everybody figures if you're in here, you're guilty. But I'm not a criminal. Nobody cares if I die in here, but if I live, I tell you one thing: I'm not going to keep quiet."

If in the next round of clemency hearings on March 10, Governor Lawton Chiles grants Collins or any other battered woman clemency, Florida will join 26 other states in a national movement to take another look at the cases of abuse

---

 From *Time*, January 18, 1993, pp. 38-45. © 1993 by Time Inc. Magazine Company. Reprinted by permission.

victims who kill their abusers. Just before Christmas, Missouri's conservative Republican Governor John Ashcroft commuted the life sentences of two women who claimed they had killed their husbands in self-defense. After 20 years of trying, these women have made a Darwinian claim for mercy: Victims of perpetual violence should be forgiven if they turn violent themselves.

More American women—rich and poor alike—are injured by the men in their life than by car accidents, muggings and rape combined. Advocates and experts liken the effect over time to a slow-acting poison. "Most battered women aren't killing to protect themselves from being killed that very moment," observes Charles Ewing, a law professor at SUNY Buffalo. "What they're protecting themselves from is slow but certain destruction, psychologically and physically. There's no place in the law for that."

As the clemency movement grows, it challenges a legal system that does not always distinguish between a crime and a tragedy. What special claims should victims of fate, poverty, violence, addiction be able to make upon the sympathies of juries and the boundaries of the law? In cases of domestic assaults, some women who suffered terrible abuse resorted to terrible means to escape it. Now the juries, and ultimately the society they speak for, have to find some way to express outrage at the brutality that women and children face every day, without accepting murder as a reasonable response to it.

But until America finds a better way to keep people safe in their own homes or offers them some means of surviving if they flee, it will be hard to answer the defendants who ask their judges. "What choice did I really have?"

HOME IS WHERE THE HURT IS

Last year the A.M.A., backed by the Surgeon General, declared that violent men constitute a major threat to women's health. The National League of Cities estimates that as many as half of all women will experience violence at some time in their marriage. Between 22% and 35% of all visits by females to emergency rooms are for injuries from domestic assaults. Though some studies have found that women are just as likely to start a fight as men, others indicate they are six times as likely to be seri-

ously injured in one. Especially grotesque is the brutality reserved for pregnant women: the March of Dimes has concluded that the battering of women during pregnancy causes more birth defects than all the diseases put together for which children are usually immunized. Anywhere from one-third to as many as half of all female murder victims are killed by their spouses or lovers, compared with 4% of male victims.

"Male violence against women is at least as old an institution as marriage," says clinical psychologist Gus Kaufman Jr., co-founder of Men Stopping Violence, an Atlanta clinic established to help men face their battering problems. So long as a woman was considered her husband's legal property, police and the courts were unable to prevent—and unwilling to punish—domestic assaults. Notes N.Y.U. law professor Holly Maguigan. "We talk about the notion of the rule of thumb, forgetting that it had to do with the restriction on a man's right to use a weapon against his wife: he couldn't use a rod that was larger than his thumb." In 1874 North Carolina became one of the first states to limit a man's right to beat his wife, but lawmakers noted that unless he beat her nearly to death "it is better to draw the curtain, shut out the public gaze and leave the parties to forget and forgive."

Out of that old reluctance grew the modern double standard. Until the first wave of legal reform in the 1970s, an aggravated assault against a stranger was a felony, but assaulting a spouse was considered a misdemeanor, which rarely landed the attacker in court, much less in jail. That distinction, which still exists in most states, does not reflect the danger involved: a study by the Boston Bar Association found that the domestic attacks were at least as dangerous as 90% of felony assaults. "Police seldom arrest, even when there are injuries serious enough to require hospitalization of the victim," declared the Florida Supreme Court in a 1990 gender-bias study, which also noted the tendency of prosecutors to drop domestic-violence cases.

Police have always hated answering complaints about domestic disputes. Experts acknowledge that such situations are often particularly dangerous, but suspect that there are other reasons for holding back. "This issue pushes buttons, summons up personal emotions, that almost no other issue does for police and judges," says Linda Osmundson,

who co-chairs a battered wives' task force for the National Coalition Against Domestic Violence. "Domestic violence is not seen as a crime. A man's home is still his castle. There is a system that really believes that women should be passive in every circumstance." And it persists despite a 20-year effort by advocates to transform attitudes toward domestic violence.

While most of the effort has been directed at helping women survive, and escape, abusive homes, much of the publicity has fallen on those rare cases when women resort to violence themselves. Researcher and author Angela Browne points out that a woman is much more likely to be killed by her partner than to kill him. In 1991, when some 4 million women were beaten and 1,320 murdered in domestic attacks, 622 women killed their husbands or boyfriends. Yet the women have become the lightning rods for debate, since their circumstances, and their response, were most extreme.

WHAT CHOICE DID SHE HAVE?

"There is an appropriate means to deal with one's marital problems—legal recourse. Not a .357 Magnum," argues former Florida prosecutor Bill Catto. "If you choose to use a gun to end a problem, then you must suffer the consequences of your act." Defense lawyers call it legitimate self-protection when a victim of abuse fights back—even if she shoots her husband in his sleep. Prosecutors call it an act of vengeance, and in the past, juries have usually agreed and sent the killer to jail. Michael Dowd, director of the Pace University Battered Women's Justice Center, has found that the average sentence for a woman who kills her mate is 15 to 20 years; for a man, 2 to 6.

The punishment is not surprising, since many judges insist that evidence of past abuse, even if it went on for years, is not relevant in court unless it occurred around the time of the killing. It is not the dead husband who is on trial, they note, but the wife who pulled the trigger. "Frankly, I feel changing the law would be authorizing preventive murder," argued Los Angeles Superior Court Judge Lillian Stevens in the Los Angeles *Times*. "The only thing that really matters is, Was there an immediate danger? There can't be an old grievance." And even if a woman is allowed to testify about past violence, the jury may still condemn her response to it. If he was really so savage, the prosecutor typically asks, why didn't she leave, seek shelter, call the police, file a complaint?

"The question presumes she has good options," says Julie Blackman, a New Jersey-based social psychologist who has testified as an expert witness in abuse and murder cases. "Sometimes, they don't leave because they have young children and no other way to support them, or because they grow up in cultures that are so immersed in violence that they don't figure there's any place better to go, or because they can't get apartments." The shelter facilities around the country are uniformly inadequate: New York has about 1,300 beds for a state with 18 million people. In 1990 the Baltimore zoo spent twice as much money to care for animals as the state of Maryland spent on shelters for victims of domestic violence.

Last July, even as reports of violence continued to multiply, the National Domestic Violence Hotline was disconnected. The 800 number had received as many as 10,000 calls a month from across the country. Now, says Mary Ann Bohrer, founder of the New York City-based Council for Safe Families, "there is no number, no national resource, for people seeking information about domestic violence."

The other reason women don't flee is because, ironically, they are afraid for their life. Law-enforcement experts agree that running away greatly increases the danger a woman faces. Angered at the loss of power and control, violent men often try to track down their wives and threaten them, or their children, if they don't come home. James Cox III, an unemployed dishwasher in Jacksonville, Florida, was determined to find his ex-girlfriend, despite a court order to stay away from her. Two weeks ago, he forced her mother at gunpoint to tell him the location of the battered women's shelter where her daughter had fled, and stormed the building, firing a shotgun. Police shot him dead. "This case illustrates the extent to which men go to pursue their victims," said executive director Rita DeYoung. "It creates a catch-22 for all battered women. Some will choose to return to their abusers, thinking they can control their behavior."

"After the law turns you away, society closes its doors on you, and you find yourself trapped in a life with someone capable of homicide. What choice in the

end was I given?" asks Shalanda Burt, 21, who is serving 17 years for shooting her boyfriend James Fairley two years ago in Bradenton, Florida. She was three months pregnant at the time. A week after she delivered their first baby, James raped her and ripped her stitches. Several times she tried to leave or get help. "I would have a bloody mouth and a swollen face. All the police would do is give me a card with a deputy's name on it and tell me it was a 'lover's quarrel.' The battered women's shelter was full. All they could offer was a counselor on the phone."

"I didn't mean to kill him. He had hit me several times. Something inside me snapped; I grabbed the bottle and swung."

Two weeks before the shooting, the police arrested them both: him for aggravated assault because she was pregnant, her for assault with a deadly missile and violently resisting arrest. She had thrown a bottle at his truck. Her bail was $10,000; his was $3,000. He was back home before she was, so she sent the baby to stay with relatives while she tried to raise bail. The end came on a Christmas weekend. After a particularly vicious beating, he followed her to her aunt's house. When he came at her again, she shot him. "They say I'm a violent person, but I'm not. I didn't want revenge. I just wanted out." Facing 25 years, she was told by a female public defender to take a plea bargain and 17 years. "I wanted to fight. But she said I'd get life or the electric chair. I was in a no-win situation."

It is hard for juries to understand why women like Burt do not turn to the courts for orders of protection. But these are a makeshift shield at best, often violated and hard to enforce. Olympic skier Patricia Kastle had a restraining order when her former husband shot her. Lisa Bianco in Indiana remained terrified of her husband even after he was sent to jail for eight years. When prison officials granted Alan Matheney an eight-hour pass in March 1989, he drove directly to Bianco's home, broke in and beat her to death with the butt of a shotgun. Last March, Shirley Lowery, a grandmother

of 11, was stabbed 19 times with a butcher knife by her former boyfriend in the hallway of the courthouse where she had gone to get an order of protection.

THE MIND OF THE VICTIM

Defense lawyers have a hard time explaining to juries the shame, isolation and emotional dependency that bind victims to their abusers. Many women are too proud to admit to their family or friends that their marriage is not working and blame themselves for its failure even as they cling to the faith that their violent lover will change. "People confuse the woman's love for the man with love of abuse," says Pace's Dowd. "It's not the same thing. Which of us hasn't been involved in a romantic relationship where people say this is no good for you?"

It was Denver psychologist Lenore Walker, writing in 1984, who coined the term battered-woman syndrome to explain the behavior of abuse victims. Her study discussed the cycle of violence in battering households: first a period of growing tension; then a violent explosion, often unleashed by drugs or alcohol; and finally a stage of remorse and kindness. A violent man, she argues, typically acts out of a powerful need for control—physical, emotional, even financial. He may keep his wife under close surveillance, isolating her from family and friends, forbidding her to work or calling constantly to check on her whereabouts. Woven into the scrutiny are insults and threats that in the end can destroy a woman's confidence and leave her feeling trapped between her fear of staying in a violent home—and her fear of fleeing it.

Many lawyers say it is virtually impossible to defend a battered woman without some expert testimony about the effect of that syndrome over time. Such testimony allows attorneys to stretch the rules governing self-defense, which were designed to deal with two men caught in a bar fight, not a woman caught in a violent relationship with a stronger man.

In a traditional case of self-defense, a jury is presented a "snapshot" of a crime: the mugger threatens a subway rider with a knife; the rider pulls a gun and shoots his attacker. It is up to the jurors to decide whether the danger was real and immediate and whether the response was reasonable. A woman who shoots her husband while he lunges at her with a knife should have little trouble claiming that she acted in self-defense. Yet lawyers still find jurors to be very uncomfortable with female violence under any circumstances, especially violence directed at a man she may have lived with for years.

Given that bias, it is even harder for a lawyer to call it self-defense when a woman shoots a sleeping husband. The danger was hardly immediate, prosecutors argue, nor was the lethal response reasonable. Evidence about battered-woman syndrome may be the only way to persuade a jury to identify with a killer. "Battered women are extraordinarily sensitive to cues of danger, and that's how they survive," says Walker. "That is why many battered women kill, not during what looks like the middle of a fight, but when the man is more vulnerable or the violence is just beginning."

"Delia was driven to extremes. The situation was desperate, and she viewed it that way."

A classic self-defense plea also demands a fair fight. A person who is punched can punch back, but if he shoots, he runs the risk of being charged with murder or manslaughter. This leaves women and children, who are almost always smaller and weaker than their attackers, in a bind. They often see no way to escape an assault without using a weapon and the element of surprise—arguing, in essence, that their best hope of self-defense was a pre-emptive strike. "Morally and legally a woman should not be expected to wait until his hands are around her neck," argues Los Angeles defense attorney Leslie Abramson. "Say a husband says, 'When I get up tomorrow morning, I'm going to beat the living daylights out of you,' " says Joshua Dressler, a law professor at Wayne State University who specializes in criminal procedures. "If you use the word imminent, the woman would have to wait until the next morning and, just as he's about to kill her, then use self-defense."

That argument, prosecutors retort, is an invitation to anarchy. If a woman has survived past beatings, what persuaded

her that this time was different, that she had no choice but to kill or be killed? The real catalyst, they suggest, was not her fear but her fury. Prosecutors often turn a woman's history of abuse into a motive for murder. "What some clemency advocates are really saying is that that s.o.b. deserved to die and why should she be punished for what she did," argues Dressler. Unless the killing came in the midst of a violent attack, it amounts to a personal death-penalty sentence. "I find it very hard to say that killing the most rotten human being in the world when he's not currently threatening the individual is the right thing to do."

Those who oppose changes in the laws point out that many domestic disputes are much more complicated than the clemency movement would suggest. "We've got to stop perpetuating the myth that men are all vicious and that women are all Snow White," says Sonny Burmeister, a divorced father of three children who, as president of the Georgia Council for Children's Rights in Marietta, lobbies for equal treatment of men involved in custody battles. He recently sheltered a husband whose wife had pulled a gun on him. When police were called, their response was "So?" Says Burmeister: "We perpetuate this macho, chauvinistic, paternalistic attitude for men. We are taught to be protective of the weaker sex. We encourage women to report domestic violence. We believe men are guilty. But women are just as guilty."

He charges that feminists are trying to write a customized set of laws. "If Mom gets mad and shoots Dad, we call it PMS and point out that he hit her six months ago," he complains. "If Dad gets mad and shoots Mom, we call it domestic violence and charge him with murder. We paint men as violent and we paint women as victims, removing them from the social and legal consequences of their actions. I don't care how oppressed a woman is; should we condone premeditated murder?"

Only nine states have passed laws permitting expert testimony on battered-woman syndrome and spousal violence. In most cases it remains a matter of judicial discretion. One Pennsylvania judge ruled that testimony presented by a prosecutor showed that the defendant had not been beaten badly enough to qualify as a battered woman and therefore could not have that standard applied to her case. President Bush signed legislation in October urging states to accept expert

testimony in criminal cases involving battered women. The law calls for development of training materials to assist defendants and their attorneys in using such testimony in appropriate cases.

Judge Lillian Stevens instructed the jury on the rules governing self-defense at the 1983 trial of Brenda Clubine, who claimed that she killed her police-informant husband because he was going to kill her. Clubine says that during an 11-year relationship, she was kicked, punched, stabbed, had the skin on one side of her face torn off, a lung pierced, ribs broken. She had a judge's order protecting her and had pressed charges to have her husband arrested for felony battery. But six weeks later, she agreed to meet him in a motel, where Clubine alleges that she felt her life was in danger and hit him over the head with a wine bottle, causing a fatal brain hemorrhage. "I didn't mean to kill him," she says. "He had hit me several times. Something inside me snapped; I grabbed the bottle and swung." The jury found Clubine guilty of second-degree manslaughter, and Judge Stevens sentenced her to 15 years to life. She says Clubine drugged her husband into lethargy before fatally hitting him. "It seemed to me [the beatings] were some time ago," Stevens told the Los Angeles *Times*. Furthermore, she added, "there was evidence that a lot of it was mutual."

It is interesting that within the legal community there are eloquent opponents of battered-woman syndrome—on feminist grounds—who dislike the label's implication that all battered women are helpless victims of some shared mental disability that prevents them from acting rationally. Social liberals, says N.Y.U.'s Maguigan, typically explain male violence in terms of social or economic pressures. Female violence, on the other hand, is examined in psychological terms. "They look to what's wrong with her and reinforce a notion that women who use violence are, per se, unreasonable, that something must be wrong with her because she's not acting like a good woman, in the way that women are socialized to behave."

Researcher Charles Ewing compared a group of 100 battered women who had killed their partners with 100 battered women who hadn't taken that fatal step. Women who resorted to violence were usually those who were most isolated, socially and economically; they had been the most badly beaten, their children had been abused, and their husbands were drug or alcohol abusers. That is, the common bond was circumstantial, not psychological. "They're not pathological," says social psychologist Blackman. "They don't have personality disorders. They're just beat up worse."

Women who have endured years of beatings without fighting back may reach the breaking point once the abuse spreads to others they love. Arlene Caris is serving a 25-year sentence in New York for killing her husband. He had tormented her for years, both physically and psychologically. Then she reportedly learned that he was sexually abusing her granddaughter. On the night she finally decided to leave him, he came at her in a rage. She took a rifle, shot him, wrapped him in bedsheets and then hid the body in the attic for five months.

Offering such women clemency, the advocates note, is not precisely the same as amnesty; the punishment is reduced, though the act is not excused. Clemency may be most appropriate in cases where all the circumstances of the crime were not heard in court. The higher courts have certainly sent the message that justice is not uniform in domestic-violence cases. One study found that 40% of women who appeal their murder convictions get the sentence thrown out, compared with an 8.5% reversal rate for homicides as a whole. "I've worked on cases involving battered women who have talked only briefly to their lawyers in the courtroom for 15 or 20 minutes and then they take a plea and do 15 to life," recalls Blackman. "I see women who are Hispanic and don't speak English well, or women who are very quickly moved through the system, who take pleas and do substantial chunks of time, often without getting any real attention paid to the circumstances of their case."

The first mass release in the U.S. came at Christmas in 1990, when Ohio Governor Richard Celeste commuted the sentences of 27 battered women serving time for killing or assaulting male companions. His initiative was born of long-held convictions. As a legislator in the early '70s, he and his wife helped open a women's center in Cleveland and held hearings on domestic violence. When he became lieutenant governor in 1974 and moved to Columbus, he and his wife rented out their home in Cleveland as emergency shelter for battered women. He and the parole board reviewed 107

cases, looking at evidence of past abuse, criminal record, adjustment to prison life and participation in postrelease programs before granting the clemencies. "The system of justice had not really worked in their cases," he says. "They had not had the opportunity for a fair trial because vitally important evidence affecting their circumstances and the terrible things done to them was not presented to the jury."

The impending reviews in other states have caused some prosecutors and judges to sound an alarm. They are worried that Governors' second-guessing the courts undermines the judicial system and invites manipulation by prisoners. "Anybody in the penitentiary, if they see a possible out, will be claiming. 'Oh, I was a battered woman,' " says Dallas assistant district attorney Norman Kinne. "They can't take every female who says she's a battered woman and say, 'Oh, we're sorry, we'll let you out.' If they're going to do it right, it's an exhaustive study."

Clemency critics point to one woman released in Maryland who soon afterward boasted about having committed the crime. Especially controversial are women who have been granted clemency for crimes that were undeniably premeditated. Delia Alaniz hired a contract killer to pretend to rob her home and murder her husband in the process. He had beaten her and their children for years, sexually abusing their 14-year-old daughter. The prosecutor from Skagit County, Washington, was sufficiently impressed by the evidence of abuse that he reduced the charge from first-degree murder and life imprisonment to second-degree manslaughter with a sentence of 10 to 14 years. In October 1989, Governor Booth Gardner granted her clemency. "Delia was driven to extremes. The situation was desperate, and she viewed it that way," says Skagit County public defender Robert Jones. "The harm to those kids having a mom in prison was too much considering the suffering they went through. As a state, we don't condone what she did, but we understand and have compassion."

THE ALTERNATIVES TO MURDER

There is always a risk that the debate over clemency will continue to obscure the missing debate over violence. "I

grew up in a society that really tolerated a lot of injustice when it came to women," says Pace University's Dowd. "It was ingrained as a part of society. This isn't a woman's issue. It's a human-rights issue. Men should have as much to offer fighting sexism as they do racism because the reality is that it's our hands that strike the blows." The best way to keep battered women out of jail is to keep them from being battered in the first place.

In a sense, a society's priorities can be measured by whom it punishes. A survey of the population of a typical prison suggests that violent husbands and fathers are still not viewed as criminals. In New York State about half the inmates are drug offenders, the result of a decade-long War on Drugs that demanded mandatory sentences. A War on Violence would send the same message, that society genuinely abhors parents who beat children and spouses who batter each other, and is willing to punish the behavior rather than dismiss it.

Minnesota serves as a model for other states. In 1981 Duluth was the first U.S. city to institute mandatory arrests in domestic disputes. Since then about half the states have done the same, which means that even if a victim does not wish to press charges, the police are obliged to make an arrest if they see evidence of abuse. Advocates in some Minnesota jurisdictions track cases from the first call to police through prosecution and sentencing, to try to spot where the system is failing. Prosecutors are increasingly reluctant to plea-bargain assault down to disorderly conduct. They have also found it helpful to use the arresting officer as complainant, so that their case does not depend on a frightened victim's testifying.

Better training of police officers, judges, emergency-room personnel and other professionals is having an impact in many cities. "We used to train police to be counselors in domestic-abuse cases," says Osmundson. "No longer. We teach them to go make arrests." In Jacksonville, Florida, new procedures helped raise the arrest rate from 25% to 40%. "Arrests send a message to the woman that help is available and to men that abuse is not accepted," says shelter executive director DeYoung, who also serves as president of the Florida Coalition Against Domestic Violence. "Children too see that it's not accepted and are more likely to grow up not accepting abuse in the home."

Since 1990 at least 28 states have passed "stalking laws" that make it a crime to threaten, follow or harass someone. Congress this month may take up the Violence Against Women bill, which would increase penalties for federal sex crimes; provide $300 million to police, prosecutors and courts to combat violent crimes against women; and reinforce state domestic-violence laws. Most women, of course, are not looking to put their partners in jail; they just want the violence to stop.

A Minneapolis project was founded in 1979 at the prompting of women in shelters who said they wanted to go back to their partners if they would stop battering. Counselors have found that men resort to violence because they want to control their partners, and they know they can get away with it—unlike in other relationships. "A lot of people experience low impulse control, fear of abandonment, alcohol and drug addiction, all the characteristics of a batterer," says Ellen Pence, training coordinator for the Domestic Abuse Intervention Project in Duluth. "However, the same guy is not beating up his boss."

Most men come to the program either by order of the courts or as a condition set by their partners. The counselors start with the assumption that battering is learned behavior. Eighty percent of the participants grew up in a home where they saw or were victims of physical, sexual or other abuse. Once imprinted with that model, they must be taught to recognize warning signs and redirect their anger. "We don't say, 'Never get angry,' " says Carol Arthur, the Minneapolis project's executive director. "Anger is a normal, healthy emotion. What we work with is a way to express it." Men describe to the group their most violent incident. One man told about throwing food in his wife's face at dinner and then beating her to the floor—only to turn and see his two small children huddled terrified under the table. Arthur remembers his self-assessment at that moment: "My God, what must they be thinking about me? I didn't want to be like that."

If the police and the courts crack down on abusers, and programs exist to help change violent behavior, victims will be less likely to take—and less justified in taking—the law into their own hands. And once the cycle of violence winds down in this generation, it is less likely to poison the next. That would be a family value worth fighting for.

—**Reported by Cathy Booth/Miami, Jeanne McDowell/Los Angeles and Janice C. Simpson/New York**

WHEN MEN HIT WOMEN

A program for battered women in Duluth, Minn.—though widely considered the model for the rest of the country—has enjoyed only limited success. Nothing speaks more eloquently to the intractability of the problem.

Jan Hoffman

Jan Hoffman, a staff writer for The Village Voice, *recently completed a journalism fellowship at Yale Law School.*

This Saturday night shift has been excruciatingly dull for the police in Duluth, Minn., a brawny working-class city of 90,000 on the shoreline of Lake Superior. The complaints trickle into the precinct, the callers almost embarrassed: black bear up a tree; kids throwing stuffed animals into traffic. But it's 1 A.M. now, and the bars are closing. People are heading home.

1:02 A.M.: Couple arguing loudly. Probably just "verbal assault," the dispatcher tells the car patrols.

1:06 A.M.: Two squad cars pull up to the address. A tall blond man opens the door as a naked woman hurriedly slips on a raincoat. The man looks calm. The woman looks anything but.

"We were just having a squabble," he begins.

"He was kicking the [expletive] out of me," she yells.

"Let's go in separate rooms and talk," says one of the officers, following the Duluth Police Department procedure for domestic disputes.

In the living room, George G. tells his side of the story. "We've been trying to work on things. And so we were talking. And wrestling."

How does he explain the blood oozing from the inside of her mouth? "She drinks, you know. She probably cut

herself." From inside the bedroom, Jenny M., whose face is puffing up, screams: "Just get him out of here! And then you guys leave, too!"

The police officers probe for details, telling her that something must be done now, or there will probably be a next time, and it will hurt much worse. Jenny M. glares, fearful but furious. "He slapped me and kicked my butt. He picked me up by the hair and threw me against the wall."

"She lies, you know," George G. confides to an officer, who remains stone-faced. Jenny M. starts crying again. "I don't want him hurt. This is my fault. I'm the drinker. He's not a bad guy."

Following protocol, the officers determine that the couple live together. And that she is afraid of him. Next, they snap Polaroids of her bruised face, and of his swollen, cut knuckles. Then the police head toward George G. with handcuffs. He looks at her beseechingly. "Jenny, do you want me to go?"

An officer cuts him short. "George, it's not her choice."

George G. thrusts his chin out and his fists deep into the couch. "But this is just a domestic fight!"

One cop replies: "We don't have a choice, either. We have to arrest you." They take him away, handcuffed, leaving Jenny M. with leaflets about the city's Domestic Abuse Intervention Project (D.A.I.P).

By 1:34 A.M. George G. has been booked at the St.

From the *New York Times Magazine*, February 16, 1992, pp. 23-27, 64-66, 72. © 1992 by the New York Times Company. Reprinted by permission.

Louis County jail, where he will sit out the weekend until arraignment on Monday morning. Within an hour, a volunteer from the city's shelter will try to contact Jenny M., and in the morning, a man from D.A.I.P. will visit George and explain the consequences in Duluth for getting into "a domestic fight."

It was 10 years ago this summer that Duluth became the first local jurisdiction in America to adopt a mandatory arrest policy for misdemeanor assaults—the criminal charge filed in most domestic-violence cases. But the arrest policy alone is not what makes Duluth's perhaps the most imitated intervention program in the country. Its purpose is to make every agent of the justice system—police, prosecutors, probation officers, judges—deliver the same message: domestic violence is a crime that a community will not tolerate. The program's centerpiece is D.A.I.P., which acts as a constant, heckling monitor of all the organizations. The project, which also runs batterers' groups and supervises custody visits between batterers and their children, chugs along on $162,000 a year. Financing comes from the state's Department of Corrections, foundation grants and fees for D.A.I.P.'s manuals and training seminars.

The Duluth model—pieces of which have been replicated in communities throughout Minnesota, in cities like Los Angeles, Baltimore, San Francisco, Nashville and Seattle, and in countries like Canada, Scotland, New Zealand and Australia—has been admiringly described by Mary Haviland, a New York City domestic-abuse expert, as "an organizing miracle."

Typically, a first-time offender is incarcerated overnight. If he pleads guilty, he'll be sentenced to 30 days in jail and put on probation, pending completion of a 26-week batterer's program. If he misses three successive classes, he is often sent to jail. Men who are served with civil orders of protection are routinely sent into the same treatment program. Staff members and volunteers from the shelter maintain contact with victims throughout the process.

Many experts regard Duluth as embodying the best of what the almost 20-year-old battered-women's movement has sought to achieve. The movement, inspired by the grass-roots feminist campaign that opened rape-crisis centers in the late 60's, sprang up in the mid-70's as a loose coalition of emergency shelters. Duluth's own shelter, the Women's Coalition, was founded in 1978. Reflecting the national movement's multiple approaches a few years later, Duluth activists then prodded local law-enforcement agencies to take the issue seriously and eventually urged that batterers be offered treatment as well as punishment.

Nowadays in Duluth, women who seek help from the legal system do receive some protection, and their batterers are usually held accountable. After a decade of many trials and many errors, Ellen Pence, one of the

project's founders and its national proselytizer, estimates that 1 out of every 19 men in Duluth has been through the program. During that same period, not one Duluth woman died from a domestic homicide. Given the rate of Duluth's domestic homicides in the 70's, says Pence, "there are at least five women alive today that would have otherwise been killed."

The results from Duluth are not, however, wholly triumphant. One study shows that five years after going through the Duluth program and judicial system, fully 40 percent of the treated men end up reoffending (or becoming suspects in assaults), either with the same woman or new partners. Pence thinks the real number may be closer to 60 percent. And the number of new cases each year that come before either criminal or family court judges has remained constant—about 450 a year.

"The changes in the country have been enormous," says Elizabeth M. Schneider, a Brooklyn Law School

---

... while intervention may be possible, prevention seems all but unimaginable.

---

professor and expert on battered women. "But we seriously underestimated how wedded our culture is to domestic violence." Upward of four million American women are beaten annually by current and former male partners, and between 2,000 to 4,000 women are murdered, according to the National Woman Abuse Prevention Center. C. Everett Koop, the former Surgeon General, has identified domestic violence as the No. 1 health problem for American women, causing more injuries than automobile accidents, muggings and rapes combined. The connection with child abuse in a family has been well documented: between 50 and 70 percent of the men who physically harm their partners also hit their children.

At this point, while intervention may be possible, prevention seems all but unimaginable. Despite the community's exceptional efforts, as Pence flatly admits: "We have no evidence to show that it has had any general deterrent effect. The individual guy you catch may do it less. But in Duluth, men don't say, 'Gee, I shouldn't beat her up because I'll get arrested.' After 10 years, we've had a lot of young men in our program whose dads were in it.

"I have no idea where the next step will come from," she adds. "We're too exhausted just trying to stay on top of things as they are."

Ellen Pence's commitment to ending family violence is hard-earned. An aunt was shot to death by her husband, a sister is a former battered wife and, one night about 20 years ago, a neighbor fleeing an abusive partner left her boy with Pence, who subsequently helped raise him. In 1981, D.A.I.P. received a $50,000 state grant for Pence's bold new experiment. Duluth was chosen for a simple but powerful reason: the city's judges and police chief were the only ones in Minnesota willing to take her proposal seriously. A Minnesota native, Pence, now 43, is an exasperating, indefatigable earthshaker, who, by dint of her salty wit and impassioned outbursts, simply will not be denied.

Duluth, she concedes, is not exactly the mayhem capital of the Midwest. In 1990, homicides hit a record high of three. The local scourge is predominantly alcoholism, not drug addiction. The people are mostly Scandinavian and Eastern European, with a modest minority of Ojibwa Indians, blacks and Southeast Asians. With fir-dotted hills that swoop sharply down to the largest fresh-water lake in the world, Duluth appears to be a pretty decent place to live–particularly for those with a fondness for ice fishing and months of subfreezing weather. Its incidence of domestic violence is probably no worse than anywhere else in the country, and, a decade ago, was treated just as casually. In 1980, there were just 22 arrests for domestic assault, and only four convictions.

First, Ellen Pence took on the cops.

Traditional practice: If an officer doesn't witness a misdemeanor assault, the officer won't arrest.

New practice: If an officer has probable cause, including a victim's visible injury, to believe a misde-

---

. . . women just want their abusers out of the house but not sent to jail . . .

---

meanor domestic assault occurred within four hours of the arrival of the police, the officer must arrest. In 1990, the Duluth police arrested 176 men and 23 women for misdemeanor domestic assaults–of whom almost all were convicted. (Experts agree that violence by women against men is usually in self-defense or retaliation, and is often less severe.)

Over the years, mandatory arrest has become increasingly popular, having been adopted, though inconsistently enforced, in dozens of municipalities and 15 states–although recent studies have called into question whether police arrests are the best way to protect domestic-abuse victims.

Still, mandatory arrest earns favorable reviews from police and prosecutors, and a D.A.I.P. survey found that 71 percent of the victims approved of the Duluth police's handling of their situations. But some battered-women's advocates remain skeptical, particularly because the policy can be disproportionately tough on poor minority families. Most experts point out that while battering occurs across all races and classes, poor people are more likely to be reported to authorities and punished than men from middle-class households. "For people who are more disadvantaged economically, like Native Americans, blacks and Hispanics, there are higher levels of all kinds of victimization, including family violence," says Angela Browne, the author of "When Battered Women Kill."

Another significant problem with mandatory arrest is that it can backfire: on occasion, when faced with two bloodied people accusing each other of attacking first, police have arrested the woman as well as the man. When this happens, children may be sent into foster care. In Connecticut, which has one of the country's toughest domestic-violence policies, the dual-arrest rate is 14 percent.

Many police are still reluctant to arrest because prosecutors tend to put the cases on the back burner. Prosecutors, in turn, blame their lack of action on the victims, who, they say, often refuse to press charges, fearing a batterer's revenge or believing his promise of reformation. Duluth, however, has what officials call a "flexible no-drop" policy: regardless of the victim's wishes, the prosecutor will almost always pursue the case.

"I assume that victims won't cooperate," says Mary E. Asmus, the chief prosecutor of Duluth's city attorney's office. Asmus has a working procedure for obtaining evidence independent of the victim's cooperation. At trial, she'll offer police photographs, tapes of calls to 911 and medical records. She also subpoenas all victims. If the victim recants on the stand, Asmus, making unusual use of a state rule of evidence, will offer the woman's original statement to police–not to impeach her witness, but to assert the facts of the incident. In her nine years as a Duluth prosecutor, Asmus has lost only three domestic-violence cases in court.

Nationwide, some of the most aggressive domestic-violence prosecutors are in Philadelphia, San Francisco and San Diego, which files at least 200 new cases each month. To pressure women to testify, some prosecutors have gone so far as charging them with filing false police reports and perjury, issuing contempt-of-court citations, and, in rare instances, even jailing them. The no-drop policy has ignited fiery debate. One prosecutor argued in a recent national District Attorneys Association Bulletin that it "smacks of the worst kind of paternalism." In Westchester County, N.Y., Judge Jeanine Ferris Pirro retorts, "Some jurisdictions allow a victim to drop charges, and that's sending a subtle message that they don't take the crime seriously."

Not surprisingly, a no-drop policy often puts prosecutors at odds with the same activists who are demanding that the justice system go after batterers. Susan Schechter, author of "Women and Male Violence," contends that such a policy can erode a battered woman's sense of self-esteem and control, "particularly when

---

"If she'd been raped by a stranger, would you expect her to live with him, too?"

---

she has a good sense of her own danger and what's best for her and the kids." Pence says that in Duluth, D.A.I.P. has managed to cut the dual-arrest rate way down. "We trust our system," she says, "so we're willing to force a woman into it." But Pence doesn't condone mandatory arrest or no-drop prosecutions unilaterally.

While tougher policies have diverted more cases into criminal court, women just want their abusers out of the house but not sent to jail seek relief through a different route: the civil order of protection, which limits the batterer's contact with the woman and her children. Applying for such an order can be a labyrinthine undertaking—even on a good day. Every jurisdiction has its own criteria for who qualifies, as well as for the duration of the protection order. Women with mixed feelings about getting the order in the first place can quickly become frustrated.

And judges become frustrated with them. Gender-bias studies of various state court systems have sharply criticized judges for penalizing battered women. In Duluth, the D.A.I.P. targeted the judiciary. "We explained why they were seeing what they were seeing," Pence recalls. "They were interpreting a woman's fear as ambivalence and masochism. We showed them what happened in cases when they just gave a guy a lecture or a fine." Now she occasionally trots out one or two Duluth judges on her judicial-training sessions around the country. One grumbles fondly that "Ellen Pence is turning us into feminist tools."

Judge Robert V. Campbell of Duluth's District Court presides over most of its order-of-protection hearings. If a woman fails to appear in court because her abuser may be present, "I'll continue the order for a month or so, on the theory that she's being intimidated," Campbell says. A Duluth woman named Brenda Erickson, whose request for an order against her husband alleged that he'd raped her, had her first brush with the

justice system before Judge Campbell. Her husband's attorney argued that his client could not have raped her. "Your honor," Erickson remembers the lawyer protesting, "she's his wife!"

The judge, she says, all but leaped down from the bench, sputtering, "If she'd been raped by a stranger, would you expect her to live with him, too?" "And I thought, Oh God, he understands how I feel," Erickson says.

Six glum faces, 12 crossed arms—nobody thinks they did anything wrong, so why do they have to be here? Ty Schroyer, a D.A.I.P. group leader, assumes an expression of determined cheeriness as he greets this week's recruits, all ordered by the court to the batterer's program. Some ground rules:

"We don't call women 'the old lady,' 'the wife,' 'that slut,' 'that whore,' 'the bitch,' 'that fat, ugly bitch.' . . ." The list quickly becomes unprintable.

"So what should we call her—'it'?" says a man who calls himself Dave, as the others snicker.

"How about her name?" snaps Schroyer, who himself was arrested nearly a decade ago for pounding his wife's head against a sidewalk.

Trying to change a batterer's behavior toward women makes pushing boulders uphill look easy. Nonetheless, at least 250 different programs around the country, filled with volunteer and court-referred clients, are having a go at it. Among them, no consensus has emerged about philosophy or length of treatment: Phoenix courts send their batterers to 12 weeks or more of counseling sessions; San Diego batterers must attend for a year.

Edward W. Gondolf, a Pittsburgh sociologist who has evaluated and developed batterers' programs for 12 years, says, "We're making a dent with garden-variety batterers"—first-time or sporadic offenders—"but there's another cadre, the most lethal, who are still out of our reach." Batterers who go through the legal system should be more carefully screened, he says, and some confined. Men whom he would categorize as antisocial or even sociopathic batterers—about 30 percent—not only resist intervention, but may be further antagonized by it.

He cautions women not to be taken in when their partners enter counseling. "Counseling is the American way to heal a problem," he says. "She'll think, 'If he's trying, I should support him,' while he's thinking, 'I'll go to the program until I get what I want—my wife back.' But his being in counseling may increase the danger for her because she has got her guard down."

In Duluth, when a batterer enters D.A.I.P., officials at the Women's Coalition shelter will stay in close touch with the victim; a woman who is reluctant to report another beating to police can confide in a shelter counselor, who will tell a group leader, who may confront the man in the following week's session.

Nearly half of all batterers have problems with substance abuse, especially alcohol, and D.A.I.P. group leaders often have difficulty persuading men not to blame their violence on their addictions. John J., 35, a Duluth man who once beat a marine senseless with a lug wrench, raped the women he dated and kicked the first of four wives when she was pregnant, thought he'd become violence-free after going through the D.A.I.P. batterers' program and Alcoholics Anonymous. One night several years later, though sober, he shoved his third fiancée so hard that she went flying over a coffee table. "Men have more courage when we're drunk," he says, teary-eyed with shame, during an interview. "But the bottle didn't put the violence there in the first place."

Why do men hit women? "Men batter because it works," says Richard J. Gelles, director of the Family Violence Research Program at the University of Rhode Island. "They can not only hurt a woman but break down her sense of self-worth and belief that she can do anything about it."

Some programs use a therapeutic approach, exploring family history. Others employ a model inspired by the psychologist Lenore Walker's "cycle of violence" theory of battering: the man goes through a slow buildup of tension, explodes at his partner and begs her forgiveness during a honeymoon period.

But Pence criticizes both approaches for failing to confront a batterer's hatred of women, as well as his desire to dominate them. Duluth's 26-week program is divided in two sections. The first, usually run by a mental-health center, emphasizes more traditional counseling that tries to teach men to walk away from their anger. The second, run by D.A.I.P., provokes men to face up to their abuse and to identify the social and cultural forces underlying it. (In 1990, Duluth sent 350 men through its program. By comparison, Victim Services in New York City sent 300.)

Bill, 30, admits that he once believed "you were allowed to hit a woman if you were married—the license was for possession." A sense of entitlement pervades the men's groups: when Schroyer asked one man why he cut telephone cords in his house, the man shouted, "Why should she talk on something I paid for?"

Duluth batterers don't necessarily have to slap, punch, choke, kick with steel-toed boots or crush empty beer cans against a cheekbone to keep their partners terrified. During arguments, abusers will floor the gas pedal, clean hunting rifles or sharpen knives at the kitchen table, smash dishes and television sets, call her office very two minutes and hang up. One man smeared a peanut butter and jelly sandwich in his wife's hair. One woman's ex-husband wrote her phone number in the men's rooms of Duluth's seediest bars, with an invitation to call for a good time.

Then there are the outright threats. If she leaves him, he'll tell child-welfare services that she's a neglectful mother. Or he'll kill her. Or himself.

Schroyer and the other group leaders stress that when the violence does erupt, contrary to a batterer's favorite excuse, he has not lost control. "You chose the time, the place, the reason, how much force you'd use," Schroyer tells them. "She didn't."

But convincing men that they are better off without that control is perhaps the most challenging impediment to treatment. One night a batterer huffily asked, "Why should men want to change when we got it all already?"

Brenda Erickson, one of the Duluth women who appeared before Judge Campbell, had been thinking about leaving her husband, Mike, for a long time. Mike had always told her that she was fat, ugly and stupid, and besides, no man would want a woman with three children, so she'd better stay with him. Brenda never thought she was a battered woman, because Mike had never punched her.

The social psychologist Julie Blackman points out that a byproduct of the attention given to the Lisa Steinberg tragedy several years ago is that the public now mistakenly associates battered women with the smashed, deformed face of Hedda Nussbaum. Susan Schechter finds that many abused women who are not as bloodied as the character portrayed by Farrah Fawcett in "The Burning Bed" do not believe they deserve aid. "Many battered women see themselves as strong, as keeping together a family, in spite of what's going on," Schechter says.

Mike often assured Brenda that if he went to jail, it wouldn't be for wife-beating—it would be for her murder. When he was angry, he would shatter knickknacks or punch a hole in the wall right next to her head. Brenda is 5 foot 1 and Mike is 6 foot 3. "Imagine an 18-wheeler colliding with a Volkswagen," she says. "So I learned how to say 'yes' to him, to defuse situations."

Over the eight years of their marriage, the family subsisted on welfare and Mike's occasional earnings as a freelance mechanic. In the final years, Brenda cooked in a restaurant, worked as an aide for Head Start and cared for their three sons. According to Brenda, Mike chose not to seek a full-time job in order to keep an eye on her. She couldn't even go to the grocery store alone.

Frequently, he raped her. "He'd rent pornographic films and force me to imitate them," Brenda says. The sex was often rough and humiliating. "He thought that if we had sex a lot I wouldn't leave him." Mike acknowledges that there was "mental abuse" in their marriage, but not what he'd call rape. "I'm oversexed, but there's nothing wrong with that."

A friend at work, sensing Brenda's distress, gave her the number of the Women's Coalition shelter. Brenda would call anonymously, trying to figure out if she could possibly escape. Finally, she just picked a date: Feb. 9, 1988.

That morning, she told Mike she was taking the kids to school. Once there, a shelter official picked them up. When Brenda walked into the handsome Victorian house filled with women and children, she felt an overwhelming sense of relief.

Women stay in abusive relationships too long for many reasons. Susan Schechter says it can take years before physical abuse starts, even longer for a woman to learn "not to blame herself or his lousy childhood for

---

Women stay in abusive relationships too long for many reasons.

---

his violence." Brenda refused for years to believe her marriage wasn't working. Another Duluth woman, who endured a decade of stitches and plaster casts, sobbed, "We did have some wonderful times, and he was my entire world."

Some women stay because they may have reasonable expectations that they will die leaving. As many as three-quarters of the domestic assaults reported to authorities take place after the woman has left.

Some women stay because they can't afford to leave–or because, long since alienated from friends and family, they have no place to go. There are about 1,200 shelters scattered across the country, many reporting that they must turn away three out of every four women who ask for help. Duluth's shelter can house up to 30 women and children; the shelter in Las Vegas, Nev. (population: 850,000), has only 27 beds.

But when Brenda finally made the decision to leave, she had more options than most battered women in the country–the full resources of the shelter and D.A.I.P. were available to her. Shelter staff members screened her phone calls, and Pence spoke with Mike on Brenda's behalf; she joined a women's support group, and a counselor led her through the first of what would be many appearances before Judge Campbell in family court. But things did not go smoothly.

Mike did manage to complete the batterers' group program and made several passes through substance-abuse treatment. Yet, even though Brenda had filed for three separate orders of protection, the net effect was negligible: she claims to have suffered harassing phone calls, slashed tires and broken car windows. D.A.I.P. officials pressed police to investigate, but because the officers never caught Mike on the premises, he was never arrested.

After the divorce was granted, they continued to battle over visiting the children. Brenda had ultimately left Mike because of her children–the eldest, then in kindergarten, was already angry and trau-

matized. Research indicates that children exposed to family violence are 10 times as likely to be abused or abusive in adult relationships.

Two years ago, D.A.I.P. opened a visitation center at the Y.W.C.A. for noncustodial parents whom the court has granted supervised time with their children. The entrances and exits are such that neither parent has to see the other, and, under the watchful gaze of a D.A.I.P. staff member, parent and children have the run of two large living rooms, a small kitchen and a roomful of toys. This is where Brenda's boys have been seeing their father and his new wife.

Brenda Erickson is now an honor student at the University of Minnesota in Duluth, majoring in family life education. "Mike has some good qualities," she allows, "but this sure as hell beats walking around on eggshells. The boys and I are so much more relaxed and able to love each other. And I found a strength I never knew I had."

On a Friday night last fall, Mike Erickson was finally arrested for domestic assault and violently resisting arrest. The victim was not Brenda, however, but his new wife, Deborah, and her teen-age son. In the ensuing brawl, it took four officers and a can of Mace to get him into the squad car, as he howled: "I wasn't domesticating with her. I was drinking!" He pled guilty to all charges and served 36 days on a work farm. Mike is now enrolled in the D.A.I.P. program. "That night I pushed my stepson and backhanded my wife because she pulled the phone out and I got irritated," he says. "It's hard for me to shut up when I get going."

But Deborah Erickson refused to file charges against Mike or even to speak to a volunteer from the Women's Coalition. She has been in abusive relationships before, but she's certain this marriage is different. "I told the cops, 'Hey, it happened, but it's not happening again.'"

Those who are in a position to help battered women tend to deny the gravity of the problem. "Doctors still believe the falling-down-stairs stories, and clergy still tell women to pray and go to a marriage counselor," says Anne Menard of the Connecticut Coalition Against Domestic Violence.

But Congress has begun to act. In 1990, it passed a resolution, adapted by 30 states, urging that domestic violence by a parent be a presumption against child custody. The most dramatic policy reform, however, may be Senator Joseph R. Biden Jr.'s pending Violence Against Women Act, which proposes, among other things, to stiffen penalties for domestic abusers.

But while the use of the criminal-justice system to quash domestic violence has gained currency around the country, Ellen Pence's advice to women in battering relationships is simply this: leave. Leave because even the best of programs, even Duluth's, cannot insure that a violent man will change his ways.

INCEST

A Chilling Report

Do you want to know what incest is? What it really is? No euphemisms, evasions, excuses, or intellections? Are your sure? Then read this. Every word of it is true. The horror is unimaginable. But in the end, at least you will know.

Heidi Vanderbilt

Heidi Vanderbilt is an award-winning writer who lives in New England.

Where there is no last name identifying details have been changed.

The Children

I am five. The July sun shines on my shoulders. I am wearing a dress I have never seen before, one I don't remember putting on. The door opens and a little girl runs to me her face delighted. I have never seen her before. I am completely terrified and try to hide behind my astonished and irritated mother.

"But she's your best friend!" my mother says, and tells me that I played at the girl's house just yesterday. I don't remember. When my mother tells me her name, I've never heard it before.

Other children arrive. I remember some of them, but from long ago. They're older now. They've grown. Some have lost their teeth.

I pretend that everything is all right.

At night I lie awake as I have for years, listening. I hear footsteps coming down the hall. I hold my breath. I watch the edge of the door to my bedroom. I watch for the hand that will push it open. If it is my mother's hand or my father's, I am all right. For now. If it is the hand of the woman who lives with us and sticks things into me, I move out of my body. I disappear into a painting on the wall, into my alarm clock with its rocking Gene Autry figure, into imaginary landscapes. Usually I come back when the woman leaves. But not always.

I am eight. I have spoken French from the time I was three. I attended a French kindergarten, and now the Lycée Français. I have just spent the summer in France. My French is fluent when we leave Nice. Four days later, after my return to the woman who hurts me, I can no longer understand or speak a single word of French. Sitting at my gouged wooden desk, my classmates sniggering around me, I feel terrified and ashamed, certain that whatever is wrong is my fault.

She told me she would cut out my tongue. She told me I would forget. I remember how tall she was, how she wore her hair pulled

---

CASE STUDIES

Rikki and Nick's parents were members of a satanic cult. The children were sexually abused and tortured. When the parents left the cult, they got their children into therapy. Rikki is three. Nick is four. Both have full-blown multiple personality disorders.

Lauren was five when she told her mother that a family friend who often took care of her had "fooled" with her. Her mother was relieved when the doctors found no physical evidence of sexual abuse. She wondered if her daughter's story was true. Then Lauren told her mother that the friend had taken photos of her. The photos were found; they revealed that Lauren had been raped and sodomized over a period of more than a year.

Sharon's mother masturbated her to sleep from the time she was born. As Sharon grew older, her mother would sometimes stare at her for long periods. "I love you too much," she would repeat, over and over. Now 44, Sharon says, "I still don't know where my mother ends and I begin."

"I take responsibility for what happened," she says. "I bought into it. I know my mother shouldn't have done it, but I'm responsible, too."

"How could you be responsible for something that began when you were only a baby?" a friend asks.

"I just am," she insists.

Sharon has been in Freudian analysis for 15 years.

First published in *Lear's Magazine*, February 1992, pp. 49-64. © 1992 by Heidi Vanderbilt. Reprinted by permission of the author.

back with wisps breaking loose at the temples. I knew then that I would never forget.

I am 40. There are things I have always remembered, things I have forgotten, things that exist in shadows only, that slip away when I try to think about them. I can't remember all that she did that sent me "away." Nor do I know what I was doing while I was "away." I only know that these episodes began with periods of abuse so frightening, painful, and humiliating that I left my body and parts of my mind.

I rarely talk about what happened to me. I have never discussed the details with my parents, my husband, or anyone else. Whenever I think of telling, she returns in my dreams.

I dream that I am a child and she chases me with a sharp knife, catches me, and gouges out my eyes. I dream that I have to protect little children at night, even though I am alone and a child myself. I tuck in the other children and get into my bed. Her arm reaches for me and pulls me down. I dream that I run for help, enter a phone booth, hear a dial tone. When I reach up I see the phone has been torn from the wall. I dream of animals skinned alive while I scream.

Sometimes when I sleep I stop breathing and can't make myself start until I wake gasping, my fingers blue.

Incest can happen to anyone: to rich and to poor; to whites, blacks, Asians, Native Americans, Jews, Christians, and Buddhists. It happens to girls and to boys, to the gifted and to the disabled. It happens to children whose parents neglect them, and those—like me—whose parents love and care for them.

What exactly is incest? The definition that I use in this article is: any sexual abuse of a child by a relative or other person in a position of trust and authority over the child. It is the violation of the child where he or she lives—literally and metaphorically. A child molested by a stranger can run home for help and comfort. A victim of incest cannot.

Versions of this definition are widely used outside the courtroom by therapists and researchers. In court, incest definitions vary from state to state. In many states, the law requires that for incest to have taken place, vaginal penetration must be proved. So if a father rapes his child anally or orally he may be guilty of child sexual abuse but may not, legally, be guilty of incest.

I believe that if incest is to be understood and fought effectively, it is imperative that the definition commonly held among therapists

and researchers—the definition I have given here—be generally accepted by the courts and public. I am not alone in this belief. As therapist E. Sue Bloom, for one, writes in *Secret Survivors: Uncovering Incest and Its Aftereffects in Women*: "If we are to understand incest, we must look not at the blood bond, but at the emotional bond between the victim and the perpetrator. . . . The important criterion is whether there is a real relationship in the experience of the child."

"The crucial psychosocial dynamic is the *familial* relationship between the incest participants," adds Suzanne M. Sgroi, M.D., director of the Saint Joseph College's Institute for Child Sexual Abuse Intervention in West Hartford, Connecticut, writing in the *Handbook of Clinical Intervention in Child Sexual Abuse*. "The presence or absence of a blood relationship between incest participants is of far less significance than the kinship roles they occupy."

Incest happens between father and daughter, father and son, mother and daughter, mother and son. It also happens between stepparents and stepchildren, between grandparents and grandchildren, between aunts and uncles and their nieces and nephews. It can also happen by proxy, when live-in help abuses or a parent's lover is the abuser; though there is no blood or legal relationship, the child is betrayed and violated within the context of family.

No one knows how many incest victims there are. No definitive random studies on incest involving a cross section of respondents have been undertaken. No accurate collection systems for gathering information exist. The statistics change depending on a number of variables: the population surveyed, the bias of the researcher, the sensitivity of the questions, and the definition of incest used. This is an area "where each question becomes a dispute and every answer an insult," writes Roland Summit, M.D., a professor of psychiatry at Harbor-UCLA Medical Center in Torrance, California, in his introduction to *Sexual Abuse of Young Children*. "The expert in child sexual abuse today may be an ignoramus tomorrow."

As recently as the early '70s, experts in the psychiatric community stated that there were only 1 to 5 cases of incest per one million people. When I began work on this article, I thought that maybe one person in a hundred was an incest victim. How wrong I was. Sometimes called "rape by extortion," incest is about betrayal of trust, and it accounts for most child sexual abuse by far. To be specific:

In 1977, Diana E. H. Russell, Ph.D., professor emeritus at Mills College in Oakland, California, and author of *The Secret Trauma: Incest in the Lives of Girls and Women* and *Sexual Exploitation: Rape, Child Sexual Abuse and Workplace Harassment,* questioned 930 San Francisco women and found that 38 percent had been sexually abused by the time they had reached the age of 18. She further found that of those women who were victims, 89 percent were abused by relatives or family acquaintances. Using Russell's figures as my guide—they are widely cited by other authorities in the field and have been duplicated in other studies—the estimate of the incidence of incest that I came up with is one in three; which is to say that incest happens to about one person in three before the age of 18.

Incestuous acts range from voyeurism and exhibitionism to masturbation, to rape and sodomy, to bestiality, to ritualized torture in cults. Incest may or may not include penetration, may or may not be violent. It may happen only once or continue for decades. It usually exists in secret, but not always.

Kim Shaffir was four and a half years old when her divorced mother remarried. Her stepfather, John Hairsine, showed Kim pornographic photographs and read aloud to her from pornographic novels. He took Polaroids of himself and Kim's mother having sex and showed Kim the pictures. He arranged for her to watch him and her mother having intercourse; he told her when they would be doing it and left the door open. Hairsine kept Kim quiet with the threat that if she told anyone, her mother would send her away.

From exhibitionism and voyeurism, Hairsine moved on to fondling. He made Kim perform oral sex on him. Then he forced her to have anal sex. As he had photographed himself with her mother, he now photographed himself with Kim.

When Kim was 13 her mother discovered the blurred backings of the Polaroid pictures of her husband and Kim. She broke the camera as a symbolic statement. "We're going to put it all behind us," she announced. But she was wrong.

Hairsine made peepholes throughout their Maryland house so he could spy on Kim. He drilled through the bathroom door. Kim repeatedly stuffed the hole with soap and toilet paper, which he would remove and she would replace. For three years she tried to avoid showering when her mother was out of the house.

Every morning, under the guise of waking

her for school, Hairsine entered her room and masturbated in her presence. Kim, now 30 and living in Washington, D.C., says, "That's how I'd wake up, to him coming into a dish towel as he stood by my bed."

One reason for the imprecise nature of the incest statistics is that when children try to tell, they aren't believed. Another is that many victims don't recognize certain behaviors as abusive. My parents would never have let anyone abuse me—if they had known. They didn't know because I didn't know to tell them.

Small children understand very little about sex. Even kids who use "dirty" words often don't understand what those words mean. And as little as they know about normal sex, they know less about deviant sex. They simply trust that whatever happens to them at the hands of those who take care of them is supposed to happen. Children know that adults have absolute power over them, and even in the face of the most awful abuse, they will obey.

The victim who does tell is almost always asked: Why didn't you tell sooner? The answers are:

I didn't know anything was wrong.
I didn't know it was illegal.
I didn't know who to tell.
I did tell and no one believed me.
I was ashamed.
I was scared.

The abuser keeps the incest secret through threats:

If you tell, I will kill you.
If you tell, you'll be sent away.
If you tell, I'll kill your little sister.
If you tell, I'll molest your little brother.
If you tell, I'll kill your dog.
If you tell, it will kill your mother.
If you tell, no one will believe you.
If you tell, then you will go to the insane asylum.
If you tell, I'll go to jail and you'll starve.
If you tell, they'll give you to someone who will really hurt you.
If you tell, you'll go to hell.
If you tell, I won't love you anymore.

Many abusers make good on their threats, but most don't need to. "Small creatures deal with overwhelming threat by freezing, pretending to be asleep, and playing possum," says Dr. Roland Summit, the Harbor-UCLA Medical Center psychiatrist who, in a paper titled "The Child Sexual Abuse Accommodation Syndrome," sets forth a widely accepted explanation of how children behave when molested.

The classic paradigm for an incestuous union is between an older male (father or stepfather or grandfather or uncle) and a younger female. The male is pictured as seduced by a conniving and sexually precocious child who wants sex, power, and presents. Or he is seen as a snaggletoothed tree dweller with an IQ below freezing who rapes his daughter because she is female, his, and nearer to hand than a cow. Yet Massachusetts therapist Mike Lew, author of *Victims No Longer: Men Recovering from Incest and Other Sexual Child Abuse*, told me that as many as 50 percent of victims may be boys. As therapist Karin C. Meiselman, Ph.D., writes in *Resolving the Trauma of Incest*, "The fact that many males are abused as children and adolescents is only beginning to receive adequate professional attention."

Difficult as it is for girls to talk about their abuse, it is even harder for boys. Boys are taught that they must be strong and self-reliant. For a boy to report that he was abused, he must admit weakness and victimization. If he was molested by a male, he will fear that this has made him homosexual.

Then, too, many boys simply don't know they have been abused. Deborah Tannen, Ph.D., professor of linguistics at Georgetown University and author most recently of *You Just Don't Understand: Women and Men in Conversation*, suggests that girls and boys are raised in different cultures. The world expects one set of behaviors and attitudes from girls and another, quite different set from boys.

We teach girls to avoid sex, to wait, and to protect themselves. We teach them that men are not allowed to do certain things to them. But we teach boys that any sex—any heterosexual sex—is good, the earlier the better. We tell them they "scored," they "got lucky." But consider the impact when a boy "gets lucky" with his mother.

"My first really clear memory," says Michael Smith, 30, "is of my mother performing oral sex on me. I was seven. My parents would make me watch them have sex before or after my mother had oral sex with me."

Ralph Smith, the family patriarch, is now 65 years old. His wife, Betty, is 58. They are gray-haired, churchgoing, God-fearing people whose eight children range in age from 20 to 40. The Smiths say they tried to give their kids a good childhood.

"What happened to me was bad," says Michael, "but it was nothing compared to

what happened to Lisa." Lisa is Michael's sister. Her earliest memory is of being five and her father fondling her and performing oral sex on her. She told her mother. "I was in the bathtub when I told her," Lisa says. "She slapped me around. She said, 'You're dirty. Don't ever say that again.' "

Lisa's parents had sex in front of her, and when she turned 12 her father had intercourse with her—a pattern he continued until she turned 23 and left home. "I didn't like it," she says. "But he said it was right. He said it even said in the Bible that it was okay to have sex with your children and sex with your parents. He quoted Job. I begged my mother not to leave me alone with him anymore. She said, 'I know you love him.' I asked her to help me, but she wouldn't."

Lisa's sister Michelle slept in a room next to Lisa's. She would hear her father go into Lisa's bedroom at night. "I would hear Lisa crying and screaming and telling him no," Michelle recalls.

Ralph and Betty Smith made Michael and Lisa perform oral sex on each other while they watched and gave instructions. "They said they were teaching us about sex," Michael says. "They were teaching us how to be good mates when we grew up, how to keep a mate satisfied. I would know how to please a woman. I could stay married."

Ralph and Betty kept the children silent by beating them and threatening to kill them and their brothers and sisters. Ralph Smith regularly held a gun to Lisa's head while he had intercourse with her.

Lisa believed that she and Michael were the only ones being molested. She believed that her being abused was protecting her younger siblings. "Until Michelle came and told me she was also being molested," Lisa says, "I thought I had protected them. My whole goal was to protect them. When I found out they had all been abused . . . " Her voice trails off. "We were afraid of our parents and the outside world. The very few people we tried to tell didn't believe us or only believed a little, not enough to do anything."

"I even told a priest once," Michael says. "He gave me a bunch of leaflets and told me to go home and work it out with my family."

Abused children assume that they are responsible for the abuse, believing they brought it on themselves. One man said to his 13-year-old victim, "I'm sorry this had to happen to you, but you're just too beautiful." Some victims feel guilty because they accepted presents or felt pleasure. Victims who experience orgasms while being molested suffer excruciating guilt and conflict.

While there have been articles by pedophiles arguing that incest is good and natural and that its prohibition violates the rights of children, psychiatrist Judith Lewis Herman, M.D., writes in her pioneering book, *Father-Daughter Incest,* that the actual sexual encounter, whether brutal or tender, painful or pleasurable, "is always, inevitably, destructive to the child." And Maryland psychotherapist Christine A. Courtois, Ph.D., author of *Healing the Incest Wound: Adult Survivors in Therapy,* is firm in her belief that incest "poses a serious mental-health risk for a substantial number of victims."

Mariann's father began taking her into his shower when she was five. He washed her and taught her to wash him. He took her into his bed for snuggling, which turned into fondling. He taught her to masturbate him and made her perform oral sex on him. When she was ten he forced her to have vaginal and anal intercourse.

Mariann's father told her he was teaching her about sex. He said he was teaching her to control her sexual feelings so she wouldn't get swept away. He told her that if she was ever with a boy and got sexually aroused, she was to come to him and he would "help" her.

When Mariann's mother caught her husband fondling their daughter, she called Mariann a whore and accused her of trying to seduce her father. Yet when Mariann's father got a job in another state that required him to move early one spring, her mother stayed behind until summer but insisted that Mariann go with him.

As Mariann grew older her father experienced periods of impotence. When he could no longer manage penetration, he masturbated between his daughter's breasts, ejaculated onto her chest, and rubbed his semen over her.

"There was no escaping it, no safety," Mariann remembers. "I started to feel crazy. I wanted to be crazy. I remember thinking, I want to take LSD and go crazy so they'll lock me up and I can stay there for the rest of my life." At 17, Mariann cut her wrists. The wounds were superficial, but she bled into her sheets all night and came down to breakfast with Band-Aids lined up along her arms. No one asked what had happened.

In spite of her objections and efforts to avoid her father, he continued to have sex with her, until he died when she was in her 20s. She has been hospitalized several times for severe depression and suicidal impulses. "I was invisible," she says. "That's all I was—a vagina. Nothing else existed."

If incest can lead to suicide, it can also lead to homicide. Witness Tony Baekeland. Tony's mother, Barbara, seduced him when he was in his early teens. She openly boasted of their affair, and Tony talked of it as well. When he became violent in his late teens and early 20s, neither of his parents got him psychiatric help. At 26, Tony stabbed his mother to death in their apartment. He was incarcerated at a facility for the criminally insane. His grandmother rallied friends and family to have him released. It took six years. Once freed, Tony stabbed his grandmother eight times at her apartment in New York. She survived. He was imprisoned on Rikers Island, where he suffocated himself with a plastic bag.

In young children who are victims of incest, the vast array of physical and psychological symptoms suffered include injuries to the mouth, urethra, vagina, and anus; bedwetting and soiling; fear of everyone of the perpetrator's gender; nightmares and/or sleep loss; compulsive masturbation, precocious sexual knowledge, and sexual acting out; running away, suicide attempts, and sexually transmitted diseases. Judge Jeffry H. Gallet of the New York State Family Court, sitting in Manhattan, perhaps best known as the judge who heard the Lisa Steinberg case, told me he had once seen a baby with pelvic inflammatory disease so severe that as an adult she will never be able to conceive. And as is well known to health workers and court officials, not all AIDS babies contract the virus before they are born.

It is not at all unusual for victims to grow up with sexual problems. Some can't touch or be touched. Others become wildly promiscuous. Or act out in other sexual ways. That was the case with my friend Nina, who told me that she had been her "father's mistress."

Nina then went on to defend her father. "I hate it," she said, "when people say, 'Any man who'd do that is sick.' He wasn't sick. Except for the incest my dad was totally reliable and helpful and loving. He was the only loving parent I had. He was my role model when I was growing up. He taught me about morals and gave me all the important lessons of my life. If I have to give up my love for my father, what will I have left? I hate what he did, but I love him."

In what she now understands was an unconscious need to reenact in adulthood her secret, duplicitous life with her father, Nina became a bigamist. She married two men, maintained two households, and simultaneously raised three children—two of them in one house and a stepchild in the other.

Some victims become prostitutes. Others

believe that incest forced them into lifelong sexual behaviors that they would not have chosen for themselves, including homosexuality. Victims experience not only guilt, shame, fear, and a broad range of psychosocial disorders. They are unable to trust. They have severe problems maintaining intimate relationships, including those with their children.

Journalist Betsy Peterson, in *Dancing with Daddy: A Childhood Lost and a Life Regained,* describes how incest with her father affected her relationship with her sons. "To know how much I love them is to know what I didn't give them, what they missed and what I missed," she writes. "I use my hands to stuff the sobs back in, to eat the terrible grief . . . because I spent their childhood as I spent my own, trying to protect myself."

Michigan therapist Kathy Evert, author of the autobiographical *When You're Ready: A Woman Healing from Childhood Physical and Sexual Abuse by Her Mother,* recently completed a study of 93 women and 9 men abused by their mothers. She found that almost a fourth of the men and more than 60 percent of the women had eating disorders. "I can't tell you the number of women I've seen who weigh over five hundred pounds," Evert says. One woman told her she ate to get bigger and more powerful than her mother. Another woman in the group weighed more than 600 pounds. "Food was my weapon against her," she said of her mother.

More than 80 percent of the women and all the men in Evert's study had sexual problems as adults that they attributed to the abuse by their mothers. And almost two thirds of the women said they rarely or never went to the doctor or dentist because to be examined was too terrifying for them. Thus they are unable to avail themselves of the diagnostic benefits of modern medicine, such as pelvic exams, PAP smears, breast examinations, and mammography.

Some victims are unable to feel physical pain. Some self-mutilate—they burn or cut themselves. Mariann told me that the impulse to cut herself is almost constant and almost uncontrollable. "You get to feeling like your body is full of something rotten," she says. "If you can make an opening, somehow the pressure will be relieved and everything will come out."

Dr. Roland Summit says that a victim of incest "will tend to blame his or her own body for causing the abuse." Some victims may go so far as to seek repeated cosmetic surgeries in an attempt to repair physically the damage that was done to them psychologically, according to a 1990 paper written

2. VICTIMOLOGY

by Elizabeth Morgan, M.D., a plastic surgeon, and Mary L. Froning, who holds a doctorate in psychology. (Dr. Morgan herself had made headlines in the late '80s, when she sent her daughter into hiding to keep her away from the father that Dr. Morgan alleged had sexually abused the child.) Perpetual plastic surgery, in fact, was to become one of the consequences of incest for Cynthia, who was raped by her father and her brother Eugene but had blocked all memory of the assaults.

Even when her brother sexually abused Cynthia's daughter Kit, Cynthia failed to recall her own assaults. Kit was three and a half when Eugene came to visit and, one afternoon, took her upstairs to the bathroom. When Cynthia discovered them, both were naked. Kit was sitting on the sink and Eugene, standing between her legs, was slowly rocking back and forth. Cynthia threw her brother out of the house. Then she said to the confused child, "This never happened. Understand? Forget it ever happened." By the time Kit was 20, she had only vague memories of childhood trips to the doctor for pelvic examinations and ointments.

Cynthia spent years in psychoanalysis, which didn't seem to help her severe depressions—nor restore her memory of having been sexually assaulted as a child. She kept telling Kit—who didn't understand why she was being told—that incest is so rare that it almost never happens. Kit was in her 30s when she remembered that afternoon in the bathroom with her uncle, and she understood then that he had probably given her a sexually transmitted disease.

Cynthia began to have plastic surgery in her middle 40s. She approached each operation as if it were The Solution, and she was briefly delighted with the results. Within months of each lift, tuck, or suction, however, she began to prepare for the next one. Cynthia didn't remember her own abuse until she was in her late 60s and a grandmother. Now in her middle 70s, she is planning on having a breast reduction as soon as she can find the right surgeon.

Also prevalent among incest victims is post-traumatic stress disorder (PTSD), which I discussed at length with Mary W. Armsworth, Ed.D., the author of dozens of articles on incest and its aftermath, as well as a professor of educational psychology at the University of Houston who teaches one of the few courses in this country on trauma. In the early '80s, Armsworth noticed that incest patients, who "live in a bath of anxiety," had the same PTSD symptoms demonstrated by some Vietnam War veterans and most victims of torture. These symptoms include but are not limited to amnesia, nightmares, and flashbacks. People who have PTSD may "leave their bodies" during the abuse, and they may continue to dissociate for decades after the abuse ends.

(In 1990, *The New York Times* reported that Dennis Charney, M.D., a Yale psychiatrist and director of clinical neuroscience at the National Center for Post-Traumatic Stress Disorder, had found that even one experience of overwhelming terror permanently alters the chemistry of the brain. The longer the duration and the more severe the trauma, the more likely it is that a victim will develop PTSD.)

Most of the dreams told to me by victims of incest involve being chased and stabbed, suffocated, made immobile and voiceless. I myself have a recurring dream of a man who gouges out my eyes and of a woman who rips out my tongue. One woman who has been in long-term therapy owing to years of abuse by her aunt, uncle, and mother told me she dreamed she was at a beautiful, crowded picnic in the woods when she vomited feces. The dream so revolted and shamed her that she had never before told it to anyone, not even her therapist.

Children forced to perform fellatio may grow up to be adults with flashbacks triggered by the smell of Clorox, the feel of melted butter, the sight of toothpaste in their mouth. It is difficult for people who don't have flashbacks to know what one is like. Flashbacks are not memories—memories have distance, are muted and selective. A flashback is a memory without distance. It can bring all the terror of an original event, triggered by something utterly innocuous.

A few months ago I was daydreaming in a friend's kitchen. Her husband, on his way to get the mail, came up quietly behind me, speaking softly to himself. The sensation of being approached (sneaked up on) from the rear by a much larger person who was muttering triggered a flashback—terror so acute that I had to get him away from me with the same urgency I would feel if my shirt were on fire.

Flashbacks can be almost continuous and overwhelming. People who experience them without knowing what causes them can feel crazy. An incest survivor's friend, seeing her run to hide for no apparent reason, might agree that she is. When flashbacks come less frequently, they can be handled almost as fast as they happen. The man who accidentally terrified me never knew it, and I was able to check back in with where I really was and what had really happened almost as quickly as I had checked out.

At the extreme edge of post-traumatic stress disorder lies multiple personality disorder (MPD). It was once thought to be rare and is still disbelieved entirely by some (one of the more noted skeptics is Paul McHugh, M.D., head of psychiatry at Johns Hopkins in Baltimore). But while MPD has been called the UFO of psychiatric disorders, a growing number of cases are being treated.

Researchers believe that children develop multiple personalities as a way of coping with abuse so violent and sadistic that the mind fractures. Each assault is then handled by one or more personalities—"selves," or "alters." Some personalities hold pain, others grief, others rage. Even happiness may be segregated into a discrete "self." The personalities often have no knowledge of one another, so a person with MPD "loses time" when one personality gives way to another, and can "come to" hours or years later without any way of knowing what had happened in the interim.

Brad, a victim of incest who suffers MPD, has learned to recognize a particular feeling that warns him he is about to switch into one of his alters. It happens under stress, he says. "My eyes all of a sudden blur and everything goes to gauze."

I met another sufferer of multiple personalities—a young woman—the day after she fled a cult. My husband and I were guests of the people she ran to, and I sat up with her until early morning because she was afraid to be alone. She had been sexually tortured by her father, brothers, and other cult members for all of her 28 years. As we talked, she switched personalities.

One of her alters was suicidal. Another wanted to call her family and tell them where she was. One was very young, five or six. One knew the dates of satanic holidays and the rituals she had performed on them. At one point during the night she closed her eyes, then opened them again and looked at me with such an evil stare that the hair on my neck stood up. Later, she asked me to put my arms around her and hold her, and I did.

"I was my mother's gift to my father," says Sylvia, yet another woman who suffers multiple personalities. "My dad's a pedophile. He had sex with me until I was seven. My mom's a sociopath. She tried to suffocate me many, many times. She slept with my brother until he was fourteen. She made him her husband, even though my father lived with us. The last time I saw her was twenty years ago. I came by the house where she was living with my brother. He opened the door with a gun in his hand. She had told him to shoot me."

Sylvia and her family lived in a cult that practiced blood sacrifices. When she was three, she was ritualistically raped and sodomized by the cult leaders. Her life was so torturous that she split into alternate selves who carried on when she couldn't.

"The one thing a child learns from sexual abuse," Dr. Summit told me, "is how to be abused." Sexually abused children teach themselves to endure assault. Instead of learning to protect themselves, they learn that they *can't* protect themselves. As adults they can be blind to dangers others would find obvious. They may freeze or go limp when threatened. Someone who has never been abused can say no, can walk or run away, can scream and fight. The incest victim often doesn't know what to do except to wait for the danger to be over.

Child incest victims often become adult rape victims. Almost one quarter of the incest victims Mary W. Armsworth studied went on to be sexually abused by their therapists. Many incest victims as adults choose abusive partners.

Judy, who was abused from infancy by her grandmother, grew up with what she describes as free-floating feelings of shame. "I always felt there was something wrong about me," she says, "something loathsome."

She married a violent man. She believed that when he beat her it was her fault and what she deserved. She believed the beatings were a sign of his love. She stayed with him for more than a decade, leaving him only when she became afraid that her suicidal feelings would overwhelm her and that she would die, leaving her child alone and in danger from his father.

Only later did Judy remember the abuse at the hands of her grandmother. "Every night, I lay awake listening for the sound of her feet on the hall carpet," she now recalls. "I taught myself to leave my body when she came into the room, and to forget. I forgot so well that whole years vanished from my life."

When victims do finally remember their abuse, they are often hushed by friends and told to "put it in the past," to "forgive and forget." But that is precisely what they unwittingly had done so very long ago. In *Incest and Sexuality: A Guide to Understanding*

and Healing, psychotherapists Wendy Maltz and Beverly Holman point out that "many women (estimates run as high as 50 percent) do not remember their incestuous experiences until something triggers the memory in adulthood."

"Sometimes my body remembered," says therapist Roz Dutton of Philadelphia, "and sometimes my mind remembered." Roz was an infant when her father began coming into her room at night. He placed one hand on her back and inserted a finger in her anus. He continued doing this until she was two and her baby sister was born. As a teenager and young woman Roz had no conscious memory of these events, though her life had been punctuated with "nudging feelings and disturbing thoughts."

Roz became a therapist with a thriving practice. In working with her clients, she noticed that she had "triggers"—things she heard or saw that sent her into a dissociative state. These things tended to have to do with certain settings but included once the unexpected sight at a professional meeting of a man's hairy hands. Though she questioned herself for years in therapy and in clinical supervision, it wasn't until she was in her early 40s that a chance remark to a colleague about brainwashing—and the colleague's reply that maybe Roz was afraid of brainwashing herself—evoked memories of her father.

Says Roz: "As I talked about myself and my symptoms—eating disorders, depression, inability to protect myself from emotional danger, dissociating emotionally—I began to make clear connections between myself and other abuse victims." Roz's memories were of early infancy. She remembered feelings of dread and terror associated with her father coming into her room. Images came to her of his hands reaching over the slats of her crib, and she experienced body memories from infancy of being held facedown and penetrated.

Just how reliable are memories? Can they be manufactured? How reliable, especially, is the memory of a child? Do leading questions by parents, therapists, or investigators—or the use of anatomically detailed dolls in the questioning of children who may have been abused—create false accusations that lead to false convictions? These were the sort of questions addressed by Gail S. Goodman, a psychologist at the State University of New York, Buffalo, and her colleagues in studies designed to test not only the accuracy of children's recall under stress and over time but also how children respond to leading or strongly suggestive questions devised to bring

about false accusations. "If children are indeed as suggestible as some have claimed, then we should be able in our studies to create false reports of abuse," Goodman writes in the chronicle of her studies, published in 1990. Child-abuse charges, after all, have often been dismissed by judges on this ground.

The scenes acted out in one of Goodman's studies were based on actual child-abuse cases. Pairs of four- and seven-year-olds were taken into a dilapidated trailer where they encountered a man who talked to them while using hand puppets. Then he put on a mask. While one of the children observed, he played a game of Simon Says with the other child, during which he and the child touched knees. He photographed the children and played a game where one child tickled him while the other child watched. All of this was videotaped through a one-way mirror so that researchers could have a precise record.

Ten to 12 days later the children were asked the kinds of questions that might lead to a charge of sexual abuse: "He took your clothes off, right?" The seven-year-olds remembered more than the four-year-olds, but whatever both groups remembered they remembered accurately and could not be led into sexualized answers. They became embarrassed by the leading questions, looked surprised, covered their eyes, or—according to Goodman—"asked in disbelief if we would repeat the question."

Goodman and her colleagues used anatomically detailed dolls when questioning the children to see if the dolls would encourage false reports. The study's conclusion on this point: "Whether or not the children were interviewed with anatomically detailed dolls, regular dolls, dolls in view, or no dolls did not influence their responses to the specific or misleading abuse questions."

Because some people believe that a child under stress can't remember accurately and may escalate what really happened in order to match the stress felt, Goodman also studied children who had to go for shots at a medical clinic. "We know of no other scientific studies in which the stress levels were as high as they were for our most stressed children," she writes. The children had to sit in the clinic waiting room and listen to other children scream as they got a needle, knowing they would get one, too.

"These children's reports were completely accurate," Goodman writes. "Not a single error in- free recall was made." The most stressed children remembered best and in the greatest detail. One year later Goodman and her colleagues reinterviewed as many participants as they could find. Even after the children had listened repeatedly to leading questions, most persisted in reporting the incident exactly as it had taken place. "Child abuse involves actions directed against a child's body," Goodman writes. "The violation of trivial expectations would probably not be very memorable. The violation of one's body is."

The Offenders

Jerry "Bingo" Stevens was born in 1910 in New Orleans. He was the third of five children and the first and only boy, hence his nickname. Bingo's father, Joe, was tall, handsome, redheaded, and smart. A supremely successful real estate developer, Joe believed that men should be strong and that women should smell good, keep the house clean, and serve dinner on time. He smoked a cigar and drank quietly and steadily from the moment he came home from the office until he went to bed.

Bingo's mother, Trudy, sometimes took the boy to bed with her to relieve her loneliness. She snuggled him in the dark, trying to block the sounds Joe made on his way into the girls' rooms, and any sounds that came later.

Joe died of cirrhosis of the liver when Bingo was 13. "You're the man of the house now," his mother told him.

By the time Bingo was 30, he had molested not only his sisters but most of their children. Trained from infancy to keep sexual abuse a secret, they never talked about it, even among themselves.

Bingo fell in love and married. The marriage was, apparently, a happy one. He had three daughters of his own, a son, and, eventually, an infant granddaughter. When his wife died he mourned. Then, after an interval, he married again and had a happy second marriage. He owned and operated a successful real estate business. In addition, he was a champion polo player and a member of the Explorers Club.

Bingo died of a heart attack in 1988 while sailing on Lake Pontchartrain with the nine-year-old daughter of his best friend.

He was, as anyone who knew Bingo was quick to say, brilliant, funny, charming, gifted, and successful with women. There was nothing about him that would have identified him as an incestuous father, brother, uncle, cousin, and grandfather. I am one of the children he abused.

After Bingo's death I visited his psychiatrist. "Bingo was one of my favorite patients ever," he told me.

"He molested me," I said.

"He molested everyone," his psychiatrist said. "Why not you?"

Everyone reading this article probably knows—whether aware of it or not—more than one incestuous man or woman. "Offenders don't have horns and a tail," says incest survivor Kim Shaffir. "They look like nice guys. They are not strangers. Everyone tells you to say no to strangers. No one tells you to say no to your family."

In *Broken Boys, Mending Men: Recovery from Childhood Sexual Abuse,* incest survivor Stephen D. Grubman-Black points out that "perpetrators who commit sex crimes are rarely the wild-eyed deviants who stalk little boys. They are as familiar and close by as the same room in your home, or next door, or at a family gathering."

Offenders come from the ranks of doctors, construction workers, hairdressers, building contractors, teachers, landscapers, philosophers, nuclear physicists, and women and men in the armed forces. David Finkelhor, Ph.D., director of the Family Research Laboratory at the University of New Hampshire, and his associate, Linda Meyer Williams, Ph.D., had just concluded *Characteristics of Incest Offenders,* their landmark study of incestuous fathers, when they saw nearly half of their subjects sail off to the Persian Gulf to serve their country.

Some offenders prefer girls, others boys. Some abuse both. Some are interested only in adolescents, or preteens, or toddlers, or newborns. Some, though not most, molest only when they are drinking or depressed or sexually deprived. Some don't abuse until they are adults, but more than half start during their teens.

Like Bingo, some victims go on to become abusers. Seventy percent of the incestuous fathers in the Finkelhor study admitted that they were abused during their own childhood. Judith V. Becker, Ph.D., a professor of psychiatry and psychology at the University of Arizona College of Medicine who has supervised or been involved in the assessment and/or treatment of more than 1,000 abusers, reports that some 40 percent said they had been sexually abused as children. Ruth Mathews, a psychologist who practices with Midway Family Services—a branch of Family Services of Greater St. Paul—has seen a similar number of adolescent offenders, male and female, and has arrived at a similar conclusion.

Mathews went on to tell me about a girl whose father abused her with vibrators after her mother's death. He also brought in other men to abuse her and, with his new wife, had sex in front of her. When she was 12, a city agency, acting on a neighbor's complaint, removed her from her father's house and placed her in a foster home. There she inserted knitting needles into her foster sister's vagina. Asked why, she replied, "For fun." In therapy, asked to draw a picture of herself, she chose a black magic marker and wrote, over and over again, the words *hate, disgust,* and *hell.*

In another instance of children acting out their own abuse on other children (animals are also frequent targets), one little boy was referred for therapy because he tried to mount most of the children in his kindergarten. His parents told the therapist that they made him ride on his father's back while they had intercourse. They said that this excited them.

Although we want to believe that we can spot evil when we confront it, the truth is that nothing about a perpetrator would alert us. Offenders are good at hiding what they do. They are master manipulators, accomplished liars. Those few who aren't get caught; the others molest dozens or even hundreds of children over many decades.

On January 15, 1991, 67-year-old Raymond Lewis, Jr., a retired aerospace designer, son of the founder of the Lewis Pharmacies in Los Angeles, wrote to his middle-aged daughter Donna that he "was the father who begat you; the knight on a white horse who protected you. The guy who had no lover other than your mom till well past his teens. A no smoking, no drinking, no drugs man of restraint."

This man of restraint had raped his five daughters (Donna's first memory of abuse is of her father molesting her while he was taking her to her first day of school in the first grade) and each of the female granddaughters he had access to—five out of seven. In the letter, Lewis wrote: "What is going on in Marlon's twisted mind when he tells of me, deathly ill and post-operative from my prostectomy, licking Nicole's vagina making slurping noises? . . . Why would I *lick* a female? Wrong modus operandi. Wrong age. And a relative! A grandchild! Totally insane! Granddaughters have fathers and no father would permit such a thing to happen. Nor would any mother. Had it happened, hell would have been raised."

But for more than 40 years, hell had not been raised. When Lewis's daughters tried to avoid him, when they cried and told him it hurt, when they threatened to tell on him, he showed them photographs of decapitated murder victims. They endured his rapes in silence, convinced from earliest childhood that they were protecting one another and themselves.

Says DeeDee, now 38: "My father said, 'People who betray their father are like people who betray their country. They should be executed.' He carried a gun in his car, in some black socks. He also kept a gun between the mattress and box spring.

"At first he'd molest me in the bathtub. He'd say, 'I'm the baby. Clean me up. Here's the soap.' Every time before he molested me and my sisters, he'd put his foot on the bed and beat on his chest like King Kong. He penetrated me when I was eight. When I was thirteen he bought me a ring. He told me we could cross out of California and get married, because I was illegitimate. He said exactly the same thing to my daughter when *she* was thirteen. I fooled around with the first boy I could. I got pregnant. I thought, Thank goodness, Dad won't touch me now. For a while, he didn't.

"When my little sister was fifteen she was living alone with Dad. I waited one day until he'd gone out, and went in the house. I found her in a corner, naked, crying. She said, 'I'll be okay. Don't tell. Don't tell.' I thought that if I told, Dad would find out and kill me."

One daughter broke away from Lewis when she was in her 30s and went into therapy. Then, recognizing signs of sexual abuse in her five-year-old niece, Nicole, DeeDee's youngest child, she reported her father to the authorities. In his letter to Donna, Lewis wrote about Nicole: "I fooled with the petite perjurer's pudendum! She said it! Crazy story! Totally insane!" He denied that he had done anything. At first his other daughters defended him. Then they began to talk—16 relatives, including his daughters, told the same story.

Most of his crimes were wiped out by the statute of limitations. He was charged with only four counts of child sexual abuse against his five-year-old granddaughter, and one count of incest—a lesser charge in California, as in most states—against her mother, DeeDee, whom he had coerced into sex when she was a grown woman by promising to leave her daughter alone.

During the trial Lewis's daughters—all professional women, one a college professor—were unable to meet his gaze in the courtroom. It fell to his five-year-old granddaughter

to face him. Although Lewis had threatened that he would kill her if she ever talked about what he had done, the judge ordered her to tell the truth. Seated on the witness stand, shaking and crying, she testified for two days. Lewis denied everything.

Three times the judge asked him if there wasn't anything he was sorry for. "How could they say such terrible things about me?" Lewis asked by way of an answer. "I drove a rusted wreck of a car so that I could give them good cars."

"Isn't there something you think you did to make your family say these things about you?" the judge asked.

"Well, maybe," Lewis replied. "A long time ago."

The five-year-old handed the judge a note she had written. "My granddaddy is a bad man," it read. "I want him to go to jail for two hundred years."

Lewis was convicted of one count of incest against his daughter and three counts of lewd acts, including oral copulation, involving his granddaughter. Expressing the opinion that Raymond Lewis, Jr., represented a threat to all females and that the only place where he would have no access to them was in prison, Superior Court Judge Leslie W. Light sentenced him to the maximum: 12 years and 8 months. But with time off for good behavior, he will probably serve only half his sentence, which means that he will be released from Mule Creek Prison in 6 years.

Says DeeDee: "Until I was twenty-three, I thought I was retarded. He told me I was brain damaged. He told me I was neurotic, manic-depressive, a damaged genius. He thought he was a genius. He said we could have a child together and it would be a genius. Six months before going to jail, he offered me one hundred thousand dollars to bear his child.

"I always hoped he would love me. I just wanted to be his daughter. But now I have my own home, my own checking account. I give sit-down dinners. I feel special. I have knowledge. I am a great mom and I'll be a great grandmom. I love myself, finally. And now I can die without that secret."

Lewis never said he was sorry. In the letter to Donna—one of a stream that he continues to send to his daughters—he wrote: "Loneliness was the reason that I had enslaved myself in my youth to raise kids, and now in the illnesses of old age 14 of my loved ones had abruptly dumped me! *Licked!* How bizarre! A puzzle."

Lack of empathy for the victim is typical of offenders. Every therapist I spoke to commented on this characteristic. All said that for offenders to be rehabilitated they must take responsibility for what they did and develop empathy for their victims. With one possible exception, not one of the offenders I interviewed had done this.

I am talking to Joe. His daughter accused him of sexually abusing her. He pleaded nolo contendere. "But I didn't do it," he says. His sentence: four years probation, with therapy. He has been in treatment for two years. "When I first came to therapy," he says, "I had an attitude that I was being punished for what I didn't do. I had no rights, when you got right into it."

I ask how he feels about the therapy he is required to undergo now. "It's a little inconvenient," he says, "but it helps me in dealing with other people to understand them. I think it would be helpful if a lot of people could go through a program to give them understanding and another outlook, instead of being negative or feeling put down."

I ask him again about his daughter. "I never touched her," he says.

Later I talk with Joe's therapist. "Is he in denial?" I ask.

"Denial," the therapist replies, "is when someone says 'She asked for it' or 'She didn't say no.' Joe's not in denial. He's lying."

I am talking to Chris. His sentence: 8 to 23 months in jail plus 5 years probation, with therapy. He has served 8 months and has been in therapy for 2 years.

"My stepdaughter and I had an affair when she was thirteen," he says. "It lasted a year. I got sick and had to go on dialysis. My wife was working. My stepdaughter was taking care of me. She was like the wife. She never refused me or anything. I really believe she fell in love with me. More than like a father. She met a boy and fell in love. He was into selling cocaine. I didn't want him in the house. I slapped her. She ran to her grandmother and told. She didn't want to take it to court, didn't want me to go to jail. But her grandmother and Women Against Rape stepped in. The grandmother never did like me anyway. They blew it out of proportion and it got all stinky. I did what I could to keep it out of the paper. I could have beat it. I have to come here [to therapy] or I'd have to serve all my time. But if I didn't have to come, I wouldn't."

"Is there a message you would like me to pass on to the people who read this?" I ask him. "Can you tell me something that would help them?"

"Yes!" he replies. "I want you to tell them that if their child gets a boyfriend, don't stand in the way. Don't say no. If I hadn't said no to her, this would never have happened."

I am talking to Bob. He, too, is in court-ordered therapy. Two and a half years ago he was convicted of indecent assault on his girlfriend's 15-year-old daughter. "She was curious about drinking," he says. "Her mother and I decided we would all get together and drink. Better at home, you know?"

The first time, all three drank together. But later the drinking took place when Bob's girlfriend was away. "The first time it went okay," he says. "Then two weeks later, we did it again. I talked her into giving me a back rub. Then I gave her one. I felt her breasts. She didn't say no. I was very attracted. She got up and went upstairs. She got on the phone, but she didn't say 'Stop.' Then she pretended to fall asleep facedown. I fondled her buttocks, pulled her pants down, felt her vagina.

"She was crying. I started to get scared. For myself. I really got scared. I'm trying to figure out how to react. I ask her, 'You want me to leave?' She says to me, 'No. Mom loves you.' She went outside and didn't come back. She called her girlfriend whose mom works at the courthouse. The cops showed up. I was thinking, Oh shit, this is real."

Bob was given a two-year probation, with therapy. (The sentence was light because this was his first offense and the molestation hadn't progressed beyond fondling.) "She would have dropped it," Bob says, "but the courts already had it."

I ask Bob about his therapy. "I have a lot more knowledge now than I had," he replies—"about how many lives I can screw up. Every time she goes through something in the future I'm going to have to ask myself, 'Was I responsible for that?'"

Males who molest children have traditionally been lumped into two broad categories, violent and nonviolent. Included in the latter are offenders who are fixated and regressed. Psychologist A. Nicholas Groth, Ph.D., founder of the Sex Offender Program at the Connecticut Correctional Institution at Somers, describes fixated offenders as adult men who "continue to have an exclusive or nearly exclusive sexual attraction toward children." Regressed offenders are attracted to their peers, but under

A PIONEERING NEW

David Finkelhor, Ph.D., and Linda Meyer Williams, Ph.D., who are sociologists at the Family Research Laboratory of the University of New Hampshire, have recently completed the most thorough study to date of men who have sexually abused their daughters. The sample consisted of 118 incestuous fathers—55 men in the U.S. Navy and 63 civilians from treatment centers around the country—and a carefully matched control group of nonincestuous fathers.

In this landmark study on the characteristics of incest offenders, Finkelhor and Williams set out to determine whether men are socialized to see all intimacy and dominance as sexual, whether fathers separated from their daughter for long periods soon after birth are more likely to molest her than fathers who have not been absent, and whether incestuous men had themselves been abused as children more than had nonoffenders. The researchers also sought to learn each man's feelings about his daughter, his outlook on sex, and his attitudes toward incest.

Many theories have been posited about why fathers molest their daughters. Everything from alcoholism to a frigid wife has been blamed. With this study, Finkelhor and Williams have shed new light on the subject and produced much new insight. They have established, for example, that there are distinct differences in the onset of abuse: Daughters ranged in age from 4 weeks to 15 years old when the incest began. "Fathers were more likely to start abuse when their daughter was four to six years old or ten to twelve years old," the study reveals, "than to initiate abuse when she was seven, eight, or nine years old." Men reported various behaviors leading up to the abuse. Some of the fathers said they had masturbated while thinking of their daughter, had exposed themselves to her, or had made her touch their genitals before they began touching hers. A substantial percentage of the men—63 percent—had been sexually attracted to their daughter for a period of years before the abuse began. Most significantly, the findings reveal that there are many paths to incestuous behavior and that there is not just one type of man who commits such abuse.

Each man was interviewed for at least six hours and was asked hundreds of questions. The results—many presented here for the first time—dispel some common myths and prompt the following typology.

Type 1.

SEXUALLY PREOCCUPIED

Twenty-six percent of the fathers studied fell into this category. These men had "a clear and conscious (often obsessive) sexual interest in their daughters." When they told what attracted them to their daughter, they talked in detail about her physical qualities—the feel of her skin, for example, or the smell of her body.

Type 1 subcategory: *Early sexualizers*

Among the sexually preoccupied fathers, many regarded their daughter as a sex object almost from birth. "One father reported that he had been stimulated by the sight of his daughter nursing and that he could never remember a time when he did not have sexual feelings for her. . . . He began sexually abusing her when she was four weeks old."

Many of the offenders were themselves sexually abused as children.

STUDY OF INCESTUOUS FATHERS

"These men are so sexualized that they may simply project their sexual needs onto everybody and everything. . . . The children may be those who are most easily manipulated to satisfy the preoccupations."

Type 2.
ADOLESCENT REGRESSIVES

About a third of the fathers—33 percent— became sexually interested in their daughter when she entered puberty. They said they were "transfixed" by her body's changes.

For some the attraction began when the daughter started to act more grown up, before her body changed. Some of the fathers in this group became aroused by a daughter after having been away from her for a long time. Her new maturity and developing body caught them by surprise. Sometimes the fathers let the attraction build for years, masturbating to fantasies of the daughter, before they acted.

These men acted and sounded like young adolescents themselves when they talked about their daughter. One said, "I started to wonder what it would be like to touch her breasts and touch between her legs and wondered how she would react if I did."

"The father-adult in me shut down," said another offender, "and I was like a kid again."

Type 3.
INSTRUMENTAL SELF-GRATIFIERS

These fathers accounted for 20 percent of the sample. They described their daughter in terms that were nonerotic. When they abused her, they thought about someone else—their wife, even their daughter as an adult.

In contrast to the sexually preoccupied and adolescent-regressive fathers who focused on their daughter, the instrumental self-gratifiers blocked what they were doing from their mind: "They used their daughter's body as a receptacle." The fact that they were abusing a daughter or that a daughter was so young was actually "a distracting element" that these fathers had to work to ignore. While one man was giving his seven-year-old a bath, she rubbed against his penis. "I realized that I could take advantage of the situation," he said. "She wasn't a person to me." Another man said, "I abused her from behind so I wouldn't see her face."

Instrumental self-gratifiers abused sporadically, worried about the harm they were causing, and felt great guilt. To alleviate the guilt, some convinced themselves that their daughter was aroused.

Type 4.
EMOTIONALLY DEPENDENT

Just over 10 percent of the sample fit this category. These fathers were emotionally needy, lonely, depressed. They thought of themselves as failures and looked to their daughter for "close, exclusive, emotionally dependent relationships," including sexual gratification, which they linked to intimacy and not to their daughter's real or imagined sexual qualities.

One man, separated from his wife, saw his five-year-old daughter only on weekends. "It was companionship," he said. "I had been alone for six months. We slept together and would fondle each other. The closeness was very good and loving. Then oral sex began."

The average age of the daughter when the incest began was six to seven years. But it happened with older daughters as well. The fathers of older daughters described the girls as their "best friends," and the relationships had a more romantic quality: The men described their daughter as they might have described an adult lover.

Type 5.
ANGRY RETALIATORS

About 10 percent of the men were in this category. These fathers were the most likely to have criminal histories of assault and rape. They abused a daughter out of anger at her or, more often, at her mother for neglecting or deserting them. Some denied any sexual feelings for the daughter. One father of a three-year-old said, "My daughter has no sex appeal for me at all. What I did was just an opportunity to get back at my daughter for being the center of my wife's life. There was no room for me."

Sometimes the daughter was abused because she resembled her mother, sometimes because of the father's desire to desecrate her or to possess her out of an angry sense of entitlement. Some angry retaliators tied up, gagged, beat, and raped their daughter and were aroused by the violence.

OTHER FINDINGS Alcohol and drugs: While 33 percent of the men reported being under the influence of alcohol when the abuse occurred, and 10 percent reported that they were using drugs, only 9 percent held alcohol or drugs responsible. "Preliminary analysis indicates that the incestuous fathers are not more likely than the comparison fathers to have drug or alcohol abuse problems, although they may use alcohol or drugs to lower their inhibitions to abuse."

Marital discord: Forty-three percent of the men felt that their relationship with their wife was part of the reason for the incest. "However, the wife was rarely the only factor mentioned. . . . Different men probably come to incestuous acts as a result of different needs, motives, and impairments."

Sexual abuse of the offender as a child: Significantly, 70 percent of the men said they themselves had been sexually abused in childhood. Half were physically abused by their father and almost half—44 percent—had been physically abused by their mother. "Although not all who are abused go on to become perpetrators, it is critical that we learn more about how child sexual victimization affects male sexual development and male sexual socialization."

RECOMMENDATIONS Finkelhor and Williams suggest, considering the "intergenerational transmission of sexual abuse," men be given improved opportunities for positive fathering—including paternity leave and more liberal visitations in cases of divorce or separation. Also that they be encouraged to be intimate in nonsexual ways, beginning in boyhood. The study argues that, based on the evidence, it's very likely that people can become more aware of the precursory signs of incest. "It is conceivable," Finkelhor and Williams conclude, "that the sequence of events that leads to abuse can be interrupted."

stress—illness, loss of job or spouse—turn to children as substitutes.

To refine these categories, Robert A. Nass, Ph.D., a Pennsylvania therapist who treats sex offenders, suggests a third group: quasi-adult sex offenders—men who yearn for a loving relationship with another adult but, because of their own immaturity, are unable to have one and turn to children instead.

In researching *Characteristics of Incest Offenders*, the most detailed study of male perpetrators to date, David Finkelhor and Linda Meyer Williams of the University of New Hampshire questioned 118 incestuous fathers in exacting detail. Based on the men's explanations about why and how the incest started and how the men felt about what they had done, the researchers identified five distinct types of incestuous father: the sexually preoccupied—men who are obsessed about sex and tend to sexualize almost every relationship; adolescent regressives—men who have adolescentlike yearnings for young girls generally and direct them toward their daughter; instrumental self-gratifiers—men who molest their daughter while fantasizing about someone else; the emotionally dependent—men who turn to their daughter for emotional support they feel deprived of from others; and angry retaliators—men who assault their daughter out of rage at her or someone else.

And what of the women who sexually abuse children in their care? What patterns, if any, are they cut from? Psychologist Ruth Mathews of St. Paul, in a study of more than 100 female sex offenders—65 adult women and 40 adolescent girls—found that they fall into four major categories.

The first is teacher-lover—usually made up of older women who have sex with a young adolescent. This category often goes unnoticed by society as well as by the offender because the behavior is socially sanctioned. For confirmation, one has only to look to films such as *The Last Picture Show, Summer of '42,* and *Le Souffle au Coeur.*

The second category is experimenter-exploiter, which encompasses girls from rigid families where sex education is proscribed. They take baby-sitting as an opportunity to explore small children. Many of these girls don't even know what they are doing, have never heard of or experienced masturbation, and are terrified of sex. One girl who had seen a movie with an orgasm scene said, "I wondered if *I* could get that 'ah' feeling. I was waiting for the 'ah' to happen, then I got into all this trouble."

The third category is the predisposed,

meaning women who are predisposed to offend by their own history of severe physical and/or sexual abuse. The victims are often their own children or siblings. As one woman in this category said, "I was always treated as an animal when I was growing up. I didn't realize my kids were human beings."

Mathews's final category is male-coerced women—women who abuse children because men force them to. These women were themselves abused as children, though less severely than the predisposed. As teens they were isolated loners but anxious to belong. Many are married to sex offenders who may abuse the kids for a long time without the wife's knowledge. Ultimately, she is brought into it. Witness a typical scenario.

He: "Let's play a game with the kids."
She (*surprised and delighted*): "Great!"
He: "Let's play spin the bottle."
She: "No!"
(*He slaps her face, then beats her head on the floor. The child tries to stop him.*)
Kid (*yelling*): "Mom, do it. *He's* been doing it for years."

Deeply dependent and vulnerable to threats, these women are easily manipulated. As one of them said, "If he would leave me, I would be a nobody." Once such a woman molests a child, however, she may go on to offend on her own. As the mother of a five-year-old put it, "Having sex with my son was more enjoyable than with my husband."

While more than a third of the survivors I interviewed told me that they had been molested by women, true female pedophiles, Mathews says, are relatively rare—about 5 percent of her sample. Those she interviewed had themselves been abused from approximately the age of two onward by many family members. They received virtually no other nurturing—most of the nurturing they received was from the offender—and came to link abuse with caring.

Like male offenders, some females molest many, many children, their own and those in their care. But Mathews feels that women may take more responsibility for their acts than men do. Only one girl she worked with blamed her victim. Seventy percent of the females took all the blame if they acted alone. One half took 100 percent of the responsibility if they molested with a man. Where the men minimized what had happened—"We were only horsing around"—the women were "stuck in shame."

In Atlanta at a poetry reading, the woman sitting next to me asks what I write about. When I tell her, she leans close. "I molested my son," she whispers. I ask if she wants to

talk about it. "No," she says. "But I will say that it will take me the rest of my life to even begin to deal with it."

Therapist Kathy Evert of Michigan, extrapolating from her 450-question survey of 93 women and 9 men who were abused by their mothers, sees a more general problem. "I believe that no one, including me," she says, "knows the extent of sexual abuse by females, especially mothers. About eighty percent of the women and men reported that the abuse by their mothers was the most hidden aspect of their lives. Only three percent of the women and none of the men told anyone about the abuse during their childhood." Instead they endured their own suicidal and homicidal feelings.

A. Nicholas Groth, the Connecticut psychologist, suggests "the incidence of sexual offenses against children perpetrated by adult women is much greater than would be suspected from the rare instances reported in crime statistics." He further suggests that women offenders may not be recognized as such because it is relatively easy to get away with abusive behavior under the guise of child care.

Female offenders wash, fondle, lick, and kiss the child's breasts and genitals, penetrate vagina and anus with tongue, fingers, and other objects: dildos, buttonhooks, screwdrivers—one even forced goldfish into her daughter. As one survivor told me, "My mom would play with my breasts and my nipples and insert things into my vagina to see if I was normal. 'I'm your mother,' she'd say. 'I need to know you're growing properly.' She'd give me enemas and make me dance for her naked. It lasted until I was twenty. I know it's hard to believe, but it's true. I was petrified of her. Absolutely."

It has long been believed that any woman who sexually abuses a child is insane and sexually frustrated but that her abuse is less violent than a man's. None of this is true. Only a third of the women and men in Kathy Evert's study, for example, said they thought that their mother was mentally ill. (According to Ruth Mathews, a tiny percentage of abusing mothers are severely psychotic.) Not only were most of the mothers in the study sane, but almost all had an adult sexual partner living with them. Furthermore, the mothers in Evert's study abused their daughters violently, beat and terrorized them, and raped them with objects. But they treated their sons like substitute lovers. Evert postulates that the abusing mothers projected self-hate from their own history of sexual abuse onto their daugh-

---

CASE STUDIES

When Anne-Marie's 17-year-old daughter, Maureen, left home, she told an aunt that her father had molested her and her brothers and sisters. While the case was being investigated, Maureen's father killed her mother. Out on bail pending trial, he moved back in with his younger children. When a child-welfare worker came to question him, he said, "Get out of my face or I'll do to you what I did to my wife."

Jenny, who had been sexually abused as a child, refused to believe it when a neighbor filed a complaint charging that her ten-year-old had been molested by Jenny's husband, Norman. Then her own child, five-year-old Emma, told Jenny that her father had abused her and her baby brothers while Jenny was at work. Norman went to prison.

Jenny poured gasoline over herself and her children and struck a match. The mother and both sons were enveloped in flames, but Emma was able to escape. Jenny, two-year-old Adam, and three-year-old Gerry burned to death.

Alison was eight when she was raped by her stepfather, Buddy, a drug user. HIV positive, Buddy had infected his wife, who later gave birth to an HIV-positive son and, the following year, a second daughter, who is HIV negative. In 1987, Alison's mother, who was carrying twins at the time, died of AIDS in her seventh month of pregnancy. Convicted of Alison's rape, Buddy is currently serving time. From prison he is seeking visitation rights to his son and daughter, who are now in foster care.

---

ters. "This causes rage and anger that don't go away," she says.

Not all incest is intergenerational, committed by adult against child. "There is more sibling incest than parent-child," David Finkelhor told me. And in *Sibling Abuse: Hidden Physical, Emotional, and Sexual Trauma,* Vernon R. Wiehe, Ph.D., professor of social work at the University of Kentucky, writes: "There is evidence . . . that brother-sister sexual relationships may be five times as common as father-daughter incest."

There are problems with numbers and definitions in this area, as in others. How, for example, does one define consensual versus forced sexual contact between siblings? Finkelhor says that an age gap of five years implies coercion. Others feel that a five-year gap is too wide. What about children who are close in age but different in size? What about children who have much more or much less power in the family? What about children who are more gifted or less gifted physically or intellectually?

Coercion aside, "sibling abuse has been ignored in part," writes Vernon Wiehe, "because the abusive behavior of one sibling toward another is often excused as normal behavior. Sibling rivalry must be distinguished from sibling abuse."

Certainly, sibling sexual abuse is no different from other sexual abuse in that it is self-perpetuating. According to the Fin-

kelhor study: "The role of physical and emotional abuse in childhood should not be overlooked. . . . Arousal to very young children may be the result of early sexual victimization."

The Finkelhor study has profound implications for the possible prevention of father-daughter incest. Over 50 percent of the men in the study reported that their sexual interest in the daughter developed slowly. Is it possible that prevention programs could have helped them clarify and deal with their feelings about her before sexual contact occurred? According to the researchers, "It is conceivable that men can interrupt the sequence of events which led to the abuse."

Currently, the statistics on recidivism are predictably dismal. The rehabilitation of offenders has always been approached as a matter of jail, probation, or court-ordered therapy. Only some few medical institutions in the country—notable among them, Baltimore's Johns Hopkins—offer impressive inpatient treatment involving drugs and therapy, but treatment is expensive, and not all medical-insurance plans will cover it.

While some nonmedical rehab programs claim up to a 95 percent "cure" rate, they are misleading in their optimism. Jim Breiling of the National Institutes of Mental Health says

that the results of many studies are suspect owing to the unreliability of statements by offenders, many of whom lie. According to one study, a 38 percent dropout of participants can be anticipated in any program. Of those who receive the full course of treatment, 13 percent reoffend during the first year. After that, who knows?

The rare offender who voluntarily seeks help can get trapped in a bind. Therapists are legally required to inform the local police if they hear about a specific child-abuse crime. Massachusetts therapist Mike Lew cautions his clients at the outset that if they tell him they have offended, he must report them. Even so, the authorities tend to look more favorably on those who turn themselves in than on those who get caught or accused.

Ruth Mathews believes that women may be easier to rehabilitate than men because, as noted, they may feel more empathy for their victims than male offenders do. But she points out that her opinion is based on the women she sees, who have come voluntarily for treatment. A sample of women in prison for sex crimes would probably yield very different results. Child offenders who receive treatment, on the other hand, do much better than adults. They need less long-term help and are less likely to reoffend.

Mental-health providers are key to spotting and treating offenders and their victims. But, says psychologist Mary W. Armsworth, the Houston trauma specialist, "we don't train mental-health providers properly." Incest victims who need psychiatric care are often misdiagnosed. Victims of child sexual abuse who suffer symptoms of post-traumatic stress disorder have been hospitalized for everything from manic depression to schizophrenia and have been subjected to shock treatments, insulin shock, and other inappropriate therapies.

Misdiagnosis occurs because the therapist, psychiatrist, or doctor doesn't know what to look for, doesn't consider childhood sexual abuse a possibility, or doesn't believe the patient's account of what has occurred. For almost a century, Freud and his followers have led us astray.

Vienna, Austria. April 21, 1896. Sigmund Freud stands before his colleagues at the Society for Psychiatry and Neurology, reading his paper "The Aetiology of Hysteria." He informs his listeners that mental illness is the result of childhood sexual abuse. The words he uses to describe the abuse are *rape, assault, trauma, attack.*

He has based his findings—which he has used to formulate what he terms the seduction theory—on the testimony of his patients. These are both women and men who have told him of their childhood abuse, often by their fathers. He has listened to them, understood them, and believed them. He has reason to. As he has written to his friend and colleague Wilhelm Fliess, "My own father was one of these perverts and is responsible for the hysteria of my brother . . . and those of several younger sisters."

But Freud is soon under attack by his colleagues, many of whom denounce his argument. He retracts the seduction theory. The accounts of incest, he now says, were fabricated by hysterical women who were not assaulted. Like Oedipus, he says, they yearned for intercourse with one parent and wanted to murder the other, and these yearnings produced such a profundity of guilt and conflict that they caused a lifetime of mental illness.

Unlike the seduction theory, for which Freud was ostracized, the Oedipal theory finds favor with the great majority of his colleagues. It becomes the cornerstone, the bible, of all psychoanalysis to come.

Jeffrey Moussaieff Masson, Ph.D., former project director of the Sigmund Freud Archives in Washington, D.C., and a self-described "former psychoanalyst," has written three books detailing first his affection for, then his disaffection from, Freud and his teachings. According to Masson, Freud's reversal of his position represented a monumental loss of moral courage that served to save his professional skin to the detriment of his patients.

In *Banished Knowledge: Facing Childhood Injuries*, Alice Miller, Ph.D., like Masson a former Freudian psychoanalyst, argues that Freud suppressed the truth to spare himself and his friends the personal consequences of self-examination. "Freud has firmly locked the doors to our awareness of child abuse and has hidden the keys so carefully that ensuing generations have been unable to find them."

Miller goes on to make a startling revelation about Freud's great friend Wilhelm Fliess. She writes that many decades after Freud suppressed his data, Wilhelm's son Robert found out that "at the age of two,

[Robert] had been sexually abused by his father and that this incident coincided with Freud's renunciation of the truth."

Some scholars have expressed the wish that the seduction theory and the Oedipal theory could work together. But they can't. The seduction theory states that child sexual abuse is the cause of most—or even all—mental illness. The Oedipal theory, on the other hand, states that child sexual abuse almost never happens, that a person's memories are false, and that mental illness and neuroses come from a child's conflicted desires for sex and murder.

Ever since Freud, the Oedipal theory has been used to refute claims of child sexual abuse. In *Healing the Incest Wound*, Dr. Christine Courtois, the Maryland psychotherapist, writes that "many survivors report that they were medically examined and treated for their various symptoms, but for the most part the symptoms were never attributed to abuse even when the evidence was obvious. Instead, symptoms were most frequently described as psychosomatic or without basis or another diagnosis was given." Some therapists still tell their patients that their memories—no matter how degrading, detailed, or sadistic—are really their wishes. Freud placed the responsibility for the deed and the memory not with the offending adult but with the child victim—and his adherents continue the sham. As Alice Miller writes: "I often hear it said that we owe the discovery of child abuse to psychoanalysis. . . . In fact it is precisely psychoanalysis that has held back and continues to hold back knowledge of child abuse. . . . Given our present knowledge of child abuse, the Freudian theories have become untenable."

But most people don't know this. To accept that Freud lied means that nearly a century of child rearing, analytic training, law enforcement, and judicial and medical attitudes must be reconsidered. As the matter rests now, the men and women who should be able to identify abuse and help prevent and punish it have never even learned the basics. Our doctors, analysts, and judges have been taught to mistake victim for offender. They allow offenders to remain untreated, free to infect the next generation.

Alice Miller writes that Freud "wrote volume after volume whose style was universally admired and whose contents led humanity into utter confusion." His legacy has been in part to blind us to the prevalence of incest, to make the offenders in our midst invisible.

At the Sexual Abuse Center of the Family Support Line in Delaware County, Pennsylvania, therapists who work with perpetrators and survivors showed me paintings done by children aged 7 to 12 who had participated in an incest survivors' support group.

Monica, 10, had drawn the outline of an adult, six feet tall, on butcher paper. With the help of her therapist she titled it *Diagram of a Perpetrator*. She drew in hair, a brain, eyes, ears, nose, mouth, shoulders, big hands, a heart, and a penis. Next to each feature, down each finger, and around the penis, she wrote the things her father had said to her:

TRUST ME.

I'LL PROTECT YOU.

I'M NOT GOING TO HURT YOU.

IT'LL FEEL GOOD.

DON'T FIGHT ME.

DON'T MOVE.

THEY'RE SOFT.

I THINK WITH MY PENIS.

I DON'T CARE WHAT YOU SAY.

I NEED SOME.

BETTER ME THAN SOMEONE ELSE.

IT'LL MAKE YOU A WOMAN.

I'M BIG.

Editor's note: This is a four-part report, of which two parts are included here. Parts two and three addressing the courts and recovery factors may be found in the February 1992 issue of *Lear's*.

MURDER NEXT DOOR

Complacent Canadians are shaken by a new kind of random violence

Rae Corelli

To the white middle class of Canada, indoctrinated by detective novels and TV cop shows to look for motive and opportunity, violent crime used to follow patterns. Bandits robbed banks because that's where the money was. Husbands and wives (seldom from the middle class) killed one another in drunken rages. Burglars broke into the homes of the wealthy because they contained valuable things to steal. If a citizen got mugged, many Canadians might well conclude that he had been in the wrong part of town and should have known better. For years, the middle class—shaken only rarely by murder in its midst—was a spectator, complacent within its anonymity to the ugliness of the times. Not any more. There is a new kind of crime evident across the land. Its motivation seems to be no more than violence itself. It is irrational. It is deadly. Its enemy often is anyone who gets in the way. Which is why middle-class people are no longer just spectators. They have become targets as well.

From the East Coast to the West, in cities large and small, hardly a week passes without newspaper or TV accounts of another drive-by shooting, home invasion or brutal smash-and-grab robbery of a charity bingo or fast-food restaurant—crimes virtually unknown just a few years ago. On March 27 in Ottawa, Nicholas Battersby, a 27-year-old British engineer, was killed as he walked along a street by a short fired from a passing Jeep. The grief and outrage touched off by Battersby's death had not subsided when, three days later in Hamilton, 25-year-old McMaster University student Joan Heimbecker was mortally wounded by a shotgun blast, allegedly fired by an ex-boyfriend.

But the senseless killing was not over. Last week in Toronto, three men invaded a popular midtown dessert parlor. The intruders demanded money and beat those who hesitated. Then, seemingly at random, one of them fatally wounded 23-year-old Georgina Leimonis with a shotgun blast before they fled. An angry police

Chief William McCormack warned of spreading urban terrorism, and Toronto City Councillor John Adams declared: "It's a loss of innocence for the whole community."

Behind the bleak warnings, heated emotion and strident demands for tough measures to protect ordinary people, there is some reassurance about the nature of Canadian society that may, given current passions, be overlooked. For example, the latest crime figures from Statistics Canada show that the annual national murder rate of two per 100,000 population hasn't changed since 1988, except for 1991 when it was three. And although the rate for all crimes of violence in 1992 was nearly 25 per cent higher than in 1988, Statistics Canada reported that part of the increase may be due to the greater willingness of Canadians, particularly sexually assaulted women, to report per-

BODY COUNTS

This chart shows the murder rate per 100,000 people for selected North American cities in 1992, the latest year for which statistics are available.

CANADA		U.S.A.	
St. John's	0.6	Seattle	11.0
Ottawa-Hull	1.4	Boston	12.7
Winnipeg	2.0	Denver	19.3
Toronto	2.3	Philadelphia	26.5
Halifax	2.5	New York City	27.0
Montreal	3.3	Los Angeles	30.0
Vancouver	3.7	Miami	34.2
Edmonton	3.8	Dallas	37.0
Calgary	4.6	Detroit	57.0
Thunder Bay	5.6	Washington	75.2

SOURCES: THE CANADIAN CENTRE FOR JUSTICE STATISTICS
AND THE U.S. FEDERAL BUREAU OF INVESTIGATION

From *Maclean's* magazine, April 18, 1994, pp. 14-18, 20. © 1994 by Maclean Hunter, Ltd. Reprinted by permission.

sonal crimes to the police. On top of that, the Canadian statistics pale beside American ones. The Canadian robbery rate, for instance, is 121 per 100,000 population; in the States, it is 590. The Canadian assault rate is 850 per 100,000; the American, 2,550.

However, it is the *kind* of crime that moulds public perception–and what the Canadian public evidently perceives is bad news. In a *Maclean's*/CTV poll conducted by Decima Research and published in the Jan. 4, 1993, issue of this magazine, fully half of adult Canadians said they felt more threatened by crime than they had five years before. Perhaps most disturbing of all was that of those who felt more threatened by crime, 42 per cent looked upon increased immigration as "a bad thing." When it became known that the three men involved in the killing of Georgina Leimonis were black, some callers to Toronto radio phone-in shows demanded that police begin identifying suspects by race.

The public perception, of course, is based on much more than interracial suspicion. Television is probably a significant factor. Night after night, American TV network and syndicated crime and cop dramas, documentaries and lurid tabloid programs remind viewers of their vulnerability, shape their attitudes towards their surroundings. "My community is blanketed by Detroit television," says Saskatoon police Chief Owen Maguire. "There's a whole generation of seniors afraid to leave their houses because they think life is like that."

TV may also serve as a video classroom for thugs open to suggestion, and they have been quick to learn. Last week in Prince Albert, Sask., somebody in a car opened fire on a man and his granddaughter as they left their home. Neither was hit. "I don't rule out a copy-cat incident," said police Staff Sgt. Dave Demkiw. On Dec. 30, 1992, in the Vancouver suburb of Richmond, three men burst into the home of retailer David Sarraf, pistol-whipped, stabbed and seriously wounded him and his wife.

The dismal chronicle is endless: on March 27, six hoodlums, some of them armed, forced their way into a charity club casino in the Toronto suburb of Scarborough; they pistol-whipped and disarmed a security guard and forced 150 patrons to lie on the floor and surrender their wallets. In Montreal, restaurant manager Ahmad Doughan was driving home at 4 a.m. one morning last August when a man in the car beside him fired a shot through his passenger-side window, hitting him on the finger, and then sped away. In Metropolitan Toronto, police say there were 150 home invasions in 1993, and last week a couple in neighboring Mississauga were tied up and terrorized in front of their three small children during a home invasion. "If the motivation is theft, it doesn't make sense," said sociologist Vincent Sacco of Queen's University in Kingston, Ont. "The ability to terrorize residents in the home somehow seems to be part and parcel of the crime." Statistically, it is just another robbery. But more than that, it is brand new and it is frightening.

TRAIL OF TEARS

The brutal slayings of three young people have touched off outpourings of grief, fear and rage

'It could have been us'

They came to pay their respects to someone they never knew. Following the brutal killing of 23-year-old Georgina Leimonis during an armed robbery last week at Just Desserts, a trendy café in midtown Toronto, dozens of residents dropped off bouquets of flowers outside the empty restaurant. Many of the flowers bore yellow ribbons declaring "In memory of Georgina" and cards such as the one that read: "You're best off where you are; it's a safer world there." Among the spontaneous mourners was David Hemmings, a real estate broker who had often brought his wife and two young children to Just Desserts. "It's horrible," said Hemmings as he peered in the restaurant's darkened windows. "An innocent young woman goes out to enjoy a quiet moment and gets blasted away by a thug wielding a shotgun. What frightens me most is that it could have been my family in there. It could have been us."

It could have been us. That phrase, more than any other, sprang from the mouths of Torontonians last week as they grappled with the violent death of the young woman known to friends and to her Greek immigrant family as "ViVi." The fact that Leimonis was fatally shot while sipping coffee and munching cheesecake along with 30 other patrons in an affluent neighborhood known as the Annex came as a rude shock. "This just shows that you don't have to go to the bad part of town to get into trouble," said Carolyn Schwartz, a 28-year-old saleswoman at Palma Brava, a store next door to Just Desserts. "It's all a matter of luck."

Luck was clearly not on Leimonis's side as she and a friend ordered a late-night sweet on April 5. As a videotape recorded by the restaurant's surveillance camera later showed, four black males who appeared to be in their early 20s arrived at the café shortly before

11 p.m. They briefly looked over the crowd, then left. About 10 minutes later, three of the men returned, one carrying a sawed-off, doublebarreled shotgun in a gym bag. According to police and witnesses, two of the men started to corral customers into the rear of the café, demanding their wallets and purses, while the third pulled out his gun. When two male customers refused to hand over their money, they were assaulted and received minor injuries. Then, in what police described as "a deliberate shooting," the gunman lowered his weapon and fired, apparently at random, into the crowd.

Leimonis, who was standing in the front line of the huddled patrons, took the full blast, the bullets tearing through her heart and lungs, injuring several organs. After the thieves fled, taking less than $1,000 in stolen loot, Leimonis lay conscious and alert, while customers tried to comfort her. She died three hours later in hospital, while undergoing surgery.

Following the fatal robbery, some people who live and work near the scene of the crime talked brashly about buying guns to defend themselves. Others warned that such actions would only make a bad situation worse. "The backlash worries me most," said David Currie, who runs a French bistro around the corner and who still considers his neighborhood—and his city—relatively safe. "What am I going to do: hire an armed guard to stand there while people eat their meal? It doesn't make sense."

By week's end, police had released pictures of the four suspects taken from the surveillance tape. They had also recovered a wallet stolen from one of the café patrons from a North York housing project. A break in the case could not come soon enough for Leimonis's grieving relatives who, following a Greek tradition, will bury the slain woman this week in the wedding dress she never got a chance to war in life. Friends and family spoke proudly of how Leimonis, despite holding down two jobs as a hair stylist and a telephone operator, always found time to comfort and cheer anyone going through tough times. And they declared that Toronto, and the country, must learn from her murder. "It's got to stop here," said the victim's brother, Tom. "This has ripped apart this city and no one should be able to forget." While it could have happened to anyone, this time it was their beloved ViVi—and that loss will surely haunt them the rest of their lives.

'Not as protected as we thought'

On the afternoon of the last day of her life, Joan Heimbecker spent six hours in the science library at McMaster University in Hamilton poring over evidence that vitamins A and E can extend the lifespan of rats. Returning to her campus apart-

ment in Bates Residence, the 25-year-old master's student in physical education burst into the bedroom of roommate Tara Gilbert and excitedly recounted her findings. "Then," recalls Gilbert, "she looked at me and said, 'I've never taken a vitamin before, but today I took my very first one.'" Remembering that conversation in an interview with *Maclean's,* Gilbert began to weep quietly, before recounting the events that followed.

At around 6 p.m. on March 30, the two women shared dinner with their two apartment mates. Then, Heimbecker and one of the other women settled in for a night of studying, while Gilbert and the fourth roommate headed out to class. At about 11 p.m., as Gilbert returned to the residence, a TV cameraman told her that someone inside had been murdered. "Do you know who?" Gilbert asked the man. "I think her name began with 'J,'" he replied. Soon after, Gilbert learned that Joan Heimbecker had been shot in the back, abdomen, arms and legs, and that police had issued a warrant for the arrest of Rory Eldon Foreman, with whom Heimbecker had recently ended an 18-month romance.

In fact, Gilbert had seen Foreman arriving at the apartment at about 9 o'clock, just as she was heading out the door. "But," she recalls, "he just seemed a little quiet, not scary at all." About one hour later, Jamie Twiselton, who lived in the next apartment, heard what he thought was "a frying pan being knocked against the wall." When he and a roommate went to investigate, they saw a man leaving Heimbecker's apartment—and a sawed-off shotgun, which police now suspect was obtained in Toronto, lying in her doorway. Pushing into the apartment, they found Heimbecker lying in a pool of blood, and her roommate, who had not been physically injured, frantically trying to stem Heimbecker's bleeding with a sleeping bag. Later that night, police now say, Foreman, a third-year nursing student at Conestoga College in Kitchener, Ont., crossed the U.S. border near Kingston, Ont., in a light blue Ford Taurus. The following day, he was spotted at a restaurant in New Brunswick, where Heimbecker's only sibling, Donna, attends university in Fredericton. Although police did not know if there was any connection, they placed Donna under protection.

Harry and Marlene Heimbecker, of Clifford, Ont., near Kitchener, declined to comment on the death of their daughter, who one year earlier had graduated from Wilfrid Laurier University, in Waterloo, Ont., with the highest marks in her class. But in a brief interview, Donna, 22, said that she blamed her sister's death in part on "too easy accessibility of guns, especially in an underground way." She added that the violent way in which Joan died "was as hard to accept as the fact that she died at all."

At McMaster, Heimbecker's friends and colleagues also struggled to come to terms with her murder. "People joke and say they're in school to avoid the real world," said Bates resident Mark Parolin. "It's made us realize that maybe we're not as protected, as isolated from what society is becoming, as we had thought." Twiselton, meanwhile, said that the incident has left him utterly shaken. "It's not like TV," he noted grimly. "I could smell the smoke, I could see the blood—this was real violence. People want to know what I saw, but I would give anything not to have seen it at all."

At the heart of campus a fence surrounding the Nina DeVilliers Garden, named for the McMaster student who was abducted and murdered in 1991, is covered with hundreds of white ribbons—symbols of violence against women—that were placed there during a ceremony in Heimbecker's honor last Wednesday. But across campus, people were wearing black and green ribbons as well. "There was some discussion that we should just have white ribbons, but we wanted to mourn the death of Joan, the individual woman," explains Bates hall-master David Palmer. "Black, of course, speaks of our grief—and green was her favorite color, and the color of her eyes."

'An inquiring mind and a basic kindness'

The card attached to a bunch of red roses, placed with care on a busy downtown Ottawa sidewalk, reads: "To innocence lost." It was there, outside a popular Elgin Street nightclub called The Penguin and within the protection of a crowded street in a presumably safe city, that Nicholas Battersby was shot to death by strangers at 7:29 p.m. on Sunday, March 27. The 27-year-old British-born engineer, walking home to his apartment, was struck in the chest by a bullet from a sawed-off, .22 calibre rifle fired from a passing white Jeep Cherokee. The irony was horrific: Battersby chose a job in Ottawa over one in Los Angeles last November because of its crime-free reputation. "I lived in L.A. for 14 years," said aerospace engineer Vivek Joshi, a friend and co-worker of Battersby at Bell-Northern Research Ltd. "I didn't even know of a friend who had a friend who got shot. My very first six months in Canada, and this happened. It is a case of disbelief."

The randomness of Ottawa's first drive-by killing—preceded by a 20-minute shooting spree during which three central Ottawa storefronts were shattered by bullets—jolted a smug city that once believed that violent crime happened somewhere—anywhere—else. The arrest three days later of three suspects, all under the age of 18, fuelled debate at Parliament's doorstep about toughening the Young Offenders Act. In fact, Crown prosecutors in Ottawa planned to ask this week that the trials of the trio—a 16-year-old youth, charged under the act with second-degree murder, and two others, aged 16 and 17, facing manslaughter charges—be moved into adult court.

The shock of Battersby's death, and the poignant story of how he came to be at the wrong place at the worst possible time, has provoked more than outrage. At a memorial service on Easter Monday, 500 people crowded into St. John's Anglican Church, with another 1,500 spilling onto the street. Among those at the service were Battersby's parents, Charles and Gay, and his brother James, 25, from the southern English town of Brackley. In Ottawa, the family had made a pilgrimage to the spot where Nicholas died and where every day last week passers-by added new bunches of flowers. From friends, they learned that the young engineering doctoral graduate had been on his way home to attend a friend's birthday party across the hall from his apartment on nearby Somerset Street. He had made those plans with Joshi over lunch at his office earlier that day. "I told him I would knock on his door around 8 o'clock," Joshi told *Maclean's* last week. "I kept knocking, and didn't hear anything, until a neighbor came up and said that he had been shot."

Incredibly, no one at the scene could provide a licence-plate number or identify the assailants. The shots were lost in the bustle of street activity on the warm spring night; a dozen witnesses lining up outside the nightclub thought at first that Battersby had merely tripped and fallen. Only later did police piece together the tragedy. The white Jeep, later discovered to have been stolen, had been recorded by a video camera as it sped away from one of the three convenience stores hit by rifle fire. The owner and three customers inside one store were showered with glass. The Jeep then drove along Elgin Street, its occupants apparently searching indiscriminately for targets.

Only hours after they were told of Nicholas's death, the Battersbys received a letter he had mailed last month. He had proudly written that his job as a researcher working with semiconductors was going well, and that he had made new friends. He added that he had survived his first Canadian winter and had learned how to ski and skate. In a moving tribute to his son, Charles Battersby said that "Nick achieved more in his 27 years of life through hard work, an inquiring mind and a basic kindness and humanity than many people achieve in a whole lifetime." He also said that the "crazy and senseless events that took place could have happened anywhere in the world." That it happened in Ottawa is still difficult for many in the city to grasp.

BRIAN BERGMAN in *Toronto*, **VICTOR DWYER** in *Hamilton* and **E. KAYE FULTON** and **LUKE FISHER** in *Ottawa*

Battered Women

AND THE CRIMINAL JUSTICE SYSTEM

MARGARET MARTIN

Margaret E. Martin is Associate Professor in Residence, University of Connecticut School of Social Work, West Hartford, Connecticut. She has been active in the battered women's movement since 1977 as a community activist, shelter director, and researcher. Formerly she was President of the Connecticut Task Force on Abused Women.

Advocates for battered women have played an historically important role in redefining the rights of women, challenging traditional concepts about the privacy of the family, and providing real alternatives to violence in the home. A social movement by and on behalf of battered women has provided safety and support to thousands of battered women and their children, but it also has prompted the arrest, detention, mandated treatment, and occasionally the incarceration of the battering men, and sometimes even of the women victims.[1] It is ironic that a feminist social movement, grounded in humanist values and revulsion for the abuse of power and the use of violence, has embraced the coercive social control mechanisms of the state to advance the goals of security and equality. Can the immediate needs of safety for battered women be achieved through legal solutions that are community focused and respectful of the civil rights of all the parties?

Acts of violence occurring between persons who were in intimate relationship have been considered acts of private violence, outside the purview of the criminal justice system. Although such violence was technically criminal, policy and practice provided no real protection for women battered by intimates. Yet the problem of violence is serious and widespread. Estimates are that three to four million American women are injured and fifteen hundred women murdered each year by their husbands or male partners. But during the last decade battered women's advocates have succeeded in changing criminal justice policy. Almost every state has altered its criminal code to include some form of recognition of crimes in the family. Mandatory arrest or preferred arrest for crimes in the family, for newly defined family violence crimes, or for violation of protective orders are the most common solutions. But many other alterations of the criminal code are current and pending, such as requirements that prosecutors state in writing their refusal to prosecute cases; the provision of alternative sentencing programs or pre-trial diversion programs for first-time domestic violence offenders; interstate apprehension, arrest and transfer of domestic violence offenders; mandatory sentences; or the denial of bail for domestic violence offenders deemed at risk of further violence.

The battered women's movement targeted the criminal justice system for reform soon after it began in the 1970s. It successfully achieved a network of shelters and supports to provide for the immediate safety of battered women. But its strongest press for change came during a period of conservative activism which demanded increasing criminalization of behaviors and more serious penalties for those convicted of crime. The pressure to reform the criminal justice system's response to

Women of Color for Reproductive Freedom rally in Roxbury, Massachusetts.

family violence arose not only from individual women who sought the physical protection afforded by police but from other women's advocates who attempted to reframe the relationship of the state to women.

The criminal justice system was identified early in the battered women's movement as a major barrier to women's safety in the home. All levels of the system were challenged, but the police, as the gatekeepers to the system, were targeted for their general refusal to respond to domestic violence calls and, in the instances when they did respond, their usual failure to arrest the violent man. Importantly, much of the demand for police response came from women who sought shelter or called battered women hotlines. Some studies suggest that one-third to one-half of all women who experience multiple acts of violence in a relationship call police for assistance. The police are the most commonly requested source of help for women, for they are available constantly and are legitimate authorities who, it is hoped, could control a violent partner. Battered women want,

and feel that they deserve, the security and safety that the state provides to all its citizens.

In fact, the earliest feminist arguments promoting arrest of domestic violence offenders were based on grounds of equality. Police failed to assist battered women because of legal traditions which allowed husbands to physically chastise wives and treat a husband and a wife as a single legal entity. By extending these concepts, women who were abused by a man who was or had been in an intimate relationship with her, were similarly unprotected. Police policy was to act as mediators or social workers in the situation, to "cool off" the man, to refer the couple for counseling, or to do nothing. Practice ranged from these activities to overtly supporting the batterer or threatening the victim. Battered women and their advocates demanded that they be given the same rights to protection that all citizens received. Others argued that because of battered women's special vulnerabilities (the perpetrator often had legal access to her, her children and her possessions, and often

The Clothesline Project. Shirts symbolize women who have survived rape, battery, and sexual assault.

repeated his pattern of assaults) that they be given special protection and consideration by the legal system.

Feminist demands for equality joined with other economic, political and social factors to enact legislation that redirected the social control apparatus of the state on behalf of battered women. A highly publicized civil rights case, the Thurman case, found the city of Torrington, Connecticut in violation of federal civil rights guarantees and liable for the failure of its police department to provide the same protection to battered women as it provided to other citizens. The city, located in the state which is home to the nation's insurance industry, exemplified what can happen when a city faces financial liability for the failure of its police to arrest batterers. Concurrently, a federally sponsored policing experiment in Minneapolis apparently demonstrated that of a variety of police responses to domestic violence, arrest appeared to be the most effective in deterring the offender from additional violence in the short-term (although subsequent studies have challenged these findings). In addition, the state gave increasing credence to victim rights advocates who promoted new rights for victims in the criminal justice process.

Each of these social forces: the burgeoning political power of the women's movement, and the battered women's movement specifically; the potential fiscal liability of all municipal police departments; and the apparent deterrent effect of arrest, coalesced during the

1980s when the general public called for increasing criminal sanctions and more government attention to law and order. During this period states and the federal government created new categories of crime, expanded the scope of existing crimes, broadened the powers of police, and lengthened sentences, while reducing social welfare programs and other compassionate approaches to social problems and needs.

Ironies of the criminal justice response

It is without question that battered women are unprotected by the state and that there is a great need for police to actively respond with legitimate authority to protect them. At least in the United States, the police may be a necessary part of a solution. Often the violence occurs in private: the batterer's behavior known only to the victim. But even when others are aware of the violence, there is little to curtail his actions. Because of the extreme levels of violence in this culture, and because of social norms that promote both patriarchal violence and individualism, informal sources of social control such as the family, churches, peer groups and close-knit neighborhoods fail to influence individual violent behavior and do not effectively intervene when a violent person needs help.

Feminists in the United States have been ambivalent about the role of the state, embracing it to promote rights and decrying it for fostering inequality. But feminists in other countries have a greater

2. VICTIMOLOGY

Thousands join Boston march against domestic violence in October of 1992.

skepticism or fear of using the state to coercively intervene in family violence and have decided not to depend on the police. British feminists are attempting to thwart efforts on the part of the national justice system to promote arrest and prosecution. Swedish feminists are so wary of state control that they repudiated federal efforts to promote arrest, hid the shelters from the state, and attempted to develop an underground movement. They refuse to promote the state's use of violence to end violence. But other countries, such as India and Brazil, have, through the prompting of feminists, established domestic violence units in police departments and worked to increase penalties for these offenders.

New domestic violence laws in the United States have not only sanctioned the use of traditional policing and court responses in family violence cases but have expanded their legal authority. In at least 13 states police are legally mandated to arrest when probable cause of a crime or violation of a restraining order exists. As a reaction to the failure of police to protect battered women, legislation has now reduced the prerogative of the police and in effect ensured that all persons who have violated the law will be arrested. A perverse consequence of this policy is that dual arrest, the arrest of both the man and the woman, has become common practice in some jurisdictions. In Connecticut, for instance, at least one-quarter of the arrests that involve adult domestic violence are dual arrests. In exchange for such new demands on the police, some states have offered police protection from prosecution for unlawful

---

Although many battered women want behavioral change rather than punishment for the batterer, few options are available in the courts. Perhaps most profoundly seen in this crime, there is no need to pit victim against offender to produce justice.

---

arrest. Police in Connecticut are exempt from civil suits that result from personal injury or property damage incurred during the arrest.

Because of a concern that the domestic violence offender will retaliate against his victim for arrest, battered women's advocates have argued that accused batterers be detained before arraignment and denied bail based on grounds of presumed dangerousness. In Massachusetts, new legislation promoted on behalf of battered women reformed the bail system to allow dangerousness to be included in the determination of bail. This reform affects all accused. Ironically, both clinical and statistical predictions of dangerousness are not accurate and even the best methods are seriously ineffective in predicting family violence. Even the methods used to study the problem and develop solutions can be oppressive. A federally sponsored experiment in Milwaukee was recently conducted to determine whether detaining misdemeanant domestic violence offenders for short periods, of about three hours,

or longer periods, of about 11 hours, would deter future violence. The persons held were "predominantly unemployed suspects concentrated in black ghetto poverty neighborhoods." (Longer arrests were not more effective.) Although prompted by a concern for the victim's safety, these solutions restrict civil liberties and Constitutional protections for the accused, and set dangerous precedents for the use of police detention and the denial of bail. Certainly other solutions that protect the victim and do not violate the rights of the accused could be found. Police could ensure that the victim received shelter or was provided with adequate police protection if she remained in her own home. In addition, the police might accompany the accused to his home with the victim to promote the victim's safety. Although these solutions may not be as economical as preventive detention, they certainly would be more just.

The new treatment given to cases of domestic violence that are brought to court expands the role of the courts and promotes concern about the civil liberties of victim and offender. New strategies that are conceptualized as nonpunitive, compassionate and rational approaches to family problems may create serious violations of constitutional guarantees and standards of justice. For example, court-based family services require arrested persons to describe the family violence arrest incident, their history of violence, criminal record and other factors to officers of the court without the presence of the accused's attorney, and sometimes before entering a plea. When the person accused of family violence is eligible for a pre-trial diversion program he often has limited information about his rights to refuse the diversion and about the realistic expectations about his fate in court should he reject treatment. Many women who are caught in dual arrests are not informed about the option to press legitimate claims to self-defense and also, as first offenders, are likely to be sent to pre-trial diversion programs for counseling. Pre-trial diversion programs are certainly preferable to the formal imposition of a conviction and sentence; however, their administration and management must assure that they do not widen the net of correctional control. They must ensure that only those be diverted who most likely would be convicted, and that the courts adhere to the highest legal standards.

New protections afforded battered women have also meant perpetuation of inequalities that are common in the criminal justice system. Although studies have not shown that discrimination prevails in the treatment of domestic violence cases in the criminal justice system, overall studies of policing, prosecution and sentencing suggest that racism, sexism and classism and other forms of discrimination exist. A study that I conducted on the treatment of family violence cases in the Connecticut courts showed that primarily legal factors, such as the seriousness of the crime, the injury incurred, and the criminal history of the defendant were the factors that predicted the court outcome, not race or ethnicity. However, because blacks were more likely to have criminal histories (related both to poverty and to the over-surveillance of poor communities by police), they were also more likely to be prosecuted, convicted and punished by the courts than their white counterparts. Should the protection of battered women place some persons, particularly those most oppressed in this society, at higher risk of criminal penalty than others?

The police and the courts frequently treat battered women as members of an impersonal entity known as Battered Women and not as persons. Women articulate a variety of needs and wants in their calls to police. Some want an immediate cessation of the violence which can be brought about by an authority on the scene; some want safe passage to shelter or medical care; and others want more long term benefit. Some women use the threat of police intervention, an arrest record, a court appearance, conviction or even incarceration as a point of leverage in gaining some control in their relationship. Others want the imposition of these sanctions to deter future violence or to ensure retribution and punishment. Others see sanctions as a way to achieve safety and protection.

Our criminal justice system cannot respond to the multiple dimensions of social need evident here. Because of the focus on the crime, and not the persons accused of and affected by the crime, and because of the concomitant expectation of equality, it becomes impossible to address the particular needs of a battered woman. As the police and courts assume additional responsibility for family violence crimes, their response becomes increasingly paternalistic. Arrests will be made regardless of the wishes of the woman and, although still a rare outcome, prosecution will proceed with or occasionally without the woman's endorsement. Battered women are often subpoenaed to testify against their batterers "for their own good." In some jurisdictions there is an attempt to empower women as much as the system allows, even producing, as in Connecticut, the anomaly that offenders who have caused the most serious injuries are less likely to be prosecuted because their victims are more likely not to desire this outcome. But empowerment of individual women, although ideal in an restorative model of justice, is an unlikely goal of the current justice process.

The current legal process relies on retribution and punishment rather than on notions of restorative justice which is based in community, not individualistic values. Although many battered women want behavioral change rather than punishment for the batterer, few options are available in the courts. Perhaps most profoundly seen in this crime, there is no need to pit victim against offender to produce justice. Many battered women do want a new relationship with the batterer, one that is free of abuse, and others do not want a continued relationship, although they desire that the abuser no longer use violence against others. In many ways, major gains have been made toward a restorative mode in the treatment of family violence, only because of the belief that many families want to reunite in spite of the violence. For minor forms of violence and for first offenders, many states and locales have instituted treatment programs for the offenders and work closely with community programs to assist the victims. Although they have very weak success rates, the attempt to treat the batterer is founded on community and humanistic values. But beyond these approaches, most locales have resorted to punitive practices such as mandatory sentences, which provide no integration of the victim's wishes into the criminal justice outcome and attempt no strategies to eliminate the violent behavior.

Because this approach relies on the use of power and control to deter, restrain, and punish battering men, it reinforces the very mechanisms of violence and coercive control that form the foundation of battering in the family. Battering men routinely believe that they have the right to exercise violent control over members of their families and they use violence instrumentally to achieve their goals. Battering is about the abuse of power. The criminalization of family violence attempts to redefine acts seen as legitimate as now illegitimate. The act of inviting the state to exercise more legitimate control in the family arena, however, may place all of us at greater risk of perpetuating a misuse of power by official sources.

Finally, the present legal response to violence in the family reframes the problem of violence in the family as a problem of a pathological or uncontrolled man, or even as a problem of a pathological family, rather than as a socio-political problem that has its roots in the oppression of women and in the socially sanctioned use of violence in this society.[2] Because the legal system individualizes the problem and has no mechanisms for treating social ills, it reinforces the notion that the problem can be solved by punishing or treating a few deviant men. The solution is to promote a social context that equalizes men and women and facilitates the nonviolent resolutions to conflicts.

The willingness of states to use new control mechanisms on behalf of battered women therefore is problematic in many regards. It expands the power of the

---

We should not allow our efforts to protect women to expand systems of injustice and to curtail the civil liberties of all.

---

police and the courts in new and encompassing ways; it provides new protections which promote inequities; it fosters the treatment of individuals as members of groups; it idealizes notions of individually-based retributive justice rather than community-based restorative justice; it reinforces the use of violence and coercive control which are the underpinnings of violence in the family; and it redefines a social problem that requires social solutions to be an individual problem that involves either pathological men or dysfunctional families.

Solutions

Feminist demands that the criminal justice system respond to battered women emerged from arguments about equal protection and safety. But there are numerous feminist voices and others who advocate for battered women. Increasingly additional goals have been articulated which tend to reinforce the role of the criminal justice system as a utilitarian or retributive social vehicle. Legislation has been promoted by criminal justice practitioners and others who have argued that arrest and detention work as deterrents to future violence in the family. Also, some of the power and anger propelling new legislation for battered women comes not only from concern for the women's well-being, but from an anger at a system of justice that continues to treat crime against property as seriously, or more seriously, than crimes against people. It is grossly unfair, in a humanistic value system, that a person who has passed a bad check or damaged another's property be given harsher sentences than a person who has injured another person. In a quest for "fairness," some advocates con-

tinue to increase the demands for more punishment in a system that seems to continue to raise sentence levels to appeal to yet another interest group.

Policies and practices that have been generated by demands for equality may have provided both greater rights of protection and an erosion of civil liberties for battered women and their families. This predicament provides a profound challenge and unique opportunity to the criminal justice system. In battered women's dilemma with the justice system lay the foundations for a restorative justice. Many feminist advocates for battered women recognize the inherent contradictions within current legal standards and practices and understand the system's limitations in transforming the social conditions that promote violence in the family. This awareness can be used to prompt advocates to reject the traditional victim rights ideology which posits that criminal justice practice is a zero sum game, with one winner and one loser, and more importantly, to forge alliances with persons seeking to transform the criminal justice system into a mechanism for restoring relationship, empowering oppressed people and fostering community values. By using civil rights and human rights as working parameters, advocates can fashion solutions that are creative responses to the conditions of exploitation that battered women face. As example, battered women and their advocates should hold positions on police review boards which will hold the police accountable for their responsibilities to protect battered women and for the appropriate and just use of arrest. Where there are no such review boards they should be created.

Battered women's advocates recognize that the criminal justice system ultimately cannot free women from violence or equalize the status of women and men. The legal system reflects current power relationships, especially the dominance of men over women. Yet feminists attempt to alter the system's values and practices in order to protect and empower women. Feminist values are consistent with a conception of justice that seeks individual wholeness and community fairness but such values are not consistent with tactics that will limit Constitutional liberties. We should not allow our efforts to protect women to expand systems of injustice and to curtail the civil liberties of all.

[1] In this paper I will refer to battered women and battering men. This is the primary mode of adult, intimate violence. But it is known that in under 5% of the cases, some family violence is primarily characterized by woman to man violence and violence in gay and lesbian relationships.
[2] See Patricia A. Morgan, "Constructing Images of Deviance: A Look at State Intervention into the Problem of Wife-Battery" in *Marital Violence*, Norman Johnson, ed., Sociological Review Monograph 31, London: Routeledge & Kegan Paul, 1985.

Police

The police officer of today is caught in a crossfire of demands. People want crime suppressed, but at what cost? Should constitutional rights be diminished, or should more force be used? Should more expensive technologies be employed? What is the cost to the individual officer? In the article "Officers on the Edge," Nancy Gibbs discusses the problem of police suicides.

"Police Work from a Woman's Perspective" presents another aspect of stress in policing. James Daum and Cindy Johns explore the problems still facing female police officers as they assume a greater policing role.

People who live in high crime areas are desperate for safety solutions. One controversial proposal would allow police to search apartments in public housing projects without warrants. The article "Public Safety and Crime: Are Warrantless Searches for Guns in Public Housing Projects Justified?" presents two opposing viewpoints.

In "A LEN Interview with Professor Carl Klockars of the University of Delaware," an interesting interview with a renowned expert in policing is presented.

Police are always looking for alternatives to the use of deadly force. One popular alternative has been *pepper spray.* Following reports of deaths following the use of pepper spray, a study was conducted by the International Association of Chiefs of Police (IACP), and the results are presented in "Pepper Spray and In-Custody Deaths."

Looking Ahead: Challenge Questions

Is there "community policing" in your area? Is it working? Why or why not?

Should the police be given broader search powers? Defend your answer.

What alternative uses of force are in place in your police agencies?

Are women police officers being accepted by their male peers and supervisors? By the community? Explain your answers.

Unit 3

OFFICERS ON THE EDGE

A spate of suicides has departments reviewing how to help cops cope with pressures on—and off—the job

NANCY GIBBS

ANN MARIE HALL SAT NEXT TO HER husband on the green sofa, trying to talk the gun out of his hands. "You know you can't kill yourself," she said. "Think about the boys, and your mother, and your brother and me. How will we feel?"

Michael admitted he wasn't thinking straight. "It's not about anything but you and me," he said. Even as cops' marriages go, theirs was badly bruised. They had fallen in love fast; he proposed five months after they met, on bended knee atop the Empire State Building, and they were married eight years ago. But since then, the fights had become more frequent, as Ann Marie learned what it meant to marry into the force.

She remembers a night they spent cruising up the Hudson River at a wedding reception on a yacht. "Mike and I went up on deck, and we were the only two up there," she recalls. "We were slow dancing, and I was thinking about how romantic it was. And then Mike says, 'Do you have any idea how many dead bodies there are in this river?' "

Michael had grown quiet, withdrawn, in the days leading up to that Sunday afternoon in July. She glanced at the heavy flashlight on the stone fireplace and thought of grabbing it, hitting him on the head and getting the gun away. But she was afraid something would go wrong, so she stayed where she was. He put the gun to his head.

"Don't be ridiculous," she said, "put that thing down."

"Oh, I'm ridiculous?" When he pulled the trigger, the bullet passed through his skull and lodged in the wall behind the couch.

Their three small children were playing in the next room. When they heard the shot, they came running, saw the red stain spreading over the sofa and didn't say a word.

MICHAEL HALL, AN OFFICER IN THE 46TH precinct in the Bronx, became the seventh of 10 New York City cops to kill themselves so far this year, already tying the record set in 1987. No one has an adequate explanation of what finally drove him over the edge, and so the speculation runs a predictable course: it was the danger, the pressure, the grinding sorrows embedded in the daily routine. Last week the New York police department released the results of a three-year study that found that cops were more than twice as likely to kill themselves as were members of the general population. Though every case is different, the experts do see some patterns: male officers are far more likely to kill themselves than female ones, alcohol often plays some role, and corruption scandals within the department are usually followed by a spate of suicides.

The cops themselves rarely blame the obvious culprit—the tension of living forever in the cross hairs. Veteran officers and the experts who study them agree that the pressure on police officers actually comes from some surprising sources. The most crushing battles, they argue, often occur not on the streets but in the rundown precinct houses, and the courtrooms, and the privacy of their own homes. Too often, police complain, the commanders and commissioners who cops imagined would guide and protect them seem to ignore or betray them instead. "Frequently, officers feel that somewhere on the line between lieutenant and captain, these people change," says Scott Allen, clinical psychologist for the 3,200-member Metro-Dade police department in Florida. "The command loses touch with the soldiers."

Many cops on the street charge that they are being asked to do more with less; just getting the equipment they need requires a major bureaucratic struggle. "A car that breaks down while you're pursuing a suspect? That's stress. A gun that may not work? That's stress," says John Johnston, a 20-year veteran of the Los Angeles police department. The criminals, he takes in stride: "Dealing with bad guys is why I became a cop. What gets you down is the bureaucracy." In his office in the L.A.P.D.'s Northeast division, which includes the grimiest stretch of Hollywood Boulevard, the computers are antique, the shotguns routinely fail during practice and the cars in the lot are monuments to budgetary restraints: the odometers read 132,000 miles, 136,000, 148,000 . . .

Just as punishing to police morale is the problem of punishment: it is common for officers to risk their lives arresting suspects whom they meet again on the streets within days. "That's the main stress," Seattle Detective Nathan Janes says, "like the fact that the violent criminal doesn't even go to jail." He recalls a thug who attacked a fellow officer a few years ago, wrestled his gun away, jammed it under the officer's bulletproof vest and tried to fire. "He wanted to kill him, but the cop got his hand in between the hammer and the firing pin," Janes says. "I took this guy to jail, and he was joking that he'd do it again if he got the chance. Anyway, 18 months later, I was involved in a car chase. I finally stopped the car, and there he was. He didn't even serve 18 months for trying to kill a cop. That can cause some stress all right."

When so much of the day's job involves exposure to the darkest corners of human nature, cynicism and denial serve as a handy emotional vaccine. But that coldness can take a personal toll; and at worst, the day's violence bleeds into the home. In a study by Arizona State University sociologist Leanor Boulin-Johnson of 728 officers in two East Coast departments, some 40% responded that "they had gotten out of control and behaved violently against their spouse and children." Last week in Alexandria, Louisiana, deputy sheriff Paul Broussard shot his estranged wife Andrea five times because she was filing for divorce.

From *Time*, September 26, 1994, pp. 62-63. © 1994 by Time Inc. Magazine Company. Reprinted by permission.

He fled across the street to a bank, still waving his gun, as police moved in and sealed the area. Surrounded by sharpshooters, Broussard talked to a priest for more than two hours. A friend and a police chaplain tried to persuade him to surrender as well. "Nothing worked," said Lieut. Tommy Cicardo. Broussard finally put the .45 to his jaw and pulled the trigger, as the local TV cameras rolled.

"AT BEST, BEING A POLICE OFficer places terrific stress on a family," says Harvey Schlossberg, the former director of psychological services for the New York City police department and a 20-year veteran himself. Cops "tend to feel very uncomfortable outside the company of other police officers," he observes. "They tend to be very clannish." The hypervigilance that keeps them alive on the street is hard to shed once they're home. "It's as if you become a cop 24 hours a day," says the ex-husband of a New Mexico cop. "That's the way you treat everyone—commanding, suspicious, paranoid. She'd gone into the cop role so much that she regarded any challenge to her authority as an attack."

Though urban cops may feel that they are the ones patrolling a war zone, rural officers often long for the anonymity of the big cities. At a crime scene, the odds are high that they will know both the victim and the suspect. It is impossible to go off-duty; like the small-town doctor, the local cop is constantly pressed for help and advice. "Community members expect the officer and their family to be free from family conflicts," explains psychologist Ellen Scrivner, an expert on police stress. "Moreover, children are expected to behave differently when their parent is a police officer."

Twenty years ago, it was the rare police department that had any formal mechanisms for helping officers or their families cope with the demands of the job. Now more and more have instituted programs ranging from peer counseling to diet and exercise plans, designed to teach stress management. The L.A.P.D. has seven full-time psychologists working out of an old bank building in Chinatown, where cops can visit without fear of being seen by their colleagues or superiors. Since 1990, there has been a 103% increase in the number of counseling sessions conducted there, to a projected 3,734 sessions in 1993, and a 44% increase in the number of clients seen.

But the experts acknowledge it is hard for police officers to admit when they need help. If an officer visits a counselor and is put on psychological leave, notes William Nolan, president of the Chicago Fraternal Order of Police, "they take him off the street because the city doesn't want the liability of an officer with stress on the streets. So if an officer is willing, or man enough, to admit it, they'll take away your gun and star, and you won't get them back until you can prove you're O.K." Nolan would prefer a more anonymous system, where officers could seek help without feeling a stigma or risking a career.

The Halls' white clapboard and brick house is half empty; there's a FOR SALE sign in the yard, and the path to the door is strewn with Tonka Trucks. Ann Marie is inside packing, to move closer to her family in Connecticut. She hasn't been sleeping well, and has lost weight. Michael's dress uniform hangs in plastic in the closet. A carpenter has been in to fix the hole where the police dug the bullet from the wall. Michael's partner came by with the contents of his locker. Three-year-old Danny, who loves playing cop, went rummaging through the box, then came running upstairs to his mom, wearing his father's dark blue hat. "After we were married," Ann Marie says, "he told me he had a dark side and that I'd better pray that I never see it." Now she must wonder how long it will take to get the vision out of her mind.

—Reported by Hannah Bloch and Massimo Calabresi/New York and Elaine Lafferty/ Los Angeles

Police Work From a Woman's Perspective

James M. Daum, Ph.D., Police Psychologist, Lippert, Daum and Associates;
and Lieutenant Cindy M. Johns, Cincinnati Police Division

Since women have joined the ranks, much attention has been paid to their impact on the police organization and the community. However, comparatively little research has been conducted to determine how the police organization and the community have affected the female police officer. Common wisdom might lead one to believe that becoming a police officer would bring about a more radical change in a woman's life than in a man's. Police work remains a predominantly male occupation, and there is still a remnant of the traditional belief that assertiveness, aggressiveness, physical capability and emotional toughness are "male" characteristics necessary to perform competently as a police officer. When a woman displays these very same characteristics, she is often perceived as "cold," "pushy" or somehow in violation of the role socially prescribed for her gender.

For a man, a career in law enforcement is an option he can select without question. To become an officer, he must demonstrate that he possesses the knowledge, skills and abilities to do the job. In contrast, a woman aspiring to become a police officer is often viewed as unusual. This makes her "different" from other women. In order to become an officer, she must not only prove that she has the "KSAs", but also deal with the obstacles posed by being a true minority. Rather than proving that she can be as good as any other officer, she has to prove that she is as good as any *male* officer. In other words, there is pressure for her to be what she is not—which is male.

She also faces the problem of not being taken seriously as an officer. Although this lack of respect occurs most frequently among her fellow (male) officers, she sometimes encounters this same problem in the community, from citizens who request a male officer after she responds to the call. Although legal and formal organizational barriers no longer exist, a woman is still subjected to the stereotype of being one of "the weaker sex" and therefore not as capable as a man. As such, she must fight a steep uphill battle to gain acceptance as an officer.

What type of impact might such barriers and pressures have upon the female police officer? One might expect a high stress level, along with such side effects as undesirable changes in personality, health, job performance and home life. However, it could also be argued that working to combat stereotypes and gain acceptance has reward value, and that job success might provide a greater feeling of accomplishment. All that can be stated with certainty is that for women, being socialized into a police organization presents a considerable challenge.

Procedure

Eighty-one of the 122 female police officers of a metropolitan police department completed surveys while attending a one-day workshop that addressed issues of women in policing. Participation in this workshop was voluntary, so 41 of these police women did not attend. Thus, the survey results do not represent all of the female members of the department. However, it can be asserted that those who filled out the surveys have an interest in women's issues in policing, and are therefore probably aware of gender-related problems facing female officers.

Of the 12 supervisors and 69 officers who responded, 51 worked in patrol, with the remaining 30 serving in a non-patrol capacity. Eighteen respondents had been with the department for two or fewer years, 23 had been police officers for three to five years, 12 had been officers for six to 10 years and the remaining 27 had been with the division for more than 10 years. Fifty-two respondents were white, 28 were African-American and one was Hispanic.

Results

It is important to note that these findings represent the perceptions of the women who completed the surveys. Their opinions were not verified by consulting outside sources of information, such as performance evaluations, disciplinary records or other documentation. The focus of this study is not on the police department itself, but rather the perceptions, attitudes and behaviors developed among female officers through their exposure to police work.

Acceptance

Asked whether they felt accepted by other officers, supervisors, civilian city employees and the public, very few reported having difficulty being accepted by civilian employees (7 percent) or the public (10 percent). Likewise, there was general agreement that they were accepted by other female officers, as well as by female supervisors. However, 42 percent did not feel accepted by male officers, and 55 percent expressed the opinion that male supervisors did not accept them.

To assess the female officers' confidence on the job, they were asked to compare their job performance with that of male officers. The vast majority (76 percent) felt that they perform the job as well as male officers. It is significant to note, however, that almost one-fourth (24 percent) expressed the opinion that they do a better job than do male officers.

More than two-thirds (68 percent) of the female officers surveyed felt that they had to do a lot more work to receive the same credit as their male counterparts; only 30 percent believed that they were given just as much credit for their work as their male counterparts.

Asked to compare the code of conduct for male and female officers, only 4 percent felt that male officers had a stricter code of conduct, whereas 58 percent believed

Reprinted with permission from *The Police Chief* magazine, September 1994, pp. 46-49. © 1994 by the International Association of Chiefs of Police, Inc., P.O. Box 6010, 13 Firstfield Road, Gaithersburg, MD 20878. Further reproduction without express written permission from IACP is strictly prohibited.

female officers faced tougher standards; 38 percent saw no difference. Some respondents expressed the opinion that grooming standards were stricter for females, and that their behavior was more closely scrutinized than that of males.

Another issue related to acceptance is the attitude of the recruit's field training officer (FTO). Respondents were split fairly evenly on this question, with slightly over half (52 percent) reporting that they experienced no reluctance on the part of the FTO and the remaining 48 percent reporting having sensed some displeasure about having a female as a partner.

Although the majority (57 percent) saw no difference in morale between male and female officers, a substantial percentage (35 percent) felt that morale was lower among female officers. Several respondents noted that, since the majority of officers are men and they prefer to work and socialize with each other, women tend to be left out and feel disenfranchised from the organization; others observed that there are more "men-only" outings among male officers.

Many respondents expressed the need for the department to realize that female officers have different needs and to adjust its thinking accordingly; others stressed the need for official recognition that women do the job just as well, albeit differently. There were also comments about not wanting to be pampered or given the "quiet beats."

A number of respondents expressed the desire to be treated as equals and receive more support, as well as appreciation for doing a good job. "Just let me feel good about being a female cop," noted one respondent, perhaps summarizing what most female officers felt.

Changes in Attitude and Behavior

Ninety-seven percent of the female officers surveyed firmly agreed that becoming a police officer has changed them in significant ways. Although most of the group were generally pleased with these changes, there were a substantial number who were displeased. Some like feeling more self-confident and less naive. Others mentioned having more distrust of others. Being able to relate more easily to people was listed as a desirable change, whereas being colder, more skeptical and less tolerant were mentioned as undesirable changes. Common themes were that the job produces a negative outlook, less patience, more forcefulness and greater irritability. Overall, there seemed to be a general awareness that exposure to life's harsher realities has significantly changed perceptions and attitudes.

Asked if being a police officer has affected relationships outside the police department, many of these officers reported feeling set apart from others and subjected to stereotypes put forth by the media. Others mentioned that the shifts they work afford little time for relationships, or that it is more difficult to start a relationship because a potential date is uncomfortable with a "cop."

It might be expected that a stressful job would have an impact on the officer's tendency to curse, smoke or use alcohol. Respondents reported the following changes in these behaviors:

	Never Have	More	Less	Same	Quit
Smoking	57%	6%	5%	13%	19%
Drinking	16%	13%	29%	35%	7%
Cursing	3%	63%	8%	24%	2%

It could be said that becoming a police officer appears to have had some positive impact in the areas of smoking and drinking, in that 24 percent have either quit smoking or smoke less than previously, and a total of 36 percent have either decreased their alcohol intake or quit altogether. It is obvious that most of these women find that they curse more now than they did before.

These officers also noted unpleasant changes in sleeping and eating habits, as well as attitude. Changes in sleeping or eating habits were usually attributed to shift work and the corresponding need to alter one's daily schedule. A negative eating habit mentioned by several officers is having to eat more "fast food" instead of home-cooked meals.

Sixty-five percent of respondents reported regularly engaging in one or more stress-reducing activities, including playing team and individual sports, walking, reading, spending time with family, bike riding and doing aerobics. Also mentioned were tending to animals (household pets, horses), exercising, talking out problems and enjoying outdoor activities.

Sexual Harassment

Respondents considered several behaviors to be part and parcel of sexual harassment, including jokes, inappropriate touching, requests for sex, sexually degrading comments or gestures and other threatening behaviors. Some respondents also mentioned being treated differently because of their sex.

Sixty-two percent of the survey respondents had experienced some form of sexual harassment (as defined above)

from a co-worker or supervisor. Of these, one-third confronted the offender, and 6 percent talked to their supervisors about it. A few contacted a representative of the EEOC, but 21 percent took no action at all. Very few took strong measures to address the problem.

Job Goals

Given the difficulties facing female police officers, one might expect discouragement and disenchantment. However, 80 percent stated that they plan to work for the department until retirement. There were very few with definite plans to leave within the foreseeable future, although some mentioned getting another position after finishing college. Only one respondent stated that she sees better opportunities for advancement and promotion outside of a police career. Fifty-six percent of the patrol officers planned on working toward promotion, and 31 percent were seeking a specialized assignment. Only 13 percent preferred to stay on as patrol officers.

There was substantial confidence among female officers that they will be able to succeed in garnering a promotion or preferred assignment—implying either that no major organizational obstacles are perceived or that female officers have confidence in their ability to surmount whatever obstacles there might be. Such confidence may also result from the department's policy of encouraging placement of minorities in preferred assignments.

Seventy-one percent reported that if they had to start over again, they would still become police officers. Therefore, most felt that they had made the right choice and were receiving enough reward and satisfaction from their careers. The 29 percent who would have pursued another career stated that they have remained on the job primarily due to the salary, benefits and job security. A few said they have continued as police officers because they were taught to "tough it out," or that they enjoyed the status that comes with the profession.

Summary

The results of this survey suggest that female police officers continue to struggle to gain acceptance from their male counterparts. The prevailing opinion among respondents to this survey is that they do not receive equal credit for their job performance, even though they believe that they are as capable as male officers. They also sense some degree of ostracism from the male social network, which has a negative impact on their morale. They feel a need to be accepted as female officers, rather than being evaluated according to "male" criteria. Many have experienced some form of sexual harassment from co-workers and supervisors, but did not assertively address the problem.

Exposure to police work produces a change in social attitudes for female officers. Some become more confident, more socially comfortable and less naive, but others become colder, less trusting and less tolerant of others. Most of the officers who responded to the survey regularly engage in healthy activities to relieve stress. Many have decreased their smoking and use of alcohol. Their sleeping and eating habits are adversely affected because of lifestyle adjustments to shift work.

Despite these problems, most do not regret the decision to become a police officer. They plan to continue with the job and are optimistic about career advancement. For these officers, the career is worth the struggle, and although they have yet to gain full acceptance, they see themselves as making valuable contributions to their departments and communities.

Public Safety and Crime

Are warrantless searches for guns in public housing projects justified?

Instead of being a haven of stability for people on government assistance, the nation's public housing in some cities has turned into storm centers for crime.

With the Clinton administration backing such measures as asking tenants to permit searches of apartments, the debate over fighting crime and defending the Constitution is growing as loud as the sounds of nighttime gunfire in the projects.

The issue reached the White House and the nation's public housing officials this spring after the American Civil Liberties Union went to court for some Chicago Housing Authority residents claiming civil liberties violations. Since then, the CHA and the administration have backed off from their position that tenants must sign waivers to searches in their leases.

The ACLU's Harvey Grossman says floor-by-floor patrols and beat policing are more effective in the long run than warrantless searches.

Robert Teir of the Washington, D.C.-based American Alliance for Rights and Responsibilities, a communitarian group that represented tenants objecting to the ACLU suit, maintains that searches are not unreasonable because they save lives and help to restore security.

Yes: Living without fear is the most important right

ROBERT
TEIR

Robert Teir is general counsel for the Alliance for Individual Rights and Responsibilities.

In a meeting held during a bitterly cold morning in February, tenants elected to the Central Advisory Council of the Chicago Housing Authority voted unanimously (with one absent) to oppose the ACLU in court over proposed security initiatives. These residents were in favor of metal detectors at entrances, a visitor sign-in requirement, and complete searches (or "sweeps") of buildings after a barrage of gunfire when the police cannot determine where the shots originated.

Despite a massive snowstorm, over 5,000 residents signed petitions to support the council. After a federal judge's ruling that sweeps are permissible with tenant consent, the CHA proposed a lease provision expressly authorizing these safety measures, but has since vacillated on whether the waiver should be voluntary or mandatory.

In frequent meetings and discussions with CHA residents, I learned that they did not view the CHA's original proposal as an offer to sacrifice constitutional rights for personal safety. Rather, they saw the lease terms as consistent with both.

Metal detectors and visitor sign-in requirements are so widely used in government buildings as to make the ACLU's arguments against these programs quixotic and obstructive. The requirement that tenants consent to the search policy also rests on solid legal grounds.

First, federal courts routinely permit conditions—some quite intrusive—on government benefits. Here, those receiving public housing units must contribute to the safety of the community by agreeing to occasional searches in emergency situations. If residents find the sweeps objectionable, they can simply move. No one is subject to a sweep involuntarily, or without advance notice.

Reprinted with permission from the *ABA Journal*, July 1994, pp. 40-41. © 1994 by the American Bar Association.

It seems clear that a private landlord could impose such a lease condition. Indeed, condominium associations routinely impose entry authorizations in emergencies. CHA residents, desiring the same security enjoyed by residents of Chicago's Gold Coast, want to do the same thing.

Second, the Fourth Amendment protects citizens against unreasonable searches. One indicator of reasonableness is the response of the people being searched. Here, the people subject to the searches are the ones calling for them.

Third, a warrant or particularized suspicion is not a prerequisite for searches where there is a special governmental need. The Supreme Court, for instance, allowed searches without particularized suspicion of homes of those on probation, homes of welfare recipients for unregistered live-ins, cars near immigration checkpoints, and of drivers for sobriety.

Chicago public housing tenants asserted a "special need," demonstrated by parents disassembling bunk beds to keep children out of the line of fire, mothers putting children to bed in bathtubs for fear of random gunfire, and grandparents paying gang members to be allowed to "pass" with groceries.

The goal of the law-abiding CHA tenants and their landlord is not to have more sweeps. Rather, it is to deter gang members from taking over these buildings through violence and intimidation. As one eighth-grader said: "They're shooting at kids and putting them in fear. We need to have sweeps. They're killing my friends. Don't people understand what's going on?"

The tenant leaders and the CHA do understand, and a lease term allowing new security measures will save lives. Long-term measures are also needed to make the searches unnecessary, but step one is to regain control. This is why the residents pushed the CHA for the lease change, as part of their right to petition the government for redress of a deadly grievance.

No: Police sweeps make residents second-class citizens

HARVEY
GROSSMAN

Harvey Grossman is the legal director of the American Civil Liberties Union of Illinois.

Mark Pratt did not predict how devastating it would be for his son to watch him being frisked by Chicago Housing Authority police while other CHA workers searched their home. Shortly afterward, the boy began having nightmares. That's when Pratt decided to challenge the CHA's policy of conducting warrantless weapons searches of its tenants and their apartments.

The ACLU, on behalf of Pratt and other CHA dwellers, has sought to protect both the safety and the constitutional rights of Chicago's public housing residents. Our clients, all of whom have lived in public housing for more than 20 years, know firsthand the deplorable living conditions and violence CHA residents endure. They also know that they have the same rights to have adequate police protection and be free from warrantless searches as residents of private housing.

In the summer of 1993, the CHA implemented a warrantless search policy that authorized its police to search all apartments in a building whenever there was persistent gunfire or a weapons-related incident. These searches were conducted without warrants or individualized suspicion that a particular apartment contained weapons and regardless of whether tenants consented.

After four days of searching more than 1,500 apartments, only 23 weapons were obtained. Most were found in vacant apartments and common areas, which the CHA may search without a warrant. Only four weapons were subsequently identified as being found in apartments, and the CHA said it obtained consent to search those apartments.

Court testimony showed that the weapons came right back into buildings after the searches because of lax security guards, described by CHA chairman Vincent Lane as not being worth "two dead flies." This was further proof that the warrantless search policy is not only unconstitutional but also ineffective. It is surely no substitute for adequate police protection.

On April 7, U.S. District Judge Wayne R. Anderson ordered a halt to warrantless, nonconsensual apartment searches. Denied the use of unconstitutional and impotent sweeps, the CHA and the city of Chicago have started using approaches long advocated by law enforcement experts and the ACLU. Teams of police are conducting "vertical patrols," walking each floor at CHA high-rise buildings, inspecting common areas and doing surveillance.

In the first few days of operation at Robert Taylor Homes, these officers recovered more weapons than in the illegal searches. Again, the weapons were found mostly in common hallways and vacant apartments.

The federal government recently pledged $10 million for 180 additional police officers to patrol CHA buildings and to secure lobbies. Although insufficient, this positive development was overshadowed by President Clinton's proposal requiring tenants to consent to searches as a condition of their lease. This would have set a dangerous precedent—requiring the forfeiture of the most basic protection of a person's home. Fortunately for CHA tenants, the Clinton administration now has proposed merely asking tenants for consent.

No housing authority should adopt an involuntary search policy, for it can only perpetuate second-class law enforcement in public housing and second-class citizenship for its residents. If we truly care about the violence plaguing public housing, we must address the problem honestly. We must move beyond the quick fixes and provide adequate law enforcement. Only then will we bring a sense of security and community to all citizens.

A LEN interview with
Prof. Carl Klockars of the University of Delaware

"The police have been extraordinarily open to researchers. Police are anxious for input when they become convinced that the people working with them are sincere and are not there to do some kind of hatchet job."

Law Enforcement News Interview
by Marie Simonetti Rosen

LAW ENFORCEMENT NEWS: You've been thinking about crime for about two decades now. What changes, if any, do you see in the role of police now compared to the past?

KLOCKARS: My entire perspective on police stems from a single fundamental observation, namely that what distinguishes police from every other domestic institution is that they exercise a general right to use coercive force. That general right to use coercive force is exactly what makes them so valuable to us in society. It's what makes them able to handle situations which no other institution can. That central core of the police role is constant and it always will be; it's what defines police and what makes them worth having in society. So in that way the role of the police is the same.

Now the question becomes, why does society need an institution with that general right to use coercive force? The answer is that there are a whole bunch of situations which ought not to be happening, and about which something ought to be done now, either it's a car that has to be moved from the street after an accident, or people standing in the way when a fire truck is trying to get to a fire. Those are situations that can't await a later resolution. If the people won't move or the motorists won't move their vehicles, we need someone with the right to use coercive force to attend to that situation and move those people or those vehicles out of the way. We invest no other institution in society with that responsibility. And it's an awesome responsibility because essentially what it says is you have

this right to use coercive force in virtually any situation that you see needing it, and no one has the right to resist your use of force when you think it's appropriate. So we invest police with a tremendous and awesome responsibility and one that is absolutely necessary in a democratic society, but fundamentally different from the right we give to any other institution.

LEN: Does society expect something different from police now than it did in the past?

KLOCKARS: I think that what society expects from police is, to a great extent, influenced by what police encourage them to expect. If police promote themselves as engaged in a war on crime, if they take credit when the crime rate goes down, the public's expectation is that police will do something to prevent crime. If they go to city councils asking for more police officers or money in their budgets in an effort to control crime, then the public's expectation is going to be that they do it.

There's a long history of claims that have been made as to why we need police and what police can do—that police make us safe, that they will prevent crime, that they will do various kinds of things. In the United States, certainly, the public has come to accept that a defining role of police is to do something about crime. Unfortunately, criminologists like myself have found only very rare occasions, on which police can make much difference at all in the actual levels of crime in the community. Police can respond to crime when it happens, and they are more or less successful in making arrests when crimes occur. But I know of very few studies which show that police can have any kind of sizable impact on the reduction of crime, no matter what they do—the rare exceptions being extremely high-intensity crackdowns in very small areas, which produce temporary reductions and probably a displacement. Short of that, even though the major mandate and the basis on which the police have sold themselves and the public expectation for police has been to do something about crime, to stop crime, or to wage a war on crime, the evidence is pretty strong that they only make a marginal difference in that effort.

LEN: One of the newest wrinkles has been community policing, with its almost inherent promise that it will make a locality safer. Given what you've just said about the police and their inability to prevent crime, how do you think this new approach stacks up?

KLOCKARS: Actually, the people who have written as advocates of community policing have been very cautious about claims to reduce crime. If you look at the work by Skolnick and Bailey, Mark Moore, George Kelling, Trojanowicz and others, what you'll find is that they're very, very cautious on any kinds of promises to control crime. They say the goal of community policing is crime prevention. But, of course, prevention is one of those strange things; it's very hard to know what prevents something because the idea of preventing is that something

---

"The police won't reduce crime. More prisons are probably not going to reduce crime. The types of things that cause the levels of crime that we have in society are not situations that we'll be able to control by more gun legislation or by punishing more people."

---

doesn't happen. So they've been very cautious about making those promises to reduce crime, probably because we found such rare occasions on which police can do so. I don't blame the police for that failure; it's simply that the kinds of things which determine whether or not there will be more or less crime in society at any time are things over which the police have very little control. For example, the age distribution of the population—how many males in their late teens do you have? If you have a lot of them, you're going to have more crime. There's the level of freedom that we accord people, the extent to which moral, cultural and religious restraints prevail in a population, the status of the economy—all of those things, any criminologist will tell you, are the big-ticket items which determine whether or not we have more or less crime in society at any time. The police at best are a small and marginal influence on the level of crime, and no criminologist I know has much faith that the institution of police is going to be able to change things. We don't give police the means to change those things, and we wouldn't.

DESPERATE MEASURES

LEN: If, as you point out, proponents of community policing hedge their best when it comes to crime reduction,

why do you think so many police executives and politicians have embraced community policing so thoroughly?

KLOCKARS: Politicians—and I include police chiefs in that group—are absolutely desperate to show people who are unhappy with the current crime situation that they are doing something about it. It almost doesn't matter whether that something is actually having an effect; in the face of a public demand that you do something, if you don't know what to do, then you ought to do something anyway simply to satisfy that public. Just look at the dozens of things that are going on that no criminologist I know of would maintain would have any impact on crime, yet they get an enormous amount of political play: gun buyback programs—absolutely no effect; the attempts to introduce more and more gun-control legislation—there's tons of evidence that those kinds of things simply are not going to make an impact in any way on the crime rate. The politicians are desperate and the public is clamoring for it. The police won't reduce crime. More prisons are probably not going to reduce crime. The types of things that cause the levels of crime that we have in society are not going to be situations that we'll be able to control by more gun legislation or by punishing more people.

LEN: If there were fewer weapons in the hands of civilians—a measure that goes further than the Brady Law—might that have a potential for reducing crime?

KLOCKARS: If tomorrow we could snap our fingers and all weapons would vaporize, then I think there would be an effect, probably a dramatic effect, in the reduction of use of handguns in crimes. But we probably have more weapons than people in this country. It is literally impossible to take those away. Any effort to take those away will result in largely the law-abiding citizens surrendering their weapons. Certainly the last people to give them up will be people who intend to use them in crimes. The laws that we have already, such as prohibiting people from doing things like committing armed robberies, don't deter armed robbers, even with extraordinarily severe penalties. Why should we believe that an additional law which says that they can't have handguns would deter them any more? We have 20,000 gun laws on the books. A new handgun comes off the assembly line every 10 seconds, and we have programs in which politicians and police chiefs get their pictures on the front page of the paper because for a couple of weeks they had people turn in 200 weapons. It's sheer political imagery, which will have no impact whatsoever on crime.

WHAT DOES WORK?

LEN: So what *do* you think would reduce crime?

KLOCKARS: There are many ways to answer that question. There are many conditions which encourage a society to have more or less crime: the quality of education in society, the quality of moral education at home, family stability, the amount that society moves around and is dislocated, whether the ethos of society is one that finds citizens subordinated to authorities, to manners, to respect for people, versus a society that celebrates self-expression and individualism. That kind of society is more likely to be criminogenic.

The causes of crime are a densely packed collection of many, many things. You can't pull one out and say this is a cause; it's a product of our entire culture. One of the ironies is that among the things which cause crime are lots of good things that we don't want to give up—like individual freedom, values of self-expression, resistance to authority. Crime may be one of the prices we pay for the individualism that we have in this society and for the type of culture that we have. I'm not going to tell you if you want to stop crime, do X or Y; it's far more complicated than that, although I think that a lot has to do with the moral education of children, and the quality of home life that children experience. The major criminal element in our society is males in their late teens to early 20's. I think what you do is look largely toward their adolescent experience and pre-adolescent experience and you ask, what is it that's going to change that level of behavior?

It is very important to understand that the level of crime we have today, by the best estimates of the social sciences, has been relatively stable. To listen to politicians talk, it looks like we're undergoing a massive boom in violent crime. But in fact, from National Crime Survey data, which is the best that we have, our level of violent crime has been going down gradually, and it's been relatively stable. What has happened is that you have an absolute media explosion in the coverage of crime. The thesis for the evening news is: If it bleeds, it leads. Every day you and I can watch some murder or other terrible crime, and in a society with 240 million people, with the kinds of communication that we have, it's certainly possible to give us a diet of a new murder every day. Just the other night I watched a program on child abduction and we find a legislator in New York introducing legislation to make it mandatory in the schools to teach children how to avoid being abducted. We have between 50 and 100 of those abductions totally each year in the United States. The chance of a child being abducted and murdered in the United States is far less than winning the state lottery jackpot. One of the great things about modern media is that it allows us sitting in our homes in Delaware or New York to worry about a child in South Dakota, another one in California, another one in Maine, another one in upstate New York, as if they were part of our community. In fact, those experiences are extraordinarily rare.

"I'm an advocate of accountability for tax dollars. There's an enormous role in criminal justice for finding out whether the strategies used by police have any effect whatsoever."

LEN: In a number of localities over the past several years, when police chiefs and politicians sell the public on "doing

something" about crime it has entailed levying new taxes specifically for crime-control efforts. These higher taxes would seem to mean higher expectations as well. Do you think there could be any backlash if heightened expectations go unfulfilled?**

KLOCKARS: The issue always is whether or not we have the capacity to measure if that money has somehow paid off. As I look at the criminal justice system, I see enormous expenditures in all sorts of different ways, for which we have no idea whether or not those expenditures are in any way effective. We go to the citizenry to ask for more police officers, and there's no evaluation of whether it makes any difference on crime. Look at the billions and billions of dollars we have spent on the war on drugs. On the face of it, drug use has been absolutely immune to the multibillion-dollar enforcement and incarceration effort; it's as if it made no difference whatsoever. I'm an advocate of accountability for tax dollars. If some government institution or some politician tells me that he wants my tax dollars to make something happen, I want to see an evaluation to know whether or not that's money well spent. Very often there's either no evaluation made whatsoever, or if there is any kind of evaluation, it falls into the hands of people who have a vested interest in saying how successful it was. I think there's an enormous role in criminal justice for simply finding out whether or not the strategies that are used by police have any effect whatsoever.

EXHAUSTED BY CHANGE

LEN: In an earlier article, you observed that the prevailing wisdom in police management warns the successful administrator of organizational resistance to change. You went on to surmise that it's not so much resistance to change as it is the fact that police may be exhausted by it. Could you explain?

KLOCKARS: There are many myths associated with police, and one of the greatest is that the police are resistant to change. In fact, police agencies are one of the most rapidly changing institutions. They certainly have changed in many ways much faster than, say, colleges and universities have changed. They probably change faster than many contemporary businesses have changed, although I don't have any data to back me up. If you look at how quickly police have shifted from things like team policing, into foot patrol, into community policing, you find that police agencies are enormously open. They're enormously receptive in many, many respects to citizen input. They respond differently in different neighborhoods as those neighborhoods change. They're certainly receptive to all sorts of technological changes. I mean police departments have undergone dramatic computerization in many aspects; they've undergone civilianization radically in many respects. It's part of the nature of policing to be in a sort of constant exchange with the communities they police. That's a very good thing. And police departments very often are not given credit for the amount of change they do engage in.

Twenty years ago, the assumption was that any criminologist studying police was studying one of two things: corruption or brutality. And there was a kind of enmity between criminologists and police. Today, virtually all top quality research on police is research *with* police. It's researchers and police working together. They're finding problems together; the police have been extraordinarily open to researchers, far more than virtually any other industry I can think of. Police are willing and anxious for input when they become convinced that the people working with them are sincere and are not there to do some kind of hatchet job. Many of the people who run police agencies these days are my students! They ought to be receptive to research because many of them have backgrounds in which they have been educated in the importance of research, and have come out of very serious and good criminal justice training.

A SHERIFF'S VIRTUES

LEN: You've been working with sheriffs lately. Given the fact that sheriffs are elected, do you believe they have more insight into the needs of a community?

KLOCKARS: I had no experience with sheriff's departments, and frankly I had harbored the impression that the sheriff system was a kind of an antiquated way of doing police business, and that the really progressive way to get policing done was with a department with an appointed professional chief. I've come to realize over the last five years that the sheriff system has a lot of virtues to it, and many of them are quite in line with things that have been said about community policing. Sheriffs are inherently interested in the community that they serve. They're interested in keeping communications open with as many sectors of the community as possible. They're interested in serving the community and seeing that the community believes itself to be well served. Those things spring directly from the fact that the sheriff is an elected figure. I find in sheriffs' offices a very attractive attitude toward the public because it's widely understood by the sheriff—and that attitude trickles down through the troops—that the people out there are the ones that are going to determine whether or not that sheriff stays in office. As a result, there is a level of responsiveness, a level of involvement with the community in many informal ways that to me characterizes the sheriff's departments. They are virtues of the sheriff's system which, as far as I am concerned, make it a very attractive system.

LEN: In the last year of elected officials' terms, they're often too busy campaigning to be an effective presence in office. On top of that, there is the whole issue of campaign financing and what that can entail. How do sheriffs fare in that particular arena?

KLOCKARS: I think sheriffs get public support not so much by campaigning, but by doing a job day in and day out that pleases the public, and dealing in a responsive way with complaints that the public has. The sheriff system, it seems to me, is a kind of the-buck-stops-where-it-ought-to system. In a normal municipal or county government, the police are but one part of a large bureaucracy, and citizens don't really have the opportunity to evaluate that part independently. You can kick out the mayor, but that's not an evaluation of the police function. The sheriff system makes it possible for citizens to evaluate their police service independently of other government services. So you may have a sheriff who is doing a good job in a county in which the trash removal is terrible and the schools have problems and the rest of government is falling apart and deserves to be kicked out. It gives the citizens an opportunity to selectively make that evaluation of police services, and I think that's a good thing. But the thing that most impresses me about it, again, is a kind of tone within the sheriff system in which the politics are very well known, and that politics says, "We want to keep the citizens happy; we want to make them believe that they are getting a good quality service." Any sheriff with any salt is going to see to it that that attitude prevails, because that's the kind of thing that gets a sheriff re-elected.

NO EXPERIENCE NECESSARY

LEN: Sheriff's don't necessarily have to have any kind of law enforcement background to be run for or hold office. Is that necessarily a good thing?

KLOCKARS: It's a mixed thing, and let me elaborate. I don't think it's a fault that most people we send to our legislatures, or who occupy executive positions, don't have degrees in political science. I think a police chief, depending upon the size of the agency, is a person who is heavily a policy-maker. And a sheriff who is elected can summon about himself or herself whatever professional and technical expertise is necessary. Most sheriffs who are elected come to that post with police experience of one kind or another, but on those occasions when someone is elected with little police experience, you certainly can hire people who have that experience. What people want in a police chief and in a sheriff is leadership, a commitment to integrity, a person who can communicate with the community, and a person who is able to administer a police agency, or at least surround himself or herself with competent administrators. I think the head of a police agency is a very important political figure, and the difference between sheriffs and police chiefs is that, in the case of sheriffs, that politics is largely public, whereas for police chiefs the politics is much more difficult to understand because it happens inside the bowels of government bureaucracies, rather than out there in front of the people.

LEN: Look at the issue another way, then. Do you think police chiefs ought to be elected?

KLOCKARS: I don't want to take a position either way. I think that there are lots of virtues to the sheriff system, and the distinguishing feature of the sheriff system is that the sheriff is an elected official. That could be a very, very good thing. We also have, of course, absolutely superb police chiefs who are appointed. I don't think either situation guarantees a high-quality department. However, I do think there are a lot of things to recommend the sheriff's system.

A QUESTION OF FORCE

LEN: In a 1992 article for LEN on police use of force, you suggested that changes were needed to establish standards

that go beyond—as you put it—conduct that is criminal, civilly liable, or scandalous. Could you describe a model policy for police departments that wish to go one step beyond the norm?

KLOCKARS: Right now, police agencies have three standards that control their use of force, and that society has to control police use of force: the criminal law, the civil law, and the fear of scandal. By and large these are the major mechanisms that we have to set the standards for controlling excessive force by police. In no other occupation would we set the standards so low. If I told you I was looking for a doctor, and you said, "I recommend Dr. Jones because he's never been arrested for anything and he's never been sued and he's never done medicine so badly that it caused a scandal," I'd hardly be satisfied with Dr. Jones. The only place any profession like police can go to set the standards for the use of that thing which distinguishes them as a profession is into the profession itself.

So if you want to define the problem of excessive force in policing, you have to look to the skills of policing to set that standard. What I've done in a number of pieces I've written is argue for a standard that defines excessive force as any more force than a highly skilled police officer would find necessary to use. And I set this as a standard for police agencies to work to achieve, not a standard beneath which policemen should be punished.

LEN: Could you elaborate?

KLOCKARS: Every one of the approaches that police now have for defining excessive force is one that says, "If you use more force than this, you're going to be punished for it." Either you'll be punished criminally, or you'll be punished by being sued along with your agency, or you're going to be punished because it's caused a scandal. Well, as long as you define the problem of excessive force in this punitive way, you're going to be forced to define excessive force at the lowest possible level, because anything that falls beneath it is going to merit punishment.

It seems to me that the proper approach to the idea of excessive force is to ask, what does really skilled policing consist of? What does policing by the most skilled officer imaginable consist of? Let's try to direct police work toward that standard, rather than constantly engaging in cover-your-ass behavior, or all those kinds of defensive responses that police engage in to avoid the lowest standard. The whole problem in police agencies is that their approach toward the use of force is largely punitive, largely focused toward keeping police officers from violating those low standards, rather than encouraging them to work in ways that highly skilled police officers do to minimize the use of force.

GREAT EXPECTATIONS

LEN: An increasing number of departments have established civilian review boards. Does the approach you suggest necessarily preclude civilian involvement?

KLOCKARS: It does, but perhaps for exactly the wrong reason that you're suspecting. We have a fair amount of

research now which shows that civilian review boards are less demanding of police than are other police officers. The problem with civilian review boards is that they don't know enough about police to expect more of them. It would be like me trying to evaluate the behavior of a physician. I don't know enough about medicine to distinguish between highly skilled medicine and medicine which is unskilled. The people who really know the difference between good and bad policing, between highly skilled policing and less than highly skilled policing, are other police officers. The trick in police administration is to find ways to get police officers to mobilize the expectations of high police skill on themselves and others. For a whole variety of reasons, police departments don't do that. Police officers are reluctant to demand those skills from fellow officers. They're reluctant to speak out critically. Actually it all has to do with the fact that the police approach to the control of excessive force is largely punitive. Consequently, there's this defensive mentality that grows up, quite reasonably so on the part of police officers, vis-a-vis the administration in the area of use of force.

"The ATF handling of the [Waco] situation was a catastrophe. The ATF made mistake after mistake in handling that situation, and it's just unforgivable. The behavior of the FBI was even more offensive to anyone who is concerned about the use of force."

INSULT & INJURY

LEN: Last year's debacle in Waco has been characterized by some as the most extreme application of deadly force in recent times, and many police say privately that the siege and the subsequent Justice Department investigation were thoroughly mishandled. Would you agree with those assessments?

KLOCKARS: There were of course, two police events in Waco. The first was the ATF handling of the situation. It was a catastrophe, and one of an almost typical police kind; that is, it involved poor planning. I don't think police are generally very good at those kinds of mass assaults. Police are not like the military in pulling off an assault like that; policing is to a great extent an individual occupation, with police as solitary workers. The ATF just made mistake after mistake after mistake in handling that situation, and it's just unforgivable.

To my way of thinking, though, the behavior of the FBI was even more offensive to anyone who is a student of policing, and to anybody who is concerned about the use of force. The FBI had all the time in the world to make the decision that it did. It seems to me that what the FBI managed to do in that situation is, for a variety and political and organizational reasons, simply talk or think its way out of the value of the lives of those children who were hostages there. The only way that the FBI could come to conclude that the strategy they used to assault that building would be acceptable is to simply discount the potential harm to those children. There is no way in the world that if Chelsea Clinton were one of those hostages, or if a child of any one of those members of the FBI team were in that building, they would have proceeded in that fashion. It was an assault to maximize the danger to the hostages; it minimized the danger to police, but the price of it, as we see, is that something like 26 perfectly innocent children ended up getting killed. How Janet Reno can justify that, and how Bill Clinton could stand behind that decision is simply incomprehensible to me.

On top of that, I am absolutely appalled by the investigation or evaluation which was done of that subsequently by Ed Dennis. It is a whitewash of a catastrophic incident that never should have happened. The whole idea of policing is to accomplish what needs to be accomplished in ways that minimize the use of force. The FBI did not use the skill that it should have, and the consequence was that it resulted in the death of absolutely innocent children. In any hostage situation the rule that you should use to decide whether or not you ought to do something—and hostage people will tell you this—is, would I do this if it were my child or my wife or my spouse that was being held hostage? There's no way they could have reconciled that behavior if it was a person of value like that?

LEN: How else might the evaluation have been handled?

KLOCKARS: A really fascinating study of this incident would have been one that tried to answer the question of how the best and brightest most highly trained police we have—the FBI—came to devalue the lives of those children so much that they could entertain this strategy. What organization dynamics, what political dynamics, what pressures were present that brought about that transformation? We could have learned a great deal, it seems to me, from a careful study of the Waco incident over time, but I doubt that that would be possible at this date.

LEN: One would guess that the Department of Justice would not be eager to give you the money for a study like that.

KLOCKARS: Oh, no. They're already done their studies, and the tragedy is, they didn't learn anything from them. Their studies came out and vindicated the FBI and they vindicated Janet Reno, and they concluded that David Koresh was a bad guy. What they didn't take out was the question of how these highly trained, highly educated police officers could have made such a catastrophic decision. As a criminologist, and as an expert on police and police use of force, I'd like to understand that whole process of what went on in the organization, what went on in the minds of the people there that let them reach these extraordinary conclusions about what they ought to do.

FERTILE GROUND FOR RESEARCH

LEN: A moment ago, in discussing criminal justice research, you mentioned that such research now tends to be conducted *with* police. What areas do you think offer the most fertile ground for research at this time?

KLOCKARS: My own particular interest is in the use of force, and one of the things that I'd like to do is give police agencies a capacity to analyze their own use of force. Most police agencies in this country can't tell you whether they have more force this year than last. They have no capacity to analyze the incidents in which they have used force; there's no capacity to compare the levels of the use of force in the Los Angeles Police Department with Philadelphia, with New York, with Baltimore County. That is, there's no capacity to do any interagency comparisons because the way those departments record and analyze and handle the record-keeping on use of force makes those comparisons utterly impossible. A major area in which police departments can advance for research purposes is in the analysis of the use of force. From that kind of analysis we can learn, for example, that certain approaches to handling certain types of situations will over the long run produce less injury to citizens and less injury to police officers.

Let me also reiterate an important distinction that I made in a previous writing and is now, I think, having some influence. It's the difference between the use of excessive force—that phrase—and the excessive use of force. You can have excessive use of force, even though you have no use of excessive force. Let me explain what I mean. You can pursue a strategy of handling, let's say, domestic violence incidents. Let's say that you allow officers to handle those complaints singlehandedly—that is, you allow a single officer to handle domestic-violence complaints. One of the things you may find as a consequence is that those officers find themselves in lots of use-of-force situations. Now, they may perfectly justify those individual officers in using force in those situations—they may use it in self-defense, for example—but what you find is that if you assign two officers to those domestic-violence complaints, those officers may not have to use force at all. So it's possible to discover ways of handling situations so as to avoid having to use force. That's what we call the problem of excessive *use* of force, though not a use of *excessive* force. There are probably lots of opportunities in policing for police agencies to discover that handling certain types of situations in certain types of ways will reduce the need to use force. but it's only when you're able to collect data on use-of-force incidents over time that you begin to see these problems.

LEN: The Police Foundation recently published a study of use of force, and the IACP, which was involved in the study, voiced some concern about precisely the use of the phrase "excessive force." Their concern was that you can't really analyze the available data and make comparisons from department to department because you don't know how they interpret that phrase. Should the Federal Government get more involved in this area, in a sense of trying to come up with standardization of terms?

KLOCKARS: What I would like to see the Federal Government support is a uniform force-reporting system. That is, I would like to see the Federal Government develop—with the cooperation, let's say of a small group of police agencies to start out with—a way of recording use-of-force incidents that would be standard across police agencies. The whole idea of this is not to pick on any police agency; there could be very good reasons why one police agency uses force at a higher rate than another. I don't have any problem with that. But if we're going to learn about use of force by police, then we have to have some mechanism of recording those incidents and allowing the analysis of those incidents to occur. If you have all sorts of different reporting systems, with different definitions and rules, you simply can't do that analysis. So I'd like to see the Federal Government involved in creating a kind of model system for record and analyzing use-of-force incidents. That would be a great help to police. You see, it's exactly the same thing as medical researchers in evaluating the use of surgery, and whether or not one surgical procedure is more effective than another. If medical science is to advance, it has to have that kind of information on the outcomes of its practices, and the same is absolutely true of police.

THE POLITICS OF RESEARCH

LEN: Based on your long involvement with criminal justice research, to what extent do you think politics plays a role in the allocation of Federal research funds?

"We have to have some mechanism of recording [use-of-force] incidents and allowing the analysis of those incidents to occur. If you have all sorts of different reporting systems, definitions and rules, you simply can't do that analysis."

KLOCKARS: Most of my experience has been in working with the National Institute of Justice, and for that agency I have reviewed grant proposals of one kind or another in various program areas for probably 20 years I'm only one of four or five people who reviews grants for police, and my experience on those grant-review panels has left me extraordinarily impressed with the quality of work that the reviewers put in, with the sincerity of the reviewers' comments and evaluations, and with that part of the peer-review process.

Beyond that, there is a substantial amount of politics that affects the awarding of grants. That is, peer review is one part of the process, and an advisory one at that. Political considerations govern to a substantial extent the setting of the NIJ agenda.

At the core of Carl B. Klockars's two decades of studying law enforcement is a single fundamental observation—a central principle that he says applies to police "everywhere and at all times." It is that "what distinguishes police from every other domestic institution is that they exercise a general right to use coercive force." The problem, he says, is that the three standards currently used to define and control excessive force—the criminal law, the civil law and the fear of scandal—are set too low to be particularly useful.

What Klockars advocates is "a standard that defines excessive force as any more force than a highly skilled police officer would find necessary to use." It would then fall to capable police leaders "to find ways to get police officers to mobilize the expectations of high police skill on themselves and others." But because the control of excessive police force is "largely punitive," a defensive mentality exists that prevents a higher standard from being achieved.

While Klockars is considered to be one of the country's leading experts on police use of force, his scholarly research and writings cover a wide spectrum of areas. One of his earliest works, "The Professional Fence," was the result of 18 months of observing and interviewing a fence—a stolen-property broker, not a real-property marker. This book, based on a doctoral dissertation that earned him a Ph.D. from the University of Pennsylvania in 1973, was selected as one of the "outstanding academic books" of 1975, and to this day it continues to sell more than 1,000 copies annually. Since then Klockars has written several other well-received books, in-

cluding "The Idea of Police" and "Thinking about Police"—considered to be touchstones in police literature—and scores of articles and research reports. In addition to his writing and teaching at the University of Delaware, where he has been a member of the faculty since 1976, Klockars also reviews grants for the National Institute of Justice.

Of late, Klockars's scholarly interests have come to include the sheriffs' departments of the United States—a system that, he says, "has a lot of virtues to it and many of them are in line with a lot of things that have been said about community policing." One such virtue that he particularly likes is that the position is an elected one. This fundamental difference between sheriffs and police chiefs leads to a different type of political environment, says Klockars. For sheriffs, "that politics is largely public, whereas for police chiefs the politics is much more difficult to understand because it happens inside the bowels of government bureaucracies, rather than out there in front of the people." The community's evaluation of public safety efforts, in the case of sheriff's departments, takes place in the form of casting a ballot.

The ever-precise, often-controversial Klockars puts a good deal of emphasis on evaluation—or to be specific, the lack of it in the criminal justice system. He opines, "I see enormous expenditures in all sorts of different ways, for which we have no idea whether or not those expenditures are in any way effective." And when it comes to money, Klockars is firm: Throwing it hand-over-fist at crime problems just won't work.

3. POLICE

There are also relationships that grow up between the National Institute of Justice and groups like the Police Executive Research Forum and the Police Foundation, who are regular recipients of NIJ grants. In defense of those agencies, though, they're right there in Washington, they're geared up for it, they have research staffs that are focused on those issues, and we can expect a high degree of success by institutions of that kind in grant-getting in the areas in which they are specialized. If the agency is good at it, and produces—well, nothing succeeds like success. If I were the NIJ director, I don't know that I would do anything different.

LEN: If you were given a blank check, any amount of money you'd care to write in, and were told you could do with it anything in policing that you wanted to, what would you do?

KLOCKARS: I'd tell you to hold your check. The problem with policing is not money. Crime is not going to go away or get better if we throw more money at it. It's not going to go away buying more police, or more police cars, or more computers. So I'd tell you to keep your money.

Pepper Spray and In-Custody Deaths

John Granfield, Jami Onnen and Charles S. Petty, M.D.

Introduction

Responding to the need for a less-than-lethal alternative, police departments throughout the country have adopted Oleoresin Capsicum (OC) or pepper spray as a force option. OC is a naturally occurring inflammatory agent found in cayenne peppers. OC causes almost immediate swelling and burning of the eyes and breathing passages. When the agent is inhaled, the respiratory tract is inflamed, and breathing is restricted. Effects do not support high levels of physical activity such as fighting with the police.

Anecdotal reports of agent effectiveness are favorable: significant reductions in officer/arrestee injuries and in use-of-force complaints have been reported. Moreover, studies indicate that the risk of injury or death is statistically improbable (for discussion of this, see Onnen, 1993). However, cases have recently been reported where deaths have occurred subsequent to OC use. These deaths have created some concern among those in the law enforcement community, as well as among others, with regard to OC's possible role. As a result, some agencies contemplating production adoption are reluctant to begin use, while agencies using the product are seeking information affirming product safety and effectiveness.

To address this concern, the National Institute of Justice (NIJ) asked the International Association of Chiefs of Police (IACP) to collect data on in-custody death incidents where pepper spray had been used in the arrest procedure and to assess from this aggregated data whether there is a possibility that OC could be a factor in these deaths. This report will cover information resulting from the examination of these specific incidents.

Reported Incidents

An incident involving a sudden death while in police custody is not a distinct category of information reported by local, state or federal law enforcement agencies. Therefore, in order to collect some representative data on the incidents where death followed the use of OC spray, four sources of information were used: news media services, California POST, the American Civil Liberties Union of Southern California and networking among IACP members.

A total of 30 incidents were found between August of 1990 and December of 1993 in which the death of a subject occurred following a spraying with OC. The earliest incident

in this study occurred on August 27, 1990; except for one incident in 1991 and two in 1992, the remaining 26 took place in 1993. Although there is no way of knowing all the incidents that have taken place, it is logical to conclude that most occurrences would be fairly recent since the substantial growth in OC use has been over the last two years. With knowledge of 30 occurrences from 13 states, information was obtained to review the cause of death and to determine commonalities among the cases. To investigate these cases, the following procedure was used:

1. A review of the incident reports of the law enforcement agency involved.

2. A review of the medical-legal investigative office (coroner or medical examiner) records, including investigation reports and autopsy reports, together with toxicologic information and conclusions as to the cause of death.

3. A comparison of all cases where complete details existed to determine what patterns were present in the nature of the confrontations.

Information from the 30 cases revealed the following:

Age:	*Range: 24-53 years*
	20s 7
	30s 14
	40s 8
	50s 1
Gender:	Male 30
	Female 0
Race:	White 12
	Black 13
	Hispanic 5
Behavior:	Violent/Bizarre 30
Struggle:	Yes 28
	No 0
	Unknown 2
Effectiveness of OC:	Effective 4
	Ineffective 18
	Partially Effective 7
	Unknown 1

(continued)

From *Science and Technology*, March 1994, pp. 1-5. © 1994 by the International Association of Chiefs of Police. Reprinted by permission.

3. POLICE

Restraint Techniques:	Hog-tying 5
	Handcuffs 6
	Cuff/Leg Restraint 15
	Strapped to Stretcher 4
Drug/Alcohol Involved:	Yes 23
	No 5
	Unknown 2
Significant Disease Present:	Yes 12
	No 18
	Unknown 0

The 30 cases, all involving male decedents, share several commonalities. All subjects behaved in a combative and/or bizarre manner and struggled with the police. Drugs and/ or alcohol were involved in most cases. In the majority of cases, OC spray was either ineffective or less than totally effective. Generally, restraint techniques were employed subsequent to spraying, and with one exception, all deaths occurred either immediately or soon after the confrontation.

Sufficient information was obtained in 22 of the 30 cases to allow for a thorough review of the incident so a reasonable conclusion as to the cause of death could be determined. Specifically, an autopsy and the police report were necessary so an entire incident could be reviewed to ensure that all causal and/or contributory factors to the death were examined. **The reviews' results indicate that OC was not the cause of death in any of the cases.**

In the one case where OC was listed in the autopsy report as a factor in the death, the review did not substantiate that opinion. Our review concluded that, in these cases, OC was not a factor in any of the deaths and that something else caused the subject to die. More specifically, it was concluded that in 18 of the 22 cases, positional asphyxia was the cause of death, with drugs and/or disease also being contributing factors. In the remaining four cases, three involved a drug (cocaine)-related death, and one involved a drug (cocaine)/ disease-related death.

The circumstances leading to positional asphyxia in many cases were probably initiated by handcuffing subjects (behind the back) and having them on their stomachs or in a position that allowed them to end up on their stomachs. In some cases, ankle restraints were concomitantly employed with hog-tying and/or pressure on the back by an officer. Subjects were also often transported in a prone position, and a number of them were markedly overweight with "big bellies."

In such a prone, secured position, it is very difficult for any individual to breathe. In most instances, drugs (including alcohol), disease and obesity made the subject even more vulnerable to being denied proper breathing.

In conclusion, in none of the 22 cases was OC considered to be a cause of, or a contributor to, the deaths. Rather, the cause of death in the majority of cases was determined to be positional asphyxia, aggravated by drugs, disease and/ or obesity.

Custody-Related Deaths

Although OC was not implicated as a lethal factor in the reported deaths, further discussion of sudden death in custody is warranted because of the potential for certain individuals to die in police custody. While subsequent evaluation of civil and criminal liability is often incumbent on the courts, an extensive investigation by the individuals charged with determining the cause of death is also required (Mittleman and Davis, 1991). To reasonably establish the cause of death, a broad range of factors must be considered:

- Nature of the confrontation
- Weapon(s), if any, employed by officers
- Amount and duration of physical combat
- System or type of restraint employed
- Transportation of the subject
  —Destination
  —Duration
  —Mode of transport (police car, EMS vehicle)
  —Position of subject during transport
- Emergency room observations and actions
- Postmortem examination (autopsy) of subject
  —Nature of injuries
  —Diseases present
  —Drugs present
  —Other physical factors

While custody deaths are rare, they tend to share common elements which occur in a basic sequence. Subjects will often display bizarre or frenzied behavior. Almost always, the subjects are intoxicated by drugs and/or alcohol. Usually, subjects will engage in a violent struggle with the police, requiring the officers to employ some type of restraint technique. During or immediately after the struggle, the subject becomes unresponsive, goes into cardiopulmonary arrest and does not respond to resuscitation.

Experts postulate that often the mechanism of sudden custody death is an abnormal heart rhythm produced by one or more of the following: the arrhythmogenic potential of catecholamines released during the struggle, certain drugs (e.g. cocaine, amphetamines) and alcohol. All of these substances work directly on the heart and can produce fatal arrhythmias (DiMaio and DiMaio, 1989). In addition, certain restraint techniques (i.e., hog-tying and prone positioning) combined with intoxicants and catecholamines can contribute to death (DiMaio and DiMaio, 1989; O'Halloran and Lewman, 1993).

Determination of cause of death is often problematic regardless of the causative conclusions rendered. Attesting to the perils of investigating and certifying custody death, Luke and Reay contend that "there is no more slippery slope than death in custody" (1992, 98). Such deaths often follow violent struggles with police and create the potential for significant legal and departmental ramifications. Witnesses may misinterpret such events as police brutality. Family members, the news media and concerned citizens' groups may become involved and demand further case investigation and even outside case intervention. The potential complications are exacerbated by the fact that often little pathological evidence is demonstrated at the autopsy (Luke and Reay, 1992; DiMaio and DiMaio, 1989; Reay et al., 1992). When negative findings are reported, accusations of conspiracy or incompetence may be directed at the medical examiner's/coroner's office. Involved police officers may be similarly accused and subsequently required to further justify their actions.

Moreover, due to the lack of or difficulty in interpreting pathological evidence, the cause of death may be misattributed to police action (see Mittleman and Davis, 1991, for an excellent discussion of this possibility). Wetli (1991, 3) cautions that "sole reliance upon anatomical findings for the determination of the cause and manner of death is fraught with error" as "death certification must rely upon physical evidence and witness testimony." Hirsch and Adams (1993, 140) similarly warn that "the pathologist who focuses solely on anatomic causes of death is doomed to fail . . . equally important are the evaluations of the history, circumstances surrounding death, and the fatal environment."

Based on these considerations, law enforcement personnel must be aware of and familiar with deaths in custody. The benefits of such understanding are twofold: police may potentially avert death by recognizing symptomatology and thus rendering/obtaining assistance; or if a fatality does occur, police will be familiar with the problems associated with custody death investigation and certification.

General Conditions

Research suggests that four conditions may account for the majority of custody-related deaths: positional asphyxia, cocaine intoxication, excited delirium and neuroleptic malignant syndrome. Each condition is subsequently discussed, so law enforcement personnel will have a basic familiarity with some of the various presentations of these general types of custody deaths.

Positional Asphyxia. Positional asphyxia occurs when body position interferes with respiration, resulting in asphyxia (Reay et al., 1992). Positional asphyxial deaths tend to occur in a similar manner: maximally restrained subjects, unless seated upright in police vehicles, may become quiet and inactive after several minutes of transport. Respiratory difficulty is exhibited, and subjects subsequently stop breathing.

Certain factors can render individuals more susceptible to sudden death due to positional asphyxia. Such predisposing factors include drug/alcohol intoxication (Bell et al., 1992); excited delirium (O'Halloran and Lewman, 1993); and violent muscular activity. Acute alcohol intoxication is a major risk factor because respiratory drive is reduced, and subjects do not realize they are suffocating. Excited delirium combined with certain restraints (e.g., hog-tying) can also increase the susceptibility to sudden death by placing catecholamine stress on the heart. Subjects who have engaged in violent

activities are rendered more vulnerable to subsequent respiratory muscle fatigue. Such fatigue may prove fatal to a restrained subject whose movement is restricted.

Experts (Reay et al., 1992; O'Halloran and Lewman, 1993) contend that maximal, prone restraint techniques can have sudden lethal consequences. This potential is increased in intoxicated, delirious and/or violent individuals. Law enforcement personnel should employ alternative restraint methods (e.g. upright, seated positioning) whenever feasible. In situations where prone restraints are necessary, subjects should be closely and continuously monitored.

Cocaine Abuse and Toxicity. Cocaine is an agent that stimulates both the central nervous and the cardiovascular systems. Pharmacologically, cocaine constricts blood vessels, elevates heart rate, raises blood pressure and increases body temperature. Such effects have produced lethal anatomic catastrophes in individuals without underlying preexisting anatomic disease(s). Mittleman and Wetli (1991) note that the medical literature clearly documents cocaine-induced vasoconstriction, vasospasm and hypertension that has culminated in spontaneous intracranial hemorrhage and infarcts of the cerebrum (i.e. strokes), kidney and intestinal tract. Cocaine may also be the cause of death in cardiovascular incidents where there is no anatomic abnormality (Mittleman and Wetli, 1987). Likewise, these effects can substantially compromise an already diseased heart or vascular system, and potentially culminate in fatalities (Mittleman and Wetli, 1987).

Of further concern is the fact that there is not an individual minimal lethal dose since fatalities have been associated with a wide range of concentrations including very low concentrations (Mittleman and Wetli, 1987). For example, the sudden occurrence of seizures and death has been documented in recreational users who chronically use even small amounts of cocaine (Fishbein and Pease, in press). Apparently, this phenomenon is the result of a kindling effect, a reverse tolerance whereby the sensitivity of the brain to cocaine is increased, and the brain's seizure threshold is lowered. Fishbein and Pease (in press) note that such potentially lethal seizures may occur any time.

Alcohol substantially increases the risk of sudden death when combined with cocaine. Researchers (Escobedo et al., 1991) suggest that the cardiotoxic effects of alcohol potentiates the cardiotoxic effects of cocaine, thus increasing the risk of overdose death. Wetli (1993) indicates that the risk of sudden death is increased 18-fold when cocaine is used in combination with alcohol. This may be due to the production of cocaethylene, a result of this combination.

Mittleman and Wetli (1987) note that recreational cocaine use may be lethal via its pharmacologic effects. They argue that the role of cocaine in precipitating a hypertensive or cardiovascular crisis must seriously be considered when investigating sudden death in a population where cocaine abuse is prevalent. Police should be aware of the potential lethality of cocaine use.

Cocaine-Induced Excited Delirium. Excited delirium is an acute mental disorder characterized by impaired thinking, disorientation, visual hallucinations and illusions (Wetli and Fishbain, 1985). Behavior is consistent, purposeless and often violent. Significantly increased body temperature (hyperthermia) is part of the syndrome (O'Halloran and Lewman, 1993). Excited delirium may be part of the spectrum of manic-depressive psychosis, chronic schizophrenia and/or acute drug intoxication (cocaine, PCP and amphetamines).

The most serious psychiatric consequence of cocaine abuse is cocaine-induced excited delirium (cocaine psychosis), which may be associated with sudden death (Wetli and Fishbain, 1985). Although most individuals will respond to treatment, cocaine-induced excited delirium is usually regarded as a potentially lethal medical emergency. Wetli (1992) notes that hyperthermia is a negative prognostic factor frequently associated with sudden, unexpected cocaine-induced delirium deaths.

Cocaine-induced excited delirium fatalities tend to occur in a stereotypic manner, with subjects exhibiting similar behaviors. Generally, symptoms begin with an acute onset of intense paranoia, immediately followed by violent and/or bizarre behavior. Such behaviors include displaying violence toward inanimate objects (particularly glass), running, screaming and stripping off clothing (Wetli, 1992). Subjects appear psychotic, exhibit great strength and appear to have a significantly diminished sense of pain. Police must necessarily restrain such individuals, and a violent struggle generally ensues; however, force used by police often has minimal effects. Sudden death occurs either during or immediately after the struggle. Wetli (1992) explains that the mechanism of death is uncertain, and autopsy findings are generally nonspecific, revealing only injuries sustained from the struggle with the police.

Police officers should be aware of the potential for sudden unexpected death resulting from cocaine-induced excited delirium. Police should be able to immediately recognize attendant symptoms, including any one or combination of the following:

- bizarre and/or aggressive behavior
- shouting
- paranoia
- panic
- violence toward others
- unexpected physical strength
- sudden tranquility

Subjects exhibiting any of these symptoms should be promptly transported to a nearby medical facility. Close and constant monitoring during transit is warranted.

Neuroleptic Malignant Syndrome. Neuroleptic malignant syndrome (NMS) is another recognized cause of sudden, unexpected death. This syndrome presents characteristics in a manner very similar to excited delirium (Reay et al., 1992). Neuroleptic malignant syndrome generally occurs in psychiatric patients who are taking antipsychotic medication (i.e., neuroleptics). Physical exhaustion, dehydration and organic brain disease are additional predisposing factors. Symptoms include hyperthermia, fluctuating levels of consciousness and hypotonicity (i.e. limpness) of skeletal muscles.

NMS may also occur in individuals who are not being treated with such medication. This specific form is often diagnosed as acute exhaustive mania. The condition is poorly understood and may be related to a cardiac event due to psychological stress (Reay et al., 1992). Hirsch and Adams (in Spitz, 1993) contend that the common lay term "scared to death" is literally true: psychological stress can induce fatal cardiac arrhythmias. However, autopsy findings are generally negative, seldom revealing a pathological cause of death (Reay et al., 1992).

Anyone exhibiting symptoms of NMS or acute exhaustive mania should be taken immediately to a medical facility for evaluation. Optimally, this transport should involve two officers, thus allowing for the close and constant monitoring of the subject in custody.

Conclusion

Sudden death in custody is neither a new phenomenon nor attributable to the use of OC spray. Rather, sudden custody death can occur at any time for a variety of reasons. Any law enforcement agency may experience a sudden custody death, regardless of OC involvement. Consequently, officer awareness and recognition of risk indicators are necessary to ensure subject safety and minimize the risk of sudden custody death. These indicators generally include:

- bizarre/violent activity
- obesity—especially "big bellies"
- drug and/or alcohol involvement
- apparent ineffectiveness of spray

Diligent observation and constant monitoring of subjects displaying any one or a combination of the indicators are procedurally warranted. Furthermore, the use of maximal, prone restraint techniques should be avoided. If prone positioning is required, subjects should be closely and continuously monitored. By implementing such procedural protocols, the potential for custody deaths may be lessened.

References

Bell, M.D., V.J. Rao, C.V. Wetli and R.N. Rodriguez. "Positional Asphyxiation in Adults: A Series of 30 Cases from the Dade and Broward County Florida Medical Examiner Offices from 1982 to 1990." *The American Journal of Forensic Medicine and Pathology.* 1992. 13(2): 101-107.

DiMaio, D.J. and V.J. DiMaio. *Forensic Pathology.* New York: Elsevier. 1989.

Escobedo, L.G., A.J. Ruttenber, M.A. Agocs, R.F. Anda and C.V. Wetli. "Emergency Patterns of Cocaine Use and The Epidemic of Cocaine Overdose Deaths in Dade County, Florida." *Archives of Pathology* and Laboratory Medicine. 1991. 115: 900-905.

Fishbein, D. and S. Pease. The Dynamics of Drug Abuse. Needham Heights, Massachusetts: Allyn & Bacon, Inc. In press.

Hirsch, C.S. and V.I. Adams. "Sudden and Unexpected Death from Natural Causes in Adults." In W.U. Spitz, ed., Medicolegal Investigation of Death. Springfield, Illinois: Charles C. Thomas, 1993. pp. 137-174.

Luke, J.L. and D.T. Reay. "The Perils of Investigating and Certifying Deaths in Police Custody." The American Journal of Forensic Medicine and Pathology. 1992. 13(2): 98-100.

Mittleman, R.E. and J.J. Davis. "Death From Custody?" Forensic Pathology. 1991. 33(2): 1-4.

Mittleman, R.E. and C.V. Wetli. "Cocaine and Sudden 'Natural Death.'" Journal of Forensic Sciences. 1987. 32(1): 11-19.

Mittleman, R.E. and C.V. Wetli. "The Pathology of Cocaine Abuse." In Advances in Pathology and Laboratory Medicine. St. Louis, Misssouri: Mosby-Yearbook, Inc., 1991. pp. 37-73.

O'Halloran, R.L. and L.V. Lewman. "Restraint Asphyxiation in Excited Delirium." The American Journal of Forensic Medicine and Pathology. 14(4): 289-295, 1993.

Onnen, J. Oleoresin Capsicum. Alexandria, VA: International Association of Chiefs of Police, 1993.

Reay, D.T., C.L. Fligner, A.D. Stilwell and J. Arnold. "Positional Asphyxia During Law Enforcement Transport." The American Journal of Forensic Medicine and Pathology. 1992. 13(2): 90-97.

Wetli, C.V. "Supplement to ASCP Check Sample FP 91-2 (FP-175)." Forensic Pathology. 1991. 33(2).

Wetli, C.V. "The Pathology of Cocaine: Perspectives From the Autopsy Table." National Institute on Drug Abuse Research Monograph 123: 173-182, 1992.

Wetli, C.V. Personal Communication. December 10, 1993.

Wetli, C.V. and D.A. Fishbain. "Cocaine-Induced Psychosis and Sudden Death in Recreational Cocaine Users." Journal of Forensic Sciences, 30(3): 873-880, 1985.

The Judicial System

The American people really got an inside look at the American judicial system in 1994 as hour upon hour the television screen was filled with scenes from the O. J. Simpson hearings, the murder trial of the Menendez brothers (Erik and Lyle), and the malicious wounding trial of Lorena Bobbitt. The various players in the system, judges, prosecutors, and defense lawyers were scrutinized, and some articles in this unit present several negative viewpoints concerning the attorneys in the court process. "The Abuse of Power in the Prosecutor's Office" is a critical analysis of the position of the prosecutor. It is offered, not as an indictment of all prosecutors, but to stimulate discussion of possible areas of abuse. On the other hand, "Why Lawyers Lie" presents a discussion of the ethical problems faced by defense lawyers in controversial cases. "The Trials of the Public Defender" presents a sympathetic view of the problems faced by this overworked professional.

The problems of selecting a jury and the deliberation process of the jury has also been the focus of much discussion. The article "Inside the Mind of the Juror" discusses a study concerning the way death penalty juries reach decisions, and "Jury Consultants: Boon or Bane?" presents pros and cons concerning this growing technique in jury selection.

What impact, if any, do television talk shows have on the judicial process? In "Fault Lines" the author explores some of the results in recent controversial cases, such as the Menendez brothers' mistrial and the Lorena Bobbitt trial, and she discusses how these cases were handled by the television talk show media.

The articles "Inside the Mind of the Juror" and "Racial, Ethnic, and Gender Bias in the Courts: *What Progress Have We Made, and What Can Be Done?*" indicate that there are still signs of bias in the court system.

Looking Ahead: Challenge Questions

Is there too much television coverage of high-profile criminal cases?

Should lawyers refrain from being "spin doctors" on television?

Is the American jury system in peril as our communication network expands?

ABUSE OF POWER IN THE PROSECUTOR'S OFFICE

Bennett L. Gershman

Bennett L. Gershman is professor of law at Pace University. He is the author of Prosecutorial Misconduct *and several articles on law dealing with such topics as entrapment and police and prosecutorial ethics. For ten years, he was a prosecutor in New York.*

The prosecutor is the most dominant figure in the American criminal justice system. As the Supreme Court recently observed, "Between the private life of the citizen and the public glare of criminal accusation stands the prosecutor. [The prosecutor has] the power to employ the full machinery of the State in scrutinizing any given individual." Thus, the prosecutor decides whether or not to bring criminal charges; whom to charge; what charges to bring; whether a defendant will stand trial, plead guilty, or enter a correctional program in lieu of criminal charges; and whether to confer immunity from prosecution. In jurisdictions that authorize capital punishment, the prosecutor literally decides who shall live and who shall die. Moreover, in carrying out these broad functions, the prosecutor enjoys considerable independence from the courts, administrative superiors, and the public. A prosecutor cannot be forced to bring criminal charges, or be prevented from bringing them. Needless to say, the awesome power that prosecutors exercise is susceptible to

abuse. Such abuses most frequently occur in connection with the prosecutor's power to bring charges; to control the information used to convict those on trial; and to influence juries.

The prosecutor's charging power includes the virtually unfettered discretion to invoke or deny punishment, and therefore the power to control and destroy people's lives. Such prosecutorial discretion has been called "tyrannical," "lawless," and "most dangerous." Prosecutors may not unfairly select which persons to prosecute. But this rule is difficult to enforce, and the courts almost always defer to the prosecutor's discretion. In one recent case, for example, a prosecutor targeted for prosecution a vocal opponent of the Selective Service system who refused to register, rather than any of nearly a million nonvocal persons who did not register. The proof showed that the defendant clearly was selected for prosecution not because he failed to register but because he exercised his First Amendment rights. This was a legally impermissible basis for prosecution. Nevertheless, the courts refused to disturb the prosecutor's decision, because there was no clear proof of prosecutorial bad faith. Many other disturbing examples exist of improper selection based on race, sex, religion, and the exercise of constitutional rights. These

This article first appeared in *The World & I,* June 1991, pp. 477-487. Reprinted by permission of *The World & I,* a publication of the Washington Times Corporation. © 1991.

cases invariably are decided in the prosecutor's favor. The reasoning is circular. The courts presume that prosecutors act in good faith, and that the prosecutor's expertise, law enforcement plans, and priorities are ill suited to judicial review.

Unfair selectivity is one of the principal areas of discretionary abuse. Another is prosecutorial retaliation in the form of increased charges after defendants raise statutory or constitutional claims. Prosecutors are not allowed to be vindictive in response to a defendant's exercise of rights. Nevertheless, proving vindictiveness, as with selectiveness, is virtually impossible. Courts simply do not probe the prosecutor's state of mind. For example, prosecutors often respond to a defendant's unwillingness to plead guilty to a crime by bringing higher charges. In one recent case, a defendant charged with a petty offense refused to plead guilty despite prosecutorial threats to bring much higher charges. The prosecutor carried out his threat and brought new charges carrying a sentence of life imprisonment. The court found the prosecutor's conduct allowable. Although the prosecutor behaved in a clearly retaliatory fashion, the court nevertheless believed that the prosecutor needed this leverage to make the system work. If the prosecutor could not threaten defendants by "upping the ante," so the court reasoned, there would be fewer guilty pleas and the system would collapse.

Finally, some prosecutions are instituted for illegitimate personal objectives as opposed to ostensibly valid law enforcement objectives. Such prosecutions can be labeled demagogic and usually reveal actual prosecutorial malice or evil intent. Telltale signs of demagoguery often include the appearance of personal vendettas, political crusades, and witch hunts. Examples of this base practice abound. They have involved prosecutions based on racial or political hostility; prosecutions motivated by personal and political gain; and prosecutions to discourage or coerce the exercise of constitutional rights. One notorious example was New Orleans District Attorney James Garrison's prosecution of Clay Shaw for the Kennedy assassination. Other examples have included the prosecutions of labor leader James Hoffa, New York attorney Roy Cohn, and civil rights leader Dr. Martin Luther King.

HIDING EVIDENCE

A prosecutor's misuse of power also occurs in connection with legal proof. In the course of an investigation, in pretrial preparation, or even during a trial, prosecutors often become aware of information that might exonerate a defendant. It is not unusual for the prosecutor to have such proof, in view of the acknowledged superiority of law enforcement's investigative resources and its early access to crucial evidence. The adversary system relies on a fair balance of opposing forces. But one of the greatest threats to rational and fair fact-finding in criminal cases comes from the prosecutor's hiding evidence that might prove a defendant's innocence. Examples of prosecutorial suppression of exculpatory evidence are numerous. Such conduct is pernicious for several reasons: It skews the ability of the adversary system to function properly by denying to the defense crucial proof; it undermines the public's respect for and confidence in the public prosecutor's office; and it has resulted in many defendants being unjustly convicted, with the consequent loss of their liberty or even their lives.

Consider the following recent examples. Murder convictions of Randall Dale Adams in Texas, James Richardson and Joseph Brown in Florida, and Eric Jackson in New York all were vacated because the prosecutors hid crucial evidence that would have proved these defendants' innocence. The Adams case—popularized by the film *The Thin Blue Line*—depicts Texas "justice" at its worst. Adams was convicted in 1977 of murdering a policeman and sentenced to die largely on the testimony of a juvenile with a long criminal record who made a secret deal with the prosecutor to implicate Adams, and the testimony of two eyewitnesses to the killing. The juvenile actually murdered the policeman, as he later acknowledged. At Adams' trial, however, the prosecutor suppressed information about the deal and successfully kept from the jury the juvenile's lengthy record.

4. THE JUDICIAL SYSTEM

The prosecutor also withheld evidence that the two purported eyewitnesses had failed to identify Adams in a line-up, and permitted these witnesses to testify that they had made a positive identification of Adams. A Texas court recently freed Adams, finding that the prosecutor suborned perjury and knowingly suppressed evidence.

Richardson—whose case was memorialized in the book *Arcadia* was condemned to die for poisoning to death his

tor misrepresented to the jury that ballistics evidence proved the defendant's guilt, when in fact the prosecutor knew that the ballistics report showed that the bullet that killed the deceased could not have been fired from the defendant's weapon.

Eric Jackson was convicted of murder in 1980 for starting a fire at Waldbaum's supermarket in Brooklyn in which a roof collapsed and six firefighters died. Years later, the attorney who repre-

---

Abuses most frequently occur in connection with the prosecutor's power to bring charges, to control the information used to convict those on trial, and to influence juries.

---

seven children in 1967. The prosecutor claimed that Richardson, a penniless farm worker, killed his children to collect insurance. A state judge last year overturned the murder conviction, finding that the prosecutor had suppressed evidence that would have shown Richardson's innocence. The undisclosed evidence included a sworn statement from the children's babysitter that she had killed the youngsters; a sworn statement from a cellmate of Richardson's that the cellmate had been beaten by a sheriff's deputy into fabricating his story implicating Richardson; statements from other inmates contradicting their claims that Richardson confessed to them; and proof that Richardson had never purchased any insurance.

Brown's murder conviction recently was reversed by the Eleventh Circuit. Brown was only hours away from being electrocuted when his execution was stayed. That court found that the prosecutor "knowingly allowed material false testimony to be introduced at trial, failed to step forward and make the falsity known, and knowingly exploited the false testimony in its closing argument to the jury." The subornation of perjury related to the testimony of a key prosecution witness who falsely denied that a deal had been made with the prosecutor, and the prosecutor's misrepresentation of that fact to the court. In addition, the prosecu-

sented the families of the deceased firemen in a tort action discovered that one of the prosecutor's expert witnesses at the trial had informed the prosecutor that the fire was not arson related, but was caused by an electrical malfunction. At a hearing in the fall of 1988, the prosecutor consistently maintained that nothing had been suppressed and offered to disclose pertinent documents. The judge rejected the offer and personally inspected the prosecutor's file. The judge found in that file two internal memoranda from two different assistant district attorneys to an executive in the prosecutor's office. Each memorandum stated that the expert witness had concluded that the fire had resulted from an electrical malfunction and had not been deliberately set—and that the expert's conclusion presented a major problem for the prosecution. None of this information was ever revealed to the defense. On the basis of the above, the court vacated the conviction and ordered the defendant's immediate release.

To be sure, disclosure is the one area above all else that relies on the prosecutor's good faith and integrity. If the prosecutor hides evidence, it is likely that nobody will ever know. The information will lay buried forever in the prosecutor's files. Moreover, most prosecutors, if they are candid, will concede that their inclination in this area is not to reveal information that might damage his or her case. Ironically, in this important area in which the prosecutor's fairness, integrity, and good faith are so dramatically put to the test, the courts have defaulted. According to the courts, the prosecutor's good or bad faith in secreting evidence is irrelevant. It is the character of the evidence that counts, not the character of the prosecutor. Thus, even if a violation is deliberate, and with an intent to harm the defendant, the courts will not order relief unless the evidence is so crucial that it would have changed the verdict. Thus, there is no real incentive for prosecutors to disclose such evidence.

Hopefully, in light of the recent disclosures of prosecutorial misconduct, courts, bar associations, and even legislatures will wake up to the quagmire in criminal justice. These bodies should act vigorously and aggressively to deter and punish the kinds of violations that recur all too frequently. Thus, reversals should be required automatically for deliberate suppression of evidence, and the standards for reversal for nondeliberate suppression relaxed; disciplinary action against prosecutors should be the rule rather than the exception; and legislation should be enacted making it a crime for prosecutors to willfully suppress evidence resulting in a defendant's conviction.

MISBEHAVING IN THE COURTROOM TO SWAY THE JURY

Finally, the prosecutor's trial obligations often are violated. The duties of the prosecuting attorney during a trial were well stated in a classic opinion fifty years ago. The interest of the prosecutor, the court wrote, "is not that it shall win a case, but that justice shall be done. As such, he is in a peculiar and very definite sense the servant of the law, the twofold aim of which is that guilt shall not escape or innocence suffer. He may prosecute with earnestness and vigor—indeed, he should do so. But, while he may strike hard blows, he is not at liberty to strike a foul one."

Despite this admonition, prosecutors continually strike "foul blows." In one leading case of outrageous conduct, a prosecutor concealed from the jury in a murder case the fact that a pair of undershorts

with red stains on it, a crucial piece of evidence, was stained not by blood but by paint. In another recent case, a prosecutor, in his summation, characterized the defendant as an "animal," told the jury that "the only guarantee against his future crimes would be to execute him," and that he should have "his face blown away by a shotgun." In another case, the prosecutor argued that the defendant's attorney knew the defendant was guilty; otherwise he would have put the defendant on the witness stand.

The above examples are illustrative of common practices today, and the main reason such misconduct occurs is quite simple: It works. Indeed, several studies have shown the importance of oral advocacy in the courtroom, as well as the effect produced by such conduct. For example, a student of trial advocacy often is told of the importance of the opening statement. Prosecutors would undoubtedly agree that the opening statement is indeed crucial. In a University of Kansas study, the importance of the opening statement was confirmed. From this study, the authors concluded that in the course of any given trial, the jurors were affected most by the first strong presentation that they saw. This finding leads to the conclusion that if a prosecutor were to present a particularly strong opening argument, the jury would favor the prosecution throughout the trial. Alternatively, if the prosecutor were to provide a weak opening statement, followed by a strong opening statement by the defense, then, according to the authors, the jury would favor the defense during the trial. It thus becomes evident that the prosecutor will be best served by making the strongest opening argument possible, thereby assisting the jury in gaining a better insight into what they are about to hear and see. The opportunity for the prosecutor to influence the jury at this point in the trial is considerable, and many prosecutors use this opportunity to their advantage, even if the circumstances do not call for lengthy or dramatic opening remarks.

An additional aspect of the prosecutor's power over the jury is suggested in a University of North Carolina study, which found that the more arguments counsel raises to support the different substantive arguments offered, the more the jury will believe in that party's case. Moreover, this study found that there is not necessarily a correlation between the amount of objective information in the argument and the persuasiveness of the presentation.

For the trial attorney, then, this study clearly points to the advantage of raising as many issues as possible at trial. For the prosecutor, the two studies taken together would dictate an "action-packed" opening statement, containing as many arguments as can be mustered, even those that might be irrelevant or unnecessary to convince the jury of the defendant's guilt. The second study would also dictate the same strategy for the closing argument. Consequently, a prosecutor who through use of these techniques attempts to assure that the jury knows his case may, despite violating ethical standards to seek justice, be "rewarded" with a guilty verdict. Thus, one begins to perceive the incentive that leads the prosecutor to misbehave in the courtroom.

Similar incentives can be seen with respect to the complex problem of controlling evidence to which the jury may have access. It is common knowledge that in the course of any trial, statements frequently are made by the attorneys or witnesses despite the fact that these statements may not be admissible as evidence. Following such a statement, the trial judge may, at the request of opposing counsel, instruct the jury to disregard what they have heard. Most trial lawyers, if they are candid, will agree that it is virtually impossible for jurors realistically to disregard these inadmissible statements. Studies here again demonstrate that our intuition is correct and that this evidence often is considered by jurors in reaching a verdict.

For example, an interesting study conducted at the University of Washington tested the effects of inadmissible evidence on the decisions of jurors. The authors of the test designed a variety of scenarios whereby some jurors heard about an incriminating piece of evidence while other jurors did not. The study found that the effect of the inadmissible evidence was directly correlated to the strength of the prosecutor's case. The authors of the study reported that when the prosecutor presented a weak case, the inadmissible evidence did in fact prejudice the jurors. Furthermore, the judge's admonition to the jurors to disregard certain evidence did not have the same effect as when the evidence had not been mentioned at all. It had a prejudicial impact anyway.

However, the study also indicated that when there was a strong prosecution case, the inadmissible evidence had little, if any, effect. Nonetheless, the most significant conclusion from the study is that inadmissible evidence had its most prejudicial impact when there was little other evidence upon which the jury could base a decision. In this situation, "the controversial evidence becomes quite salient in the jurors' minds."

Finally, with respect to inadmissible evidence and stricken testimony, even if

---

In one leading case of outrageous conduct, a prosecutor concealed from the jury in a murder case the fact that a pair of undershorts with red stains on it, a crucial piece of evidence, was stained not by blood but by paint.

---

one were to reject all of the studies discussed, it is still clear that although "stricken testimony may tend to be rejected in open discussion, it does have an impact, perhaps even an unconscious one, on the individual juror's judgment." As with previously discussed points, this factor—the unconscious effect of stricken testimony or evidence—will generally not be lost on the prosecutor who is in tune with the psychology of the jury.

The applicability of these studies to the issue of prosecutorial misconduct, then, is quite clear. Faced with a difficult case in which there may be a problem of proof, a prosecutor might be tempted to try to sway the jury by adverting to a matter that might be highly prejudicial. In this connection, another study has suggested that the jury will more likely consider inadmissible evidence that favors conviction.

Despite this factor of "defense favoritism," it is again evident that a prosecutor may find it rewarding to misconduct himself or herself in the courtroom. Of course, a prosecutor who adopts the unethical norm and improperly allows jurors to hear inadmissible proof runs the risk of jeopardizing any resulting conviction. In a situation where the prosecutor feels that he has a weak case, however, a subsequent reversal is not a particularly effective sanction when a conviction might have been difficult to achieve in the first place. Consequently, an unethical courtroom "trick" can be a very attractive idea to the prosecutor who feels he must win. Additionally, there is always the possibility of another conviction even after an appellate reversal. Indeed, while a large number of cases are dismissed following remand by an appellate court, nearly one-half of reversals still result in some type of conviction. Therefore, a pros-

moral standards, the problem of courtroom misconduct will inevitably be tolerated by the public.

Moreover, when considering the problems facing the prosecutor, one also must consider the tremendous stress under which the prosecutor labors on a daily basis. Besides the stressful conditions faced by the ordinary courtroom litigator, prosecuting attorneys, particularly those in large metropolitan areas, are faced with huge and very demanding caseloads. As a result of case volume and time demands, prosecutors may not be able to take advantage of opportunities to relax and recover from the constant onslaught their emotions face every day in the courtroom.

Under these highly stressful conditions, it is understandable that a prosecutor occasionally may find it difficult to face these everyday pressures and to resist temptations to behave unethically. It is not unreasonable to suggest that the conditions under which the prosecutor works can have a profound effect on his attempt to maintain high moral and ethical standards. Having established this hy-

An unethical courtroom ''trick'' can be a very attractive idea to the prosecutor who feels he must win.

ecutor can still succeed in obtaining a conviction even after his misconduct led to a reversal.

An additional problem in the area of prosecutor-jury interaction is the prosecutor's prestige; since the prosecutor represents the "government," jurors are more likely to believe him. Put simply, prosecutors are the "good guys" of the legal system, and because they have such glamor, they often may be tempted to use this advantage in an unethical manner. This presents a problem in that the average citizen may often forgive prosecutors for ethical indiscretions, because conviction of criminals certainly justifies in the public eye any means necessary. Consequently, unless the prosecutor is a person of high integrity and able to uphold the highest

pothesis, we see yet another reason why courtroom misconduct may occur.

WHY PROSECUTORIAL MISCONDUCT PERSISTS

Although courtroom misconduct may in many instances be highly effective, why do such practices continue in our judicial system? A number of reasons may account for this phenomenon, perhaps the most significant of which is the harmless error doctrine. Under this doctrine, an appellate court can affirm a conviction despite the presence of serious misconduct during the trial. As one judge stated, the "practical objective of tests of harmless error is to conserve judicial resources by enabling appellate courts to cleanse the judicial process of prejudicial error without becoming mired in harmless error."

Although this definition portrays harmless error as having a most desirable consequence, this desirability is undermined when the prosecutor is able to misconduct himself without fear of sanction. Additionally, since every case is different, what constitutes harmless error in one case may be reversible error in another case. Consequently, harmless error determinations do not offer any significant precedents by which prosecutors can judge the status of their behavior. Moreover, harmless error determinations are essentially absurd. In order to apply the harmless error rule, appellate judges attempt to evaluate how various evidentiary items or instances of prosecutorial misconduct may have affected the jury's verdict. Although it may be relatively simple in some cases to determine whether improper conduct during a trial was harmless, there are many instances when such an analysis cannot be properly made but nevertheless is made. There are numerous instances in which appellate courts are deeply divided over whether or not a given error was harmless. The implications of these contradictory decisions are significant, for they demonstrate the utter failure of appellate courts to provide incentives for the prosecutor to control his behavior. If misconduct can be excused even when reasonable judges differ as to the extent of harm caused by such misbehavior, then very little guidance is given to a prosecutor to assist him in determining the propriety of his actions. Clearly, without such guidance, the potential for misconduct significantly increases.

A final point when analyzing why prosecutorial misconduct persists is the unavailability or inadequacy of penalties visited upon the prosecutor personally in the event of misconduct. Punishment in our legal system comes in varying degrees. An appellate court can punish a prosecutor by simply cautioning him not

to act in the same manner again, reversing his case, or, in some cases, identifying by name the prosecutor who misconducted himself. Even these punishments, however, may not be sufficient to dissuade prosecutors from acting improperly. One noteworthy case describes a prosecutor who appeared before the appellate court on a misconduct issue for the third time, each instance in a different case.

Perhaps the ultimate reason for the ineffectiveness of the judicial system in curbing prosecutorial misconduct is that prosecutors are not personally liable for their misconduct. During the course of a trial, the prosecutor is absolutely shielded from any civil liability that might arise due to his or her misconduct, even if that misconduct was performed with malice. To be sure, there is clearly a necessary level of immunity accorded all government officials. Without such immunity, much of what is normally done by officials in authority might not be performed, out of fear that their practices would later be deemed harmful or improper. Granting prosecutors a certain level of immunity is reasonable. Allowing prosecutors to be completely shielded from civil liability in the event of misconduct, however, provides no deterrent to courtroom misconduct.

For the prosecutor, the temptation to cross over the allowable ethical limit must often be tremendous, because of the distinct advantages that such misconduct creates with respect to assisting the prosecutor to win his case by effectively influencing the jury. Most prosecutors must inevitably be subject to this temptation. It takes a constant effort on the part of every prosecutor to maintain the high moral standards necessary to avoid such temptations. Despite the frequent occurrences of courtroom misconduct, appellate courts have not provided significant incentives to deter it. Inroads will not be made in the effort to end prosecutorial misconduct until the courts decide to take a stricter, more consistent approach to this problem.

THE TRIALS OF THE
Public
Defender

**Overworked and underpaid lawyers serve up a brand of
justice that is not always in their clients' best interests**

JILL SMOLOWE

EVERY DAY, AS HE AMBLES through the cobwebbed halls of the New Orleans criminal court building, public defender Richard Teissier feels he violates his clients' constitutional rights. The Sixth Amendment established, and the landmark *Gideon* Supreme Court case affirmed, the right of poor people to legal counsel. At any given moment, when Teissier is representing some 90 accused murderers, rapists and robbers, his office has no money to hire experts or track down witnesses; its law library consists of a set of lawbooks spirited away from a dead judge's chambers.

With so many clients and so few resources, Teissier decided he could not possibly do justice to them all. So he filed suit against himself. He demanded that the court judge his work inadequate, and find more money for more lawyers. A judge agreed and declared the state's indigent-defense system unconstitutional. The ruling is now on appeal before the Louisiana Supreme Court. "This is a test of whether there is justice in the United States," Teissier says. "If you're only going to pay it lip service then get rid of *Gideon.*"

Thirty years ago last week, the Supreme Court unanimously voted in favor of Clarence Earl Gideon, an uneducated gambler and petty thief who insisted on his right to legal counsel. "Any person

haled into court who is too poor to hire a lawyer cannot be assured a fair trial unless counsel is provided for him," wrote Justice Hugo Black. "This seems to us to be an obvious truth." Over the next two decades the court expanded the protection to apply to all criminal cases and stressed that the representation must be "effective." But today, as defenders of indigents handle a flood of cases with meager resources, the debate rages on whether the promise of *Gideon* has been fulfilled.

Most public defenders think not. In Memphis, lawyers lament the plead-'em-and-speed-'em-through pace. "It reminds me of the old country song we have here in Tennessee: 'We're not making love, we're just keeping score,'" says chief public defender AC Wharton. Across the country, lawyers watch with frustration as the bulk of criminal-justice funds goes to police protection, prisons and prosecutors, leaving just 2.3% for public defense services. "We aren't being given the same weapons," says Mary Broderick of the National Legal Aid and Defender Association. "It's like trying to deal with smart bombs when all you've got is a couple of cap pistols."

During the war on crime of the '70s and the war on drugs of the '80s, funneling money to defend suspects was a low priority. Meanwhile, the ranks of police and prosecutors were beefed up, leading to

more arrests, more trials and more work for public defenders. "Indigent defense is a cause without a constituency," says Stephen Bright, director of the Southern Center for Human Rights. Over the years, states have unenthusiastically devised three strategies to handle indigent cases: public defender offices, court-appointed lawyers and contract systems. In all cases, the emphasis is on holding costs down. Justice—and sometimes people's lives—can get lost in the mix.

PUBLIC DEFENDERS: NO RESPECT

"Felonies worry you to death, misdemeanors work you to death," says Mel Tennenbaum, a division chief in the Los Angeles public defenders' office. "We're underappreciated and misunderstood." L.A. lawyer David Carleton had his teeth loosened by a client who didn't like his plea arrangement. Manhattan's Judith White needs all seven days of the week to handle her load of drug cases—a task she continues to tackle even since a crack addict murdered her father four years ago. When Lynne Borsuk filed a motion with Georgia's Fulton County Superior Court seeking to reduce her load of 122 open cases, she was demoted to juvenile court. She was lucky; others have been fired for similar actions.

Across the country, the lawyers who staff big-city public defender offices strike a common note: they get no respect. "Clients figure if we were really good, we'd be out there making big money," says Maria Cavalluzzi, a Los Angeles public defender. In courthouse waiting areas—known variously as the Tombs, the Pits, the Tank—defendants cavalierly dismiss their free counselors as "dump trucks," a term that reflects their view that public defenders are more interested in dumping cases than mounting rigorous defenses.

The typical public defender is underpaid and overwhelmed. When Jacquelyn Robins was appointed New Mexico's state public defender in 1985, there were six lawyers in Albuquerque's Metro court to handle the annual load of 13,000 misdemeanor cases. Three years later Robins persuaded state legislators to put up funds for three more lawyers. Even then, lawyers could manage only cursory conferences with clients just 30 minutes before their court appearance. In 1991 Robins again went begging for dollars. When she was accused of having a "management problem," she quit. The move caused such a furor that the Governor promised additional funds. Albuquerque's chief public defender, Kelly Knight, now has 16 lawyers, but the pace is still grueling. "I'm 34, not married, and I have no children," Knight says. "But I'm really, really burned out." She plans to take a sabbatical next year—whether she is granted one or not.

In Los Angeles, which boasts one of the best public defender programs in the country, salaries start at $42,000 and go as high as $97,000. A staff of 570 lawyers juggles roughly 80,000 cases a year. The work is often thankless, but every so often a case upholds the promise of *Gideon*. Earlier this month Frank White, 36, a tall, muscular man covered with tattoos, landed in L.A. County court, accused of murdering a tiny Korean woman with his bare fists. White, diagnosed as a paranoid schizophrenic, refused to take his medication and grew angry when the deputies would not remove his handcuffs. White glared as he stalked into the courtroom and dropped heavily into the seat beside public defender Mark Windham. Without a word, Windham slid his chair closer to his explosive client until they were touching shoulders. And there he stayed throughout the proceeding. "Male bonding," a sheriff's deputy quipped. But to everyone's astonishment, White quieted down. "I did it to make him and everyone else in the room feel better," Windham explained.

Seasoned defense lawyers know the value of the small gesture. And the large. Anticipating the guilty verdict returned by the jury two weeks ago, Windham built a parallel argument that White was not guilty by reason of insanity. If the jury agrees, White will be locked up in a hospital instead of being imprisoned.

ASSIGNED ATTORNEYS: NO EXPERIENCE

In smaller cities, defendants are usually assigned attorneys by the court. Often these lawyers, who tend to be young and inexperienced or old and tired, receive only $20 to $25 an hour. Capital cases go for as little as $400. At Detroit's Recorder's Court, lawyers are paid a flat fee: $1,400 for first-degree murder, $750 for lesser offenses that carry up to a life sentence. "The more time you spend on a case, the less money you make," says attorney David Steingold, a 14-year veteran. Hence lawyers have learned to plead cases quickly and forgo time-consuming motions, a phenomenon known among lawyers as the "plea mill."

Slapdash pleas are sometimes less brutal than the farcical trials that can result when ill-prepared lawyers are thrown in over their heads. In 1983 a man named Victor Roberts and an accomplice stole a car and drove to an Atlanta suburb hunting for a house to burglarize. Posing as insurance salesmen, they entered the home of Mary Jo Jenkins. A skirmish ensued and a gun went off, shooting Jenkins through the heart. H. Geoffrey Slade, a lawyer for 13 years, was assigned to handle the capital case. When he realized he was in over his head and requested co-counsel, the court appointed Jim Hamilton, 75, who had almost no criminal experience.

Their efforts, while well intended, served no one's interests. They conducted no investigation. They interviewed no witnesses in person. They never visited the crime scene. During the trial they introduced no evidence in Roberts' defense. The prosecution, meanwhile, trotted out gory photographs of Jenkins—taken after she had been autopsied. Slade knew enough to object, but he was overruled. The jury deliberated only 45 minutes; Roberts found himself on death row. A federal judge subsequently ordered a new trial, on the ground that the first had been "fundamentally unfair," in part because Roberts' lawyers had failed to "adequately and effectively investigate" the crime. Pretrial proceedings are scheduled to get under way this month—10 years after Roberts' arrest.

CONTRACT LAWYERS: NO SATISFACTION

A variation on court-appointed attorneys, popular in rural areas, is a contract system under which lawyers receive a flat rate. The fee is usually so meager that these attorneys maintain a private practice on the side. Such a system, says Bright, results in "lawyers who view their responsibilities as unwanted burdens, have no inclination to help the client and have no incentive to learn or to develop criminal trial skills." When expenses mount, they economize by refusing the collect calls of their jailed clients. Under a contract system, says L.A.'s Tennenbaum, "you don't investigate, you don't ask for continuances, you plead at the earliest possible moment."

Or worse. In Indiana's Marion County, which includes Indianapolis, reform was sparked after a 1991 study documented abuses in a system where the six superior court judges hired defense lawyers for $20,800 a year to handle the area's indigent work on a part-time basis. Bobby Lee Houston, a truck driver, hired a private counselor whom he couldn't afford when he was arrested in 1989 on charges of child molestation. The lawyer urged him to plead guilty and serve five years; Houston insisted he was innocent. He wrote to a judge complaining of delays and, after 14 months, was assigned David Sexson, one of the contract lawyers. Sexson suggested that Houston plead guilty and get off with time served. Houston was firm: no dice.

One month later, Houston's case was dismissed—but no one bothered to tell him. It would be four more months before Houston learned that he was a free man. After 19 pointless months in a jail cell, Houston has his own bottom line: "Justice is a money thing."

That is precisely what Clarence Earl Gideon complained of in 1962 when he put pencil to lined paper in his Florida cell and and wrote the Supreme Court: "The question is very simple. I requested the court to appoint me attorney and the court refused." Since then, lawyers and judges have stated and restated Gideon's assertion of a fundamental right to adequate representation. Chief Justice Harold Clarke of the Georgia Supreme Court warned state legislators earlier this year, "We need to remember that if the state can deny justice to the poor, it has within its grasp the power to deny justice to anybody." Richard Teissier and his fellow public defenders surely would agree with Judge Clarke: Justice on the cheap is no justice at all. —*Reported by Julie Johnson/ Washington, Michael Riley/New Orleans and James Willwerth/Los Angeles*

WHY LAWYERS LIE

If the O. J. Simpson case has taught anything, it's that finding out the truth isn't always the highest priority in a criminal trial. Winning is. That's the way the system is built.

Floyd Abrams

Floyd Abrams, a partner in the New York law firm of Cahill Gordon & Reindel, tries cases and argues appeals in constitutional law.

As the O. J. Simpson case has transfixed the public, it has also taught it. Not only have the attorneys in the case been on constant public display, but other lawyers have served as television commentators, explaining, critiquing and judging the performance of their colleagues. Never before has so wide a swath of the public been subjected to such detailed, thought-by-thought analysis of how real lawyers think and what they do.

It is not always an attractive portrait, even to lawyers themselves. Viewed through my own prism of almost 35 years of practice, the Simpson case raises broad questions about just what it is our society asks lawyers to do, and the rather breathtakingly amoral way in which they do it.

Consider first the rules that govern the conduct of lawyers. They are not quite given James Bond's license to kill. But as lawyers, they have a license that requires them to defend their clients whether they are guilty or not; their responsibility is to attack those who have accused them, whatever the truth of those accusations. Regardless of whether Simpson committed the murders of which he is accused, it is Robert Shapiro's *job* as Simpson's lawyer to attack the validity of the DNA tests, to impugn the credibility of the police and, if useful and at all plausible, to attack the character of Simpson's former wife whom he is accused of murdering. Only lawyers are expected to do such things.

Lawyers are not asked to do justice. They participate in what everyone hopes is a system of justice, a system that seeks justice by asking lawyers on both sides to represent their clients zealously. Lawyers are the legal embodiment of – the spokesmen for – those clients. Subject only to the constraints of criminal law (a lawyer may not break open a mailbox as the Paul Newman character did in the movie "The Verdict") and the canons of legal ethics (a lawyer may not plant a spy within the camp of opposing counsel as the James Mason character did in the same movie), a lawyer is supposed to do whatever can be done to defend and vindicate the client's position in a case.

Those are wide, extraordinarily wide, boundaries. Within them, lawyers for rapists and murderers have accused their clients' victims of being responsible for their plight. Lawyers for warring husbands and wives have dropped the equivalent of tactical nuclear weapons on families, destroying all within range – children included.

All, all for clients. Prosecutors are, at least in theory, supposed to be governed by somewhat different standards. Although no less zealous than defense counsel, they are supposed to indict only those they think guilty and to understand that, as the Supreme Court put it 60 years ago, the interest of the government "in a criminal prosecution is not that it shall win a case but that justice shall be done." It is not always so. Certainly the potentially prejudicial comments of the Los Angeles District Attorney, Gil Garcetti, on "This Week With David Brinkley" suggesting that Simpson might well admit to the killings of which he is accused – and proffer some form of Menendez brothers-like psychological defense – offered little basis for thinking so.

From the *New York Times Magazine,* October 9, 1994, pp. 54-55. © 1994 by the New York Times Company. Reprinted by permission.

Public statements of prosecutors and defense counsel alike must be viewed with the greatest skepticism. The Robert Shapiro who asserted, in one of his unending series of interviews, that Simpson was innocent was not the Shapiro one might have met before he was retained by Simpson. He is now Simpson's Shapiro, Simpson's representative, sometimes Simpson's flack. What he says is said for Simpson's benefit, not because it is true.

So with Alan M. Dershowitz, when he was representing Mike Tyson. The frequent public assertions by Dershowitz of Tyson's innocence after he began to represent him were not those of the Bill of Rights-protecting Harvard Law School Professor Alan Dershowitz. The Tyson-defending Dershowitz was, in the end, little more than a better-spoken Tyson, Tyson in Harvard garb. That does not make what Dershowitz said of Tyson untrue. It does not mean that he did not mean what he said. But we should take care not to get our Dershowitzes confused.

So with all of us. Shortly after I argued before the Supreme Court representing a death row inmate in Parchman, Miss., I received a call from a newspaper in the small town in which my client had been tried, convicted and sentenced to death. "I know you only sought to persuade the Supreme Court to set aside the death sentence in the case," the reporter observed. "What I'd like to ask you is whether you believe he committed the crime."

I paused. It was true that I had only argued that the death sentence imposed upon my client was unconstitutional, a sentence the Supreme Court later set aside. It was also true that my client continued to deny his guilt. And it was true that I had never reached for myself any definitive conclusion as to his guilt.

But I was his lawyer. Silence might be taken as assent to his guilt. Even a "no comment" might have sounded as if I did not believe him. And so, without a gulp, I answered, "I believe he is not guilty."

I did what I think a lawyer was supposed to do. Whether my client was guilty or not, whether I suspected he was guilty or not, I was obliged to defend him. But you are not obliged to believe me when I do so.

Nor should you take too seriously many of the published and broadcast reactions to the Simpson case of lawyers who represent criminal defendants. Their personal posturing aside, they often confuse what might be useful for his defense with what might serve justice. When the fact was first revealed that Simpson had been interviewed for three hours by the police days before his arrest, for example, defense counsel around the country expressed shock. "It was horrendous," said Harland Braun, a Los Angeles defense counsel. "It really hems in tremendously what Bob Shapiro can do, in terms of strategy."

In terms of defense strategy, Braun is undoubtedly correct. A defendant who says one thing to the police may have difficulty persuading a jury of something else. A defendant who lies to the police about some things may not be viewed as credible by a jury when he swears to something else—his innocence, for example.

But wait a minute. Is this really a bad thing? From society's point of view, if not that of a potential defendant, is it anything but admirable when someone voluntarily speaks to the police about a crime of which he has knowledge? The individual interviewed may provide useful information which can aid the police in apprehending a criminal. He may demonstrate to the police his own innocence. He may inadvertently but justifiably incriminate himself. He may even confess.

If he does, and if the confession is true, we—if not his lawyer—should be pleased. As Justice Antonin Scalia of the Supreme Court observed in a 1990 dissenting opinion, "the procedural protections of the Constitution protect the guilty as well as the innocent, but it is not their objective to set the guilty free. . . . We should, then, rejoice at an honest confession, rather than pity the 'poor fool' who has made it."

Recall now the most telling part of Braun's statement: that the Simpson statement to the police might "hem in" what his counsel could later argue. Translate the statement into plainer English. Because Simpson has told one story to the police, if he tells another at his trial, he does so at his peril.

Or say it even more directly. Because Simpson has either told some truths or some lies to the police—or some of both—his lawyer cannot be as creative, as fertile in framing a defense. Is the public really supposed to feel sorry about that?

Lawyers are trained to think that way. Most people, when confronted with a problem, gather whatever information they can and reason toward an answer. Lawyers start with the answer—their clients' answer—and then search for evidence to support it. So, inexorably, their reasoning veers toward Braun's: if I am to argue that Simpson cannot be proven guilty, I must either maintain that he was not at the scene of the crime; or that if he was there, he either did not stab the two inconveniently dead victims or that if he did, he did so in self-defense; or that if he did kill them, there was some legally sanctioned psychological reason for doing so. All are possibilities. Anything Simpson said to the police limits my options. Isn't it awful?

The problem with all this is not its lack of logic; it is perfectly logical. It simply has nothing to do with truth. While it is not the role of Simpson's lawyer to take any step that might result in his conviction, Shapiro is not a novelist, free to create an entirely fictional world into which Simpson comes and goes—or came and went.

And so for the rest of us. Some arguments are not only implausible; they are impossible. Some scenarios are not only untrue; they could not have been true. It may be that society should ask both more and less of lawyers. More willingness to say to clients that there are some arguments that lawyers will not make, less willingness to counsel lawful conduct that is morally odious. More willingness of lawyers to view themselves as part of a system of law, less willingness to view themselves as the alter egos of their clients.

Judges need to rethink their roles as well. There are times, as Rudolph J. Gerber, an Arizona appellate judge, has observed, when "judicial spectatorship" at lawyers' antics amounts "to indefensible patience when righteous anger would be appropriate." A little

more anger directed at lawyers when they misbehave might go a long way.

Attorneys have frequently played valiant roles, defending the innocent, prosecuting the guilty, vindicating principle, settling disputes that should never have been litigated in the first place. They must continue to play those roles. But it is time to ask whether it really leads to justice to have a system in which many lawyers spend far more time avoiding truth than finding it. And it is never too late to ask whether we can continue to justify creating a sort of legal game in which the players lose sight of why they started playing in the first place and the spectators forget that what they are watching was not supposed to be a sport at all.

Inside the Mind
of the Juror

What is the process by which jurors' decisions are made?

Gordon Haas

Gordon Haas is a prisoner at MCI–Norfolk, Massachusetts, and the co-ordinator of the U. Mass Prison College program at MCI–Norfolk.

In Kentucky, 63% [of the jurors] indicated that the mere fact that the prosecutor asked for the death penalty convinced them that the case against the defendant must be strong. Of these, 38% felt that since the prosecutor sought the death penalty, the defendant must deserve the punishment . . . even before the trial began.

In 1972, the United States Supreme Court struck down capital punishment in the landmark decision of *Furman v. Georgia,* 408 U.S. 238. The reason for that court's ruling, however, was not that the court considered the death penalty to be cruel and unusual punishment, but that the arbitrary manner in which the death penalty was applied was un-constitutional.

States where politicians and law enforcement personnel favored execution found solace in the fact that the Supreme Court did not reject the death penalty as an inappropriate punishment, and rushed to develop statutes that would be acceptable to the court. In some states, laws were enacted that mandated capital punishment for certain crimes. In others, statutes were adopted that imposed sentencing standards to be followed by jurors in capital cases. As cases challenging the new death penalty laws found their way to the Supreme Court, only states such as Florida, Georgia, and Texas, which had enacted capital statutes that allowed for guided discretion through the use of sentencing standards, ensured that their statutes survived.

Georgia's statute listed eight aggravating conditions, any one of which was sufficient for a jury to impose the death penalty.

Florida chose to require a balancing test. Both aggravating and mitigating factors are enumerated and must be weighted one against the other before the jury recommends a sentence.

Texas law restricted capital punishment to cases in which a jury could answer affirmatively questions about intent, absence of provocation, and likely future dangerousness of the defendant.

Virginia, California, Oklahoma, South Carolina, Kentucky, New Jersey, Maryland, and Indiana followed the lead of Georgia, Florida and Texas.

The new death penalty statutes have spawned legions of critics who argue that they have introduced only new elements of arbitrariness. Statutory factors such as heinousness, vileness and wantonness, or future dangerousness are considered too vague and uncertain to provide meaningful guidance to jurors (Black, 1981; Rosen, 1986; Dix,1977; Marquat, et al.,1989).

Also, some supposedly mitigating factors such as mental or emotional disturbance or drug/alcohol involvement may be viewed by jurors as aggravating factors because of their presumed association with future violence (Berkman, 1989). Others assert that legal terms such as "aggravation" and "mitigation" are confusing to jurors, that instructions by trial judges about aggravating and mitigating factors are misleading

From *Odyssey,* Spring 1993, pp. 72-78. © 1993 by Odyssey Enterprises, Inc. Reprinted by permission.

and misunderstood by jurors (Haney & Cotovsky, 1988), and that a mechanistic weighing of such factors tends to diminish a juror's sense of moral responsibility for his or her decision (Weisberg, 1983).

Disparities in sentencing based upon the race of the victim were uncovered when social scientists monitored the results of the death penalty statutes. One study (Baldus, et al., 1990) found that the death penalty in Georgia was imposed 4.3 times more often when victims were white than it was when victims were black. Findings of racial disparities were presented to the United States Supreme Court in *McCleskey v. Kemp,* 482 U.S. 806 (1987). In a 5-4 decision, that court rejected such data, ruling that a defendant must demonstrate that there was actual intent to discriminate in his or her particular case in order to prevail.

Previously in *Lockhart v. McCree,* 476 U.S. 162 (1986), the Supreme Court faulted studies that used mock juries to analyze the workings of death penalty juries. The court found such a methodology to be no substitute for determining how actual jurors rendered their decisions in capital cases. Hence, the Capital Jury Project was born. One basis for the study is an effort to provide the type of information the Supreme Court found wanting in other studies. How the Supreme Court will react to the results of this study is, of course, purely speculative. Whatever that Court's decision, information about how jurors actually made decisions when they imposed the death penalty should enlighten judges, attorneys, legislators and those who care about what the death penalty *means.*

Methodology

The Capital Jury Project was designed by Dr. William Bowers and Dr. Margaret Vandiver and entails in-depth interviews with people who have actually sat on a death penalty jury. The interviews are conducted by law students or social science graduate students, and in each state a criminologist, social scientist or lawyer coordinates the process. The names of the jurors are kept confidential.

In each of 12 states, interviews are conducted with jurors who have served on 30 separate cases. Half of the jurors chosen are from cases in which juries imposed sentences of life imprisonment, the other half are chosen from juries that asked for the death penalty in cases decided after January, 1988. The 12 states chosen were California, Florida, Georgia, Indiana, Kentucky, Louisiana, North Carolina, Pennsylvania, South Carolina, Tennessee, Texas and Virginia. Cases were selected on a state-wide basis, except for California, Florida and Texas due to their size. In order to avoid disparities that could arise from a distribution within any state that is too narrowly confined, representative samplings from urban and rural locations were included.

All 12 jurors in each case chosen are contacted by letter and told about the study. They are also told that the interviews will be kept confidential and offered a $20.00 stipend for their participation. Of those jurors who agree to be interviewed, four are chosen at random.

An interview questionnaire is given to each person and the interview is taped. Only the interviewer, the coordinator, and the central office that processes the data know the names of the participants. Interviews average three hours and forty minutes. The completed interview record and the tape recording are forwarded to the College of Criminal Justice at Northeastern University in Boston, where students listen to the tapes and compare them to the individual interview records to check the accuracy of the interviewer's notes and to add anything that was not recorded. The interview is then computerized.

The interview questionnaire is designed not only to trace the decision making process throughout a trial, including voir dire, guilt and penalty phases, but also to identify those points at which various influences and possible aspects of arbitrariness might have come into play. Early results indicate that jurors are quite candid and have little difficulty understanding the questions or being responsive to probes by interviewers.

The primary goal of this project is to compile extensive data about the factors and influences, both legal and extra-legal, that lead participating jurors to reach a life or death decision. Additional objectives are:
1. To learn how jurors evaluate evidence and the arguments of counsel.
2. To learn how well jurors understand legal and statutory requirements, as well as judicial instructions, and how these are applied in specific cases.
3. To learn whether regional and/or cultural differences affect the manner in which jurors make decisions.
4. To learn whether jurors react differently in states where executions are common, as compared with states where executions are infrequent or have not occurred for years.
5. To learn what the subjective experience of serving on a capital jury is like for individual jurors.

Results

To date, less than 10% of the questionnaires and tapes have been computerized. Thus, the results are preliminary and no generalized findings can be determined until the data have been fully analyzed. Even with that caveat, however, the responses from the jurors are disturbing.

4. THE JUDICIAL SYSTEM

Pre-Trial Issues

In the responses of 24 participating jurors in Kentucky, 63% indicated that the mere fact that the prosecutor asked for the death penalty was enough to convince them that the case against the defendant must be strong. Of these same jurors, 38% also felt, *even before the trial began*, that since the prosecutor sought the death penalty, the defendant deserved capital punishment.

Prosecutors

After the trials, some jurors had high praise for prosecutors. Representative comments were:

> He just seemed to know what he wanted and how he wanted to get it. He presented his case very well.

> I remember her as being a smart cookie...I decided after the trial was over if I was to...if I wanted someone to defend me, it would be her.

> She used a lot of dramatics. She was excellent at using her female abilities. During her closing remarks, she actually dramatically walked over to the defendant and pretended she was the deceased's ghost and acted him out saying to her, 'Why did you kill me? I only loved you.'

Defense Attorneys

> They want to win. They want their clients not to get what they deserve.

> He did not seem prepared. He did remind me of a personality that was very laid back, did not get excited over matters. Maybe being a female myself I felt like he should have gotten more involved emotionally with what his job was. He made me feel like he felt like she was guilty.

> That his attorney would have come up with more of an argument against the state than what he really did. I mean, it just gave me the feeling that he felt like he's guilty and there's not much I can do to help him out.

Although subjective opinions of how well or poorly either counsel performed are clearly outside the realm of accepted evidence, obviously such opinions were significant for the particular jurors whose remarks are cited above. An interesting footnote about the last juror's comments about the defense counsel: the juror had been represented previously by the same defense attorney the juror criticized, and the juror stated that he had been "disappointed" with the attorney's performance on his behalf. Why a defense attorney would not have challenged any potential juror who had been a former client is mind-boggling.

Attitudes About Defendants

The following comments about defendants were recorded:

> No, he seemed pretty smart, you know, that he was — he put himself on the, on the, the last day he put himself on the stand. I would say he was above average as far as that race is concerned.

> I'm sure, I know they clean them up when they bring them in.

> He would stare, I noticed him trying to stare and I would find myself staring back at him for two minutes at a time. And I, I would, I refused to let him stare me down and he refused it, and I got to thinking he might hypnotize me when he'd do that...seemed to me like he wanted to be remembered as a tough cookie or something.

> By looking at her in these $300 to $500 suits, her ladylike poise...it was hard for me to believe that a beautiful lady could be doing this — these hideous crimes.

Defendants Who Did Not Testify

When defendants did not take the stand on their own behalf, individual jurors had these reactions:

> I would have thought that, guilty or innocent, a person would at least try to say something to defend themselves.

> A truly not guilty person would say something. I would have liked to have heard him. I think if he hadn't done it, he would be up there trying to save himself. I think they probably didn't put him up there because he did it.

> He didn't get up to defend himself; therefore, he was really guilty.

> I felt (failure to testify) was the icing on the cake; it was more proof.

> I felt like he was pretty guilty or he would have got up and defended himself.

Proof Beyond a Reasonable Doubt

One of the linchpins of our judicial system is that a defendant need not prove anything since he or she is presumed to be innocent. Thus, theoretically, a defendant may simply sit back, present no witnesses, and force the prosecution to prove its case beyond a reasonable doubt without this strategy being held against the defendant. Some jurors, however, either were not aware of or chose not to afford defendants this lawfully grounded protection. Representative of these jurors are the following viewpoints:

> Yeah, one of the reasons I was able to find him guilty was there were several things I thought the defense could have done if he were not guilty to prove

beyond a shadow of a doubt to us, the jury, that this wasn't the guy that did the crime.

Basically, that there was no reasonable other alternative.

That they were gonna have to come up with a whole lot more evidence on his side to keep him from being found guilty.

I mean, there were so many unanswered questions. There was someone else that was, that could've been...It just didn't add up. From the evidence presented, yes, he did it. But if you want to draw deeper than that, it's not that open and shut. *I don't think he did it.*

Racial Attitudes

One of the most troublesome aspects of the death penalty question is the clear evidence that racial considerations plague the process from beginning to end. What is also disturbing is that some jurors had no reluctance about expressing racially motivated sentiments even when being recorded on tape. In a North Carolina case in which both the defendant and the victim were African-Americans, a white juror referred to both as Niggers. The same was true for a Florida juror in which both the defendant and the victim were black. A Louisiana juror described the defendant as "...retarded, but no more so than others of his race." A Florida juror remarked that, "There are two different lifestyles. The black community which they were from was entirely different from the way I was raised and the way we lived. The value of life, it's just totally different." Another Florida juror echoed similar racist sentiments. "...he wasn't real bright. I was impressed that he had a lower value of life than I did. Sometimes I really thought racially I'm the same despite the differences between their ethic and my ethics."

Reaching a Verdict of Guilty

One presumption of our judicial system is that jurors must wait until all the evidence has been presented before they reach a verdict. The intent of jury deliberations is, of course, to discuss the evidence and then to render a verdict after all the evidence is reviewed. If jurors make up their minds before deliberations even begin, then the process is seriously flawed. Responses from jurors interviewed in Kentucky indicated that two-thirds had determined the defendant to be guilty even before deliberations had begun. As one juror, who obviously did not wait for all the evidence to make up his mind, said:

> The truth don't hurt nobody and that's the way I see it; halfway through the trial, after I saw the evidence

against the defendant, that's when I was thoroughly convinced.

Sentencing Decisions

Kentucky's death penalty statute calls for a decision to be made after a consideration of statutorily itemized aggravating and mitigating factors. If the jurors find even one aggravating factor to be present, for example, a "threshold" rather than a "balancing" statute, then the death penalty becomes a viable alternative. Of 24 jurors interviewed to date, 79% responded that if the victim were a child that was the aggravating factor that would most warrant the death penalty. Other significant aggravating factors were: a history of violent crime (55%); no remorse expressed by the defendant (57%); the possibility of the defendant being a future danger to society (54%); whether the victim had suffered (69%); and whether the body had been maimed or mutilated after death (66%). What is interesting about the last two factors, the second and third strongest as reported by the jurors, is that neither is a statutory aggravating factor in Kentucky.

Regarding mitigating factors, the most significant ones were whether or not the defendant was mentally retarded (79%) or had a history of mental illness (69%). A defendant's having a loving family or coming from a background of extreme poverty were considered to be mitigating factors by only 14% of the jurors. One other mitigating factor was that the jurors had lingering doubts about the defendant's guilt (67%). Theoretically, of course, those doubts should have been resolved during the guilt phase of the deliberations, presumably in the defendant's favor.

Of the Kentucky jurors, 89% reported correctly that "beyond a reasonable doubt" was the standard of proof for consideration of an aggravating factor, indicating that they understood the judge's instructions about those factors. They did not fare as well, however, when dealing with mitigating factors, and 75% stated, incorrectly, that all jurors had to agree about a mitigating factor for it to be considered in the sentencing decision.

Whether a capital jury used a balancing test or not, the possibility of the defendant being paroled was a significant deciding factor, despite the fact that jurors are instructed that future parole risk is not to be a consideration. The following comments indicate clearly that such instructions are simply ignored:

> I think the single most important factor was probably to make sure that he didn't get back on the street. I really believe that might have been the most important factor.

Q. When you were considering the punishment, were you concerned that the defendant might get back into society some day if not given the death penalty?
A. Yup.
Q. Greatly concerned?
A. Very, overriding, I think we listed that as the number one.
Q. When you were considering the punishment, were you concerned that the defendant might get back into society if not given the death penalty?
A. Yes.
Q. How concerned were you about that?
A. Scared to death.

Jurors' Sense of Responsibility and Distress When Serving on a Death Penalty Jury

Many jurors found the experience of sitting on a capital jury difficult, painful, and emotionally upsetting, but their sense of responsibility for making the right decision was very high. Trouble sleeping and loss of appetite were commonly reported symptoms. In one case in Virginia, of three jurors interviewed, two reported having nightmares. In the same case, two stated that they would serve again, but reluctantly; the other stated she would refuse to serve again on a death penalty case and that she wished she had lied so that she would not have served on the one she had.

A Kentucky juror commented that he "worried about this (whether the decision had been the right one) for a long time. It took one year to be comfortable with my decision." The decision had been for a life sentence.

Another Kentucky juror reported that, "(The jury) was so upset (after imposing death) we were still standing (in the parking lot) crying for about 30 minutes...About six months passed before I stopped thinking about it constantly."

For a Louisiana juror, "Vietnam was a piece of cake compared to capital jury duty." A Georgia juror simply could not "describe being in control of someone's life, regardless of guilt or innocence."

A Florida juror still anguishes over the decision. "OK — I was tired and I admit it and you could put my name on this jury project and I'd love to go before some Senate Committee or something to discuss this. I was damn tired. And, fine, guilty...But I was more interested in what they didn't present. But that's not the way the system works. Just tired. Exhausted. We all were...I would have convicted him of a lesser crime, but nobody wanted to hear that. The three of us, yeah we were tired. We were kind of stuck in and if we didn't reach a verdict, they were going to sequester us. They already

called the hotel...I'll never forget that. That's what made it a horrible experience for me."

Conclusion

The Capital Jury Project makes no attempt to evaluate the correctness of any verdicts, either individually or on a state-by-state basis. Rather, it is the process by which jurors' decisions are made that is the subject of this study. Although the final analysis and publication of the results of The Capital Jury Project is at least one year away, preliminary findings indicate a rather large discrepancy between the protection that defendants are legally entitled to and what capital jurors consider in their deliberations. This dichotomy takes on an even greater significance for death penalty cases, not only because of the higher stakes involved, but also because of the jury selection process itself.

The Supreme Court in *Wainwright v. Witt*, 469 U.S. 412, 423, (1985) ruled that during voir dire questioning, anyone who voices opposition to the death penalty on moral, ethical, philosophical or religious grounds can be excluded from the jury for cause as such views could "prevent or substantially impair the performance of his duties as a juror in accordance with his instructions and his oath." See also: *Adams v. Texas*, 448 U.S. 38 (1980). Thus, defendants in capital cases are faced with juries that are prone to imposing the death penalty once a defendant is found to be guilty. The dilemma for capital defendants does not begin, however, with the penalty phase, for death prone juries are also conviction prone. Defendants, therefore, can only hope that they will be fortunate enough to have their fates decided by jurors who scrupulously follow the principles by which verdicts in criminal trials are supposed to be rendered.

Our judicial system is based on the theory that two equal adversaries, overseen by an impartial judge, will present all the legally relevant evidence to a panel of 12 disinterested citizens. Once the evidentiary stage has been completed, the panel is expected to follow the instructions given to them by the judge, including, but not limited to, what evidence can and cannot be considered, what rights the defendant has which must be rigorously protected, and an explanation of the laws that apply to the case. Although it may well be unrealistic to demand a perfect trial every time, it is not fanciful to expect a fair one. The level of fairness, however, is directly proportional to what factors jurors use to reach their decisions.

The Capital Jury Project promises to provide the first in-depth evaluation of the processes jurors undertake to decide whether or not an accused person lives or dies. It is unrealistic to suppose that jurors faithfully execute either the letter or spirit of their constitutional duties, particularly when numerous self-reports contradict this claim. One can only hope that judges, attorneys, and those who enact criminal justice legislation will carefully review the results of this critical study and act to correct the deficiencies that this project has revealed. In capital cases, only the highest standards of juridicial conduct should be acceptable.

Bibliography

Baldus, Woodworth & Pulaski, *Equal Justice and the Death Penalty: A Legal and Empirical Analysis* (Northeastern University Press, Boston, 1990).

Berkman, E.F., "Mental Illness as an Aggravating Circumstance in Capital Sentencing," *Columbia Law Review* 89, 291-309.

Black, C.L., "Administration of the texas Death Penalty Statues: Constitutional Infirmities Related to the Prediction of Dangerousness," *Texas Law Review* 55, 1343-1414.

Haney & Cotovsky, "Capital Jury Insturctions and Death Penalty Decision Making." Paper presented at the meeting of the Amercian Psychological Association, August 1988.

Marquart, Ekland-Olson & Sorenson, "Gazing Into the Crystal Ball: Can Jurors Accurately Predict Dangerousness in Capital Cases?" *Law and Society Review* 23, 449-468.

Rosen, R.A., "The Especially Heious Aggravating Circumstance in Capital Cases: The Standardless Standard," *North Carolina Law Review* 64, 941-992.

Weisberg, R., "Deregulating Death," *Supreme Court Review* 8, 305-395.

Racial, Ethnic, and Gender Bias in the Courts:
What Progress Have We Made, and What Can be Done?

Harold Hood, Judge of the Court of Appeals, Detroit, Michigan

Studies conducted by a Commission of the Michigan Supreme Court found that more than a third of Michigan's citizens of <u>all</u> races believed that the justice system discriminated against individuals on the basis of race, gender, or ethnic origin. The Commission recommended objective studies to determine whether the public perception had any basis in fact.

On September 14, 1987, the justices of the Michigan Supreme Court responded to the Commission's recommendation by creating two separate task forces, one to examine racial and ethnic issues in the courts and the other to examine gender issues in the courts. Julia Darlow, a former president of the State Bar of Michigan, was selected to chair the Gender Bias Task Force, and I had the privilege of chairing the Race/Ethnic Bias Task Force. Each task force had 19 members, representing a cross-section of the legal, judicial, court administrative and lay communities.

Over a two-year period, both task forces conducted public hearings throughout the state of Michigan, at which oral and written testimony was presented and considered. The task force also conducted several surveys of groups involved with the system, including court employees, court users, attorneys, judges and prosecutors. Both task forces issued their final reports on December 19, 1989.[1] The reports concluded, *inter alia*, that "perceptions of bias are rooted in reality,"[2] and that "there is evidence that bias does occur with disturbing frequency at every level of the legal profession and court system."[3]

Such findings are not peculiar to Michigan. Race and ethnic bias task forces and commissions have been created in several states,[4] and at least four of the task forces have already rendered their final reports,[5] with similar conclusions. In addition, some 37 states have created gender bias task forces or commissions, many of which have rendered final reports documenting and demonstrating that bias, real or imagined, permeates the system.

The experiences of these task forces illustrate a saying often used in twelve-step recovery systems, i.e., "Denial is not a river in Egypt." For denial is what we often encountered. One of the most interesting phenomena that our task force discovered is that which we came to describe as the "two worlds syndrome." Simply put, the justice system, as viewed by women and minorities, is a totally different system from that viewed by non-minority males. The answers to some of the questions in our survey of attorneys illustrate that point. When asked how often they had

observed a judge giving unfair or insensitive treatment to a racial or ethnic minority (1) attorney (2) litigant or (3) witness, 65 percent, 64 percent and 45 percent, respectively, of minority attorneys responded "sometimes" or "usually," while 11 percent of non-minority attorneys responded similarly in each of the three categories.

Strikingly similar results were reported in the gender area in a recent *Wall Street Journal* report, which indicated that a 1990 Colorado study found that one-third of 2,500 male attorneys indicated that gender bias does not exist at all, as opposed to only three percent of 900 female attorneys who held such an opinion. Similarly, in a New Jersey study of 1,000 lawyers, one-third of the women surveyed reported hearing sexist comments, while only seven percent of the male lawyers reported frequently hearing such comments.[6]

What does all this mean, and where are we, or where should we be going? It is my belief that instances of overt and blatant gender, racial, and ethnic bias, although they obviously exist, are not the primary problem in our system of justice. Such manifestations, to the limited extent that they do exist and can be identified, are almost universally held acceptable, and can be dealt with. What is widespread, and endemic in the system, however, is unconscious insensitivity to racial, gender, and ethnic concerns, as well as conscious or unconscious stereotyping of entire groups or classes of persons. It is noteworthy that 10 of the 18 joint recommendations of our Michigan task forces were addressed not to areas or instances of overt gender, race, or ethnic bias, but to education, sensitization or consciousness-raising on the part of courts, attorneys, court personnel, and other persons involved in the justice system.

The 1986 Report of the Task Force on minorities in the Legal Profession, committee of the American Bar Association stated:

The lack of equal opportunity for minority participation in business, corporate, and professional affairs, is a grave societal problem that will not be solved by legislation and judicial decrees alone. Full and equal opportunities for racial and ethnic minorities will exist only after an informed society rejects discrimination and racism, not only because they may be unlawful, but also because they violate the moral and human values upon which our nation was founded.[7]

This is an accurate assessment, but we, as judges, have a special and compelling obligation to see that our society becomes an "informed society." We, as judges, are charged to be the ministers of the law, the guardians of its conscience,

From *Maddvocate*, Fall 1993, pp. 22-23. © 1993 by Mothers Against Drunk Driving. Reprinted by permission of the National Judicial College and Mothers Against Drunk Driving.

and teachers of fairness and equality. We, as judges, set the tone as to what is acceptable or not acceptable in our courtrooms and among our court personnel and the attorneys and citizens who come within our sphere of influence. We should be "overt" in our approach to combatting the specter of bias in our system. For starters, I suggest the following basic, non-intrusive steps:

1.   Each Supreme Court in this nation should issue a statement that "judges, employees of the judicial system, attorneys, and other court officers should commit themselves to the elimination of racial, ethnic, and gender bias in the court system."[8]

2.   Individual courts should clearly state that demeaning others on the basis of race, color, creed, or gender is inexcusable. As an example, the Livingston County Court in Michigan issued the following pronouncement in a June 1990 newsletter:

> CHAUVINISTS BEWARE! The Livingston County court system enjoys a fine reputation when it comes to treatment of minorities. Indeed, the statewide public perception that the court system and the legal profession demonstrate bias toward women, blacks, and other minorities at first seems to have no relevance to the Livingston County court situation. However, recently there have been at least two disturbing in-chambers incidents involving put-downs of female attorneys by male colleagues. What makes these situations awkward is the fact that both attorneys were longtime practitioners, well-known to each other and to the judge. How much offense is intended and how much is taken is often difficult to fathom in such situations. However, any put-down on the basis of race, color, creed or gender is inexcusable. Let it be known that there will be zero tolerance toward such incidents. The district judges and probate judges concur in condemning such nonsense.

3.   Attorney education courses should be revised to include racial, ethnic, and gender issues. It is important that these materials be integrated into all normal course materials, not set out in some separate "race/ethnic/gender" course. The fact of the matter is that gender, race, and ethnic issues are not "pigeonholed" into categories addressing only the target populations, but concern the entire legal community.

4.   Judicial education facilities should begin to integrate gender, race, and ethnic issues into their curricula. Again, I am NOT advocating some "gender/minority/ethnic" course. That accomplishes little. ALL courses should be sensitive to racial, ethnic and gender issues.

5.   Efforts should be made to seek diversity in faculty involved in judicial and attorney education.

6.   Every judge should look at his or her attitudes concerning persons who are "different," and attempt to become more conversant with race/ethnic/gender concerns. Existing resources should be utilized for self-education.[9]

7.   Consider adopting a sexual harassment policy to put all court personnel and persons coming in contact with your court on notice that sexual harassment will not be tolerated.

This is not intended to be an all-inclusive list, but merely some suggestions to focus attention on the subject. I am certain that the reader can expand the list greatly. We have an excellent judicial system in this country. Our goal as judges should be to make sure that the system does indeed produce justice for all.

References

   1. *Full copies of either or both reports may be obtained at a cost of $7 each from the office of the Michigan State Court Administrator, 611 W. Ottawa, Lansing, Michigan, 48909, Attention Margo Kortes (517-373-5596).*

   2. *Gender Task Force Report, page 1.*

   3. *Race Ethnic Task Force Report, page 2.*

   4. *As of September, 1992, at least 13 race/ethnic task forces or commissions had been created in Arizona, California, the District of Columbia, Florida, Iowa, Massachusetts, Michigan, Minnesota, New Jersey, New York, Hawaii, Oregon, and Washington.*

   5. *Florida, Michigan, New York, and Washington.*

   6. *Wall Street Journal, August 20, 1992, pp. B1 and B2.*

   7. *American Bar Association Task Force on Minorities in the Legal Profession, Report with Recommendations, January, 1986.*

   8. *Michigan Supreme Court Administrative Order 1990-3, June 12, 1990.*

   9. *The American Judicature Society, for example, has a two-tape videocassette entitled "Judicial Ethics and the Administration of Justice," which addresses some of these issues. Also, the State Bar of Michigan has produced a one-cassette work on racial, gender and ethnic issues, entitled "Respect."*

Fault Lines

Judging by the daily tales of rage and forgiveness
on TV talk shows and uncertain results in some
high-profile trials, it appears the nation has
turned from punishing crimes to excusing them.
But perception is not reality.

STEPHANIE B. GOLDBERG

*Stephanie B. Goldberg, a law-
yer, is an assistant editor of the* ABA
Journal.

Blame it on the Menendez trial. Blame it on Lorena Bobbitt. Blame it on Oprah and Phil and Sally and Geraldo.

Suddenly, America is coming to grips with what Harvard Law School professor Alan M. Dershowitz first dubbed the "abuse excuse"—a concept that's been expanded by the media to include all the so-called "soft" (read untraditional) defenses.

The perception is that courts are awash—and juries are in danger of drowning—in an alphabet soup of syndromes: premenstrual, postpartum, post-traumatic stress, black rage, cocaine-induced psychosis, xyy chromosome, battered women's and battered children's, to name a few.

All of these conditions supposedly boil down to the same thing—internal or external forces that limit individual responsibility. Sometimes they challenge well-settled rules of law: If, for example, a battered woman slays her husband when he doesn't appear to be threatening her, the distinction between victim and victimizer evaporates. Or does it?

The phenomenon has set off media alarms. A typical one was voiced by John Leo, senior editor for *U.S. News & World Report*, in an essay for the magazine. "The doctrine of victimology—claiming victim status means you are not respon-

sible for your actions—is beginning to warp the legal system."

Television disseminates this ideology, claims Leo. "The daily parade of bizarre creatures on Oprah and Geraldo has a long-term effect. It erases judgment and induces a generic tolerance for any kind of dysfunctional behavior. ... In highly publicized trials now, the defense attorney has the same function as 'Oprah'—to create and enlarge pools of sympathy for the beleaguered and allegedly victimized underdog."

Using that reasoning, it is a short trip from the Menendez brothers supposedly getting away with murder (after two juries deadlocked between first- and second-degree homicide in the first trial) to questioning the state of Western civilization. A score of op-ed writers have suggested that the verdicts in *Menendez* and *Bobbitt* inexorably prove our society's moral bankruptcy: Except for maybe Attorney General Janet Reno following the Waco shootout, we have become a nation of buck-passers.

Some of these concerns are shared by lawyers.

"The search for explanations has collapsed into a search for excuses," warns Roger L. Conner, director of the American Alliance for Rights and Responsibilities in Washington, D.C. Conner's group is the

legal arm of the communitarian movement, which advocates subordinating individual privileges to the greater social good. "I see this trend as very disturbing," he observes. "It brought down the Greek democratic experiment, it's that dangerous."

"Do any husbands get killed anymore who don't batter their wives?" wonders Yale Kamisar, who holds the Clarence Darrow Distinguished Professor chair at the University of Michigan Law School. "It's amazing how successful these defenses have been." He thinks that if he had given the facts of the Menendez case to his students in an exam 10 years ago, it would have seemed like a joke. "It makes you wonder if any defendant will ever say, 'Look, I just did it because I'm bad, okay?' That would be page-one news, wouldn't it?"

Writer and social critic Wendy Kaminer, a former criminal defense lawyer, agrees that there has been a sea change. "There's no way the Menendez brothers could have had a deadlocked jury with that defense 20 years ago," said the author of "I'm Dysfunctional, You're Dysfunctional," a critique of the recovery movement.

"William Kunstler is using 'black rage' as a defense in the Colin Ferguson [Long Island Railroad murders] case," notes Kaminer. "Well, if rage is a defense to criminal behav-

Reprinted with permission from the *ABA Journal*, June 1994, pp. 40-44. © 1994 by the American Bar Association.

ior, we might as well turn the prisons into public schools. Of course people commit crime when they're angry. It's a way of saying we're not going to hold anybody criminally liable."

Then again, it's entirely possible that these cases are anomalies that have received disproportionate media attention.

For, even if, as many seem to think, the average juror is growing more receptive to the idea that criminal impulses are sometimes excusable, there is nothing to suggest that courts share this enthusiasm. And they, after all, are the gatekeepers who decide whether this evidence gets in or not.

Consider:

▶ While testimony about battered women's syndrome is admissible in just about every state, it came as the result of a hard-fought, 15-year-long struggle, say advocates. And the battle continues. In some states, the requirement of proof of imminent danger still prevents some battered women from claiming self-defense, says Richard A. Rosen, a law professor at the University of North Carolina in Chapel Hill.

▶ The battered children's syndrome does not yet enjoy comparable acceptance. Santa Monica attorney Paul Mones, author of "When a Child Kills" and adviser to the Menendez defense team, says the conviction rate is more than 95 percent in cases in which he has represented children accused of murdering their parents.

▶ Certain defenses based on physiological conditions—premenstrual syndrome, for example—have been denied for policy reasons (they will open the floodgates) or because the proof of causation is tenuous, says Charles P. Ewing, a psychologist and professor of law at the State University of New York at Buffalo.

▶ Defenses based on compulsive gambling and alcoholism have been "a wash-out," says Peter Arenella, a professor of criminal law at the University of California at Los Angeles. He points out that the U.S. Supreme Court rejected a constitutional defense based on alcoholism and that attempts to use compulsive gambling as a defense have been generally unsuccessful.

There's no evidence suggesting the insanity defense is growing in popularity. In fact, since would-be presidential assassin John Hinckley was acquitted by reason of insanity, the trend has been for courts and legislatures to raise the burden of

proof in insanity defenses, not lower it, says John F. Decker, a law professor at DePaul University in Chicago. However, a relatively few number of defendants are affected because studies show the insanity defense is used in only one percent of all felony trials.

With the approval of the U.S. Supreme Court, three states have eliminated insanity defenses altogether. In addition, a growing number of jurisdictions allow juries to find defendants "guilty but mentally ill," Decker says.

So much for the perception that the courts are rushing to embrace a new psychology of forgiveness. The AARR's Conner sees it more as a tug-of-war between warring forces. "What we're really arguing about is when are things out of your control, when are you required to … control your impulses and desires?" He sees the communitarian movement as striking a balance in that it imposes higher standards of accountability, but only after a network of social services is in place.

Advocates for battered women and children reframe the struggle, seeing themselves as the advance guard in a war on domestic violence and their critics as echoing the media backlash against soft defenses. "The [presence of the] backlash is one way to measure your success," notes feminist scholar Sheila Kuehl, who is of counsel to the California Women's Law Center.

Ewing, who has written extensively on battered women's and battered children's syndromes, believes that the media backlash to *Menendez* is having an effect on juries. He testified recently as a defense expert in a trial in which a battered woman had shot her husband.

"It was one of the most clear-cut cases I've seen. He had tried to strangle her with a belt. The jury deadlocked 11-1 in favor of acquittal. I can't help but think that there's an example of one person who's been influenced by the media barrage [on *Menendez* and *Bobbitt*]."

Perhaps the first to herald passing the buck as a national pastime was conservative au-

thor Charles J. Sykes in his 1992 book, "A Nation of Victims: The Decay of the American Character." He declines, however, to hold lawyers responsible for the growth of "soft" defenses. The lawyer who invents a new defense is "like a burglar working a hotel. He'll go from room to room to see which door is open," says Sykes.

Most of the time the doors are locked, says UCLA's Arenella. If evidence of these conditions is being introduced to prove insanity, the lawyer must show that he has reliable proof connecting the defendant to a recognizable mental disease or defect, says the professor. That means the illness must be listed in the psychiatric diagnostic manual DSM-3R, rather than concocted to fit the facts of the case, he says.

Post-Traumatic Stress Syndrome, for example, has sufficient medical recognition for courts to admit it as evidence. Though the public associates this illness with mentally disabled veterans of the Vietnam War, PTSS actually can be caused by any number of traumatic events. "After the earthquake, it's fair to say that thousands of Los Angeles residents were suffering from it," Arenella notes.

PTSS, says Arenella, has "been used to explain hypervigilance, which is a trait of people who've been abused and consequently perceive a threat when someone else might not see it." It's also been used to exonerate battered women accused of homicide, he adds. However, its use in court is relatively rare, according to a 1993 study by the University of Massachusetts Medical Center.

The study of eight states found that only 28 out of 8,163 defendants pleading guilty by reason of insanity carried a post-traumatic stress diagnosis. It also found these defendants were no more successful in their insanity claims than those claiming to suffer from other illnesses.

But don't confuse PTSS with "urban stress syndrome," a phrase coined by Milwaukee attorney Robin Shellow to explain why teen-aged client Felicia Morgan killed another teen-ager in 1991 for her leather coat. (An adversary labeled it a

'It's scary to think anyone can raise some kind of plausible excuse for their behavior.'
— CHARLES P. EWING

The 'black rage' or racism defense is difficult for white jurors to accept.
— CHARLES OGLETREE

"defense of desperation.") "The argument was that the stress of urban life for impoverished and disadvantaged youths is such that it drives some of them to become homicidal," says Ewing, who testified as an expert for the defense. The court rejected it, but the case is on appeal.

Harvard Law School professor Charles Ogletree has used what he calls the "black rage" or racism defense to explain a defendant's insanity. Ogletree says the "black rage" defense derives from a 1968 book of the same name by two psychiatrists, Drs. William Grier and Price Cobbs. The theory, according to Cobbs, who has an educational consulting practice in Berkeley, Calif., is that "in certain individuals, the right stimuli will release an uncontrollable amount of rage." The stimuli or "rage button" is typically a devaluation or racial insult, he says.

Ogletree recalls using the rage defense unsuccessfully in the case of a black, Ivy League-educated executive who killed his boss after being fired. The defense is hard for white jurors to accept, he says. "Part of it requires understanding an individual's capacity for racism, and most people believe they're not consciously racist at some level."

Another difficulty with the defense, he says, is that it is necessary to show the defendant has been troubled by, and has reflected on, racism for quite some time. "So, the more evidence you have of prior race discrimination, the more evidence you have of first-degree murder."

The fly in the ointment for defense lawyers is that not all those who have been victimized by racism or otherwise traumatized or abused resort to violence. "Jurors will say, 'I know somebody who came back from Vietnam and he was a little messed up and maybe he smoked marijuana, but he sure didn't kill anybody," says DePaul's Decker. Even Ewing admits that while "being a victim in retrospect explains a lot, looking forward it's not predictive because 99.9 percent of battered women don't kill their abusers."

A long with the causation issue, courts must wrestle with the policy implications of allowing conditions to function as legal excuses or justifications. One indicator of their conservatism is how difficult it is to admit the same conditions, not to excuse a crime but to mitigate a sentence, which has a lower evidentiary standard.

A recent attempt to equate exposure to pornography with intoxication is telling. In *Schiro v. Clark*, 963 F.2d 962 (1992), the 7th Circuit held that acting under the influence of pornography could not be used to mitigate the defendant's death sentence for rape and murder. Defendant Schiro had experts testify to the violent effects of pornography and claimed that it deprived him of free will.

The argument struck out with the Court of Appeals, which held that making pornography "a legal excuse to violence against women" would be inconsistent with a decision striking an ordinance against the sale of sexually explicit material in *American Booksellers Ass'n, Inc. v. Hudnut*, 771 F.2d 323 (1985). "It would be impossible to hold both that pornography does not directly cause violence but criminal actors do, and that criminal actors do not cause violence, pornography does."

Feminist scholar Kuehl thinks an insanity defense would not pass muster either. "The defense would appear to be based on the fact that pornography causes one to believe that women are worthless and therefore it's okay to harm or kill them," says Kuehl. "Although that may be very instructive about what's wrong with pornography, it's not a defense because you are not supposed to take these messages in uncritically. Pornography is group libel in a way, but each person still has the individual responsibility to reject it."

The media 'back-lash is one way to measure your success.'
— SHEILA KUEHL

There also have been strong policy arguments against recognizing PMS as a legal disability. A staunch opponent was former Brooklyn District Attorney Elizabeth Holtzman, who in a series of law review articles disputed its medical basis and pointed out that it could be used as a weapon against women in custody disputes and battering cases.

"PMS must be viewed as much as a sword to be used against women as a shield to protect them," she wrote in the St. John's Law Review in 1986. Nevertheless, British courts have admitted evidence of PMS to mitigate sentences in the 1980 case of a barmaid accused of murder and the 1981 case of a woman who mowed down her lover with her car.

Coming up with principled distinctions can be difficult. "Every year," says Ewing, "I put the various syndromes on the blackboard and ask my classes to spell out theories about why a defense works. We invariably find that if the person claiming it can be tagged as responsible, it's not likely to be accepted by law."

But sometimes, it's difficult to describe behavior in those terms. Cocaine psychosis is a good example: While it results from a voluntary act (ingesting cocaine), it's a bonafide form of psychosis. For that reason, some U.S. and Canadian courts have used it to mitigate sentences, and in 1993, Massachusetts' highest court stated that it was a mental defect warranting a jury instruction for the insanity defense. The holding was based on evidence that cocaine-induced psychosis was not a brief transient state, but lasted longer than periods of actual intoxication.

A problem in basing a defense on a history of abuse is that "it's simply not containable," says criminal law scholar Kamisar. Domestic violence expert Ewing calls this "the slippery slope argument—that eventually we'll have the 'rotten life' defense because how will you ever close the door?"

He thinks the courts already have done so, however. "So far, the door has opened just a little bit and very few victims have been able to get through that small opening—and I think that's probably appropriate—but those groups that have gotten through have done so by surviving years of judicial scrutiny and legal commentary."

Ewing and others feel that the growth in acceptance of the battered women's syndrome doesn't reflect a loosening of standards so much as an attempt to rectify gender bias in the legal system and incorporate medical knowledge into the law.

Historically, raising self-defense claims for battered women has been "like fitting a square peg into a round hole," says Ewing. There were problems in proving they acted reasonably by staying in an abusive situation and by resorting to violence when there appeared to be no imminent threat of danger. What was not grasped, says Rosen of the UNC's law clinic, is that "a battered woman is always in danger. It's like being kidnapped. Even when you're asleep, you're at risk."

Legally, the only option for these women was to claim insanity in homicide cases. But that strategy changed as juries became educated about "learned helplessness"—in part, by TV talk shows and movies of the week. Juries came to understand why victims would feel as if they had no options other than lethal force.

Rosen believes that if the imminence requirement for self-defense were modified, introducing evidence of the battered women's syndrome would lessen in importance. But this would require proof that a defendant had no reasonable alternatives, which Rosen thinks is true of the woman who's being stalked by a murderous ex-spouse. It's clear, he says, that "society has not found a way to give protection to women in these circumstances."

The state of New Hampshire may be taking another approach entirely. In March, its Legislature began debating whether the battered women's syndrome should be a separate defense, somewhere between self-defense and insanity. If that happens, it would be a first: abuse as a separate defense rather than as underlying evidence.

Ewing emphasizes that these modifications in the law have benefitted a small group of people. "It's scary to think of a society in which anyone can raise some kind of plausible excuse for their behavior and the courts will take it seriously," Ewing says. "But that's not what's going on and it's not likely to happen in our lifetimes."

Jury Consultants:
Boon or Bane?

Communication Is Lawyer's Art, A Litigator Says . . .

The National Law Journal asked two prominent attorneys, one a trial lawyer and the other a jury consultant, for their views on the use of jury consultants. Both have been successful in highly publicized cases. But, as their answers show, that is where the similarly ends.

Frederick P. Furth

Frederick P. Furth is the senior partner of San Francisco's Furth, Fahrner & Mason, which specializes in antitrust litigation. Among recent cases, he represented former New England Patriots owner William Sullivan in his suit against the national Football League, convincing a jury that the NFL had broken antitrust laws in preventing Mr. Sullivan from trying to sell stock in the team. An outspoken jury-consultant critic, Mr. Furth told the Wall Street Journal *that a client said to him about jury consultants: "I thought that's what I pay you for."*

Q: You have been quoted in the past as having a rather dim view of jury consultants. Why?

MR. FURTH: Trial attorneys are using jury consultants as crutches, especially those attorneys who have not had a great deal of real-life experience. They, the attorneys, are insecure and are scared to tell their clients what they think. The attorneys are afraid that if they lose a case and didn't use a jury consultant, it will be discussed in a seminar somewhere as an example of why you should use a consultant.

Why do I want to hire someone who has a Ph.D. in jury consulting or jury research to tell me how to communicate? That's what you hire a trial attorney for. Knowledge of the law is something every lawyer has. When you hire an attorney, hopefully you're hiring someone who has been through life's ups and downs as well.

The ultimate trial is a communion between the attorney and the jury. You don't want that violated. Jury consultants tend to violate that by getting between you and your jury. I don't want someone with a degree in social studies looking over my shoulder.

Q: What about those cases in which a seasoned attorney uses a jury consultant? Does the "crutch" theory apply even then?

MR. FURTH: I don't know. Even experienced attorneys may have emotional problems and need a cheering section. If they're that weak, they can call me. I'll try the case for them and they can stay in Palm Beach.

Q: Have you ever used a jury consultant?

MR. FURTH: Yes, but my experiences with them has led to what I believe. I tried it; it's interesting. You go into analysis every night with your jury consultant. It's like having therapy.

But even if the consultant is a pleasant member of the opposite sex, it is a distraction at the end of a long day to the preparation of your case. They always tell you the good things first, but then follow it

with criticisms. They may say, "The jury really enjoyed when you said this or that, but stop picking your nose."

Q: Can you ever envision a case in which you *would* use a jury consultant again?

MR. FURTH: Yes, but it would be a very minor role. If you have a complicated or very technical case, and you're concerned about the jury understanding it, you could use a small issues panel to see how they would react to certain elements. Or you could do it with your wife and kids. They would be just as good.

Q: Do you think that the use of jury consultants helped in such publicized cases as William Kennedy Smith, the Rodney King officers, the Menendez brothers or the Branch Davidians?

MR. FURTH: I just can't say. I'm sure they all had outstanding lawyers, which probably had more to do with the results.

Q: Do you feel that jury selection has become more complicated as the result of recent decisions, such as the U.S. Supreme Court decision in *J.E.B. v. Alabama ex rel. T.B.,* and may that ultimately change your mind about the use of jury consultants?

MR. FURTH: If I was in the jury selection business, I would say yes. Guess what? I then sell more jury consulting. But no, I don't see how those cases are going to make the selection process any more difficult and I would challenge these jury consultants to tell me how it would make it tougher to pick a jury.

From *The National Law Journal,* June 6, 1994, p. C2. © 1994 by the New York Law Publishing Company. Reprinted by permission.

. . . But a Trial Consultant May Bring a Fresh Approach

Robert B. Hirschhorn

Robert B. Hirschhorn, a former trial lawyer, is lead consultant at Galveston, Texas' Cathy E. Bennett & Associates, a trial consulting firm. His high-profile clients have included William Kennedy Smith; Branch Davidian sect members who survived the burning of their Waco, Texas, compound; and U.S. Sen. Kay Bailey Hutchison, R-Texas, whose prosecution for alleged misuse of state funds was dismissed before trial. Mr. Hirschhorn is a member of the faculty of the National Criminal Defense College at Mercer Law School in Maco, Ga.

Q: Why use a jury consultant?

MR. HIRSCHHORN: A competent jury consultant is the eyes and ears of the lawyer. A lawyer cannot develop a rapport with the jury, take notes and observe the jury all at the same time.

The main reason is that when lawyers go to law school, they have a "lawbotomy." When they come out, they talk differently, dress differently and act differently. You therefore don't want to use another lawyer as your eyes and ears, because he or she had the same lawbotomy. You need someone with a clean, fresh and open-minded approach.

Q: There seems to be a growing feeling that jury consultants are losing some of the appeal they enjoyed in the 1980s. What do you attribute this to?

MR. HIRSCHHORN: The bad ones are getting weeded out, and I'm glad of that. But I'm booking trials for January of 1995. At our firm we could hire five more associates and still couldn't handle all of the cases. We reject four out of five cases. I predict in 20 years every major case will have a jury consultant—on both sides.

Q: Should attorneys use jury consultants in every complicated case, or are there instances when an attorney's own experience would be as good or better?

MR. HIRSCHHORN: The only time you should hire a jury consultant is when you want to win. If an attorney is committed to using every resource, a jury consultant should be part of it.

Q: In your most memorable cases—William Kennedy Smith, the Branch Davidians, Sen. Hutchison—would you say the result would have been the same if you had not been brought in as a consultant?

MR. HIRSCHHORN: I'm convinced that Smith would have been found not guilty with or without us. But there might have been very different results in the others if we had not been involved.

Q: Are you stacking the deck by bringing in jury consultants?

MR. HIRSCHHORN: Absolutely not. In all of the cases we've handled, we're 10 yards behind. In the William Kennedy Smith and Branch Davidians cases, everyone thought our clients were guilty. We just want to bring the client up to an equal point on the starting line.

Q: Do you see the use of jury consultants as the province only of wealthy defendants?

MR. HIRSCHHORN: No. Consulting services at our firm are available to anyone on the socioeconomic scale. If I believe in the case, I'll take it. In fact, 25 percent of our work is pro bono. We use the old Robin Hood technique of billing from those who can most afford it so we can help those who can't. Most downtrodden people accused of crimes should have the same shot as those with money.

Q: One trial attorney says that jury consultants are nothing more than "crutches" for inexperienced attorneys who have not had a great deal of real-life experience. How do you respond to that?

MR. HIRSCHHORN: I'll bet he didn't like fax machines either when they first came out. It sounds like he had a couple of bad experiences—either bad results or was overcharged.

I've spent a great deal of time with some of the greatest civil and criminal lawyers in this country. They didn't need crutches. They just wanted to win their cases.

Q: Are there any recent court decisions, such as *J.E.B.*, that will have an impact on your profession in either a positive or negative manner?

MR. HIRSCHHORN: Yes. Lawyers will now have to give gender-neutral and race-neutral reasons for their peremptory strikes. You're seeing the beginning of the end of peremptory challenges.

Lawyers are to blame for this because they brought their own prejudices into the jury selection process. People were getting struck for the color of their skin. *J.E.B.* has blown the lid off the Pandora's box of peremptory challenges.

Q: Should jury consultants be licensed in some manner?

MR. HIRSCHHORN: No, that pushes it into being an elite club. If jury consultants were required to have a Ph.D., for example, that would have excluded the godmother of this profession, our founder, the late Cat Bennett.

The number of degrees has no bearing on how good someone will be as a trial consultant. Some of the best consultants I've ever seen had only high school diplomas and some of the worst have had Ph.D. after their names.

Juvenile Justice

While recognizing the variations within specific offense categories, the overall juvenile violent crime arrest rate remained relatively constant for several decades. In the late 1980s something changed—a change which is bringing more and more juveniles into the justice system charged with a violent offense.

The juvenile justice system is a twentieth-century response to the problems of dealing with children in trouble with the law or children who need society's protection. Juvenile court procedure differs from procedure in adult courts because juvenile courts were based on the philosophy that the function of the court was to treat and to help, not to punish and to abandon the offender. More recently, operations of the juvenile court have received criticism, and a number of significant Supreme Court decisions changed the way the courts must approach the rights of children.

In spite of a few changes, the major thrust of the juvenile justice system remains one of diversion and treatment rather than adjudication and incarceration, although there is a trend toward dealing more punitively with serious juvenile offenders.

The unit's opening essay cites a federal government report, "Delinquency Cases in Juvenile Court, 1992" that establishes the extent of delinquency in the United States and covers other aspects of juvenile justice.

The article "Their Crimes Don't Make Them Adults" argues that punishing children as adults probably makes the situation worse, despite harsh public attitudes and views.

U.S. attorney general Janet Reno sketches a broad outline of her proposal focusing on children in this country in the essay "A National Agenda for Children: On the Front Lines with Attorney General Janet Reno." She asserts that understanding delinquency causation is crucial.

The mood and tenor of juvenile court judges across the country, which is reflected in "Juvenile Judges Say: Time to Get Tough," generally supports juvenile courts that are more like those found in the adult system.

"Throw Away the Key" asserts that phenomena such as increasing rates of infant mortality, child poverty, teen suicide, and incarceration in America in the 1990s are indicative of a country seriously harming its youth.

Jackson Toby identifies both causes and ways to reduce everyday school violence in his essay, "Everyday School Violence: How Disorder Fuels It."

A seasoned and respected juvenile court judge presents his views and concerns about the system in the essay "On the Front Lines: Interview with Judge David B. Mitchell."

An especially disquieting note is sounded in the closing article "American Killers Are Getting Younger." Evidence is presented that shows that the new generation of youngsters in this country is more inclined to resort to violence over trivial issues.

Looking Ahead: Challenge Questions

What are the types of reform efforts the juvenile justice system is currently experiencing?

Why doesn't the "get-tough" policy work?

What are some recent trends in juvenile delinquency?

Do you believe departure of the juvenile justice system from its original purpose is warranted?

In what ways will the juvenile justice system be affected by the present trends in delinquency?

Unit 5

Delinquency Cases in Juvenile Court, 1992

Jeffrey A. Butts, Ph.D.

This fact sheet was prepared by Jeffrey Butts, Project Manager of the National Juvenile Court Data Archive. The work was supported by OJJDP grant #92-JN-CX-0001. Joseph Moone, a Social Science Program Specialist in OJJDP's Research and Program Development Division, served as the Program Manager.

COUNTS AND TRENDS

Juvenile courts in the United States processed an estimated 1,471,200 delinquency cases in 1992. Delinquency cases involve juveniles charged with criminal law violations. The number of delinquency cases handled by juvenile courts increased 26% between 1988 and 1992. Since 1988, cases involving offenses against persons increased 56% while property offense cases increased 23%. during this 5-year period, cases involving charges of robbery and aggravated assault grew 52% and 80%, respectively. Although the number of drug law violation cases was down 12% compared with 1988, the number of drug cases increased 15% between 1991 and 1992.

These national estimates of the cases handled by juvenile courts in 1992 are based on data from more than 1,500 courts that had jurisdiction over 57% of the U.S. juvenile population in 1992. The unit of count in this Fact Sheet is a case disposed during the calendar year by a court with juvenile jurisdiction. Each case represents one youth processed by a juvenile court on a new referral, regardless of the number of individual offenses contained in that referral. An individual youth can be involved in more than one case during the calendar year. For a full description of the methodology used in collecting the data and making the national estimates, see *Juvenile Court Statistics 1992* (OJJDP, forthcoming).

DETENTION

One of the first decisions made in processing juvenile delinquency cases is whether or not the juvenile should be detained in a secure facility to await the next court appearance. Juveniles are sometimes detained to protect the community from their behavior, sometimes to protect the juveniles themselves, or to ensure their appearance at court hearings. Juveniles were securely detained in 20% of the delinquency cases processed in 1992. Detention was used in 35% of drug law violations, 24% of person offense cases, and 17% of property offense cases. Partly because of the large volume of property offenses handled by juvenile courts, 47% of cases involving detention in 1992 were property offense cases.

INTAKE DECISION

After reviewing the details of a case, a decision is made either to dismiss it, handle it informally, or formally process the case by taking the matter before a judge. More than one-fifth (23%) of 1992 delinquency cases were dismissed at intake, often for lack of legal sufficiency. Another 26% were processed informally, with the juvenile agreeing to a voluntary disposition (e.g. probation). Half (51%) of the delinquency cases handled in 1992 were processed formally, and involved either an adjudicatory hearing or a hearing to consider transferring jurisdiction to the adult court.

TRANSFER TO CRIMINAL COURT

During a transfer (or waiver) hearing, the juvenile court judge is asked to waive jurisdiction over a matter and transfer the case to criminal court so that the juvenile may be tried as an adult. Transfer decisions are usually based on the seriousness of the offense, the juvenile's prior record, and the juvenile's amenability to treatment. In 1992, 11,700 delinquency cases were transferred by a juvenile court judge. Transfers increased 68% between 1988 and 1992. Of the cases transferred in 1992, 34% involved a person offense, 45% involved a property offense, and 12% involved a drug law violation. The cases most likely to be transferred in 1992 were those involving drug law violation; 3.1% of formally processed drug law violations were trans-

From the *Office of Juvenile Justice and Delinquency Prevention*, Fact Sheet #18, July 1994. Reprinted by permission of the U.S. Department of Justice, Office of Justice Programs.

Most Serious Offense in Delinquency Cases, 1992			
	Number	Percent Change	
Offense	of Cases	'91-92	'88-92
Total	**1,471,200**	7%	26%
Person Offense	**301,000**	**13**	**56**
Criminal Homicide	2,500	-9	55
Forcible Rape	5,400	10	27
Robbery	32,900	9	52
Aggravated Assault	77,900	16	80
Simple Assault	152,800	14	47
Other Violent Sex Offense	9,900	13	60
Other Person Offense	19,800	11	63
Property Offense	**842,200**	**3**	**23**
Burglary	156,400	4	22
Larceny-Theft	361,600	1	16
Motor Vehicle Theft	73,000	2	34
Arson	8,300	10	24
Vandalism	121,700	12	50
Trespassing	58,500	2	17
Stolen Property Offense	28,900	7	-7
Other Property Offense	33,700	6	57
Drug Law Violation	**72,100**	**15**	**-12**
Public Order Offense	**255,900**	**11**	**21**
Obstruction of Justice	87,100	8	10
Disorderly Conduct	69,300	13	50
Weapons Offense	41,000	26	86
Liquor Law Violation	12,500	-7	-26
Nonviolent Sex Offense	12,900	22	19
Other Public Order	33,000	3	-8
Violent Crime Index *	**118,600**	**13**	**68**
Property Crime Index *	**599,400**	**2**	**20**

*	Violent Crime Index includes criminal homicide, forcible rape, robbery, and aggravated assault.
**	Property Crime Index includes burglary, larceny-theft, motor vehicle theft, and arson.
Note:	Detail may not add to totals because of rounding. Percent change calculations are based on unrounded numbers

formal probation, while in 28% the juvenile was placed out of the home in a residential facility, and 11% resulted in other dispositions (referral to an outside agency, community service, restitution, etc.). In most delinquency cases where the juvenile was not adjudicated, the case was dismissed by the court.

Between 1988 and 1992, the number of cases in which an adjudicated delinquent was ordered by the court to be placed in a residential facility increased 19%, while the number of formal probation cases increased 24%. In 1992, 57% of probation cases involved property offenses and 20% involved person offenses. Out-of-home placement cases, on the other hand, were slightly more likely to involve person offenses (23%) and slightly less likely to involve property offenses (48%).

GENDER

In 1992, four out of five delinquency cases involved a male juvenile (81%). This was the same proportion found in 1988. Males accounted for 79% of person offense cases, 81% of property cases, and 88% of drug law violation cases.

AGE

Compared with 1988, the delinquency cases handled by juvenile courts in 1992 involved slightly younger youth. Sixty percent of the juvenile delinquency cases processed in 1992 involved a juvenile under 16 years of age, compared with 57% in 1988. In 1992, juveniles younger than age 16 were responsible for 62% of all person offense cases, 64% of all property offense cases, and 39% of drug law violation cases.

RACE

In 1992, 80% of the juvenile population was white and 15% was black. White juveniles, however, were involved in 65% of the delinquency cases handled by juvenile courts. Black juveniles were involved in 31% of delinquency cases—27% of property offense cases and 40% of person offense cases.

FOR MORE INFORMATION

This fact sheet is based on the forthcoming report, *Juvenile Court Statistics 1992*. Copies of the report will be available from the Juvenile Justice Clearinghouse. Call (800) 638-8736 to obtain a copy. OJJDP also supports the distribution of a PC-compatible software package that contains the data from *Juvenile Court Statistics 1992*. The software is easy to use and can supplement educational and research programs. For a copy of the software, contact the National Juvenile Court Data Archive Project at the National Center for Juvenile Justice, 701 Forbes Avenue, Pittsburgh, PA 15219, (412/227-6950).

ferred in 1992, compared with 2.4% of person offense cases, and 1.3% of property offense cases.

ADJUDICATION AND DISPOSITION

Adjudicatory hearings are used to establish the facts in a delinquency case (analogous to determining guilt or innocence) and to decide whether to place the juvenile under the supervision of the court. In 1992 juveniles were adjudicated in more than half (57%) of the 743,700 cases brought before a judge. Once adjudicated, the majority of cases (57%) were placed on

Their Crimes Don't Make Them Adults

Despite harsh public views, punishing children as adults probably makes things worse.

Alex Kotlowitz

Alex Kotlowitz is the author of "There Are No Children Here: The Story of Two Boys Growing Up in the Other America" and a distinguished visitor at the John D. and Catherine T. MacArthur Foundation in Chicago.

Jacqueline Ross has handled upward of 3,000 cases in her five years as a public defender, all in Chicago's imposing Criminal Courts building. She represents mostly young men, many of whom have been in prison before. But one case still haunts her—that of Paulettta R., who, at the age of 14, was charged with first-degree murder. Pauletta and three girl-friends schemed to lure a man into an alley for sex where another companion, a man in his 20's, waited with a handgun. The robbery went sour and the young man shot the intended robbery victim.

During the trial, Ross recalls, Pauletta would sit at the defense table, her head buried in her hands, her thumb in her mouth. At other times, during partic-ularly tense moments, she would rock in her chair, childlike.

"She had very little idea what was going on," Ross recalls. "She should have been tried in juvenile court."

Pauletta is one of thousands of children who, accused of violent—and in recent years nonviolent—crimes are transferred to adult court, where retribution rather than rehabilitation is the result, if not the objective. This, according to a recent USA Today/CNN/Gallup Poll, is what the public wants. Three-quarters of those polled said children who commit a violent crime should be treated as adults.

As more and more juveniles are arrested for murder, rape and armed robbery—arrests for violent crimes went up 27 percent in the decade between 1980 and 1990—politicians, partly out of desperation, partly out of fear (for their jobs), are cracking down on kids. It is a frenzy that child advocates have labeled the "adultifica-tion" of children. Last year alone, the Colorado, Utah and Florida Legislatures passed laws making it easier to try certain youth offenders as adults. A number of other states are considering similar legislation. Sena-tor Carol Moseley-Braun, the freshman Illinois Demo-crat, has introduced a measure calling for the automatic transfer of juveniles as young as 13 who are accused of Federal crimes.

The juvenile courts were founded on the premise that they could be more flexible in working with children; there the accused would be defined less by their offenses than by their youth and their need for adult guidance and care. In juvenile court, the judge—in consultation with probation officers, psychologists and social workers—has great leeway as to what kind of treatment and punishment to impose. Children, because their personalities are still in the process of formation, are thought to be more open to rehabilita-tion than adults. The "waiving" of juveniles into adult courts protects neither the public nor the children. Consider Pauletta's case.

On the night of July 27, 1991, Pauletta drove around the streets of a tough neighborhood on the North Side of Chicago with three girlfriends and a young man named Michael Brandon. They stopped to chat with a neighborhood gang leader whom Pauletta's sister owed $100. He told Pauletta that if she didn't come up with the money, he'd hurt her. Pauletta and her friends, one of whom was also in debt to the gang leader then drew up a plan. They'd pose as prostitutes and rob a cus-tomer.

In the early hours of the next day, the four girls primped and posed on a street corner when a young man approached them for sex. They told him he could have his pick. He chose Pauletta's friend, Robin, also 14. Robin and her prey walked into a nearby alley where Brandon lurked in the shadows with a pistol. A

From the *New York Times Magazine*, February 13, 1994, pp. 40-41. © 1994 by the New York Times Company. Reprinted by permission.

struggle ensued, and Brandon shot once, killing his victim. Pauletta heard the gunshot as she walked toward a friends' house. Within hours, the police arrested Pauletta—as well as the four others. All five were charged with first-degree murder.

Given the serious nature of the crime, the prosecution asked the courts to try this eighth grader as an adult. The court psychologist, Nancy Feys, testified that Pauletta, who lived on welfare with her mother, had "serious problems with depression" and functioned "like a small child" with wide mood swings, including suicidal impulses. Pauletta had told the psychologist, "I just don't like the world," according to court documents.

Feys urged that Pauletta be placed in a long-term residential treatment center; both she and Pauletta's probation officer recommended that Pauletta remain in the juvenile system. The judge, though, sent her to adult court where, last summer, she was found not guilty of murder, but guilty of armed robbery. She received a six-year sentence that insured she would spend her formative teen-age years behind bars.

The crackdown on children has gone well beyond those accused of violent crimes. In Florida, for example, between October 1990 and June 1991, 3,248 children were transferred to adult court for offenses as serious as murder and as trivial as possession of alcohol. And Florida is not alone.

In November, I met Brian H. and his father, Leon, a supervisor at an electrical company, in Courtroom 301 of the same Criminal Courts building where Pauletta's case was heard. Brian, dressed in a gray suit and tasseled brown loafers, sat erect on the bench, nervously clenching his hands as he awaited the judge's arrival. His father leaned over to straighten his tie.

Brian is 15. He had been arrested and charged with possessing 1.9 grams of cocaine with the intent to deliver. This would be Brian's first offense, but because he was accused of selling drugs on the sidewalk near a local elementary school, he will be tried in the adult courts. Under Illinois law, any child charged with dealing narcotics within 1,000 feet of a school or public housing property is automatically transferred into the adult system.

"What does a kid know at 15?" asks his father. "How can you hold a kid at that age responsible for adulthood? There's got to be another way."

Children like Pauletta and Brian live in neighborhoods that don't allow much room for adolescent mistakes. They experience more than they should. This past summer, for instance, Brian saw a friend shot in the forearm; another schoolmate was killed in a gang shoot-out. Pauletta came from a family shattered by alcohol and domestic violence. Still, despite the wreckage caused by astronomical unemployment, daily gunfire and inadequate schools, they are just children. They hunt for snakes, ride bikes, play video games and go on dates. They are also impulsive and silly. They often make wrongheaded decisions. They're easily swayed by peers.

Treating adolescents as adults ignores the fact that they are developmentally different. "We can't rewire them," says Dr. Katherine Kaufer Christoffel, a pediatrician and director of the Violent Injury Prevention Center at Children's Memorial Medical Center in Chicago. "It seems like we're saying, 'Don't be a child in the wrong place.'"

Dr. Christoffel argues that preventing youth crime requires changing the child's environment. She cites studies indicating that the greatest impact on diminishing drunken driving among teen-agers comes from changes like curfews, alcohol-free proms and raising the driving age to 17.

Dr. Christoffel is concerned about what she perceives as a backlash toward children. "To the extent that parents and community fail, society has to back them up," she says. What has society done to back up urban children and their parents? Not much.

Brian's situation is illustrative. When he first showed signs of trouble—coming home late, failing classes, being suspended for fistfights at school and wearing expensive jewelry—his parents sought help. The assistance Brian could receive at his school is limited; there's only one full-time social worker and one part-time psychologist for 1,700 students. His parents called the juvenile detention center to ask if Brian could visit the facility. They hoped that might shake him up. Officials there don't give tours and had no suggestions for referral. His father then called the local police station to ask if an officer would come to their house to talk with Brian. But the police, according to his parents, said they couldn't do anything until Brian got into trouble.

"We wanted to frighten him," Brian's mother says. "We wanted him to get back on track. I was under the impression that as a parent if you were willing to work within the system you could get help."

Children need to face consequences, particularly if they're involved in criminal activity. They cannot be absolved of responsibility. Moreover, the painful truth is that some children need to be locked up for a long time, if for no other reason than to assure public safety. But a blanket policy of sending children like Pauletta and Brian into the adult courts is a grievously misguided policy. This law-and-order approach assumes that trying kids as grown-ups will deter crime. But longer sentences haven't necessarily reduced adult crime. Worse, these transfer laws often have an unintended consequence. The criminal courts are already so overburdened that some adult-court judges have shown a propensity to give children lighter sentences than they might receive in juvenile court.

The debate over treating juvenile offenders as adults is more than a debate over youth crime; it gets to the fundamental question of what it means to be a child, particularly in an increasingly violent world. Children need help navigating through what can be a treacherous adolescent maze. That is why children can't marry without permission of their parents, why children can't buy liquor—and why society created juvenile courts.

"What's so disturbing," says Felton Earls, a professor at the School of Public Health at Harvard University, "is to see a legal process that's lowering the age of adulthood rather than seeing this as a failure of social structures and policy towards our children."

When I met Brian and his father at court, their case was continued to another date. In the hallway, they huddled with their lawyer.

"Is it very serious?" Brian asked, is hands buried deep in his pants pockets, his eyes riveted on his tasseled shoes.

"It doesn't get much more serious than this," his attorney told him.

Because of mandatory-minimum sentencing, if found guilty, Brian—tried as an adult—will receive a sentence of at least six years. Moreover, he will carry for life the stamp of a convicted felon, making it difficult to find employment.

"I'm scared to go back," Brian told me. (He spent three weeks in a detention facility for juveniles.) "I got plans to do with my life." He says he wants to be an electrical engineer, just like his dad.

As for Pauletta she's due to be released from the Illinois Youth Center at Warrenville this July, at which time she'll be a month away from turning 18. She will re-enter society without a high-school diploma and without the kind of intense counseling the court psychologist said she needed.

Pauletta and Brian made mistakes. Were they big enough that society should snatch away their childhoods?

A National Agenda for Children: On the Front Lines With Attorney General Janet Reno

Janet Reno is the 77th Attorney General of the United States. This interview was conducted for Juvenile Justice by John J. Wilson, Acting Administrator of the Office of Juvenile Justice and Delinquency Prevention.

Juvenile Justice: Attorney General Reno, you have called for a National Agenda for Children. Could you please describe the broad outlines of such an agenda and how it would affect children in the justice system.

Attorney General Reno: I feel very strongly that it is imperative that we look beyond the role of the prosecutor and understand what causes delinquency problems in the first place. I don't think that there is any one point at which you can intervene in a child's life to make a significant difference. Instead, it is essential that we view a child's life as a continuum and provide a consistent support system for those times when the family is unable to provide that support on its own.

There are many things we can do that are far more cost-effective than waiting for the crisis of delinquency or crime to occur. First, we need to develop family preservation programs that offer support to families *before* they are in a crisis situation so they are much more likely to stay together through life's difficulties. We've got to make sure that our parents are old enough, wise enough, and financially able to take care of their children. We've

got to make a major effort against teen pregnancy in America. And we've got to offer parenting skill courses in every school so that children who have been raised without quality support from parents learn how to give it to their own children.

Second, we must provide proper preventive medical care for all children. I'm troubled that in this Nation a 70-year-old person can get an operation to extend his or her life expectancy by 3 years, but the family of a small child with no other health care benefits may make too much money to be considered eligible for Medicaid. I think that every child in America should have current immunizations, and every pregnant woman in America should have access to proper preventive medical and prenatal care.

Third, I strongly support *educare* programs—and by educare I mean safe, constructive child care for all children on a comprehensive basis, not just for those whose parents can afford a child care center or live where one is readily available. However, these types of programs are especially important for at-risk

From *Juvenile Justice*, a journal of the Office of Juvenile Justice and Delinquency Prevention, Fall/Winter 1993, pp. 2-8. Reprinted by permission of the U.S. Department of Justice, Office of Justice Programs.

children who need an opportunity to develop as strong, constructive human beings because—for whatever reason—they lack proper supervision in the home. Educare programs should be linked with expanded and improved Head Start programs that are available to all children in need. I believe that educare programs for small children are essential because the ages of 0 to 3 are the most formative time in a child's life—a time when child development experts say that children learn the concept of reward and punishment and develop a conscience.

Fourth, I support conflict resolution programs in our public schools to teach our children how to resolve conflicts peacefully. We have accomplished a great deal in developing education and prevention programs, such as DARE [Drug Abuse Resistance Education], that can deter children from drug use, and I think that we can do the same with respect to violence and guns in the school.

Fifth, we must free our teachers' time to teach. I think it would be very effective to develop full-service schools in areas where there are a significant number of children at risk—that is, schools that have social service providers on campus to address the social needs of the child. We also need to look at our curriculum to make sure we're doing everything we can to make school relevant and interesting for our children. We should develop school-to-work programs that provide career tracks that students can pursue and know that when they graduate they will have developed a skill that will enable them to earn a living wage. Early assessment of interest and aptitude should be used to chart an educational and work experience program, and summer job programs should be linked with educational and work experience programs as part of a comprehensive effort to prepare our children for the workplace of tomorrow. We also should develop afternoon and evening programs for children who are unsupervised because parents are working or otherwise unavailable. Such programs, including those that do not involve sports or recreation, could help our children get started in the right direction.

> ## It is imperative that we look beyond the role of the prosecutor and understand what causes delinquency problems in the first place.

Sixth, truancy prevention programs should be developed in every elementary school so that at the first sign of truancy, police, social service agencies, and the school join together to identify the cause and do something about it before it is too late. Unfortunately, there is a tendency for police to take a truant child to school, and if the parent doesn't come for the child, the principal often sends the child home without investigating why the child was truant. I would love for police officers, social service counselors, and public health nurses to make a home visit and find out why students were truant and what could be done to intervene with them.

> ## The juvenile justice system tends to wait until the child has been delinquent two or three times before evaluating the child's needs and developing a comprehensive intervention program.

Finally, employers should do everything they can to put the family first in the workplace so that parents have sufficient time to care for and spend quality time with their children.

Juvenile Justice: According to OJJDP's Conditions of Confinement study, three out of four confined juveniles are detained in overcrowded facilities. Overcrowding often results in violence against staff and other juveniles and an increased number of attempted suicides. It also gives rise to a lot of other problems, and security becomes an overriding concern of the institution. What do you think should be done about this issue?

Attorney General Reno: Obviously, one of the first steps that can be taken is to develop the type of preventive programs I just described, but beyond that, we must intervene earlier once the child has committed a delinquent act. The juvenile justice system tends to wait until the child has been delinquent two or three times before evaluating the child's needs and developing a comprehensive intervention program. At that point it is often too late to intervene. This occurs in the juvenile justice system not because of a lack of concern, but because the system is absolutely overwhelmed.

I would love to see us develop a means of identifying those children who are at greatest risk of continued delinquency. In those cases we must do everything we can to determine the cause of the problem and what we can do about it. A risk and needs assessment would allow us to determine what programs would best address the needs of children who may be at greater risk of continued delinquent behavior. However, we must take care that we do not label children unintentionally or inappropriately because many children are going to turn out okay.

Juvenile Justice: In fact, statistics show that 50 percent of the juveniles who have contact with the juvenile justice system for delinquency never come back a second time. The trick is to figure out which 50 percent.

Attorney General Reno: That is the great difficulty because some people want to do nothing and wait to see which of those juveniles come back. However, I think that approach runs the risk of allowing the behavior to become ingrained.

Juvenile Justice: Often it's not two or three times, it's seven or eight times. It's

seven or eight stolen cars or seven or eight aggravated assaults before anybody does anything, and by then not only has a delinquent pattern of behavior developed, but juveniles have stopped taking the system seriously. That's why OJJDP's Comprehensive Strategy calls for immediate intervention. Turning to another matter, studies indicate there is a disproportionate representation of minority youth in secure facilities. How do you think the Justice Department should address this problem?

Attorney General Reno: It is important for the Justice Department to assist States in analyzing every level at which intervention occurs to ensure that a young minority child is treated in the same way as any other child. Often I find that people react to situations without having the data to make an informed judgment. For example, in Florida we conducted an independent study of the application of Florida's Career Criminal Statute because some people felt that it unfairly discriminated against the minority population. The study indicated that only 2 of the 20 circuits did not discriminate in any way, and many of those found to discriminate were shocked to learn that they did. They wanted to take steps to avoid discrimination in the future. Consequently, I think it's important that we develop mechanisms in the juvenile and adult justice systems to show jurisdictions how we can properly apply the law to ensure that it's imposed even-handedly. I also feel that the Department of Justice needs to explore sentencing practices in the Federal system.

It's also imperative that we develop advocates for children who are entering the system. For example, if a middle-class child comes into the system with two parents who work, are devoted to the child, and are present in the courtroom with a minister and a psychologist offering alternative programs to recommend to the court, that child is going to have a better chance of staying out of the system than the child who has no advocate in court. Unfortunately, public defenders are so overwhelmed and their case loads so large that it is difficult for them to follow up on a child. Often they think they have been successful if they get a child off on a motion to dismiss or a motion to suppress. But I think it's important that they follow up through a summons—and if they are unable to do so, then members of the private bar, through pro bono services, should act as advocates for children by seeking community programs that will help them develop into successful, contributing members of society. There is a lot that can be done in this area.

Juvenile Justice: While the number of juvenile offenses has remained relatively static, the level of violent offenses has increased. How can we address the problem of the small number of serious, violent, and chronic juvenile offenders?

Attorney General Reno: I think that youth violence is probably the most serious crime problem that we face in America today. And unfortunately, I have seen too many juveniles who have lost their fear of the juvenile justice system because they don't think anything is going to happen to them.

We urgently need to develop fair, reasonable sanctions that fit the crime—no matter how old the offender. If a 13- or 14-year-old commits armed robbery, that child has got to know that there is a fair, reasonable sanction to fit the crime and that there is no justification for hurting someone or putting a gun against a person's head.

At the same time, we need to provide aftercare and followup that address the causes that generated the crime in the first place. We can't simply punish young offenders and return them to the community where the problem arose and think that they are going to succeed—particularly if they don't have a strong family system and are living in circumstances rife with risk factors. For these reasons I support programs with job training and placement, treatment, counseling ser-

vices, aftercare, and followup to help juvenile offenders reenter the community.

Juvenile Justice: Our Causes and Correlates study confirms that there is a direct link between physical child abuse and neglect and subsequent violent delinquency, and more significantly, that the amount of domestic violence to which a juvenile is exposed or victimized by is directly proportional to the violent conduct in which the juvenile later engages. What are your views on physical child abuse and neglect and its relationship to delinquency?

> *Often I find that people react to situations without having the data to make an informed judgment.*

Attorney General Reno: I am concerned that typically when we talk about child abuse and neglect, we're talking about child welfare. In my experience in the juvenile justice system, there seems to be a gap between professionals working in child welfare and those working in juvenile justice. Instead of working together in a coordinated effort to help the child and the family, they work apart, not knowing what the other is doing.

> *There is no justification for hurting someone or putting a gun against a person's head.*

I think many children coming into the juvenile justice system are there because of neglect in the sense that they have not had a strong family network. In some cases they have been unsupervised and lacked order, structure, and clear limits in their lives. In other cases they have come to think of violence as a way of life because they have observed it in the home. In either case, it is important that we look at children coming into the system and determine not only what fair, appropriate sanctions would be, but also what can be done to rebuild the fabric of society around them.

Juvenile Justice: How do you see the Department of Justice working with other Federal agencies to help children and their families remain drug-free? And

---

For too long we have forgotten and neglected our children.

---

what role do you see the Coordinating Council on Juvenile Justice playing in this regard?

Attorney General Reno: I think it is crucial that the Federal Government develop a coordinated effort among the different agencies that touch on children and families. Currently the Department of Justice is trying to develop such a comprehensive effort along with the Departments of Commerce, Education, Health and Human Services, Housing and Urban Development, and Labor. We are trying to focus on the National Agenda for Children by developing a partnership with communities.

Let's organize efforts that attract our young people and give them an opportunity to serve this Nation.

For example, we know that local communities are better able to assess their own needs than the Federal Government. We also know that the Federal Government could use its community resources more effectively if individual agencies did not have arbitrary barriers to program eligibility. The Federal Coordinating Council is in a good position to play a role as well, by bringing together the heads of various Federal agencies and looking at the broad issues facing families and children. I believe that much could be done if our limited community and Federal resources

were used in the most comprehensive manner possible. And we must begin by investing dollars up front in prevention programs. Let's encourage communities to address the children's agenda, develop job training and retraining programs for those who have lost their jobs, and create programs that enable the elderly to be more self-sufficient by remaining in their homes.

Juvenile Justice: How do you see the role of the juvenile court? How might it be strengthened?

Attorney General Reno: It is time to recognize that juvenile court judges need more say in structuring programs that fit the needs of the child. Judges would be more effective if they had a comprehensive evaluation and assessment of the child and of the child's needs. And if the social service components in youth service programs were better linked with the court and the court had more of a say in the program, the entire juvenile justice system would work together better and be more accountable to the community.

Juvenile Justice: After a relatively short period of time on the bench, juvenile court judges develop a remarkable expertise in knowing the programs and the resources that are available.

Attorney General Reno: They do develop a remarkable expertise. Yet, often those programs are overwhelmed, and judges have little say in the administration of programs that are not working.

Juvenile Justice: All too often our efforts seem to be a case of "too little, too late." How can we help children grow up to be law-abiding, contributing citizens, rather than delinquents or even adult criminals?

Attorney General Reno: I think that the problems of delinquency—drugs, youth gangs, teen pregnancy, and youth violence—are symptoms of a deeper problem in society. For too long we have forgotten and neglected our children, and there is no one specific delinquency prevention effort that can make a difference. Instead, I think it is imperative that this Nation develop the National Agenda for Children I discussed earlier and that communities, States, and the Federal Government commit themselves to meeting that agenda.

In addition, it is important that we focus on the issue of family violence and that when we see evidence of it among children, we take immediate action. The child who watches his father beat his mother inevitably comes to accept violence as a way of life.

We must encourage our children to take part in public and community service. So many children join gangs in order to belong and to participate. Let's organize efforts that attract our young people and give them an opportunity to serve this Nation and to develop a feeling of self-respect through constructive activity.

Finally, we must make sure that police officers, school teachers, and all who come in contact with young people learn how to talk with them. We must understand that children want limits, that they understand that they will be punished for wrongdoing, but that they want to be treated with respect. They don't want to be put down, and they don't want to be hassled. They want to be treated as responsible young people.

Juvenile Justice: What advice do you have for the professional working on the front line with children in crisis?

Attorney General Reno: I certainly don't presume to tell other professionals how to deal with children in crisis because I think these people are the heroes and heroines of our society. They have one of the most difficult jobs of anyone in public service.

However, I think it's important that we do everything we can to prevent crises from occurring. It's much easier and much less costly to prevent than to wait until after a crisis occurs. But when a crisis situation does occur, we need to bring

> *It's much easier and much less costly to prevent than to wait until after a crisis occurs.*

as many resources to bear to solve the problem quickly and restore that child and family to self-sufficiency in a safe, positive atmosphere.

Juvenile Justice: Thank you very much for your time and your thoughts on these important issues facing the Nation's children and their families.

Juvenile Judges Say: Time to Get Tough

NLJ poll finds the system is failing but kids can be saved.

Rorie Sherman

National Law Journal Staff Reporter

Most of the nation's juvenile court judges believe today's youths are more depraved than those of 15 years ago.

Nearly half admit today's juvenile justice system is failing.

And, by overwhelming majorities, they support tough-minded changes that would make the juvenile courts more like the adult system—so much so that some experts say the judges unwittingly are advocating steps that could lead to the elimination of juvenile courts.

Yet they strongly oppose measures to take juveniles out of their jurisdiction and into the adult system. In fact, an overwhelming 91 percent of the judges favor extending their power to supervise and incarcerate the most serious youthful offenders past the age of majority, provided they get more resources and options to do the job. Consistent with that preference, they believe the vast majority of delinquents who appear before them can be rehabilitated. At the same time, many judges favor the death penalty for murderers as young as 14.

These were among the key findings of a National Law Journal poll of 250 judges across the country who hear juvenile delinquency cases.

With violence among youths on the rise and with the public's fear of juvenile crime skyrocketing, debate over the system's future has intensified. All along, the politicians have been heard from; the NLJ poll now gives the judges who are on the front line a voice. New York's Penn + Schoen Associates Inc. conducted the survey by telephone July 13–19 [1994].

The judges' responses to the 50-question poll reveal the profound challenges they face today in the ongoing struggle to fulfill their tension-laden mission of simultaneously punishing and rehabilitating children and teenagers. Explains Patricia Puritz, director of the Washington, D.C.-based Juvenile Justice Center at the American Bar Association: "The juvenile justice system always has been schizophrenic."

Among the current crop of judges—89 percent white, 83 percent male, 91 percent older than 41—there is a hard core whose mood is so punitive that some veteran observers of the juvenile justice system were surprised.

• Two out of five judges believe there are circumstances under which juveniles should face the death penalty.

• Two out of five say courts should be able to try juveniles as young as 14–15 for murder as an adult; 17 percent said the age should be as low as 12–13.

• More than half—55 percent—say sanctions "build character."

• One-third believe the juvenile justice system is too lenient.

• One-quarter say parents should be held liable for their children's criminal acts. (The U.S. Senate version of the federal crime bill would make parents or legal guardians of juveniles convicted of a federal offense liable for a civil fine of not more than $10,000. Children's advocates adamantly oppose such a move, saying it is of questionable constitutionality.)

• Seventeen percent say they would like to be able to order the caning of children such as Michael Fay, the American who underwent that punishment in Singapore for an act of vandalism.

According to Barry Krisberg, president of the National Council on Crime and Delinquency, a San Francisco-based child advocacy organization, the belief of many juvenile judges that their system is more lenient than adult courts is mistaken. All studies show that the odds of being convicted of a violent crime are actually greater in juvenile court, as is the probability of a longer sentence, he says.

"In juvenile court, you have bench rather than jury trials, lower rules of evidence and higher rates of pleas," explains Mr. Krisberg. Moreover, there is no early release, and youths are held, he says, "at the whim of a parole board that decides when they are rehabilitated."

GETTING TOUGH

Toughening the system itself—in a break with tradition—garners overwhelming support.

• Ninety-three percent of the judges favor fingerprinting juveniles.

• Eight-five percent say juvenile criminal records should be available to adult law enforcement authorities. (Seventy-one percent, however, say such records should not be open to the public.)

• And 68 percent favor open court hearings for juveniles accused of felonies.

Measures such as these clearly would make the juvenile system—with its presumption that "children" should not be stigmatized on the road to rehabilitation—more like adult courts. And that, experts fear, could lead to the abolition of a separate system of justice for minors.

"That is exactly where these steps are headed," says Ira M. Schwartz, director of the Study of Youth Policy at the University of Pennsylvania. "If we keep eroding the juvenile court as we have been. I would not be surprised if 1999, which is the hundredth anniversary of the juvenile

From *The National Law Journal*, August 8, 1994, pp. A1, A24-A25. © 1994 by the New York Law Publishing Company. Reprinted by permission.

Major Changes in System Favored by Juvenile Court Judges

Percentage of respondents in favor

100 —

93 Fingerprint juveniles

91 Incarcerate and supervise juveniles past age of majority

85 Open juvenile records to adult law enforcement

68 Open juvenile court hearings to public

75 —

50 —

0 —

RAY VELLA

court . . . is a bittersweet event. We could well see many states legislate the juvenile courts out of existence, or there could be little difference between states' adult and juvenile courts."

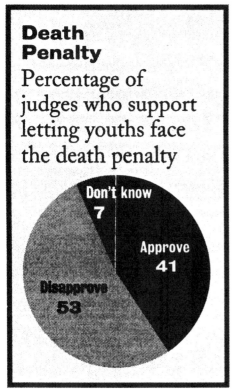

Death Penalty

Percentage of judges who support letting youths face the death penalty

Don't know 7

Approve 41

Disapprove 53

Others are less alarmed by such potential changes, seeing them more as offering improved public relations and record-keeping rather than representing any fundamental shift in philosophy.

Says Mr. Krisberg, confidentiality and prohibitions against fingerprinting are "dinosaurs." Strict confidentiality belongs more to an age when people lived in small towns, he says. Today there would be tremendous benefit to "opening the doors and the windows in the juvenile courts" so the public can see what goes on there.

KEEPING THE FAITH

The tougher judicial mood does not, however, spell an erosion of faith in the system in which these judges serve— and particularly in its potential to rehabilitate.

For example, three-quarters of the respondents say that if well-financed, first-rate rehabilitation programs were available, the majority of youths could be saved from criminality. And nearly half say that only 10 percent or less of the youths who come before them probably cannot be made into law-abiding citizens under any circumstances.

What the juvenile courts need, they say, is more resources to get the job done. Eighty-four percent complain of inadequate options available to deal with today's troubled youth. For example, 22 percent say they approve of alternative facilities such as group residences.

Judges were also unhappy with the resources they do have.

• Nearly 40 percent say that reform schools primarily help develop criminality.

• The same percentage say they are reluctant to send juveniles to reform school because of their potential to foster criminality.

• A whopping 86 percent of judges say that the agencies they rely upon to provide juveniles and their families with social services are not given adequate resources to do a reasonable job.

Meanwhile, the conditions under which judges are asked to decide young people's fate also seem hostile to justice. Thirteen percent of judges say their caseloads and work schedules are "crushing," which, according to the question put to them, means, "I do not have enough time to give most (more than half) of the cases before me the consideration they deserve." Fifty-five percent say that their days are "hectic" but that they manage to

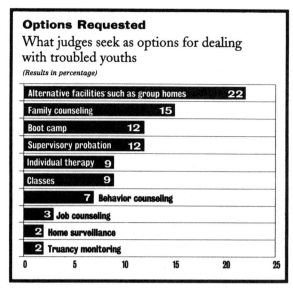

Options Requested

What judges seek as options for dealing with troubled youths

(Results in percentage)

Option	Percentage
Alternative facilities such as group homes	22
Family counseling	15
Boot camp	12
Supervisory probation	12
Individual therapy	9
Classes	9
Behavior counseling	7
Job counseling	3
Home surveillance	2
Truancy monitoring	2

dispense justice in more than half of their cases.

Only 26 percent say their workload is "reasonable," meaning they are able to give nearly every case the consideration it deserves.

Indeed, the Justice Department's latest statistics show that the number of juvenile court cases increased between 1988 and 1992 by 26 percent—to almost 1.5 million.

Overall, 48 percent of the respondents admit outright that the juvenile justice system is failing.

An additional 17 percent of judges say they don't know whether their system is failing or succeeding. According to Mark J. Penn, president of Penn + Schoen, "Judges who don't see the system as succeeding really see the system as failing. Being a 'don't know' on such a basic question usually means they don't want

to be on the record as criticizing [their] system." That would mean that 65 percent of judges really believe the system they serve in is failing.

Still, they maintain that what goes on in their own courtrooms is acceptable.

For instance, a whopping 76 percent of the judges say that most juvenile offenders who come before them are helped by their contact with the system.

Eighty-nine percent feel that the background information they receive from agencies, police and probation officers about youths and their families enables them to make sound judgments.

And a startling 99 percent characterize the quality of representation young people get in their court as adequate to excellent.

WHO'S AT FAULT?

But if judges believe in the fundamental concept of juvenile justice and have faith that they themselves are doing a good job, how do they account for the failing marks they give to today's system? In addition to a lack of resources and options, they say, today's minors are simply more troubled. And they point to social forces beyond their control.

Judges Oppose Adult Court for Kids

Juvenile court judges are up in arms over the dramatic increase in the number of juveniles being waived into adult court and over legislative proposals that would push even more minors into the adult system.

Sixty-nine percent of juvenile court judges polled by The National Law Journal say they oppose mandatory waivers to adult courts—even for cases involving serious violence or guns.

And the National Council of Juvenile and Family Court Judges is lobbying against proposed measures in the federal crime bill that threaten to bind minors as young as 13 over to adult court.

Despite their protests, however, certification of juveniles for trial in the adult system has increased dramatically in the past five years. Statistics from several major urban prosecutors' offices tell the story, and prosecutors say the situation reflects the nation's disgust with rising levels of violence among the young.

In Houston, the number of bids for adult certification has exploded at least tenfold, from just 10 cases in 1988 to 102

in the first half of 1994. Certifications in Chicago leaped from 69 in 1989 to 383 in 1992, the most recent year for statistics. And certifications in Los Angeles grew to 622 in 1993, up from 245 in 1988.

Officials in Detroit had no statistics available for 1988, the year Michigan enacted a law that expanded the offenses eligible for adult certification. But Martin Krohner, an assistant prosecuting attorney in the Wayne County office, says the figures before that time would have been minimal. In 1993, 82 of the 170 juveniles eligible for adult certification there received it. And already this year, he says, another 81 juveniles have been promoted to the adult courts.

Houston District Attorney John B. Holmes Jr. says he believes juvenile court judges might oppose increased certification because "their statutory focus is to protect the child."

But, notes Mr. Holmes, safety is a factor: "I'm not a social worker . . . the victims don't care what age the criminals are . . . I'm here for public safety."

Malcolm W. Klein, director of the Social

Science Research Institute at the University of Southern California, agrees with that assessment of the judiciary: "Juvenile court judges . . . see themselves as the last hope between salvageable kids and adult crime."

Yet according to the National Council of Juvenile and Family Court Judges, public safety is not served by sending minors into adult courts, despite Mr. Holmes' concerns.

Florida pioneered mandatory waivers in the early 1980s and since has proven that the practice does nothing to abate crime. Florida now leads the United States in violent crime, with 1,207 violent crimes for every 100,000 people.

New York, meanwhile, in 1978 passed a juvenile offender statute that gives criminal courts original jurisdiction over 13-year-olds charged with murder and anyone 14 years or older charged with other serious felonies. New York is second only to Florida in the number of violent crimes, with 1,122 for every 100,000 people.

—Gary Taylor and Rorie Sherman

5. JUVENILE JUSTICE

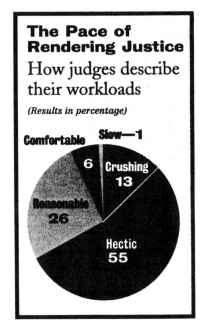

The Pace of Rendering Justice
How judges describe their workloads
(Results in percentage)

- Comfortable
- Slow—1
- Crushing 13
- 6
- Reasonable 26
- Hectic 55

Sixty-eight percent of judges believe today's youths are increasingly depraved; only 17 percent say they are "no different" from those of 15 years ago; and 5 percent actually say "less" depraved. Fifty-four percent say more juvenile males today are committing sexual abuse.

Among the causes, an overwhelming 90 percent of judges point to the media, claiming it makes youths more prone to violence.

And when asked to suggest the most significant factors contributing to juvenile violence, 26 percent of the judges cite "single parent and family breakdown," 21 percent volunteer "drugs," 15 percent "poor housing" and 17 percent "no jobs."

The judges' feeling that juveniles are committing more crime is borne out by federal statistics. But experts in the field argue that such data must be viewed n context.

The number of juvenile court cases involving serious offenses such as murder and aggravated assault jumped 68 percent between 1988 and 1992, with a total of 118,700 in the most recent year, according to the U.S. Department of Justice's Office of Juvenile Justice and Delinquency Prevention. The greatest increase came in the area of aggravated assault, up 80 percent, to 77,900, in 1992. Homicides went up 55 percent, to 2,500; robberies rose by 52 percent, to 32,900; and forcible rape cases increased 27 percent, to 5,400. Overall, juvenile court cases increased by 26 percent, to almost 1.4 million. The only decline came in the number of drug cases handled by juvenile courts: down 12 percent. The data from which the Justice Department derives these statistics come from more than 1,500 courts with jurisdiction over 57 percent of the U.S. juvenile population in 1992.

As alarming as these figures are, juveniles are no more violent than people older than 18, and their relative contribution to the violence in America has not increased. Overall, juveniles account for about 10 percent of violent crimes committed in America, and that percentage has not changed in three decades.

JUDGES' DEDICATION

Troubled children, a failing system, insufficient resources and opinions, and yet—when these judges were asked if they wanted to continue hearing juvenile matters, an overwhelming 89 percent say yes.

Hunter Hurst, director of the Pittsburgh-based National Center for Juvenile Justice, which operates the National Juvenile Court Data Archive for the U.S. Department of Justice, says the fact that so many of the respondents say they would like to stay on the juvenile court indicates to him that the poll tapped the core of juvenile justice professionals. In 26 states, including California, Washington, Colorado and Pennsylvania, he notes, judges are rotated through juvenile court. They therefore tend to develop little expertise or liking for an area on which they can have only minimal impact, he observes.

But the fact that the judges who know the system best wish to continue in it is heartening, say Messrs. Hurst and Krisberg. Mr. Hurst adds that it is especially encouraging that the judges are committed to these careers despite the fact that the juvenile court traditionally has been most lacking in prestige. Moreover, in the past decade politicians have been undermining the juvenile justice

Judges Deny System Is Racist

The majority of juvenile court judges say the system does not discriminate in favor of white minors. But experts and statistics on race and the juvenile courts suggest the judges may be wrong.

Fifty-six percent of juvenile court judges polled by The National Law Journal said there is no significant bias in favor of wealthier, white children in the juvenile justice system.

There are no current figures on the economic backgrounds of juvenile offenders. The U.S. Department of Justice's Office of Juvenile Justice and Delinquency Prevention statistics show, however, that in 1991, the last year for which data is available, black juveniles were consistently placed in training schools, which are more restrictive and larger in size, while white juveniles were sent to either halfway houses or shelters.

The answer to these discrepancies does not appear to be that blacks are committing more serious crimes than whites. Overall, white and blacks each were responsible for 49 percent of the violent crimes committed by juveniles that year.

Overall, 57 percent of the juvenile population in private facilities was white, 32 percent was black and 9 percent was Hispanic. But within the different facility types, blacks made up 48 percent of the training school population, while whites made up 61 percent of the halfway houses and 60 percent of the shelters. Similar patterns held true in public facilities.

"Minority kids track more into the back end of our system; everybody knows that," says Paul DeMuro, a Montclair,

N.J.-based juvenile justice consultant who is the lead monitor in the Oklahoma juvenile justice reform effort. Mr. DeMuro performed the same function in Florida and is a former commissioner of children and youth in Pennsylvania. White juveniles, he says, get sidetracked into abuse programs, mental institutions and residential care facilities.

Still, says Mr. DeMuro, the fact that judges fail to see their institutions as racist is understandable. "These people are generally honest . . . when they see a kid in front of them, they don't consciously operate with racism. And in an individual case they are not necessarily acting in a racist way."

—**Rorie Sherman**

Kids' Lawyers Called Capable

As 99 percent of juvenile court judges see it the quality of legal representation for youths who come before them is "adequate" to "excellent," The National Law Journal's poll of judges found.

As critics of the juvenile justice system see it, the judges are sadly mistaken.

Juveniles accused of crimes are woefully underrepresented or misrepresented in juvenile court, they say, arguing that numerous academic studies prove that when juveniles do have counsel, the attorneys are, in the words of one researcher, often "walking constitutional violations."

Hunter Hurst, the director of the Pittsburgh-based National Center for Juvenile Justice, the research arm of the National Council of Juvenile and Family Court Judges, says he was "astounded" by the judges' confidence in juveniles' legal representation. "It's been so bad for so long, all these people have lowered their standards without realizing it."

In fact, asserts University of Minnesota law School Prof. Barry C. Feld, a member of the Minnesota Juvenile Justice Task Force that conducted the nation's first multistate study of the quality of chil-

dren's representation, in many jurisdictions juveniles never see an attorney. And, adds the author of the recently published book, "Justice for Children," if they do, the quality of representation is inadequate.

According to Professor Feld's survey, published in 1988, only 37. 5 percent of juveniles in North Dakota courts had lawyers; 47.7 percent in Minnesota saw attorneys; and 52.7 percent of youths in Nebraska had counsel. He added that even if children received representation, the quality of the lawyers' work was usually unsatisfactory.

Another academic study, "Law Guardians in New York State: A Study of the Legal Representation of Children," found 45 percent of attorneys serving youths were seriously inadequate or marginally adequate; only 4 percent of the lawyers were effective. And, 47 percent of the litigators appeared to have done no or minimal preparation. In 5 percent of the cases it was clear, the study says, that the lawyer had not even met with the client. Most shockingly, in 50 percent of the cases studied, transcripts revealed appealable errors by lawyers and judges

that were left unchallenged.

Adequate legal representation for juveniles is such a hot issue, Mr. Feld notes, the General Accounting Office currently is studying it.

Perhaps, Mr. Feld adds, "When the judges talk about the quality of representation as excellent, what they really mean is that they have a lot of cooperative lawyers who are not slowing the process up by raising legal challenges." Lawyers defending youths typically handle three to four times the caseload professional standards recommend, he notes.

Judges, of course, disagree. "Most people that work in this area are more committed to helping others than in advancing their own interests," says Judge Nancy A. Konrad of Jefferson Parish, La. And while she hears criticism of juveniles' representation, the work done in her court is "excellent."

Says District magistrate Judge Richard Miller from Edwards Co., Kan.: "The courts look to protect kids." And, he notes, Kansas requires appointment of counsel regardless of whether the child can afford it.

—Peter Morrison

---

system by passing laws that pull more and more minors into the adult system. And, experts observe, funding for juvenile courts generally has not kept up with inflation.

The judges who do remain on the juvenile court bench, explains Prof. Barry C. Feld of the University of Minnesota Law School, an author of a recent revision of Minnesota's juvenile justice laws have "a profound sense that they can make a difference."

Judge Leonard P. Edwards of the Santa Clara County Superior Court in San Jose, Calif., a well-known figure in the national juvenile justice community, agrees: "We really are where the rubber hits the road."

POLL METHODOLOGY
THE NATIONAL LAW JOURNAL poll on juvenile justice consists of 50 substantive and seven demographic questions. It was conducted by Penn + Schoen Associates Inc. of New York, a national polling and political consulting firm.

A total of 250 judges, who hear juvenile delinquency cases, were interviewed by telephone between July 13 and July 19.

To ensure an appropriate representative sample of the U.S. judicial population who hear juvenile cases and to reflect the geographical distribution of juvenile arrests, respondents were selected randomly from "BNA's Directory of State and Federal Courts, Judges and Clerks" and from the membership directory of the Reno, Nev.-based National Council of Ju-

venile and Family Court Judges. The geographic distribution of juvenile arrests was derived from the "under 18" crime statistics issued by the 1992 FBI Uniform Crime Report.

The sampling error is plus or minus 6 percentage points at the 95 percent confidence level.

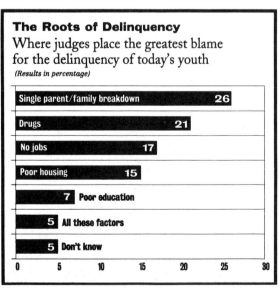

The Roots of Delinquency
Where judges place the greatest blame for the delinquency of today's youth
(Results in percentage)

Single parent/family breakdown	26
Drugs	21
No jobs	17
Poor housing	15
Poor education	7
All these factors	5
Don't know	5

Throw away the key

Juvenile offenders are the Willie Hortons of the '90s

JENNIFER VOGEL · SPECIAL TO *UTNE READER*

Jennifer Vogel is an investigative reporter for the Minneapolis-St. Paul alternative weekly City Pages.

Judged by any number of statistical yardsticks—infant mortality, child poverty, teen suicide and incarceration—America in the '90s is doing in kids at an alarming rate. It's estimated that every day, 2,700 babies are born into poverty, more than 2,000 students drop out of school, 250 kids are arrested for violent crimes, and 1,700 are abused by their parents. Youthful America's vision of its own future has never been more dire, particularly in the cities. As one 17-year-old African-American put it on his way into court: "I been dead since I was 12, so I'm not afraid of dying. I'm just waiting to get kicked into the grave."

Watching the courts and Congress, it's easy to conclude that the country is waging a battle against its children. While schools, jobs, and the social safety net continue to erode, more kids are finding themselves caught up in an ever-expanding criminal justice system. Politicians and the major media, having discovered a boom market in the public frenzy for bigger jails and longer sentences, have made juvenile offenders the Willie Hortons of the '90s.

"Over the 1980s, the United States achieved the highest rates of incarceration in the industrialized world, moving past South Africa and the former Soviet Union," notes a 1993 study by the Milton S. Eisenhower Foundation. "Because the inmates were disproportionately young, in many ways prison building became the American youth policy of choice....By the 1992 elections, one in every four young African-American males was either in prison, on probation, or on parole."

These are uncommonly honest observations compared to the reams of recent studies and white papers on "the juvenile problem." Generally speaking, young people themselves are far more candid than politicians and pundits about what lies ahead. When a national study compared the worries of high school seniors in 1979 to those of 1991, it found less concern about nuclear war, more about hunger and poverty. The numbers bear out their skepticism:

• Unemployment among teens was 19 percent in 1993, up from 15.3 percent five years earlier—and for black youths, the figure was twice that high. For those who do find jobs, the average hourly wage has fallen nearly 10 percent in the last decade.

• Since 1970, Aid to Families with Dependent Children benefits have declined an average of 45 percent in inflation-adjusted dollars, according to the Children's Defense Fund.

• In 1992, there were 14.6 million children living below the poverty line, the Children's Defense Fund says, about 5 million more than in 1973.

• Last year, there were 3 million victims of child abuse, according to the National Committee for the Prevention of Child Abuse—a rate 50 percent higher than in 1985. Studies also indicate that the majority of prison inmates were abused as children.

• Teen suicide rates increased nearly 20 percent during the 1980s.

But numbers like these are not the stuff of legislative debate, in Washington or in state legislatures around the country. Almost without exception, the trend among lawmakers is to use highly publicized incidents of brutal violence—often charged with racial stereotypes—to push for harsher penalties. In Minnesota this year, a 16-year-old black youth who broke into a suburban home and killed a white woman and her child became the poster child for juvenile justice reform. Neighbors actually circulated a petition to have him tried as an adult; 20,000 signed on. In Minnesota as elsewhere, legislators have decided to play to mob sentiments.

Of course this shift requires a rationale, and pundits have been quick to provide one. Juvenile justice laws weren't set up to deal with these new monsterlike children, they say, but to give kids stealing cookies from cookie jars a slap on the wrist. (The presumption here is that juvenile law just isn't tough enough; in fact, kids in some states tend to serve longer sentences in juvenile facilities than adults convicted of similar crimes.) While there already are numerous provisions for getting serious juvenile offenders into adult courts, the "reforms" sweeping the nation now seek to wipe out the protected

From *Utne Reader,* July/August 1994, pp. 56-60. © 1994 by Jennifer Vogel. Reprinted by permission of the author.

Rekindling the warrior

*Gangs are part of the solution,
not part of the problem*

OVER THE PAST YEAR AND A HALF, I HAVE SPOKEN to thousands of young people at schools, jails, bookstores, colleges, and community centers about the experiences addressed in my book *Always Running: La Vida Loca, Gang Days in L.A.*

What stays with me is the vitality and clarity of the young people I met, many of them labeled "at risk." They saw in my experiences and my book both a reflection of their lives and the possibility of transcendence, of change, which otherwise appears elusive. In those faces I saw the most viable social energy for rebuilding the country and realigning its resources. They are the future, but this society has no clear pathway to take them there.

For one thing, today's youth are under intense scrutiny and attack. Schools, for the most part, fail to engage their creativity and intellect. As a result, young people find their own means of expression—music being the most obvious example, but also the formation of gangs.

Despite conventional thinking, gangs are not anarchies. They can be highly structured, with codes of honor and discipline. For many members, the gang serves as family, as the only place where they can find fellowship, respect, a place to belong. You often hear the word *love* among gang members. Sometimes the gang is the only place where they can find it.

Gabriel Rivera, director of the Transitional Intervention Experience of Bend, Oregon, and a former East Los Angeles gang member, came up with a concept he calls "character in motion" to describe the essence, not the form, of gang participation.

"[Character in motion] is marked by the advertent or inad-vertent beginnings of physical, psychological, and spiritual struggle that happens for every young person," writes Rivera. "[It] is what happens when a young person responds to the inevitable inner call to embrace 'the journey,' and chooses to honor that journey above all else with a courage that relies upon connecting with one's 'warrior energy.'"

The warrior needs to be nurtured, directed, and guided—not smothered, crushed, or corralled. This energy needs to be taken to its next highest level of development, where one matures into self-control, self-study, and self-actualization. Most anti-gang measures have nothing to do with any of this. A serious effort would address the burning issue of adolescent rage. It would address a basic need for food, shelter, and clothing, but also needs for expressive creativity and community.

Sociopathic behavior exists within the framework of a sociopathic society. Under these circumstances, gangs are not a problem; they are a solution, particularly for communities lacking economic, social, and political options.

Two examples: Two years ago, I did a poetry reading in a part of eastern Ohio that was once alive with coal mines and industry but now has 50 to 70 percent unemployment in some areas. Many of the young people are selling drugs to survive. In this sense, they could be from the South Bronx or the Pine Ridge Reservation. They are, however, "white." They are listening to their own music ("Wherever kids find obstacles, I find music," an independent record producer recently told *Rolling Stone* magazine), and establishing ganglike structures to survive.

Soon after the 1992 Los Angeles rebellion, members of the Crips and the Bloods, two of the city's most notorious gangs, circulated a plan. They included proposals to repair the schools and streets and get rid of drugs and violence. At the end of the plan, they wrote: "Give us the hammers and the nails, and we will rebuild the city."

It was a demand to take responsibility, which rose from the inner purpose of Crip and Blood warrior consciousness, and a demand for the authority to carry out the plan. Unfortunately, no one took them up on it.

These young people face great barriers to educational advancement, economic stability, and social mobility—but little or none to criminal activity or violence (as everyone knows, prison is no deterrence; for some youth it is a rite of passage).

Power is the issue here. Without autonomy to make decisions that affect their lives, these young people can only attempt to approximate it, too often with disastrous results.

You want to stop the body count? Empower the youth.

—*Luis J. Rodriguez*
Special to *Utne Reader*

Luis J. Rodriguez is an award-winning poet, journalist, and critic. Always Running: La Vida Loca, Gang Days in L.A. (Curbstone Publisher, $19.95) is a memoir of growing up in the South Central and East Los Angeles areas. Rodriguez is now based in Chicago, where he directs Tia Chucha Press, a publisher of cross-cultural, socially engaged poetry. He is presently working with photographer Donna DeCesare on a book about Salvadoran gang members in Los Angeles and their impact on El Salvador.

status of juveniles as a class, making it easier to put young offenders on the road to lifelong incarceration by the age of 13 or 14.

News outlets play their part by routinely featuring images of vacant-eyed children carrying out acts of random violence. They happily parrot jacked-up statistics and stereotypes about teenagers, capping the information with headlines like "Killer Kids"—or this, from the *L.A. Times:* "Who are our children? One day, they are innocent. The next, they may try to blow your head off." One of the most prominent myths of the media is that kids are the biggest problem this country faces in its battle against crime, when in fact they make up only 16 to 17 percent of total arrests, according to one expert.

The percentage of kids arrested has remained fairly constant during the past 10 to 15 years. Though statistics is anything but an exact science, it appears that there's been a decline in juvenile property crimes such as theft, break-ins, and robberies, and an increase in murders, aggravated assaults, and other violent crimes. Even so, only a small percentage of juvenile offenses are violent crimes: about 5 percent in 1990.

Says Bob DeComo, senior program manager for the National Council on Crime and Delinquency: "I think the public perception is that [violent crime committed by juveniles] has increased much more dramatically than is really the case. It is a fact that violent crimes are up, but the extent is overstated in part because of attention to crime in general. It's still the case that the public is much more likely to be victimized by an adult."

Not that some of the numbers aren't troubling. In 1981, according to Federal Bureau of Justice statistics, youths were charged with 53,240 violent crimes; in 1992, the figure was 104,137. There's something about kids that clearly *isn't* the same as it was 20 years ago. "We're reaping the benefits of 12 years of lessening federal commitments," says Miriam Rollin, vice president for advocacy development for the National Association of Child Advocates. "I would think that if the concern was for the future, that would lead more clearly to the response that lets us invest in them. I think people are scared. I don't know that we've ever had the kind of desperation among young people, particularly in poverty, nor have we had the number of young people in poverty as we do today. I think people understand, to a certain extent, what that means. That you are potentially creating a very dysfunctional young

person. There aren't enough jails and facilities to lock up all the poor kids in this country, but that's what they are on their way toward doing."

Around the country, the most popular solutions include defining new classes of juvenile crime, making juvenile records public, creating boot camps for young offenders, tightening up curfew laws (in some cases fining parents who don't keep their kids in the house at night), and installing metal detectors in schools. One state proposed trying 12-year-olds as adults, and another has sought to eliminate age guidelines altogether.

But, like deficit spending, locking up youths may only be a way to defer the problem. In a speech before Congress in March, Michael E. Saucier, national chair of the Coalition for Juvenile Justice, said the approach "looks tough but is shortsighted." It addresses the problem of serious juvenile crime by allowing youth to be dealt with in an adult setting, a setting that is almost completely bankrupt when it comes to crime prevention, rehabilitation, or reducing recidivism.

"Juveniles in adult institutions are five times more likely to be sexually assaulted, twice as likely to be beaten by staff, and 50 percent more likely to be attacked with a weapon than youths in a juvenile facility," Saucier continued. "The most revealing research is three different studies conducted over a ten-year period that show significantly higher recidivism rates for youths tried in adult courts compared to those tried in juvenile courts for the same offenses and with similar personal profiles."

It isn't that there are no workable alternatives— just that the very concept of rehabilitation has fallen out of favor. Every year the Office of Juvenile Justice and Delinquency Prevention gives awards to particularly effective programs around the country. Those honored last year include a Nebraska program in which juvenile offenders are educated and taught independent living and family reconciliation strategies. It boasts a 50 percent reduction in recidivism. In New Hampshire, juvenile offenders are offered the chance to do community service work for local businesses or nonprofit agencies in lieu of going to jail, again resulting in very low recidivism rates.

The choice is clear, says Rollin: "Would you rather have them get out after they've had some sort of program or have them grow up in an adult facility and come out better criminals, having completed the ideal criminal mentoring program?"

EVERYDAY SCHOOL VIOLENCE: HOW DISORDER FUELS IT

JACKSON TOBY

Jackson Toby, professor of sociology and director of the Institute of Criminological Research at Rutgers University, is writing a book, Everyday Violence at School.

IN JANUARY 1989, an alcoholic drifter named Patrick Purdy walked onto the playground of the Cleveland Elementary School in Stockton, California, and, without warning, began spraying bullets from his AK-47 assault rifle. Five children died and 29 persons were wounded, some critically. In January 1992, two students at Thomas Jefferson High School in Brooklyn, New York, were fatally shot by an angry 15-year-old classmate. In April 1993, three teenagers armed with a baseball bat, a billy club, and a buck knife invaded an American Government class at Dartmouth High School, in Dartmouth, Massachusetts, a small town six miles southwest of New Bedford. They were looking for a boy they had fought with the previous Sunday. When 16-year-old Jason Robinson stood up and asked why they were looking for his friend, one of the youths fatally stabbed him in the stomach. That same month a 17-year-old Long Island high school student who had been reprimanded by her teacher poured nail polish into the teacher's can of soda. The teacher was taken to Good Samaritan Hospital; the student was arrested for second-degree assault.

The public is outraged when dramatic murders and attempted murders—as well as assaults and rapes—in or around schools are widely reported in the press and on television. Parents fear for the safety of their children and for the integrity of the educational process. People ask, "Why is there so much more school violence now than when I was in school?"

School violence is often blamed on a violence-prone society. Some urban schools *are* located—as Thomas Jefferson High School is—in slum neighborhoods where drug sellers routinely kill one another, as well as innocent bystanders, on the streets surrounding the school. More than 50 Thomas Jefferson students died in the past five years, most of them in the neighborhood, a few in the school itself. Some violence erupts inside schools like Thomas Jefferson when intruders import neighborhood violence to the schools or when students—themselves products of the neighborhood—carry knives and guns to school in order "to protect themselves." But the other

three violent incidents—in Stockton, California; Dartmouth, Massachusetts; and Deer Park, Long Island—did not occur in particularly violent communities.

The most frightening cases of school violence, those of insanely furious armed intruders such as Patrick Purdy, are, like floods or tornadoes, not easy to predict or to prevent. Although these dramatically violent acts occur at schools, the acts cannot be blamed on anything the schools did or failed to do. Such unusual cases of school violence differ from *everyday* school violence: a group of students beating up a schoolmate, one student forcing another to surrender lunch money or jewelry. Mundane non-lethal, everyday school violence is more common in big-city schools than in suburban and rural ones, but it can be found in these schools as well.

Everyday school violence is more predictable than the sensational incidents that get widespread media attention, because everyday school violence is caused at least in part by educational policies and procedures governing schools and by how those policies are implemented in individual schools. This article addresses the causes of everyday school violence and the educational policies that might be changed to reduce it.

STATISTICAL FACTS ABOUT EVERYDAY SCHOOL VIOLENCE

Partly in response to alarming newspaper, magazine, and television reports of violence and vandalism in American public schools—not just occasionally or in the central cities, but chronically and all over the United States—the 93rd Congress decided in 1974 to require the Department of Health, Education, and Welfare to conduct a survey to determine the extent and seriousness of school crime.

In January 1978, the National Institute of Education published a 350-page report to Congress, *Violent Schools—Safe Schools,* which detailed the findings of an elaborate study. Principals in 4,014 schools in large cities, smaller cities, suburban areas, and rural areas filled out questionnaires. Then, 31,373 students and 23,895 teachers in 642 junior and senior high schools throughout the country were questioned about their experiences with school crime—in particular whether they themselves had been victimized and, if so, how. From among these 31,373 students who filled out anonymous questionnaires, 6,283 were selected randomly for individual interviews on the same subject. Discrepancies between questionnaire reports of victimization and interview reports of victimization were probed to find out exactly what respondents meant when they answered that they had been attacked, robbed, or had property stolen from their desks or lockers. Finally, intensive field studies were conducted in 10 schools that had experienced especially serious crime problems in the past and had made some progress in overcoming them.

The results of this massive study are still worth paying attention to even though the data are nearly 20 years old. Because the study was conducted in schools, it remains the only large-scale national study of school violence that probed a broad range of questions about the school milieu. The other national surveys of school violence, one (McDermott, 1979) based on data collected at about the same time as the Safe Schools study, the other in 1989 (Bastian and Taylor, 1991), were based on a few questions about school victimizations in the interview schedule of the National Crime Survey—too few to throw light on why some schools seemed unable to control violent students.

The statistical picture of crime and violence in public secondary schools that emerged from these three studies placed the sensational media stories in the broader context of everyday school violence.

The report, *Violent Schools—Safe Schools,* was not mainly concerned with mischief or with foul language—although it mentioned in passing that a majority of American junior high school teachers (and about a third of senior high school teachers) were sworn at by their students or were the target of obscene gestures within the month preceding the survey. The report was concerned mainly with illegal acts and with the fear those acts aroused, not with language or gestures. Both on the questionnaires and in personal interviews, students were asked questions designed to provide an estimate of the amount of theft and violence in public secondary schools:

In [the previous month] did anyone steal things of yours from your desk, locker, or other place at school?

Did anyone take money or things directly from you by force, weapons, or threats at school in [the previous month]?

At school in [the previous month] did anyone physically attack and hurt you?

Eleven percent of secondary-school students reported in personal interviews having something worth more than a dollar stolen from them in the past month. A fifth of these nonviolent thefts involved property worth $10 or more. One-half of 1 percent of secondary-school students reported being robbed in a month's time—that is, having property taken from them by force, weapons, or threats. One out of nine of these robberies resulted in physical injuries to the victims. Students also told of being assaulted. One-and-one-third percent of secondary-school students reported being attacked over the course of a month, and two-fifths of these were physically injured. (Only 14 percent of the assaults, however, resulted in injuries serious enough to require medical attention.)

These percentages were based on face-to-face interviews with students. When samples of students were asked the same questions, by means of anonymous questionnaires, the estimates of victimization were about twice as high overall, and in the case of robbery four times as high. Methodological studies conducted by the school-crime researchers convinced them that the interview results were more valid than the questionnaire results for estimating the extent of victimization; some students might have had difficulty reading and understanding the questionnaire.

The report also contained data on the victimization of teachers, which were derived from questionnaires similar to those filled out by students. (There were no teacher interviews, perhaps because teachers were presumed more capable of understanding the questions and replying appropriately.) An appreciable proportion of teachers reported property stolen, but only a tiny proportion of teachers reported robberies and assaults. However, robberies of teachers in inner-city schools were three times as common as in rural schools, and assaults were nine times as common. Even in big-city secondary schools, less than 2 percent of the teachers surveyed cited assaults by students within the past month, but threats were more frequent. Some 36 percent of inner-city junior high school teachers reported that students threatened to hurt them, as did 24 percent of inner-city high school teachers. Understandably, many teachers said they were afraid of their students. Twenty-eight percent of big-city teachers reported hesitating to confront misbehaving students for fear of their own safety, as did 18 percent of smaller-city teachers, 11 percent of suburban teachers, and 7 percent of rural teachers.

Violence against teachers (assaults, rapes, and robberies) is more rare than violence against students. It is an appreciable problem only in a handful of inner-city schools, but, when it occurs, it has enormous symbolic importance. The violent victimization of teachers suggests that they are not in control of the school. In another segment of the Safe Schools study, principals were questioned about a variety of crimes against the school as a community: trespassing, breaking and entering, theft of school property, vandalism, and the like. Based on these reports as well as on data collected by the National Center for Educational Statistics in a survey of vandalism, *Violent Schools—Safe Schools* estimated the monetary cost of replacing damaged or stolen property at $200 million per year. Vandalism, called "malicious mischief" by the legal system, is a nuisance in most schools, not a major threat to the educational process. But vandalism of school property, especially major vandalism and firesetting, is a precursor of school violence because its existence suggests that school authorities are not in control and "anything goes."

Some of the statistics from the two national studies were reassuring. Both the 1978 Safe Schools study and the 1989 School Crime Supplement to the National Crime Survey studies showed that, in the aggregate, school crime consisted mostly of nonviolent larcenies rather than violent attacks or robberies, which were rare. In other words, the bulk of school crime is essentially

What would have been furtive larcenies in a well-ordered school can become robberies when the school authorities do not appear to be in control, just as angry words can turn into blows or stabbings.

furtive misbehavior—theft of unattended property of other students and teachers, fights between students that stop as soon as teachers loom into view, graffiti scrawled secretly on toilet walls. But schools differ in the mix of nonviolent and violent crime: In some schools, violence was appreciable—and frightening—both to students and to teachers. What apparently happens is that what would have been furtive larcenies in a well-ordered school can become robberies when the school authorities do not appear to be in control, just as angry words can turn into blows or stabbings. Under conditions of weak control, students are tempted to employ force or the threat of force to get property they would like or to hurt someone they dislike. Consequently, student-on-student shakedowns (robberies) and attacks occur, infrequently in most schools, fairly often in some inner-city schools.

Thus, school crime partly reflects weak control and is partly the cause of further disorder, which in turn leads to more crime.

HOW DISORDER PROMOTES EVERYDAY SCHOOL VIOLENCE

Everyday school violence is a visible threat to the educational process, but it's only the tip of the iceberg. Under the surface is what criminologist James Q. Wilson calls "disorder" (Wilson, 1985). Professor Wilson argues (in a more general analysis of the relationship between disorder and criminal violence) that neighborhoods ordinarily become vulnerable to the violent street crime that arouses so much fear among city dwellers only *after* they have first become disorderly. What makes a neighborhood "disorderly"? When panhandlers are able to accost passersby, when garbage is not collected often enough, when alcoholics drink in doorways and urinate in the street, when broken windows are not repaired or graffiti removed, when abandoned cars are allowed to disintegrate on the street—a sense of community is lost, even when the rate of statutory crimes is not particularly high. According to Wilson, "disorderly" means the violation of conventional expectations about proper conduct in "public places as well as allowing property to get run down" or broken. Wilson believes that the informal community controls effective in preventing crime cannot survive in a neighborhood where residents believe nobody cares:

[M]any residents will think that crime, especially violent crime, is on the rise, and they will modify their behavior accordingly. They will use the streets less often, and when on the streets will stay apart from their fellows.... For some

residents, this growing atomization will matter little, because the neighborhood is not their "home" but "the place where they live." But it will matter greatly to other people, whose lives derive meaning and satisfaction from local attachments rather than from worldly affairs; for them, the neighborhood will cease to exist except for a few reliable friends whom they arrange to meet.

Such an area is vulnerable to criminal invasion. Though it is not inevitable, it is more likely that here, rather than in places where people are confident they can regulate public behavior by informal controls, drugs will change hands, prostitutes will solicit, and cars will be stripped. Drunks will be robbed by boys who do it as a lark, and the prostitutes' customers will be robbed by men who do it purposefully and perhaps violently. Muggings will occur.

Persuasive as Wilson's thesis is with regard to *neighborhood* crime rates, it seems even more relevant to *school* crime. A school in which students wander the halls during times when they are supposed to be in class, where candy wrappers and empty soft-drink cans have been discarded in the corridors, and where graffiti can be seen on most walls, invites youngsters to test further and further the limits of acceptable behavior. One connection between the inability of school authorities to maintain order and an increasing rate of violence is that—for students who have little faith in the usefulness of the education they are supposed to be getting—challenging rules is part of the fun. When they succeed in littering or in writing on walls, they feel encouraged to challenge other, more sacred, rules like the prohibition against assaulting fellow students. If the process goes far enough, students come to think they can do *anything*. The school has become a jungle.

The Significance of Disorder

Psychologists and sociologists long have recognized that families vary both in their cohesiveness and in their effectiveness at raising children; experts regard "dysfunctional families" as a factor in juvenile delinquency, substance abuse, and the personality pathologies of young people that lead to violence. The concept of "school disorder" suggests that schools, like families, also vary in their cohesiveness and effectiveness. What school disorder means in concrete terms is that one or both of two departures from normality exists: A significant proportion of students do not seem to recognize the legitimacy of the rules governing the school's operation and therefore violate them frequently; and/or a significant proportion of students defy the authority of teachers and other staff members charged with enforcing the rules.

Although disorder is never total, at some point in the deterioration process, students get the impression that the perpetrators of violent behavior will not be detected or, if detected, will not be punished. When that happens, the school is out of control. Even lesser degrees of school disorder demoralize teachers, who make weaker efforts to control student misbehavior, lose enthusiasm for teaching, and take "sick days" when they are not really sick. Some teachers, often the youngest and the most dynamic, consider leaving the profession or transferring to private or suburban schools. A disorderly atmosphere also demoralizes the most academically able students,

Verbal abuse of a teacher, because it prevents a teacher from maintaining classroom authority, or even composure, may interfere with education more than would larceny from a desk or locker.

and they seek escape to academically better, safer schools. For other students, a disorderly atmosphere presents a golden opportunity for class-cutting and absenteeism. The proportions of potentially violent students grow in the disorderly school, and thus the likelihood decreases that violence will meet with an effective response from justifiably fearful teachers.

Disorder leads to violence partly because it prevents meaningful learning from taking place. Thus, an insolent student who responds to his history teacher's classroom question about the Civil War: "I won't tell you, asshole," merely commits an offense against school order, not a criminal offense in the larger society. Nevertheless, verbal abuse of a teacher, because it prevents a teacher from maintaining classroom authority, or even composure, may interfere with education more than would larceny from a desk or locker. The disrespectful student challenges the norm mandating a cooperative relationship between teachers and students to promote education. Under conditions of disorder, a building may look and smell like a school, but an essential ingredient is missing. Punching a teacher is only a further stage on the same road.

SOCIAL TRENDS LEADING TO DISORDERLY SCHOOLS

Part of the explanation for the greater incidence of disorderly schools in central cities is that there is less consensus in inner cities that education is crucially important. Why? Because big cities tend to be the first stop of immigrants from less developed societies where, frequently, formal secular education is less valued. (Toby, 1957; Hawaii Crime Commission, 1980) Consequently, maintaining order is easier in rural and suburban schools than those in central cities. But the problem of school disorder is not solely a problem of central cities. Social trends in American society have tended greatly to reduce the effectiveness of adult controls over students in all public secondary schools. Some of these developments have simultaneously tempted enrolled students to be unruly. It is to these trends that I now turn.

The Separation of School and Community

Historically, the development of American public education increasingly separated the school from students' families and neighborhoods. Even the one-room schoolhouse of rural America represented separation of the educational process from the family. But the consolidated school districts in nonmetropolitan areas and the

jumbo schools of the inner city carried separation much further. Large schools developed because the bigger the school, the lower the per capita cost of education; the more feasible it was to hire teachers with academic specialties like art, music, drama, or advanced mathematics; and the more likely that teachers and administrators could operate according to professional standards instead of in response to local sensitivities—for example, in teaching biological evolution or in designing a sex-education curriculum. But the unintended consequence of large schools that operated efficiently by bureaucratic and professional standards was to make them relatively autonomous from the local community. While the advantages of autonomy were immediately obvious, the disadvantages took longer to reveal themselves.

The main disadvantage was that students developed distinctive subcultures only tangentially related to education. Thus, in data collected during the 1950s Professor James Coleman found that American high school students seemed more preoccupied with athletics and personal popularity than with intellectual achievement. Students were doing their own thing, and their thing was not what teachers and principals were mainly concerned about. Presumably, if parents had been more closely involved in the educational process, they would have strengthened the academic influence of teachers. Even in the 1950s, student subcultures at school promoted misbehavior; in New York and other large cities, fights between members of street gangs from different neighborhoods sometimes broke out in secondary schools. However, Soviet achievements in space during the 1950s drew more attention to academic performance than to school crime and misbehavior. Insofar as community adults were brought into schools as teacher aides, they were introduced not to help control student misbehavior but to improve academic performance.

Until the 1960s and 1970s, school administrators did not sufficiently appreciate the potential for disorder when many hundreds of young people come together for congregate instruction. Principals did not like to call in police, preferring to organize their own disciplinary procedures. They did not believe in security guards, preferring to use teachers to monitor behavior in the halls and lunchrooms. They did not tell school architects about the need for what has come to be called "defensible space," and as a result schools were built with too many ways to gain entrance from the outside and too many rooms and corridors where surveillance was difficult. Above all, principals did not consider that they had lost control over potential student misbehavior when parents were kept far away, not knowing how their children were behaving. The focus of PTAs was on the curriculum, and it was the better-educated, middle-class parents who tended to join such groups. In short, the isolation of the school from the local community always meant that, if a large enough proportion of students misbehaved, teachers and principals could not maintain order.

Conceivably, schools can exercise effective control even though parents and neighbors do not reinforce their values through membership in PTAs or through conferences with teachers. But social control is weakened by population mobility, which creates an atmosphere of anonymity. Consider how much moving around there is in the United States. Only 82 percent of persons were living in the same residential unit in 1990 as they were in 1989. Residential mobility was much greater in the central cities of metropolitan areas. Since cities have long been considered places to which people migrate from rural areas, from other cities, and indeed from foreign countries, it may come as no surprise that during a five-year period, a majority of the residents of American central cities move to a different house. Yet the anonymity generated by this atmosphere of impermanence can plausibly explain why American society is not very successful in imposing order in urban neighborhoods. Anonymity is not confined to central cities. High rates of mobility are typical, creating the anonymity that complicates problems of social control. Schools vary of course in their rates of student turnover. In some big-city schools less than half the students complete an academic year; in some small-town schools, on the other hand, the bulk of students are together for four years of high school.

The Relentless Pressure to Keep Children In School Longer

The most important trend underlying school disorder is the rising proportion of the age cohort attending high school in all modern societies. The reason for raising the age of compulsory school attendance is excellent: Children need all the education they can get in order to work at satisfying jobs in an increasingly complex economy and to be able to vote intelligently. However, higher ages of compulsory school attendance mean that some enrolled youngsters hate school and feel like prisoners. Obviously, such youngsters don't respect the rules or the rule-enforcers as much as students who regard education as an opportunity.

Compulsory education laws vary from state to state. But they share an assumption that the state can compel not only school attendance but school achievement. In reality, compulsory education laws are successful only in keeping children *enrolled,* sometimes longer than the nominal age of compulsory school attendance. Parental consent was often written into the law as necessary for withdrawal from school before reaching 17 or 18 or a specified level of educational achievement. Parents have little incentive to consent, partly because they hold unrealistic educational aspirations even for academically marginal students, partly because they recognize the difficulties faced by adolescents in the labor market and do not want their children loitering on the streets, and partly because benefits are available from programs like Aid to Families with Dependent Children for children enrolled in school.

Like their parents, the disengaged students also have incentives to remain enrolled, although not necessarily to attend regularly. In addition to conforming to parental pressure, they are called "students" although they are not necessarily studious, and this status has advantages. The school is more pleasant than the streets in cold or rainy weather—it is an interesting place to be. Friends are visited; enemies attacked; sexual adventures begun; drugs bought and sold; valuables stolen. There are material advantages also to being an enrolled student, such as bus passes and lunch tickets, which can be sold as well as used. Consequently, many remain enrolled although they are actually occasional or chronic truants. The existence of a large population of enrolled nonattenders blurs the line between intruders and students. School officials understand this all too well, but the compulsory school attendance laws prevent them from doing much about it. (Toby, 1983)

Keeping more children in school who do not want to be there interferes with traditional learning. Consequently, functional illiteracy has spread to more students, resulting not necessarily in the formal withdrawal from school of marginal students but, more usually, in "internal" dropouts. School systems are making strenuous efforts to educate such students whom they would have given up on in a previous generation. Such students used to be described as "lazy," and they were given poor grades for "conduct." It is perhaps not surprising that the public schools have had great difficulty providing satisfaction, not to mention success, to students whose aptitudes or attitudes do not permit them to function within the range of traditional standards of academic performance. One response is to "dumb-down" the curriculum with "relevant," intellectually undemanding courses that increase the proportion of entertainment to work.

The Extension of Civil Rights to Children

A third trend indirectly affecting school order is the increasing sensitivity of public schools to the rights of children. A generation ago it was possible for principals to rule schools autocratically, to suspend or expel students without much regard for procedural niceties. Injustices occurred; children were "pushed out" of schools because they antagonized teachers and principals. But this arbitrariness enabled school administrators to control the situation when serious misbehavior occurred. Student assaults on teachers were punished so swiftly that such assaults were almost unthinkable. Even disrespectful language was unusual. Today, as a result of greater concern for the rights of children, school officials are required to observe due process in handling student discipline. Hearings are necessary. Charges must be specified. Witnesses must confirm suspicions. Appeals are provided for. Greater due process for students accused of misbehavior gives unruly students better protection against teachers and principals; unfortunately, it also gives well-behaved students less protection from their classmates.

Related to the extension of civil rights in the school setting is the decreased ability of schools to get help with discipline problems from the juvenile courts. Like the schools, the juvenile courts also have become more attentive to children's rights. Juvenile courts today are less willing to exile children to a correctional Siberia. More than 20 years ago, the Supreme Court ruled that children could not be sent to juvenile prisons for "rehabilitation" unless proof existed that they had *done* something for which imprisonment was appropriate. The 1967 *Gault* decision set off a revolution in juvenile court procedures. For example, formal hearings with youngsters represented by attorneys became common practice for serious offenses that might result in incarceration.

Furthermore, a number of state legislatures restricted the discretion of juvenile court judges. In New York and New Jersey, for example, juvenile court judges may not commit a youngster to correctional institutions for "status offenses," that is, for behavior that would not be a crime if done by adults. Thus, truancy or ungovernable behavior in school or at home are not grounds for incarceration in these two states. The differentiation of juvenile delinquents from persons in need of supervision (PINS in New York nomenclature, JINS in New Jersey) may have been needed. However, one consequence of this reform is that the public schools can less easily persuade juvenile courts to help with school-discipline problems. In some cases, the juvenile court judge cannot incarcerate because the behavior is a status offense rather than "delinquency." In other cases the alleged behavior, such as slapping or punching a teacher, is indeed delinquency, but many judges will not commit a youngster to a correctional institution for this kind of behavior, because they have to deal with what they perceive as worse juvenile violence on the streets. Thus, for its own very good reasons, the juvenile justice system does not help the schools appreciably in dealing with disorder. Only when disorder results in violence will the juvenile courts intervene; their reponse is too little, too late.

Increased attention to civil rights for students, including students accused of violence, was also an unintended consequence of compulsory school attendance laws. The Supreme Court held in *Goss v. Lopez* not only that schoolchildren were entitled to due process when accused by school authorities of misbehavior and that greater due-process protections were required for students in danger of suspension for more than 10 days or for expulsion, than for students threatened with less severe disciplinary penalties. The Court held also that the state, in enacting a compulsory school attendance law, incurred an *obligation* to educate children until the age specified in the law, which implied greater attention to due process for youngsters still subject to compulsory attendance laws than for youngsters beyond their scope. Boards of education interpreted these requirements to mean that formal hearings were necessary in cases of youngsters in danger of losing the educational benefits the law required them to receive. Such hearings were to be conducted at a higher administrative level than the school itself, and the principals had to document the case and produce witnesses who could be cross-examined.

In Hawaii, for example, which has a compulsory education law extending to age 18, Rule 21, which the Hawaii Department of Education adopted in 1976 to meet the requirement of *Goss v. Lopez,* aroused unanimous dissatisfaction from principals interviewed in the Crime Commission's study of school violence and vandalism. They had three complaints. First, in cases where expulsion or suspension of more than 10 days might be the outcome, the principal was required to gather evidence, to file notices, and to participate in long adversarial hearings at the district superintendent's office in a prosecutorial capacity, which discouraged principals from initiating this procedure in serious cases. Thus principals down-

Part of the reason for the decline of homework in public secondary schools is the erosion of teacher authority.

graded serious offenses in order to deal with them expeditiously, by means of informal hearings. Second, Rule 21 forbade principals to impose a series of short suspensions of a student within one semester that cumulatively amounted to more than 10 days unless there was a formal hearing. Although intended to prevent principals from getting around the requirement for formal hearings in serious cases involving long suspensions, what this provision achieved was to prevent principals from imposing any discipline at all on multiple offenders. Once suspended for a total of 10 days in a semester, a student could engage in minor and not-so-minor misbehavior with impunity. Third, the principals complained that their obligation to supply "alternative education" for students expelled or suspended for more than 10 days was unrealistic in terms of available facilities.

The Blurring of the Line Between Disability And Misbehavior

"Special education" serves a heterogeneous group of students, some with physical handicaps, others with behavior problems from which emotional handicaps are inferred without independent psychiatric justification. Inferring personality disturbances from deviant behavior has a long, disreputable history in the criminal courts where defense attorneys have creatively described stealing and fire-setting as "kleptomania" and "pyromania" when the behavior had no intuitively plausible explanation. In 1975 Congress passed Public Law 94-142, the Education for All Handicapped Children Act, which provided "not only that every handicapped child is entitled to a free public education, but that such an education shall be provided *in the least restrictive educational setting.*" (Hewett and Watson, 1979) Thus the philosophy of mainstreaming handicapped children—exceptional children, as they are sometimes called—became national policy. Some of the handicaps are verifiable independent of classroom behavior: deafness, blindness, motor problems, speech pathologies, retardation. But learning disabilities and behavior disorders, especially the latter, are more ambiguous. Does a child who punches other children in his classroom have a behavior disorder for which he should be pitied, or does he deserve punishment for naughtiness?

The state of Hawaii ran into this dilemma in attempting to implement Public Law 94-142. The Hawaii Board of Education promulgated Rule 49.13, which asserted that "handicapped children in special education programs may not be seriously disciplined by suspensions for over 10 days or by dismissal from school for violating any of the school's rules." This meant that there were two standards of behavior, one for ordinary students and one for "handicapped" students. But students who were classified as handicapped because of a clinical judgment that they were "emotionally disturbed" (usually inferred from "acting out" behavior) seemed to be getting a license to commit disciplinary infractions.

According to a 1980 Hawaii Crime Commission report, *Violence and Vandalism in the Public Schools of Hawaii*:

> [I]t was the consensus of 14 principals from the Leeward and Central School Districts of Oahu that the special disciplinary section under Rule 49 created a "double standard" between regular students who were subject to varying degrees of suspensions and special education students who were not. These principals believe that such an alleged double standard fosters a belief among special education students that they are immune from suspension under regular disciplinary rules and, therefore, can engage in misconduct with impunity.

"Special education" students placed in that category because of supposed emotional disturbance may have violence-prone personalities. On the other hand, they may only be assumed to have such personalities because they have engaged in inexplicably violent behavior. They might be able to control their behavior if they had incentives to do so. In formulating Rule 49.13, the Department of Education of the state of Hawaii has been explicit about denying responsibility to special education youngsters, but the same heightened concern about the special needs of presumed emotionally disturbed students is common in other American public school systems. One result of not holding some children responsible for violent behavior is that they are more likely to engage in violence than they would otherwise be.

The Erosion of Teacher Authority

The social changes that have separated secondary schools from effective family and neighborhood influences and that have made it burdensome for school administrators to expel students guilty of violent behavior or to suspend them for more than 10 days partially explain the eroding authority of teachers. Social changes are not the entire explanation, however. There also have been *cultural* changes undermining the authority of teachers. There was a time when teachers were considered godlike, and their judgments went unquestioned. No more. Doubtless, reduced respect for teachers is part of fundamental cultural changes by which many authority figures—parents, police, government officials have come to have less prestige. In the case of teachers, the general demythologizing was amplified by special ideological criticism. Bestselling books of the 1960s portrayed teachers, especially middle-class teachers, as the villains of education—insensitive, authoritarian, and even racist.

Part of the reason for the decline of homework in public secondary schools is the erosion of teacher authority. When teachers could depend on all but a handful of students to turn in required written homework, they could assign homework and mean it. The slackers could be disciplined. But in schools where teachers could no longer count on a majority of students doing their homework, assigning it became a meaningless ritual, and many teachers gave up. Professor James Coleman and his research team found that private and parochial school sophomores in high school reported doing, on the average, at least two hours more of homework per week than public school sophomores. Many teachers felt they lacked authority to induce students to do *anything* they did not want to do: to attend classes regularly, to keep quiet so orderly recitation could proceed, to refrain from annoying a disliked classmate.

A charismatic teacher can still control a class. But the erosion of teacher authority meant that *run-of-the-mill* teachers are less effective at influencing behavior in their classes, in hallways, and in lunchrooms. What has changed is that the *role* of teacher no longer commands the automatic respect it once did from students and their parents. This means that less forceful, less experienced, or less effective teachers cannot rely on the authority of the role to help them maintain control. They are on their own in a sense that the previous generation was not.

WHAT CAN BE DONE

Faced with the worrisome problem of school violence, Americans look for simple solutions like hiring additional security guards or installing metal detectors. Security guards and metal directors *are* useful, especially in inner-city schools where invading predators from surrounding neighborhoods are a major source of violence. But dealing with *student* sources of everyday school violence requires more effective teacher control over the submerged part of the violence iceberg: disorder.

Teachers, not security guards, already prevent disorder in most American high schools. They do it by expressing approval of some student behavior and disapproval of other student behavior. This is tremendously effective in schools where the majority of students care about what teachers think of them. Expressing approval and disapproval is useless (and sometimes dangerous) in schools where students have contempt for teachers and teachers know it. In such schools, particularly those in inner cities, many teachers are too intimidated to condemn curses, threats, obscenities, drunkenness, and, of course, the neglect of homework and other academic obligations. It would help enormously if all families inculcated moral values before children started school and if all teachers motivated students better in the earliest grades so that they are hooked on education by the time they reach high school. But, unfortunately, many students arrive without these desirable formative experiences.

The problem is how to empower teachers in schools where they are now intimidated by students who are not as receptive to education as we would like them to be. Teachers cannot empower themselves. Ultimately, teachers derive their authority from student respect for education and the people who transmit it. Japan provides a classic illustration of what respect for teachers, inculcated in the family, can accomplish. Japanese high school

The age limit for high school entitlement should be raised from 21, the usual age at present, to 100.

teachers are firmly in control of their high schools without the help of security guards or metal detectors. No Japanese high school teacher is afraid to admonish students who start to misbehave, because the overwhelming majority of students will respond deferentially. Japanese high school teachers know that their students care about the grades they receive at school.

Students have good reason to care. Japanese teachers give grades that employers as well as colleges scrutinize; they also write letters of recommendation that prospective employers take seriously. In short, Japanese high school students are deeply concerned about the favorable attitudes of their teachers. As a result, Japanese teachers can require lots of homework. Homework is a major factor in the superior academic performance of Japanese students in international comparisons. But effective teacher control has consequences for school safety too. Japanese high school teachers never are assaulted by their students; on the contrary, high school students pay attention to their teachers and graduate from high school in greater proportions (93 percent) than American students. They *want* to go to school because they are convinced, correctly, that their occupational futures depend on educational achievement.

It is unlikely that American high school students will ever respect their teachers as much as Japanese students do theirs. Japan's culture is more homogeneous than American culture, and Japan's high schools have a closer connection with employers than American high schools do. Japanese employers as well as Japanese colleges want to see the grades that students receive in high school, and they pay attention to letters of recommendation from teachers. Furthermore, Japan's high schools have the advantage of containing only voluntary students. (Compulsory education ends in junior high school in Japan.) But there are several measures we can take that will greatly enhance teacher control in American high schools.

The first one is to break through the anonymous, impersonal atmosphere of jumbo high schools and junior highs by creating smaller communities of learning within larger structures, where teachers and students can come to know each other well. A number of urban school districts—New York and Philadelphia among them—are already moving ahead with this strategy of schools within schools or "house plans," as they are sometimes called. Such a strategy promotes a sense of community and encourages strong relationships to grow between teachers and students. Destructive student subcultures are less likely to emerge. Problems are caught before they get out of hand; students do not fall between the cracks. And teacher disapproval of student misbehavior carries more sting in schools where students and teachers are close.

The second measure we can take—one that would significantly empower teachers—is to have employers start demanding high school transcripts and make it known to students that the best jobs will go to those whose effort and learning earn them. This idea, which John Bishop and James Rosenbaum have written about, and which Al Shanker has devoted a number of his *New York Times* columns to, is an important one. Employers currently pay little or no attention to high school transcripts. Very few ask for them. They don't know what courses their job applicants took or what grades they got. The only requirement the typical employer has is that the applicant possess a high school diploma. Whether that diploma represents four years of effort, achievement, and good behavior—or four years of seat time and surliness—is a distinction not made.

And the students know it. Rosenbaum describes the consequences:

> Since employers ignore grades, it is not surprising that many work-bound students lack motivation to improve them. While some students work hard in school because of personal standards or parental pressure or real interest in a particular subject, students who lack these motivations have little incentive since schoolwork doesn't affect the jobs they will get after graduation, and it is difficult for them to see how it could affect job possibilities ten years later.
>
> The consequences are far reaching . . . . Many kinds of motivation and discipline problems are widespread: absenteeism, class cutting, tardiness, disruptive behavior, verbal abuse, failure to do homework assignments, and substance abuse. . . .
>
> While employers ask why teachers don't exert their authority in the classroom, they unwittingly undermine teachers' authority over work-bound students. Grades are the main direct sanction that teachers control. When students see that grades don't affect the jobs they will get, teacher authority is severely crippled.

Employers, of course, would have to hold up their end of the bargain: good jobs for good grades. Once the system was credible, significant numbers of students would take heed, and teachers would be re-armed—not with hardware, but with the authority to command serious attention to the work of school.

Third, we should show that American society takes education seriously by insisting that it is not enough for a youngster to be on the school rolls and show up occasionally. Dropout prevention is not an end in itself; perhaps a youngster who does not pay attention in class and do homework *ought* to drop out. Our policy in every high school, including inner-city high schools with traditionally high dropout rates, should be that excellence is not only possible, it is expected. Those who balk at giving prospective dropouts a choice between a more onerous school experience than they now have and leaving school altogether should keep in mind that students would make the choice in consultation with parents or other relatives. Most families, even pretty demoralized ones, would urge children to stay in school when offered a clear choice. The problem today is that many families don't get a clear choice; the schools attended by their children unprotestingly accept tardiness, class cutting, inattention in class, and truancy. A child can drop out of such a school psychologically, unbeknownst to his family, because enrollment doesn't even mean regular attendance. In effect, prospective dropouts choose whether to fool around inside school or outside school. That is why making schools tougher academically, with substantial amounts of homework, might have the paradoxical effect of persuading a higher proportion of families to encourage their kids to opt for an education. Furthermore, education, unlike imprisonment, depends on cooperation from the beneficiaries of the opportunities offered. Keeping internal dropouts in school is an empty victory.

A fourth measure will demonstrate that we really meant it when we said we would welcome dropouts back when they are ready to take education seriously. School boards should encourage community adults to come into high schools, not as teachers, not as aides, not as counselors, not as security guards, but as students. A recent front-page story in the *New York Times* (November 28, 1993) illustrated the practicality of this proposal. Dropouts from an impoverished neighborhood not only hungered for a second chance at a high school education but became role models for younger students. At Chicago's DuSable High School, an all-black school close to a notorious public housing project, a 39-year-old father of six children, a 29-year-old mother of a 14-year-old son, who, like his mother is a freshman at DuSable, a 39-year-old mother of five children—returned to high school. They had come to believe that dropping out a decade or two earlier was a terrible mistake. Some of these adult students are embarrassed to meet their children in the hallways; some of their children are embarrassed that their parents are schoolmates; some of the teachers at the high school were initially skeptical about mixing teenagers and adults in classes. But everyone at DuSable High School agrees that these adult students take education seriously, work harder than the teenage students, and, by their presence, set a good example.

Adult students are not in school to reduce school violence. But an incidental byproduct of their presence is improved order. For example, it is less easy to cut classes or skip school altogether when your mother or even your neighbor is attending the school. The principal at DuSable High School observed one mother marching her son off to gym class, which he had intended to cut. Unfortunately, most school systems do not welcome adult students except in special adult school programs or G.E.D. classes. Such age-segregated programs will continue to enroll most of the high school dropouts who later decide they want a high school diploma because work or child-care responsibilities will keep all but the most deter-

mined in these age-segregated programs. But education laws should not *prevent* persons over 21 from re-enrollment in high school. The age limit for high school entitlement should be raised from 21, the usual age at present, to 100. Especially in inner-city high schools, much can be gained by encouraging even a handful of adult dropouts to return to regular high school classes. Teachers who have an adult student or two in their classes are not alone with a horde of teenagers. They have adult allies during the inevitable confrontations with misbehaving students. Even though the adults say nothing, their presence bolsters the will of teachers to maintain order.

Teenage students who feel a stake in educational achievement and adult students who have lived to regret dropping out and are eager to return to high school both empower teachers in the struggle against disorder. These secret weapons against violence are less expensive—and probably more effective—than additional security guards. Teachers need all the help they can get.

It is important also to remind ourselves that plenty of schools—including ones in the worst crime-ridden neighborhoods—are oases in the midst of despair, where teachers have managed, against all odds, to maintain a good environment for learning. America's goal must be nothing short of making all schools safe havens where children can come to learn and grow.

REFERENCES

Bastian, Lisa D. and Bruce M. Taylor, *School Crime: A National Crime Victimization Survey Report.* Washington: Bureau of Justice Statistics, 1991.

Hawaii Crime Commission, *Violence and Vandalism in the Public Schools of Hawaii. Vol. 1.* Honolulu: Mimeographed Report to the Hawaii State Legislature, September 1980.

Hewett, Frank M. and Philip C. Watson, "Classroom Management and the Exceptional Learner." In *Classroom Management,* Daniel L. Duke, ed. Chicago: University of Chicago Press, 1979.

McDermott, M. Joan, *Criminal Victimization in Urban Schools.* Washington, D.C.: U.S. Government Printing Office, 1979.

Rosenbaum, James, E., "What If Good Jobs Depended on Good Grades?" *American Educator,* Winter 1989.

Toby, Jackson, "Hoodlum or Business Man: An American Dilemma." In *The Jews: Social Patterns of an American Group,* ed. Marshall Sklare, Glencoe, Ill. Free Press, 1957.

Toby, Jackson, "Violence in School," from *Crime and Justice: An Annual Review of Research,* Vol. 4, Michael Tonry and Norval Morris, eds., 1983.

U.S. Department of Health, Education and Welfare, *Violent Schools— Safe Schools: The Safe Schools Report to the Congress.* Washington, D.C.: U.S. Government Printing Office, 1978.

Wilson, James Q., *Thinking About Crime,* pp. 75–89. New York: Vintage, 1985.

On the Front Lines: Interview With Judge David B. Mitchell

Juvenile Justice: You have become increasingly recognized as a leading juvenile court judge and as a leader in the area of juvenile justice. Why do you consider this important, and could a nonjudge do the same?

Judge Mitchell: It's important and traditional for the juvenile judiciary to take a leadership responsibility locally and, in some instances, nationally because we're the ones who see the situation in its most difficult form. In other words, the judge is always there and sees what's occurring in the community.

The judge, in most instances, is in the best position to address the needs of the families that come before the court. The judge, in many instances, is in the best position to speak to the issues because he or she is not seeking voter approval for the court's policies. The judge can go before the public and the policymakers and advocate from a position of respect and responsibility for the needs of the system as opposed to setting forth political solutions.

Juvenile Justice: It sounds like a tall order for a juvenile court judge.

Judge Mitchell: True. When you sit in the civil or criminal court, your impact is upon the litigants. That's important; however, you have no real opportunity to effect the changes needed within the

community. You may help streamline the system so that the cases move more smoothly. You may even be able to address some aspects of the problems of the community as they relate to the courts. When you sit in the juvenile court, however, you have the opportunity to speak to the broader social problems of your community, to really participate in making things better overall as opposed to what happens in this one case.

Juvenile Justice: What are the requisites for being a judge?

Judge Mitchell: Maryland has one of the unique statutes on that. It says as a general principle that no person may sit in a juvenile court unless they want to do so. Secondly, the person must have some training, experience, or interest in the field. Finally, the person requires the approval of the chief judge of the State.

Juvenile Justice: There are so many functions in the juvenile court for which the judge is responsible. Many courts delegate some of this work to referees and others. Do you? And is it a good thing?

Judge Mitchell: Unfortunately, we do. Baltimore city historically has been a master-dominated court. We have masters, who in other communities are called referees and in others commissioners. These are nonjudicial authorities. They are competent experts in what they do,

Judge David B. Mitchell is associate judge of the Baltimore (Maryland) City Circuit Court and has long been active in juvenile and family law. The interview was conducted for Juvenile Justice by Irving Slott, former director of OJJDP's Information Dissemination Unit.

From *Juvenile Justice*, a journal of the Office of Juvenile Justice and Delinquency Prevention, Spring/Summer 1993, pp. 8-16. Reprinted by permission of the U.S. Department of Justice, Office of Justice Programs.

but they do not carry the imprimatur and authority of a judge. The decision to operate the court this way is fiscally driven. As such, we have become a court that has only one judge and eight juvenile masters. There's no way for one judge to hear all those cases.

I believe cases should be heard by persons who have the final authority to make decisions, rather than have the judge act as a rubber stamp to what has happened. When it comes to the ultimate decision of what's going to happen to that child, to that family, or to the community, judges should make those decisions just as they decide whether you're going to be evicted from your home, whether you have to pay a parking ticket, or whether you are going to be separated from your family and incarcerated for the offense you have been found guilty of committing. Children and family issues are no less significant, and should be accorded the same level of responsibility.

Juvenile Justice: Let's turn to the subject of waiver, which has received quite a bit of interest lately. When should a juvenile case be waived to the criminal court? How and by whose authority?

Judge Mitchell: Only the judge should make the decision on when a case should be waived out of the juvenile system. Although some jurisdictions allow that decision to be made by the prosecutor, in most jurisdictions it is a judicial determination, and that is the way it should be. The judge is impartial. The prosecutor, no matter how competent, is a partisan in the process and subject to political and community pressures.

We use waiver too much! I'm using waiver broadly to encompass not just the judicial decision on a charge where the juvenile court has the original jurisdiction but to include cases where by statute the juvenile court no longer has original jurisdiction. For example, in Maryland, if a child is 16 years of age or older and is charged with a handgun offense, the ju-

venile court doesn't have jurisdiction in that case. It is lodged in the criminal system originally, and the juvenile court can only gain that case if a transfer or waiver occurs from the criminal system to the juvenile system.

We use waiver too much. We have not consistently addressed the needs of the juvenile system, so we blame the kids when they commit offenses that anger us. We send them to the adult system. Because of the intensity of crime in the urban setting, you find waiver being sought in a lot of cases.

Juvenile Justice: The other way juveniles who commit offenses don't go to court is through diversion. How should diversion be effected?

Judge Mitchell: Diversion is a viable tool for the juvenile justice system. Given the appropriate resources, a diversion program keeps the kid from having to come into the court system as a charged child. I don't believe it should be run by the police, and I don't think they do either. It should be run by an executive agency that will take a number of factors into consideration before a diversion decision is made.

Even after a decision has been made to charge the child, a diversion program should be available through the courts. You need the opportunity to get the attention of the family by bringing them to court and then to be able to divert the youth.

Juvenile Justice: I understand that some problems have occurred where a social work agency responsible for troubled kids does not want offenders around nonoffending youth.

Judge Mitchell: That is a problem, but I harken back to something one of my colleagues said some years ago. Many of these youthful offenders are only offenders because that's what we call them at the moment we interact with them.

Juvenile Justice: We caught them.

Judge Mitchell: Yes, we caught them or someone complained about them. It goes

Many of these youthful offenders are only offenders because that's what we call them when we interact with them.

in almost a circle. If your son takes your car, is that misbehavior on his part, or do you decide to call the authorities and make it a delinquency offense? We're not talking about the hardcore situation such as when a child seriously assaults someone. We're talking about petty thefts and acting-out behavior. I agree with you about mixing the populations, but when we examine who these kids are, they're the same kids.

Juvenile Justice: They're troubled kids.

Judge Mitchell: Yeah, they're troubled kids, and troubled kids have the same needs.

Juvenile Justice: The juvenile court originally was entrusted with determining treatment, to rehabilitate and set juveniles on the path of becoming good members of society, but since then proceedings have become more litigious to insure constitutional rights. Has this helped the juvenile? What's it done to the court?

Judge Mitchell: I think the fact we are a constitutional court is very good. I have not the slightest quarrel with that. Bear in mind, I'm from a generation that has known no difference. I started practicing law in 1970 when *Gault* had already changed the courts. I don't have a problem with lawyers in the court, but I confess to some concern about the kinds of messages kids are getting. I recall as a practicing lawyer representing a kid and being torn with a conflict whether to perform my "legal obligation" to my client and ignore what the consequences might be for this kid, or to do what I think is best for this child.

Sometimes the adversarial system is in conflict with what is in the best interest of the child. The perfect example of that is the case of two young ladies, 10 or 11,

very tender years, that I had as respondents before me about 4 years ago. They were very innocent children. Their mother was a day care provider. These young ladies had been fondling the kids who were coming to their mother for care. It was more out of curiosity than anything malicious or criminal.

The authorities discovered it, and the kids were brought before the court. They had a lawyer; the lawyer couldn't explain anything to these little girls. The State would have had difficulty prosecuting these little girls, yet these little girls needed to understand what was happening. The lawyer said to me, "Judge, I don't know what to do. If I play my role as lawyer for these children, they won't get the help they need, unless I can persuade the family to get it on a private basis."

There are critics who say that the court is not constitutional enough, that we do not uniformly provide protection for children's rights. I know that in Maryland and particularly in Baltimore city, every child that comes before the court has an attorney. Every child! In most instances when parents are brought before the court for purposes of abuse, neglect, or dependency issues, they are provided counsel. At least for the adjudication and disposition stages of the case.

Juvenile Justice: Then would you have three attorneys?

Judge Mitchell: Oh yes, three, sometimes four. Mom and Pop might be in conflict, so we'll have a representative for each one of them. We may have intervenors from the grandparents or other relatives, or even interested parties who have representative counsel. We may have six or seven lawyers here for one family.

I don't know if I would go so far as other jurisdictions and have jury trials for these kids. I think that's going too far. I have a concern about legalistic messages being sent to kids. Kids receive messages and filter them differently than adults. I'm concerned that they'll get the impression that they can hire somebody and beat the case.

Juvenile Justice: This has been a problem for prosecutors. Dedicated prosecutors have told me that they feel a responsibility for the juvenile as well as for society. It annoys them when they come against a defense attorney who really doesn't know how to handle such a case.

Judge Mitchell: It should be a specialized bar. The family will go out and hire the same lawyer that they would have hired if a 25-year-old person were charged with a crime. The needs of the person charged are completely different. Prosecutors who spend time in the juvenile court understand the differences and it frustrates them. It frustrates the court as well. We work very hard to educate the bar on the differences.

Juvenile Justice: But is there a specialized juvenile defense bar?

Judge Mitchell: If there is, it's the public defender's office. The public defender represents 80 percent, maybe 90 percent, of the kids who come before our court in delinquency matters. A specialized bar also exists for my court in dependency cases. They receive training, and they have a great deal of experience in the field. They become acquainted with what exists programmatically. They do not relinquish the rights of their clients, but they are strong advocates for the community.

Juvenile Justice: Let's turn our attention to the public. Citizens are concerned about juvenile involvement in violence, shootings, drugs, gangs. Are these your priorities?

The family will go out and hire the same lawyer as if a 25-year-old were charged. The needs are completely different.

Judge Mitchell: If you're sitting in a criminal court, violence and drugs are your priorities. If you're sitting in the juvenile court, it's the same thing. Kids are gross mirrors of the general society. They are exaggerations of what occurs generally in society.

Drugs and violence have been predominant in the criminal justice system for a couple of decades. When kids start doing the same thing, we blame them. We attack the kids as if they invented violence. There is no poppy field in Baltimore city. There is no gun factory in Baltimore city. They import drugs from other communities, but they don't bring them across the United States border.

The political process seizes upon these horrible figures and statistics. They blame the inability of the juvenile system to control the situation. Therefore you constantly have calls for reform of the juvenile system, that you're not tough enough.

Juvenile Justice: Whatever toughness means.

Judge Mitchell: Whatever toughness means. If you get tough with them, you're going to get results. Fallacious. Whatever toughness means, it's still fallacious.

Juvenile Justice: And yet the data show that violence has increased among juveniles, even among younger kids. This is disturbing.

Judge Mitchell: Yes. It has spread down to the subteen group, the adolescents. Sexual offenses against children by children has now spread in alarming rates to very young children. In Baltimore about 60 percent of the kids in the city, particularly the African-American kids, have witnessed a violent event. I'm not talking about Mom and Pop fighting or brothers and sisters fighting. I'm talking about a homicide or shooting. A huge number of people in the community know someone who has been killed or have had a member of their family who has been killed. It has an impact on ev-

If putting people in penitentiaries for decades was effective, we wouldn't have gotten to this stage.

erybody, particularly in the African-American community.

Juvenile Justice: It becomes part of normality.

Judge Mitchell: Yes, it does. Saturday I attended a funeral in Washington, D.C. The deceased was the son of a woman who was a high-school classmate of my wife. Her son was on his first date in Georgetown, the first time out with his mother's car. Someone apparently jumped out of the bushes and put a bullet in this boy's head.

It affects every one of us. I've been to a number of funerals. I have kids who have been in this court who have ended up in a violent way. It tears at the fabric of our society. I don't know what we can do about violence. I do know what does not work—incarceration. If putting people in penitentiaries for decades was effective, we wouldn't have gotten to this stage.

Juvenile Justice: That is challenged by the rare kid who simply shoots somebody without any feeling. He has never bonded.

Judge Mitchell: What imprisonment accomplishes, at the juvenile or adult level, is removal of that person from society. It provides protection for potential victims for a period of time. Unfortunately, it is not a deterrent. The other day, I sat with three drug dealers. We candidly discussed their behavior in a community forum. They understand the criminal justice system. They understand the law. They understand the possibilities not just of being caught and going to prison, but of dying. And they don't care. They are not stopping.

Juvenile Justice: Tomorrow isn't important. Next year isn't important.

Judge Mitchell: Immediate self-gratification drives them. The fact that little kids and mothers are being injured, killed in random shootings, innocent victims of turf wars, they rationalize by saying, "Well, mothers know it's dangerous out there; they shouldn't send their babies outside."

Incarcerating these individuals is not the answer alone. The process must go back further, to fundamental values that must be provided in the home. One of the drug dealers said, "I teach my children values, but I don't have any values of my own."

It must go to the educational, housing, and social opportunities we provide within that compact community that is sometimes called the inner city, sometimes called the ghetto. It is a concentration of a permanent underclass of poverty that can see the other side through the glass but doesn't know how to get there. Until we solve that problem we're going to have this one.

Juvenile Justice: You touched on the problem of juvenile sex offense before. Is that a serious problem?

Judge Mitchell: Yes. I have seen the incidents of criminal sexual behavior by kids against kids increasing at an alarming rate.

Juvenile Justice: OJJDP has just initiated a study to determine, not only how serious a problem it is, but to distinguish the types of offenses and offenders. When our fiscal year 1992 plan was issued, we received more comments on that, all positive, than on the entire rest of the plan.

Judge Mitchell: You touched a nerve I'm not sure you realized that you were about to touch. More and more, younger and younger sexual offenders are coming into the courts. They are pushing the envelope of the psychiatric community which had determined that you cannot classify a person as a pedophile below a certain age.

Juvenile Justice: Status offenses are often the first sign of antisocial behavior. Are they serious problems for the court?

Judge Mitchell: The reformist community quite accurately indicates the court has done a good job of botching this one. We've tried to use contempt authority. We've incarcerated kids. But the problem still exists. Kids do self-destructive things. They are not being brought to the attention of the courts. The reformist community has done an excellent job of convincing everyone that this is just adolescent aberrational behavior that kids will grow out of and become beautiful citizens. But every delinquent who comes before the court and is adjudicated delinquent was a status offender at some point early in his or her life.

Of course, not every status offender will become a delinquent or criminal. However, if you don't address these problems early, you're going to have to address more difficult problems later. In the same way, almost every person that comes before the juvenile and criminal systems has dropped out of school or failed to attend school. As long as you don't attack the attendance problem, you're going to cultivate a class of criminals, a class of individuals who eventually will violate the criminal justice system's laws.

> *As long as you don't address the school attendance problem, you're going to cultivate a class of criminals.*

In most urban communities you are doing well if 50 percent of the kids who enter the ninth grade graduate. Now that's a status offense, truancy. The kids get the message real early on that no one is going to do anything about it.

Juvenile Justice: Early on could be the first grade.

Judge Mitchell: Yes, that's why in Baltimore we are starting a school attendance project in the elementary schools. We're

going to bring parents whose kids aren't going to school into the courthouse. We're going to start enforcing compulsory school attendance laws.

Juvenile Justice: OJJDP has undertaken a major research project, a longitudinal cohort study of 4,000 kids. We find that kids who are dropping out later probably dropped out in the very early grades.

Judge Mitchell: When we have fiscal problems in urban communities, one of the first areas to cut in education is attendance monitors. Special education is one of the next areas. Many of the truancy cases are not brought to us until the kid has missed 120 days. That's too late. Thirty percent of the elementary pupils in Baltimore are chronic truants who miss at least 30 days, 6 weeks, from school each year.

Juvenile Justice: We talk about status offenses as a legal term. Status offenders, though, are all kinds of kids. The kid that runs home and hides under the bed is different from the one that runs away from home.

Judge Mitchell: One of the problems that the court has now is that the system does not have legal authority over those kids. It is very frustrating for judges to get calls from a family saying my child is doing this or that and we need services. What do I do? If I call the agency, they will say, "Wait till the child commits a crime." It's very frustrating.

Juvenile Justice: How difficult is it to involve the parents?

Judge Mitchell: The child does not exist in a vacuum. The problems of the child are not just the child's. The child's acting out often is nothing more than a response to stimuli from the family. We are very active in that area, but we're not always successful, and that's not an indictment of the juvenile system, it's an indictment of what is happening in our society. We have to involve the family.

Juvenile Justice: How do you involve the family when there is a limit to what government can do in intruding into a family? There ought to be some humility there. How do you say, "You can do better. Your children's future depends on you"?

Judge Mitchell: We've been somewhat coercive, in that we do a lot of lobbying and persuasion in trying to establish a base level of responsibility and authority in the family. We talk with the kids in court to make sure they understand their mother's rules aren't any different than anyone else's. In some instances we have to kind of bludgeon parents to get them motivated.

Juvenile Justice: It's almost a cliché that the status of professional juvenile justice work is low. Is this true? How can it be overcome?

Judge Mitchell: That's a very difficult question. I firmly believe that the job never gives you dignity. You give it whatever dignity or lack thereof it has.

That photograph on the wall is of the seven judges that ran for election as a team in 1986. We went around Baltimore visiting community associations. I was introduced as a juvenile court judge. They didn't ask the criminal court judges about crime. They didn't ask about civil issues or issues of rent or housing. They wanted to talk to that juvenile court judge. The community has a great deal of respect for that position.

Juvenile Justice: Well, is it the law fraternity that doesn't respect juvenile work?

Judge Mitchell: Absolutely. The law fraternity looks upon this as less than significant. You must be less talented, because if you were more talented as a judge or professional lawyer, you'd be dealing with the million-dollar cases.

Several years ago, I substituted for an administrative judge. A major civil case with quite complicated issues came up, an injunction of a restaurant. The lawyers met with me at the end of my juvenile docket, and we discussed the problem and resolved the case. Later, one

of the lawyers, in a backhanded compliment, said, "Judge, I didn't think it was possible to resolve this case, because you're sitting in juvenile."

It's the legal fraternity that has given juvenile law a low regard. It's not the social work community. This is their life. It's not the juvenile professionals or the case workers. It's their life. The legal community has made it less than significant.

You're not talking about giving someone a death sentence. You're not talking about giving someone 50 years! You're not talking about that medical malpractice case or bank dissolution. You're talking about kids. It's the same in family law. Divorces, marriage dissolutions, custody issues are given less respect in the legal community and other areas.

Juvenile Justice: How do you change that?

Judge Mitchell: You have to work with the leadership of the bar and the individual members. You have to go to the law schools. We're trying to build the responsibility of law students in this process through clinical education programs. I work with my colleagues on the bench to accept rotation to the juvenile court not as purgatory but as a challenge.

Juvenile law is a specialized area that many people don't know anything about. What they do not know, they do not understand, and what they do not understand, they do not respect. A judge who had just completed his term in the juvenile court wrote me to say that it had been the most exciting and challenging responsibility in his legal career. "I want to return, I want to stay involved," he advised me.

Juvenile Justice: My last question is: Would you predict the future? We've discussed many different problems affecting juvenile justice. Will things get better?

Judge Mitchell: One of the greatest challenges facing juvenile justice is to provide consistent services both before cases get to the court and afterwards. It is of no value for the court to work miracles in rehabilitation if there are no opportunities for the child in the community and if the child is simply going to return to the squalor from which he or she came.

For one of the first times in our Nation's history, we have a permanent underclass of poor black, white, and Hispanic kids. These kids see no opportunities. They reside in intense, comprehensive poverty. They are served by inadequate housing. They are provided with educational systems that do not function. Until we deal

---

I work with my colleagues on the bench to accept rotation to the juvenile court not as purgatory but as a challenge.

---

with the environment in which they live, whatever we do in the courts is irrelevant.

Meanwhile, fiscal constraints, if left to continue, will decimate our efforts to reform the juvenile justice system. Services will be concentrated in institutions and few resources will remain in the community. All the studies show that institutions don't work. Most juvenile institu-

---

Most juvenile institutions are simply little prisons where inmates make contacts for future criminal activities.

---

tions are simply little prisons, networking places where inmates make contacts for future criminal activities.

Innovation in community services and treatment is no longer being fostered. In fact, it's being suppressed. No one wants to pay for it. These are some of the biggest challenges facing the justice system. People expect the criminal justice system to be the savior of the community. We are not. We do not have a policy to deal with drugs. Unless a solution is found to the crisis of alcohol, drug, and substance abuse, we're going to continue to have problems.

A higher rate of kids in rural environments use cigarettes, smokeless tobacco, beer, wine, and liquor and binge drinking than kids in urban environments. Unless we recognize that substance abuse affects all of America, not just our cities, and start attacking the broad scope of the problem, the juvenile court, the criminal court, and all the courts will be irrelevant. All we shall be is conductors on the railroad to prison.

Juvenile Justice: Are there any signs of improvement?

Judge Mitchell: Not on the front end. The political community is dealing with this rhetorically. They're wringing their hands and they're pointing fingers. On the back end, there's no investment in the future. We are investing in buildings. We're building prisons, and they will not solve the problem. More and more, bigger and bigger.

Juvenile Justice: Judge Mitchell, I thank you very much.

Judge Mitchell: I thank you.

AMERICAN KILLERS
Are Getting Younger

"A 14-year-old armed with a gun is far more menacing than a 44-year-old with the same weapon. [The teen] is more willing to pull the trigger—without fully considering the consequences."

James Alan Fox and Glenn Pierce

The authors are, respectively, dean of the College of Criminal Justice and director of the Center for Social Research, Northeastern University, Boston, Mass.

BURIED AMIDST the steady stream of stories about teenage girls murdered by their obsessed boyfriends and random shootings on the streets and in the schools, the FBI actually had some good news for a change—the number of homicides in the U.S. for 1992 had fallen six percent over the previous year. Has the tide of violent crime in America finally been stemmed? Unfortunately for the nation, this trend will not last.

First, we caution against putting too much faith into single-year, so-called homicide trends. From year to year, murder rates can fluctuate much like the stock market. What goes up generally comes down, and what goes down generally comes up. The homicide count for 1992, although lower than that for 1991, still was above the murder toll for each of the previous 10 years.

Second, and far more important, the nation appears on the verge of a crime wave that likely will last well into the next century. Such pessimism is more than a case

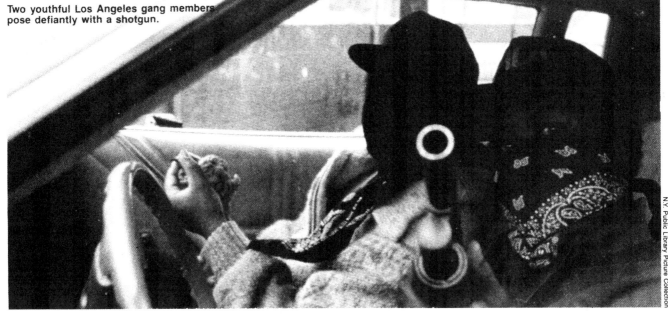

Two youthful Los Angeles gang members pose defiantly with a shotgun.

N.Y. Public Library Picture Collection

From *USA Today Magazine*, January 1994, pp. 24-26. © 1994 by the Society for the Advancement of Education. Reprinted by permission.

of "Chicken Little." Rather, there are some clear-cut social and demographic trends that make it very probable that today's shocking stories of drive-by shootings and fatal teenage romances will not go away. Even more disturbing is that the upsurge in killings has occurred during a period when violent crime should have been decreasing.

One of the authors (Fox) foretold nearly two decades ago, based on a predictive model developed in 1975 for his book, *Forecasting Crime Data*, that the rate of violent crime, including homicide, would decline from its 1980 peak until the early 1990s, when it would surge again. The premise then was simple. The explosion in lawlessness in the 1960s and 1970s, when violent crime escalated by double digits nearly every year, was in large part the result of demographics. During this time period, the post-World War II baby boomers —76,000,000 strong—had reached their late adolescence and early 20s, an age when aggressive tendencies are the strongest. As they matured into adulthood during the 1980s, however, they would have outgrown their violent ways, or at least have turned to low-risk crimes of profit. More to the point, the expected decline in the size of the population most prone to violence (teens and young adults) would have translated into a reduced level of crime.

As it happened, crime reports from the early 1980s did reflect a falling rate of violence in most parts of the country. From 1980 to 1985, for instance, the U.S. homicide rate dropped 23%. Not surprisingly, lawmakers and police chiefs were quick to claim credit for reductions in crime levels. While various programs and policies surely had some impact, the underlying cause largely was demographic.

Then, in 1986, quite unexpectedly, things began to change for the worse. The rate of violence began to rebound, despite continued shrinkage in the population of adolescents and young adults.

The forecasting model had assumed "all else being equal," but, clearly, all else was *not* equal. Although fewer in number, the new generation—the young and the rootless—was committing violent crimes at an alarming and unprecedented rate.

The statistics are scary. Whereas the rate of homicides by adults 25 and older has continued to decline steadily, the rate among 18-24-year-olds increased 62% from 1986 to 1991. Even more distressing is that murder now frequently reaches down to a much younger age group—children as young as 14-17. Murder among juveniles in that age bracket increased 124%.

Although violence has grown among both whites and blacks, the situation is particularly acute in minority neighborhoods. Black males aged 15-24, while only one percent of the U.S. population, constitute 14%

Members of the Grape Street Watts Gang, Los Angeles, pose with bandana signifying their "colors." These, in turn, denote gang affiliations.

of the victims of homicide and 19% of the perpetrators.

Adolescents, particularly those in major cities, are beset with idleness and, for some, hopelessness. A growing number of teens and pre-teens see few attractive alternatives to violence, drug use, and gang membership. For them, the American Dream is a nightmare. There may be little to hope for and live for, but plenty to die for and even kill for.

The causes of this reach well beyond demographics. There have been tremendous changes in the social context of crime over the past decade, which explain why this generation of youth is more violent than any other before it. As compared with their parents when they were young, this generation has more dangerous drugs in their bodies and more deadly weapons in their hands. According to the Department of Justice, an estimated 100,000 school children carry guns to school each day. The important role of gun availability in the increase in youth homicide can not be overstated. Since 1984, gun homicides by teenagers have tripled, while those involving other weapons have declined.

A 14-year-old armed with a gun is far more menacing than a 44-year-old with the same weapon. While the teen may be untrained in using a firearm, he is more willing to pull the trigger—without fully considering the consequences. Also, the gun psychologically distances the offender from his victim. It is all too easy—just pull

the trigger. If the same teenager had to kill his victim (almost always someone he knows) with his hands, he might be deterred. Finally, the increased firepower of today's weapons have outpaced the skills of emergency room doctors to repair damage done by gunfire.

Meanwhile, Americans can not seem to unite in opposition to guns. They are told that it is impossible ever to expect a gun-free America, so why try? They are not so skeptical, however, of the "Drug-Free America" slogan. Of course, the politics of gun control and drug control are very different. It has become politically expedient for the nation's leaders to place heavy emphasis on the drug issue—often at the expense of other equally important concerns—and to suggest drugs as the basic cause behind many of the problems faced by urban America. However, drug use is a symptom, not a cause. If the U.S. somehow were to eliminate drug use, it would not necessarily reduce crime.

Above all, the most significant change in the youth population has been in attitude. This new generation of youngsters is more inclined to resort to violence over trivial issues—a pair of Nikes, a leather jacket, or even a challenging glance—or for no apparent reason. In California, for instance, two teenaged girls murdered their best friend because they were jealous of her hair.

Part of this new attitude reflects a general trend toward a reduction in moral responsibility, affecting kids and adults alike. During the 1960s and 1970s, the U.S. fought two wars—the one in Vietnam and the war against guilt. For years, American were told not to feel guilty—do your own thing, love the one you're with. It used to be "I'm OK, You're OK." Now it's "I'm OK, You're Dead."

Another facet of this change in attitude about violence surrounds trends in the television and movie industries. Such shows as "Hard Copy," "Inside Edition," and "A Current Affair" have replaced game shows and even the early news in many markets. Programs like "Top Cops" and "Unsolved Mysteries" dominate prime time. Television docudramas glorify criminals, transforming insignificant and obscure nobodies into national celebrities. From the standpoint of crime victims everywhere, this adds insult to injury.

Consider, for example, the publicity given the "leading men" of a band of California teenagers who called themselves the "Spur Posse" and garnered points for having sex with teenaged girls as young as 13 years of age. How proud they were describing—actually bragging—about their exploits on Jane Whitney's "Nightalk." Adults were appalled, but these boys likely were heroes in the eyes of many 13- and 14-year-olds whose greatest desire was to grow up just like them.

Besides the glamorization of crime on television, VCRs have revolutionized the film industry—in certain respects for the worse. Concerned parents of the 1960s charged that motion pictures taught children a dangerous lesson—namely, that the consequences of violence are temporary and trivial. Injury and death typically were presented in a sanitized manner.

In terms of body counts, movies of today are no more violent than their counterparts 25 years ago, but their portrayal of murder no longer leaves anything to the imagination. The consequences of violence routinely are depicted as graphically as possible, without regard for how they may affect impressionable young viewers. Thanks to video cassettes, children can replay their favorite gory scenes over and over.

Parents now have a much more difficult problem—how to keep their offspring from becoming totally desensitized to human misery, mayhem, and murder. Because of the steady diet of gory films to which they are exposed, children of the 1990s slowly, but surely, are growing more tolerant of the effects of violence. They no longer are repulsed by stories of extreme brutality, even when they are real. As one teenaged bystander remarked following the 1992 murder of an MIT student, "Hey, what's the big deal . . . people die every day."

While negative socializing forces—such as drugs, guns, gangs, television, and movies—have grown more powerful, the positive forces of family, school, church, and community have grown weaker. The decline in these forms of support reflects a pervasive disinvestment in American youth over the last 30 years, documented in Glenn Pierce's *Disinvestment in America's Children and Youth.*

Social and economic changes in society, in two related respects, have diminished the contribution of women to child-rearing and socialization. As women have entered the labor force in greater numbers, they have had less time for their families, have been less able to participate in the broad range of voluntary organizations that in the past strengthened local communities, and have been less able to supervise youngsters (both their own and their neighbors') within their day-to-day activities. Equally important, as professional opportunities have opened up for females in the workforce, highly qualified women, who at one time, for lack of other options, would have gone into teaching or child care, are more likely to seek careers in law, medicine, and science.

Increasingly, kids are being raised in homes disrupted by divorce or economic stress; too many emerge undersocialized and undersupervised. This is not to imply any level of blame on partents, and mothers in particular. Most parents are well-meaning and would like to have a greater role in their children's lives, if only they could. However, many families lack the support to control and guide their offspring.

Compensating for the void

American society has not addressed the issue of how to compensate for the void left by changes in the status of women and their entry into the labor market. Society no longer can rely almost totally on the unpaid and/or underpaid time of women to socialize and supervise the nation's youth. The government has not stepped forward in the form of child care programs and better schools; the private sector has dragged its feet in parental leave and child care programs; and many men have not taken on a greater share of parenting and household responsibilities.

As a consequence of changes in the family and lack of alternative support programs for youth, children spend too little time engaged in structured activity with positive role models and too much time "hanging out" or watching savage killings on TV. The effects of the over-all disinvestment in youth are being felt in several alarming respects—increased rates of high-risk behavior among youth, from violence to drug use; reduced levels of psychological well-being, from suicide to psychiatric commitments; and lowering of academic preparedness and achievement.

At this point in time, the U.S. is due for a demographic double-whammy. Not only are violent teens maturing into even more violent young adults, but they are being succeeded by a new and larger group of teenagers. The same massive baby boom generation that, as teenagers, produced a crime wave in the 1970s has grown up and had children of their own. This "baby boomerang" cohort of youngsters now is reaching adolescence.

By the year 2005, the number of teenagers aged 15-19 will increase by 23%, which undoubtedly will bring additional increases in crime and other social ills associated with overpopulation of youth. The population growth will be even more pronounced among minorities. For example, the amount of 15-19-year-olds will rise 28% among blacks and 47% among Hispanics. Given that a large number of these children often grow up in conditions of poverty, many more teenagers will be at risk in the years ahead.

The challenge for the future, therefore, is how best to deal with youth violence—and there is little reason for optimism. America seems to be obsessed with easy solutions that won't work, such as the wholesale transfer of juveniles to the jurisdiction of the adult court or even imposing the death penalty, at the expense of difficult solutions that will work, such as providing pre-teens with strong, positive role models and quality schools.

State legislatures around the country have responded to concerns about the rising number of juvenile killings, often overreacting to certain highly publicized cases of brutal and senseless murder involving teens. In recent years, most states have made it easier—even automatic—to try juvenile killers as adults. Ignoring the immaturity of a 15- or 16-year-old, lawmakers have accepted the idea that murder is an adult crime and thus deserves an adult punishment.

Clearly, there are certain youths who are beyond the reach of the juvenile system—repeat violent offenders who are not amenable to the rehabilitative orientation of the juvenile system. On a case-by-case basis, these kids selectively should be handled outside the juvenile domain. Yet, in the effort to appear tough on crime, legislatures are making it too easy to waive youthful offenders into an adult system that is ill-prepared to handle them.

The national trend toward trying juveniles as adults in order to incarcerate them longer may address the need for justice and retribution, but it can not be counted on for dissuading kids from the temptations and thrill of street crime and gang membership. No matter how punitive society becomes and what kind or how strong of a message is sent out to the street, teens who are attracted to crime always will turn a deaf ear to deterrence. Besides, by the time a juvenile offender has "graduated" to murder, it is likely too late to reach him.

Instead, attention must be focused on the primary grades, when youngsters still are impressionable and interested in what teachers and other authority figures have to say. As Denver District Attorney Norman

S. Early, Jr., maintains, "I would rather build the child than rebuild the adult."

The nation must reinvest in youth and strive to make legitimate activity more attractive than criminal behavior. This will take time, hard work, and an awful lot of money. It is well known that positive reinforcement for pro-social behavior always will outperform punishment for anti-social behavior. Besides, it is far cheaper to hire elementary grade teachers and pay them commensurate with the importance of the

job than it is to build more prisons and hire more correctional officers later.

Tragically for America, it is unlikely that proposals focused on youngsters and pre-teens will attract much political momentum. Most politicians need to show results within four years in order to get re-elected. For them, there remains a far more immediate political payoff in advocating the "new three-R's"—retribution, retaliation, and revenge—attempting to convince voters that they are tough on crime.

Punishment and Corrections

In the American system of criminal justice, the term "corrections" has a special meaning. It designates programs and agencies that have legal authority over the custody or supervision of persons who have been convicted of a criminal act by the courts.

The correctional process begins with the sentencing of the convicted offender. The predominant sentencing pattern in the United States encourages maximum judicial discretion and offers a range of alternatives from probation (supervised, conditional freedom within the community), through imprisonment, to the death penalty. Selections in this unit focus on the current condition of the penal system in the United States and the effects that sentencing, probation, imprisonment, and parole have on the rehabilitation of criminals.

In the opening essay, "Probation's First 100 Years: Growth through Failure," Charles Lindner asserts that through the years, probation ineffectiveness has been linked to inadequate resources available to do the job.

Governments are identifying alternative ways to sentence and rehabilitate offenders, according to "Doing Soft Time." The stimulus for this approach is linked to rising crime rates and declining financial resources.

Laurin Wollan, in "Punishment and Prevention," maintains that an effective approach to fighting crime must include both prevention and control strategies. One without the other is shortsighted.

In her essay ". . . And Throw Away the Key," Jill Smolowe maintains that overcrowded prisons have failed as a deterrent to crime. Additionally, building more prisons and imposing longer sentences may exacerbate the problem.

Can private enterprise make the prison industry more effective? According to Anthony Ramirez, in "Privatizing America's Prisons, Slowly," after a questionable beginning, the future looks good for private prisons.

"Crime Takes on a Feminine Face" offers some insight as to why growing numbers of women are turning to crime. The expense of incarceration is high, and most often children are the losers.

"Psychiatric Gulag or Wise Safekeeping?" gives evidence that sex offenders, perhaps unlike any other offenders, are particularly troubling and troublesome to the justice system. Strong public sentiments against sex offenders fuel the problem.

The unit closes with " 'This Man Has Expired' " an essay focusing on the executioners themselves as they carry out typical executions.

Looking Ahead: Challenge Questions

What are the issues and trends that will be most likely faced by corrections administrators in the latter part of the 1990s?

What are some of the reasons that overcrowding is occurring in our nation's prisons in the past decade?

What should be U.S. strategy for dealing with prison overcrowding in the years ahead?

Why have prisons become so violent and difficult to manage in recent years?

Are you in favor of the death penalty? Why, or why not?

Unit 6

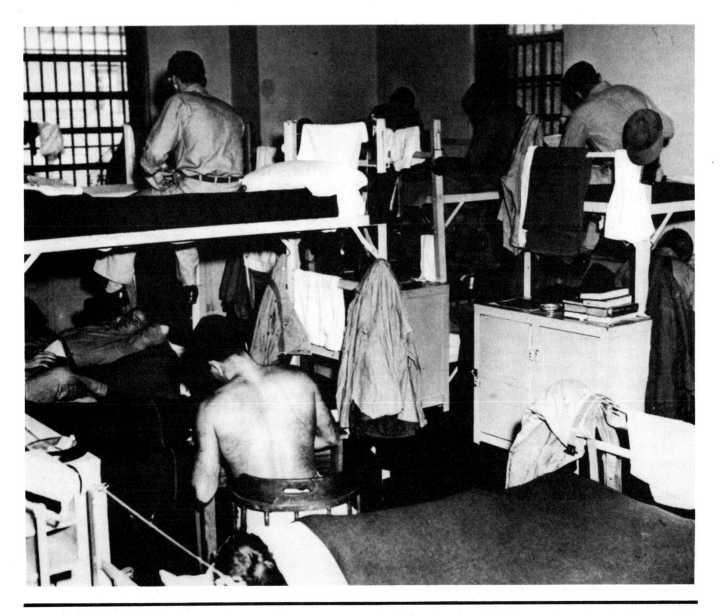

PROBATION'S FIRST 100 YEARS: GROWTH THROUGH FAILURE

Charles J. Lindner, Ph.D

Charles Lindner is a Professor of Law, Police Science and Criminal Justice Administration at the John Jay College of Criminal Justice, where he is coordinator of the Corrections Major. He has a J.D. from Brooklyn Law School and a M.S.W. from Fordham University. He has over 20 years of experience as a practitioner in the field of probation.

Professor Lindner is the author of numerous articles in professional journals, frequently addressing issues related to community-based corrections. He is a training consultant to many law enforcement agencies, including police, probation, and parole departments. Among other awards, Professor Lindner was the recipient of the American Probation and Parole Association's University of Cincinnati Award (1985) for "significant contributions to the probation and parole field."

The author is grateful to Professors Thomas Eich, John Kleinig and Maria Volpe for their constructive criticisms and insightful comments.

With the turn of the century, many of the early probation agencies will be commemorating their 100th anniversary. Over the years, probation has outgrown even the most optimistic expectations of a handful of pioneering reformers and is now the most frequently used sentencing alternative (Dawson, 1990:1). Moreover, while all correctional populations are increasing, during the years of 1982-1990 the number of sentenced offenders placed on probation surpassed any other correctional sentence (U.S. Department of Justice, 1992).

While the questions of probation's success in terms of offender rehabilitation, recidivism rates, and public safety continues to be problematic, its contribution to a perilously overcrowded criminal justice system is critical. Probation serves as a spillway for the overflowing of correctional institutions. Without the option of probation supervision, correctional institutions would be in chaos, local and state governments would be bankrupted by jail and prison costs, and inmates would of necessity be released after serving mere fractions of their sentences.

As probation becomes increasingly essential to the continued functioning of an already besieged justice system, probation agencies throughout the country are similarly facing new challenges never imagined by the early pioneers of this community-based corrections service. The probationer population has dramatically changed, so that caseloads are increasingly populated with "felony probationers" or by offenders who would have, with certainty, been incarcerated in the recent past (Petersilia, 1985; Stewart, 1986). Consistent with societal changes,

substantial numbers of probationers suffer from mental and physical illnesses, including AIDS, and regularly abuse alcohol, drugs, or both. Moreover, long-term increases in violent crimes and a proliferation of firearms on the streets of our cities, including more sophisticated and potent weapons, all contribute to the increased challenges faced by probation.

Ironically, despite the increased reliance of the justice system on probation services and the changed nature of the probationer population, many probation agencies are experiencing budgetary cutbacks. The author of this article contends that the diminution of resources at the time of increased demands upon probation agencies, is consistent with the low esteem in which probation is viewed within the criminal justice system. Moreover, in being compelled unrealistically to "do more with less," probation agencies can never really meet the dual test of increasing public safety through reduced probationer recidivism rates.

THE EARLY YEARS

The voluntary and unofficial contributions of John Augustus, "father of probation," and his small band of followers, to the creation of a probation system have been well chronicled. Based on the seminal work of Augustus, it is not surprising that the first probation law, limited to the criminal courts in the City of Boston, went into effect in the State of Massachusetts in 1878 (Chute & Bell, 1956). Vermont passed a probation law in 1898, followed by Rhode Island in 1899, and by 1910, thirty-seven states and the District of Columbia had enacted probation laws (Chute & Bell, 1956).

In retrospect, probation may have erred early on by justifying its very existence as a "cheap alternative" to other components of the criminal justice system. Augustus (1852: 100) for example made frequent reference to the savings accruable to the municipality through the use of probation as an alternative to incarceration. Unfortunately, through his own and other charitable contributions, he also set the pattern of relieving the State of the costs of probation services. At one point, for example, he bitterly denied accusations that he benefitted from his work, noting that neither the offender, nor the municipality, nor the State relieved him of the financial burdens of his volunteer efforts:

> While it saves the county or State
> hundreds, and I may say, thousands of
> dollars, it drains my pockets, instead of

 From the *Journal of Probation and Parole*, Spring 1993, pp. 1-7. © 1993 by the New York State Probation Officers Association, Inc. Reprinted by permission.

enriching me. To attempt to make money by bailing poor people would prove an impossibility (1852: 103).

The pattern of equivocating probation services in terms of financial considerations was further demonstrated with the very creation of a formal system of probation. In the Chicago Juvenile Court, for example, despite frequent judicial attributions of probation as the essential ingredient to an effective court system (Schultz, 1973), the original law establishing a juvenile court deliberately avoided the payement of salaries to probation officers, as it was feared that the cost of officer salaries might imperil the passage of such a bill (Bartelme, 1931; Schultz, 1973). To eschew the cost of professional probation officers, the early juvenile court depended upon services from civil servants, including police, court, and truant officers, all of whom were paid by their own Agency, social workers paid by private or religious organizations, and volunteers (Lindner & Savarese, 1984a). This practice was not unique to Illinois, but was also found in other jurisdictions (Linder & Savarese, 1984a), and helps to understand the proliferation of volunteers in early probation (Linder & Savarese, 1984b).

Similarly, over the years, probation was generally touted as a "cheap alternative" to incarceration. Illustrative is an early statement of the NYS Probation Commission (1906; 44-5) which cited the financial advantages, among others, of probation.

> The probation system has also another and important value to the community in its economy. The cost to the community of maintaining prisons and reformatory institutions is large. The actual saving in dollars and cents by reducing the number of persons committed to penal institutions, to be maintained therein at the expense of the public, is no inconsiderable item. The additional saving involved in the wages of men who would otherwise be unproductive is also large. Not infrequently a family has to be supported by charity while the bread winner is imprisoned.

A review of the early literature indicates that cost-savings was traditionally cited as an advantage of probation, both in official reports (NYS Probation Commission, 1907; NYS Probation Commission, 1922; and in academic publications (Morrisson, 1896), and continues to be cited today as a primary advantage of probation.

Accordingly, probation has been traditionally underfunded over the years, with chronically high caseloads from its inception to today (Mack, 1906; NYS Probation Commission, 1912; Flexner and Baldwin, 1914; NYS Probation Commission, 1915; NYS Probation Commission; 1917; Young, 1937; Rothman, 1980). Unlike institutional corrections, where even overcrowded facilities are eventually subject to the finite limitations of steel bars and concrete walls, there are no caps on the size of a probation caseload. And unlike institutional overcrowding,

often monitored by court appointed masters, probation caseloads, like watered down soup, always have room for one more. Moreover, unlike the police, probation is not considered primarily as a law enforcement organization in which there is a perception that funding is related to public safety. Finally, unlike public service organizations with a strong public constituency, as in the case of elementary schools, public support for probation services is minimal. Indeed, few lay persons can accurately articulate the difference between probation and parole, and those who are more knowledgeable of probation services, are likely to be critical of probation for being "soft on criminals."

TODAY'S PROBATION

Probation caseloads are far more difficult to manage than in the past years. Today's caseloads tend to be populated with greater numbers of violent offenders, felons, substance abusers, and physically and emotionally ill persons than every before. Moreover, many probation departments also report high numbers of recidivists on the supervision caseload, "who pose a higher risk for failure and, as such, can require more staff resources" (Irish, 1990: 90). Many of today's probationers would have been incarcerated in the recent past, and their placement on probation can be attributed only to the overcrowding of our correctional institutions. As noted by Stewart (1986), "probation departments have become spillways for overflowing prisons — an abuse of the whole probation system."

Traditionally, probation was intended to serve a misdemeanant population, generally first-time offenders who had committed non-violent acts and were believed capable of rehabilitation (Petersilia: 1985). Over the first half century of probation supervision, rarely would the number of convicted felons placed on probation exceed 10% of the total probation population. In New York State, for example, over a 14-year period ending on September 30, 1921, the number of convicted felons on probation amounted to approximately nine percent of the total population (N.Y.S. Probation Commission, 1923: 11, 20). Similarly, Rothman (1980: 108) found that "In a state like New York, a little over 90 percent of probationers in 1914 were misdemeanants and only 10 percent felons; in fact, the percentages did not vary much over the next decades."

With the insatiable demands of our correctional facilities for more space, probation nation-wide was rapidly transformed from a misdemeanant to a felony population, and by the 1980's, the term "felony probation" was popular in the literature. Petersilia (1985: 2) reported that "over one-third of the Nation's adult probation population consists of persons convicted in superior courts of felonies (as opposed to misdemeanors)." Similarly, New York State is illustrative of the dramatic increase of convicted felons under probation supervision:

> "In 1984, 47% of cases under supervision were for felony convictions. By the end of the first quarter of 1989, the felony population had increased to 54% (Seymour et al. 1989: 2).

Predictably, the growth of "felony probation" has been especially pervasive in large urban areas. In New York City, for example, the felony population in 1989 represented 70% of the total caseload, as opposed to 54% statewide (Seymour et al., 1989: 2).

Although it might be argued that "felony probation" does not of necessity pose an increased risk to public safety in that many of the felons placed on probation did not commit crimes of violence, it is in reality only an argument as to the degree of increased risk. While many felons placed under probation supervision may not have been convicted of violent crimes, it is probable that many of those who *were* convicted of violent acts would not have been placed on probation in the recent past. Moreover, a recent study of recidivism among felony probationers during the years of 1986 through 1989 found that:

> Within 3 years of sentencing, while still on probationd, 43% of these felons were rearrested for a felony. Half of the arrests were for a violent crime (murder, rape, robbery, or aggravated assault) or a drug offense (drug trafficking or drug possession) (Langan & Cunniff, 1992: 1).

Not only is supervision more difficult because of the growth of "felony probation," but studies reflect similar increases in special needs offenders. Substance abusers, for example, an especially difficult category to manage, are being placed on probation in unprecedented numbers. Smyley (1989: 34), When Commissioner of the New York City Department of Probation, reflected the concern of many urban probation departments when he estimated that between 9,000 and 13,000 crack abusers were under the supervision of his agency, with possibly as many as 40% of the probationer population "afflicted by one or more forms of chemical dependence." On the opposite coast, Nidord estimated that between 60% and 80% of the Los Angeles County probationers need drug testing and treatment programs for their addictions (Labaton, 1990).

The changed nature of the probationer population is a matter of concern to probation staff. In a nationwide study of probation/parole personnel, it was reported that "at least three-fourths of the respondents believe that the supervision needs of offenders are greater now than in the past. Thus, not only are the numbers larger, the offenders are also a more difficult group to manage." (Guynes, 1988; 8). A suburban probation agency, for example, reported that:

> More difficult offenders continued to enter the supervision program in 1990. The monitoring of undocumented aliens, mentally impaired chemical abusers, HIV positive offenders, and homeless individuals challenged supervising probation officers. The high level of recidivists or repeat offenders presented additional issues for the supervision program, as offenders with prior records pose a higher risk for failure on probation and often require increased staff

resources (Nassau County Probation Department, 1990: 19).

Recent evidence further reflects concerns as to probation officer victimization, especially as related to field activities (Ely, 1989; Holden, 1989; Parsonage, 1989; Serant, 1989; Labaton, 1990; Parsonage & Miller, 1990; Lindner, 1991; Martin, 1991; Pshide, 1991; Lindner & Koehler, 1992). Although some concern during field visits may have always existed, this is not reflected in the early literature (Hussey & Duffee, 1980; Smykla, 1984; Carter et al., 1984). Recent officer concern appears to be related not only to the new "felony probation," but their disquietude is further attributable to having to make visits to high-crime, drug ridden areas in which there is a proliferation of dangerous weapons (Linder & Koehler, 1992). As a result, many officers are reluctant to make field visits, which they view as unusually stressful and an undesirable component of their work (Ely, 1989; Parsonage, 1990; Lindner & Koehler, 1992). Probation officer victimization concerns may also be responsible, at least in part, to an increase in the number of officers carrying firearms (Brown, 1989 and 1990) and radical changes in the fieldwork policies of a number of large probation agencies (N.Y.C. Department of Probation, 1989).

A HABITUAL PAUCITY OF RESOURCES

During the 100 year existence of probation, inadequate resources have frequently been identified as an underlying factor contributing to the ineffectiveness of offender supervision. Inadequate resources are characterized by staff shortages, insufficient funding, and a lack of appropraite probationer services. The underfunding of probation, characteristic of so many of today's agencies, is especially doleful when one considers the chronic nature of the problem, little changed over the years. Moreover, since the truest test of governmental commitment to any of its public services is resource allocation, the historical underfunding of probation agencies is symptomatic of the low status awarded probation. In light of the chronic resource deprivation experienced by so many probation agencies, advocates argue that it is not that probation over the years has failed, but that it never had the opportunity to succeed. Because of chronic underfunding, inadequate resources, excessive caseloads, and policies more often shaped by politics than by reason, probation's true potential remains untested.

The historical underfunding of probation services, generally reflected in excessive caseloads and inadequate services, is well chronicled in the literature (Mack, 1906: 129; N.Y.S. Probation Commission, 1912: 87-93; Flexner & Baldwin, 1914: 116; N.Y.S. Probation Commission, 1915: 217; N.Y.S. Probation Commission: 114; Rothman, 1980). Moreover, over the years, a chronic underfunding of probation services remained the rule, rather than the exception. Lundberg's (1923: 4) contemporaneous plea for greater resources is illustrative of what is perhaps the total probation experience:

the probation staff is deplorably inadequate, both in numbers and in equipment for the work . . . in very many courts the average number of cases handled by each probation officer runs up to one hundred or even two hundred.

Some fifteen years later, Young (1937: 14) would similarly warn that "most probation officers carry too heavy a load of cases to put into practice the ideals prescribed for them," while Tappan (1960: 552) later cautioned that "much that has been written . . . has little relevance to practice and little proof of its validity because the staff in most departments carries an overload of work."

In his monumental review of the failed promise of probation, Rothman (1980: 92) recounted the chronic shortage of probation officers, inadequate salaries, and excessive caseloads, and concluded that probation failed quickly and uniformly. Interestingly, it was his contention that probation's failures were related to grandiose promises typical of the Progressive Movement, despite a "flimsy quality of reform theory" (1980: 92). Moreover, Rothman believed that the reformers failed to understand the economic and political realities of probation, in that while probation salaries were paid by local government, the primary beneficiary of diversion from prison was the State. This was because "the state government paid the costs of incarceration in state prisons, but the locality paid the costs of release on probation" (1980: 94). As a result, each case diverted from prison and placed on probation reduced state costs, but at the same time, increased municipal costs. As a result, while probtion was cheaper than incarceration, it was only the state, and not the municipality, which benefited from the diversion to probation supervision.

Finally, and perhaps most importantly, Rothman asserted that despite its many failings, probation survived because it facilitated the "specific interests of those who administered criminal justice: the prosecuting attorneys, the judges, the criminal lawyers" (1980: 98). Basically, it was the promise of a probation sentence that often convinced a defendant to accept a plea bargain, thereby expediating the process for all.

PROBATION: A PROBLEMATIC PROCESS

Whether probation will survive another hundred years is debatable. Probation supervision, as an alternative to incarceration, is ailing, and some believe that it provides neither the necessary controls to insure public safety nor offender services essential to rehabilitation. Byrne (1988: 1) argues that the crowding of probation "poses a more immediate threat to the criminal justice process and to community protection" than does prison crowding, while Lauen (1988: 33), after studying the effectiveness of a number of probation and parole programs, reported that "the evidence that probation and parole are effective correctional treatments is weak . . ." and we can conclude only that they might "have a marginal effect on some offenders for short periods of time." Morris and Tonry were

especially forceful in rejecting traditional probation supervision, which they concluded "degenerated into ineffectiveness under the pressure of excessive caseloads and inadequate resources" (1990: 6). Similar criticisms of probation effectiveness were recently expressed by other highly respected sources (Silberman, 1978; Forer, 1980; Wilson, 1983; Conrad, 1985). Most painful is the recognition that many of the criticisms of today's probation, is consistent with those expressed in the past (NYS Probation Commission, 1906; NYS Probation Commission, 1912; NYS Probation Commission, 1922; NYS Crime Commission, 1927; Glueck, 1933; Young, 1937; US Attorney General, 1939; Tappan, 1960; President's Commission on Law Enforcement and the Administration of Justice, 1967).

Unfortunately, many of the major studies of probation effectiveness have been equally discouraging. In 1976 the Comptroller General of the United States (74) concluded that "state and county probation systems are not adequately protecting the public." One year later, the Comptroller General, based on a study of five Federal Probation districts, reported a number of serious problems in the supervision of offenders, and concluded that "higher risk offenders are still not getting the required amount of personal supervision" (1977: 9-10).

More recent studies question probation's ability to effectively supervise "felony probationers." Petersilia (1985: 3) found that the emergence of "felony probation" presented "a serious threat to public safety," noting that "as far official records indicate, during the 40-month period following their probationary sentence, 65 percent of the total sample were rearrested and 53 percent had official charges filed against them." Although other studies of the supervision of felony probation caseloads were more positive (Ficter, M., Hirschburgh, P. & McGaha, J. 1987; 9), a very recent study of 79,000 felons sentenced to probation in 1986 and tracked for a 3-year period commencing with the date of sentence, is strongly supportive of the Petersilia research (Langan & Cuniff, 1992). It was found that 43% of the felons, while still on probation, were rearrested for a new felony, almost half of which were for violent crimes or a drug offense (Langan & Cuniff, 1992).

Walker (1985: 176), a critic of probation services, was especially acerbic in stating that:

> Probation supervision, in fact, is essentially a myth. The supervision amounts to little more than bureaucratic paper shuffling. The offender reports to the probation officer once a month and has a brief conversation about work, drugs, alcohol, crime, whatever. The probation officers fills out the required reports and that is that.

While some would take exception to Walker's definition of probation supervision, few would deny that probation is in need of a major overhaul. Rosecrance (1986: 25) perhaps best summarizes the desperate situation faced by probation:

Judicial support for probation services has eroded, public support has diminished; legislative backing has wavered. Probation officers themselves question the efficacy and purposefulness of their actions, while probationers seriously doubt that any good will come from their contacts with probation officials.

FUTURE PROSPECTS FOR PROBATION

The problems facing probation, as outlined above, are serious enough to raise concern as to probation's future. As stated by Conrad (1985; 421), "in the present circumstances the survival of the idea of probation as a service is in jeopardy."

At the very least, it would appear that probation's survival is linked to adequate funding, serving both to insure quality control of the offender's behavior and to provide sufficient services to make rehabilitation viable. Ideally, this would allow for manageable work loads, adequate and competent staffing, and the provision of offender services which are both plentiful and meaningful. While it is recognized that caseload size per se, as is true of the other components of this wish list, are not a guarantee of success (Champion, 1990: 284; McShane & Krause, 1993: 106), excessive caseloads, inadequate staffing, and a lack of offender services are a guarantee of failure.

Future determinations of "adequate funding" should no longer be based on the "cheap alternative" formula which has so long controlled the financing of probation agencies, but must be based on legitimate organizational needs. Obviously, this requires that budgetary decision-makers no longer view probation as an after-thought, whose status is at the very bottom of the correctional scale. Finally, it must be understood that probation costs are of necessity greater than ever, as probation now supervises a higher-risk and higher-needs population.

Unfortunately, recent indiciations, although admittedly limited, lead us to believe that many probation agencies will not only not receive increased funding, but will more likely, experience drastic budgetary reductions. Fiscal cutbacks will be justified on the basis of the financial difficulties experienced by local governments, although, as in the past probation agencies will proportionately suffer more than other criminal justice agencies. As noted by Allen (1985: 196), "in tax shortfall situations and inadequate public resource allocations, there is a tendency to underallocate resources to commununity corrections, particularly probation," Allen believes in addition that probation is considered to be of low-priority in the funding of municipal agencies:

Finally, there is some evidence that elected officials are unwilling to make the necessary hard decisions on community corrections. The easiest escape from conflicting demands is to "fund-out" all resources to meet higher priority needs (police protection, fire, mandated school

programs, cost-sharing welfare programs, and so on) . . .

Similarly, Petersilia (1988) found that the funding of probation agencies has not kept up with the increased number of offenders under probation supervision. She reported that 25 cents of every dollar spent on criminal justice goes to correction, with only three cents of that quarter spent on probation. Most important, she found that whereas most criminal justice agencies on a nationwide basis received increased funding over the past ten years, only probation received fiscal reductions.

Not only did Petersilia (1985: 2) conclude that budget cuts were experienced by probation on a nationwide basis, but she also reported that:

With Proposition 13 and other fiscal constraints, California's probation agencies may have suffered the most severe cuts of all. Since 1975, the state's probation population has risen 15 percent, while the number of probation officers has fallen by 20 percent. In the same time period, the state has spent 30 percent more on criminal justice in general, but 10 percent less on probation."

The Nassau County Probation Department experience further illustrates the funding problems noted by Allen and Petersilia, and experienced by many probation agencies. The civil servants of Nassau County, a comparatively wealthy suburb of New York City, are traditionally well compensated. Nevertheless, when faced with serious budgetary problems in the early 1990s, caused in part by a downturn in tax revenues, the County chose to substantially reduce the probation budget. It was publicly announced that the Agency faced severe staffing cutbacks, including the lay-offs of employees with years of service. These staffing reductions were planned despite increasing caseloads, a felony offender population of 34 percent of the total cases under supervision in 1991 (New York State Division of Probation & Correctional Alternatives, 1991), and the fact that "the increased numbers of high risk offenders has required more stringent standards and the use of intermediate sanctions as special conditions of probation" (Nassau County Probation Department, 1980: 7). Although public pressure caused fewer probation officers to be discharged than originally announced, the trend towards larger caseloads is apparent.:

1990 . . . . 75 cases per probation officer.
1991 . . . . 85 cases per probation officer.
1992 . . . . . . 103 cases per probation officer.

Unfortunately, because of the chronic underfunding of probation departments, even agencies that have not suffered cutbacks, fear the possibility of budget reductions. Rocco A. Pozzi, director of the Westchester County (N.Y.) Department of Probation, for example, stated to the media, that although his Agency had not experienced major cutbacks, "he feared that the final state budget could include huge cuts for probation officers" (1991: 6).

A proposed downsizing of the New York City Department of Probation, if carried out, would be even more extreme. Although not finalized, it is projected that probation officer staffing would be reduced by approximately 25 percent by 1995 (Office of the Mayor of the City of New York). Ironically, these cutbacks will be made by an Agency with a "felony probationer" population of about 70 percent (Seymour, Lockhart & Ely, 1989), and where it is estimated that the under supervision caseload includes between 9,000 and 13,000 crack abusers and "that as much as 40 percent of the probationer population may have been afflicted by one or more forms of chemical dependency" (Smyley, 1989: 34). Moreover, an Agency which has suffered from chronically high caseloads, including undifferentiated adult caseloads of approximately 200 (Lauen, 1988: 31), and where, even in a depressed economic climate, probation turnover rate was approximately 22 percent in the fiscal year ending June 30, 1991 (New York City Department of Probation, 1991). If these proposed staffing reductions come to fruition, then the New York City Department of Probation may become Jacob's classic example of a probation so watered down "that it is widely regarded as providing no punishment or control" (n.d.: 2).

At this time, the chronic underfunding of probation agencies is especially serious because of a nationwide economic downturn. In a 1991 survey of its Executive Committee, Board of Directors, and selected chief probation administrators, the American Probation and Parole Association reported that nearly half of the respondents (30 of 70) "stated that they (or their states or agencies) had experienced or anticipated cutbacks in providing services. Among the services mentioned most often as suffering cutbacks were: intensive supervision, sex offender or substance abuse treatment" (Reeves, 1991: 11).

While othe publicly funded agencies have also experienced budgetary reductions, probation is often among the departments proportionately suffering the most severe cutbacks (Allen, 1985; Petersilia, 1985). Moreover, in many instances, probation is already underfunded, struggling with high caseloads, low salaries, and insufficient programs. Most importantly, today's typical probationer caseload is likely to be populated by higher risk and special needs probationers. These types of offenders are more likely to present a multiplicity of serious problems, and as a result, usually require more intensive controls, experience the greatest likelihood of probation sentences which include intermediate sanctions, and need more extensive and expensive services.

Unfortunately, as we enter the 21st Century, the hope of adequate funding of probation agencies, is understandably pessimistic. Chronic underfunding has so diluted the quality of offender supervision, both in terms of community protection and effective treatment and services, as to debase the promise of probation. A continued diminution of an already diluted probation service may lead to its demise.

REFERENCES

Allen, H.E. (1985). The organization and effectiveness of community corrections in L.E. Travis, 111 (ed). *Probation, Parole, and Community Corrections.* Prospect Heights, Illinois: Waveland: 185-199.

Augustus, J. (1972). *John Augustus: First Probation Officer.* (S. Glueck, Introd.) Montclair, N.J.: Patterson Smith. (Original work published 1852 under the title, "A report of the labors of John Augustus."

Bartelme, M.M. (1931). *Twenty-five years ago and since.* The Yearbook. A record of the 25th Annual Conference of the National Probation Association, Minneapolis, MN, June 12 to 19, 1931. NY: The National Probation Association.

Brown, P.W. (1989). Probation and parole officers up in arms over the gun issue. Corrections Today, 51(2): 194-196.

Brown, P.W. (1990). Guns and probation officers: the unspoken reality. *Federal Probation,* 54(2): 21-25.

Byrne, J.M. (1988). *Probation.* U.S. Department of Justice, National Institute of Justice Crime File. Washington, DC: U.S. Government Printing Office.

Carter, R.N., Glasser, D., & Wilkins, L.T. (1984). *Probation, Parole, and Community Corrections.* (3rd ed.) NY: John Wiley & Sons.

Champion, D.J. (1990). *Probation and Parole in the United States.* Columbus, Ohio: Merrill.

Chute, C.L. & Bell, M. (1956). *Crime, Courts and Probation.* NY: MacMillan.

Comptroller General of the United States, General Accounting Office. (1976). *Report to the Congress: State and County Probation: Systems in Crisis.* Washington, DC: U.S. Government Printing Office.

Comptroller General of the United States, General Accounting Office. (1977). *Report to the Congress: Probation and parole activities need to be better managed.* Washington, DC: U.S. Government Printing Office.

Conrad, J.P. (1985). The penal dilemma and its emergeing solution. *Crime and Delinquency,* 31: 411-422.

Dawson, J.M. (1990). *Felons sentenced to probation in state courts, 1986.* U.S. Department of Justice, Bureau of Justice Statistics, Washington, DC: U.S. Government Printing Office.

Ely, R.E. (1989) *Report on the safety concerns of probation and alternatives to incarceration staff in New York State.* Albany, NY: New York State Division of Probation and Correctional Alternatives.

Fichter, M., Hirschburg, P. and McGaha, J. (1987). Felony probation: A comparative analysis of public risk in two states. *Perspectives.* 11(2): 6-11.

Flexner, B., & Baldwin, R.N. (1916). *Juvenile Courts and Probation.* NY: Century.

Forer, L.G. (1980). *Criminals and victims.* NY: Norton.

Glueck, S. (1933). *The signficance and promise of probation. In S. Glueck (ed.) Probation and criminal justice.* NY: MacMillan.

Guynes, R. (1988). *Difficult clients, large caseloads plague probation, parole agencies.* U.S. Department of Justice, National Institute of Justice, Research in Action. Washington, DC: U.S. Government Printing Office.

Holden, T. (1989). Point and counterpoint: Firearms-Debating the issues for probation and parole. *Perspectives.* 13(3): 6-8

Hussey, F., & Duffee, D.E. (1980). *Probation, parole and community field services.* NY: Harper and Row.

Irish, J.F. (1990) *Crime, criminal justice and probation in 1989.* Mineola, NY: Nassau County Probation Department.

Jacobs, J.B. (n.d.). Inside Prisons. *U.S. Department of Justice, National Institute of Justice Crime File.* Washington, DC: U.S. Government Printing Office.

Labaton, S. (1990). Glutted probation system puts communities in peril. *The New York Times,* AI, A16.

Langan, P.A., and Cunniff, M.A. (1992). *Recidivism of felons on probation, 1986-89.* U.S. Department of Justice: Bureau of Justice Statistics, Special Report. U.S. Government Printing Office.

6. PUNISHMENT AND CORRECTIONS

Lauen, R.J. (1988). *Community managed corrections.* American Correctional Association.

Lindner, C., (1991). The refocused probation home visit: A subtle but revolutionary change. *The Journal of Contemporary Criminal Justice,* 7(2): 115-127.

Lindern, C., & Koehler, R.J. (1992). Probation officer victimization: An emerging concern. *Journal of Criminal Justice,* 20: 53-62.

Lindner, C., & Savarese, M.R. (1984a). The evolution of probation: early salaries, qualifications and hiring practices. *Federal Probation,* 48(1): 3-10.

Lindner, C., & Savarese, M.R. (1984b). The evolution of probation: The historical contribution of the volunteer. *Federal Probation,* 48(2): 3-11.

Lundberg, E.O. (1923). *The probation officer and the community: An address.* Albany, NY: The New York State Probation Commission: 1-8.

McShane, M.D., & Krause, W. (1993). *Community Corrections.* New York, Macmillan.

Mack, J.W. (1906). *The juvenile court: The judge and the probation officer.* Proceedings of the National Conference of Charities and Correction at the Thirty-Third Annual Session. Philadelphia, Pennsylvania: Press of Fred J. Heer.

Martin, D.R. (1991). Probation and parole officer safety: Examining an urgent issue. *Perspectives,* 15(1): 20-25.

Morris, N., & Tonry, M. (1990). *Between prison and probation.* NY: Oxford University Press.

Morrison, W.D., (1975). *Juvenile Offenders.* (J.F. Short, Jr., Introd.). Montclair, N.J.: Patterson Smith. (Original work printed in 1896.)

Nassau County Probation Department. (1991). *Annual Report: 1990.* Nassau County, NY.

New York City Department of Probation. (1989). *Executive policy and procedure 40-1-89: Field activity,* NY

New York City Department of Probation. (1991). *Staffing report as of 6/28/91.* NY.

New York State Crime Commission. (1927). *Report of the Crime Commission* (New York Legislative Document No. 94.) Albany, NY: J.B. Lyon Co., Printers.

N.Y.S. Probation Commission. (1906). *Report of the Temporary State Probation Commission of 1905-6.* Brandow Printing Co., Albany, NY.

N.Y.S. Probation Commission. (1907). *A Study of Probation in Yonkers, N.Y.,* Albany, NY: J.B. Lyon Company, State Printers.

N.Y.S. Probation Commission. (1912). *Fifth annual report.* Albany, NY: J.B. Lyon Company, State Printers.

N.Y.S. Probation Commission. (1915). *Eighth annual report.* Albany, NY: J.B. Lyon Company, State Printers.

N.Y.A. Probation Commission. (1917). *Tenth annual report.* Albany, NY: J.B. Lyon Company, State Printers.

N.Y.S. Probation Commission. (1923). *Sixteenth annual report.* Albany, NY: J.B. Lyon Company, State Printers.

N.Y.S. Division of Probation and Correctional Alternatives. (1991). *All-case report; Client data system.* Albany, NY.

Nidorf, B.J. (1988). Sanction-oriented community corrections: Sales job? Sellout? Or response to reality? *Perspectives,* 12(3): 6-8.

Office of the Mayor of the City of New York. *Mayor's management report for the City of New York.*

Parsonage, W.H. (1989). Worker safety in probation and parole. Washington, DC: U.S. Department of Justice, National Institute of Justice.

Parsonage, W.H., & Miller, J.A. (1990). A study of probation and parole worker safety in the Middle Atlantic region. Middle Atlantic States Correctional Association.

Petersilia, J. (1985). Probation and felony offenders. U.S. Department of Justice, National Institute of Justice Research in Brief. Washington, DC: U.S. Government Printing Office.

Petersilia, J. (1988). Probation reform in J. Scott (ed.), *Controversial Issues in Crime and Justice.* Newbury Park, CA: Sage.

Pozzi, R.A. (1991, March 3). Probation officers adapt to a changing caseload. *The New York Times, Westchester Weekly,* 1, 6.

Pshide, W. (1991). Probation officer field safety in the 90's. *Perspectives,* 15(1): 26-27.

Reeves, R. (1991). A report of the 1991 fiscal survey results: Down, but not out. *Perspectives,* 15(4): 11-12.

Rosecrance, J. (1986). Probation supervision: Mission impossible. *Federal Probation,* 50(1): 25-31.

Rothman, D.J. (1980). *Conscience and convenience: The asylum and its alternatives in progressive America.* Boston, Mass.: Little, Brown.

Schultz, J.L. (1973). The cycle of juvenile court history. *Crime and Delinquency,* 19(4): 457-476.

Seymour, J., Lockhart, P., & Ely, R. (1989). *Felonization of the probation caseload in New York State.* Albany, NY.: N.Y.S. Division of Probation and Correctional Alternatives.

Silberman, C.E. (1978). *Criminal violence, criminal justice.* New York, NY: Random House.

Smykla, J.O. (1984). *Probation and parole: Crime control in the community,* NY: Macmillan.

Smyley, K.T. (1989). *The new probation. Perspectives* 13(2): 34-36.

Stewart, J.K. (1986). Felony probation: An ever increasing risk. *Correction Today,* 48(8): 94-102.

Serant, C. (1989). Dangerous drug visits. *New York Daily News,* 49.

Tappan, P.W. (1960). *Crime, justice and correction.* NY: McGraw-Hill.

The President's Commission on Law Enforcement and Administration of Justice. (1967). *Task force report: Juvenile delinquency and youth crime.* Washington, DC: U.S. Government Printing Office.

U.S. Attorney General. (1939). *Survey of release procedures: Vol. 2: Probation.* Washington, DC: U.S. Government Printing Office.

U.S. Department of Justice. (1992). *National Update.* Office of Justice Programs, Bureau of Justice Statistics: Vol. 1(3), Washington, DC: U.S. Government Printing Office.

Walker, S. (1985). *Sense and Nonsense about Crime.* Monterey, CA: Brooks/Cole.

Young, P. (1937). *Social treatment in probation and delinquency,* NY: McGraw-Hill.

DOING SOFT TIME

Jon Jefferson

Jon Jefferson is a free-lance writer in Knoxville, Tenn.

With 1.25 million people behind bars in the United States, even the law-abiding are prisoners of sorts. Locked into a system that spends more for jails and prisons than for job training, unemployment benefits and medical research combined, society has begun to look for an escape route.

While much of the public debate remains mired in simplistic labels—"soft on crime" or "law-and-order mentality"—more cash-starved governments are seeking new ways to curb their corrections budgets and still mete out the punishment, deterrence and security that the public demands. In New York City, where crime rates and jail crowding have forced the corrections system into the national forefront of alternatives to incarceration, the story of one young offender has an all-too-common beginning. Anthony G. grew up on the edge of Harlem, dropped out of school, and at age 18 faced one to three years in prison for beating and robbing two teen-agers. In the typical version of this story, Anthony would be behind bars.

Instead, he's at large and at "Liberty," literally: Two hundred feet below the statue's golden torch, Anthony works in the bookstore housed in the base of the nation's symbol of freedom. Amid a swarm of tourists—on peak summer days, as many as 16,000 will visit—he stocks shelves, runs the cash register, and answers questions about how the statue was built, how many stairs to the crown or how soon the next ferry leaves.

What has given Anthony's story another twist—and given him another chance—is the alternative program to which a judge sent him instead of prison. For six months, he reported to the program's Harlem office every weekday and met with a caseworker at least once a week; he also took classes, passed a high school equivalency test, learned basic computer skills and practiced interviewing for jobs. By the time he left the program, he had already landed his bookstore job.

For a now 21-year-old with a criminal record, it's a remarkable turnaround. For an overburdened prison system, it's a tiny but noteworthy measure of relief.

The nation's estimated inmate population of 1.25 million is roughly four times what it was in 1973, when a sharp 20-year climb in incarceration began. Most inmates—about 728,000—are in state prisons;

FACED WITH RISING CRIME AND FALLING REVENUES, GOVERNMENTS ARE LOOKING FOR NEW WAYS TO SENTENCE AND REHABILITATE OFFENDERS

the rest are in federal prisons and city and county jails.

The statistics, abstractly impersonal and ungraspably large, represent hundreds of overcrowded facilities, thousands of double-bunked inmates, and dozens of court orders to reduce prison crowding. They also represent the gradual ascent of a get-tough, lock-'em-up philosophy that, over the past two decades, has turned U.S. imprisonment rates into the world's highest.

In addition to those actually confined, another 3 million are on probation or parole, or are awaiting trials or appeals. When the relatively small numbers of incarcerated women, youths and elderly are factored out of the totals, roughly one of every dozen adult males in the United States is being held or watched by the criminal justice system.

"Over a lifetime, it turns out, something like a third of white men will be arrested at some point for a nontrivial crime, and something like 40 percent of black men," said Michael Tonry, a University of Minnesota law professor who also edits the bimonthly newsletter *Overcrowded Times*, which tracks the prison-population crisis and the efforts to solve it.

At an average annual price tag of $30,000 per inmate, prisons and jails now cost the nation $37.5 billion a year to operate. With the public clamoring for even tougher anti-crime measures and President Clinton backing so-called three-time-loser legislation for federal offenses, the pressures show no signs of letting up.

The best hope for relief, Tonry contended, lies in alternative sentences—or "intermediate punishments" as he prefers to call them—that mete out punishment without adding to the prison population. In a book entitled "Between Prison and Probation" (Oxford University Press, 1990), Tonry and Norval Morris, a University of Chicago law professor, urged far greater reliance on fines, community service, strictly supervised probation, electronic monitoring and day-reporting programs.

Their clear favorite is the means-based fine, or "day fine," named for the price of a day's freedom from prison. In one version of this system, a day's freedom equals a day's net income; in practice then, a convicted burglar might be fined a year's income instead of spending a year in jail.

Tonry and Morris downplayed concerns that criminals might commit additional crimes to raise cash for their fines: "No doubt some offenders will commit more crimes to pay their fines," they wrote. "If that be a serious risk, then there is merit to adding controls in the community for a period to reduce the risk. ..." They also rejected the argument that fines are unfair to the poor, citing a

Global prisoners

Incarceration rates during 1990/1991 per 100,000 population:

U.S.	455
South Africa	311
Venezuela	177
Hungary	117
Canada	111
China	111
Australia	79
Portugal	77
Czechoslovakia	72
Denmark	71
Albania	55
Netherlands	46
Rep. of Ireland	44
Sweden	44
Japan	42
India	34

Note: Nations from the former Soviet Union were not included in study.

Source: The Sentencing Project "America behind bars: One year later"

ABA Journal research by Joseph Wharton

Source: FBI

1986 analysis of fines in the Staten Island area of New York City, which showed that students and unemployed offenders who had been fined did as well at paying them as others did.

Even if day fines were limited to nonviolent offenders, Tonry explained, they still could ease dramatically the burden on prisons. "In 1991, only 27 percent of the people sent to state or federal prison had been sentenced for a violent crime," he said. "So for the other 73 percent, there's a real possibility we could do something different [impose fines] that wouldn't cost $30,000 a year, wouldn't ruin their lives, and would actually generate revenues."

Day fines are widely used in Europe. In what was West Germany before unification, for example, adoption of fines 25 years ago gradually reduced the number of short prison sentences (six months or less) by three-fourths. In 1968, just before the move to fines began, 184,000 prison sentences were handed down;

by 1989, the number had shrunk to just 48,000. During the same period, the number of criminal convictions in West Germany rose from 573,000 to 609,000.

But in the United States—which relies on the dollar for incentive and disincentive in most other arenas—fines are a form of punishment reserved almost exclusively for traffic offenses and misdemeanors. The reason, Tonry said, is "the idea that no punishment is serious unless it involves imprisonment." But if financial alternatives aren't yet helping relieve prison crowding, the same can't be said of technological ones.

Beep. "John Doe is not at home." Sounds like a message machine and it is, but not the usual sort: A version of this message has just flashed onto a computer screen at Vorec Corp., a New York company that makes electronic monitoring systems for corrections agencies. Nationwide, some 35,000 ankles are currently adorned with electronic "bracelets"; about 10 percent of them wear Vorec's version, which uses a fiber-optic circuit to increase tamper resistance. In New York, the state Department of Correctional Services has about 75 people on bracelets at a time; New York City has a similar number.

Built into the bracelet is a radio-frequency transmitter, explained David Manes, Vorec's president. The transmitter sends signals to a "smart" telephone receiver in the prisoner's home. "Typically, an individual is confined to his home for some periods of the day," Manes said. "At other times he's allowed—in fact, he's expected—to be at work, at counseling, at anger control, and so on."

A schedule of curfews and permitted travel periods is entered into the telephone unit and into the system's computers; if the bracelet moves beyond range of the phone unit during a curfew period, a computer immediately signals an operator, who notifies corrections officers. Vorec also makes a tracking antenna similar to those used to follow radio-collared wildlife that lets officers tell, simply by driving past a workplace or drug-treatment program, whether an inmate is there when required.

With a day of jail now costing $162, electronic monitoring has powerful financial advantages, said Carol Shapiro, New York City's assistant commissioner for alternatives to incarceration. The technology is cheap—

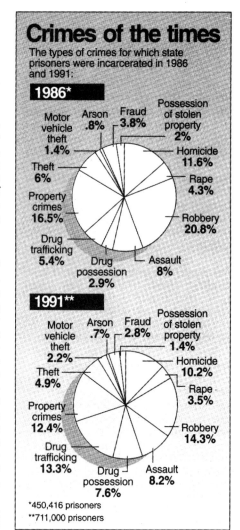

Crimes of the times

The types of crimes for which state prisoners were incarcerated in 1986 and 1991:

1986*

Motor vehicle theft 1.4%
Arson .8%
Fraud 3.8%
Possession of stolen property 2%
Homicide 11.6%
Rape 4.3%
Robbery 20.8%
Assault 8%
Drug possession 2.9%
Drug trafficking 5.4%
Property crimes 16.5%
Theft 6%

1991**

Motor vehicle theft 2.2%
Arson .7%
Fraud 2.8%
Possession of stolen property 1.4%
Homicide 10.2%
Rape 3.5%
Robbery 14.3%
Assault 8.2%
Drug possession 7.6%
Drug trafficking 13.3%
Property crimes 12.4%
Theft 4.9%

*450,416 prisoners
**711,000 prisoners

Source: FBI

"the device itself costs us $2.47 per person per day," said Shapiro—but the program as a whole averages about $75 per day. This is still $87 a day less than jail for every person wearing a bracelet.

"By the end of this year," said Shapiro, "we expect to have 100 to 150 on [electronic monitoring]. By then we'll begin to see some significant cost savings."

Electronic monitoring has another advantage, Shapiro said, as "a real support for the prisoners—we're rooting them in their communities," where they can work, stay with their families, and receive social services such as job training and drug treatment. For Shapiro, who said she believes that in this country "we overuse our capacity for imprisoning people," the community ties allowed by incarceration alternatives seem at least as important as the cost savings. "We only get [offenders] for a blink of a moment. So we really try to work with other programs and services."

In fact, other programs and services outside the corrections department provide the vast majority of New York City's alternatives to incarceration. Last year some 5,000 offenders were sent, either before trial or as part of a sentence or plea bargain, to a community-based incarceration alternative program. Services offered range from drug treatment for addicts to job training for unemployed mothers who have been arrested.

The largest of these programs is the Center for Alternative Sentencing and Employment Services (CASES), which handles more than half the city's participants in alternative programs. With 180 staffers and an annual budget of $8.5 million, the center is practically a mini-corrections system, existing in a sort of parallel corrections universe where alternative sanctions are the rule, prison the exception.

At the milder end of the center's spectrum, its Community Service Sentencing Project took in about 1,800 parole violators and chronic misdemeanants last year. Instead of going back to jail—increasingly the fate of parole violators, as New York parole officers struggle with caseloads of 200 or more—these offenders each spent 70 unpaid hours cleaning playgrounds, painting senior-citizen centers, renovating apartments or planting gardens.

The center estimates the value of this work at about $500,000 a year. That's a couple of million dollars less than the program cost. But by keeping participants out of jail—at least, the 62 percent who fulfilled the program requirements—the community service program saves on jail costs.

The center's other program, the Court Employment Project (CEP), operates at a darker end of the spectrum: prison-bound felony offenders only. When Anthony G. was arrested, for example, it was the Court Employment Project that kept him out of prison, helped him earn a high-school equivalency certificate, and arranged a job interview at the Statue of Liberty.

Begun in 1967, the project now enrolls nearly 1,000 participants a year. Like Anthony, who completed the CEP program two years ago, most are first-time youthful offenders; also like Anthony, most—nearly

two-thirds—have committed crimes involving violence or weapons.

"We're clearly the biggest alternative program in New York state," said Oren Root Jr., project director. "We also take much heavier offenders than most programs. Our 'big three' crimes are robberies, including armed robberies; drug sales; and possession of weapons."

The reasons for the project's parameters are simple: Prisons are full, and money talks. "Virtually all our money comes from the city and the state," said Root, "and their principal interest is in creating jail displacements."

At an average cost of about $9,400 per participant, the CEP program costs far less than a year in state prison ($32,000) or in the city's 20,000-bed corrections complex on Rikers Island ($59,000).

In addition—harder to calculate but maybe more valuable—there's the difference between a stint with the center and a stint behind bars. During participants' six months in the CEP program, each spends 20 to 30 hours a week in counseling, classes (at their own schools or at one of CASES' two centers), vocational training and other activities designed to land them on their feet in society.

Some, but Root conceded not enough, get jobs after graduation. Most common (but least rewarding) are fast-food jobs; more promising

are the linkages the alternative sentencing center is building with more prestigious employers, including The Nature Company, Limited Express and the Statue of Liberty.

Although it's hard for the center to track the long-term fate of its graduates, Root is convinced that the two-thirds who finish the CEP program have a better shot at going straight than if they had gone to prison. "When you're in prison," he said, "it's a lot easier to learn to be a better criminal than it is to learn to be a law-abiding citizen."

The worst nightmare for an alternative sentencing program like CASES is that a participant commits a violent crime like murder or rape while released to the program's supervision. So far, center officials said, nothing like that has happened.

"We'd be foolish to be unconcerned about the risk of violence," Root said. "But we've carved out a mission of getting the most serious cases we can into the program."

But is the center possibly playing it too safe, working what law professor Tonry called the "Milquetoast" factor?

"If a program has virtually no significant failures," Tonry argued, "what that tells you is not that the program is magically perfect; what that tells you is that they're creaming off incredibly lightweight offend-

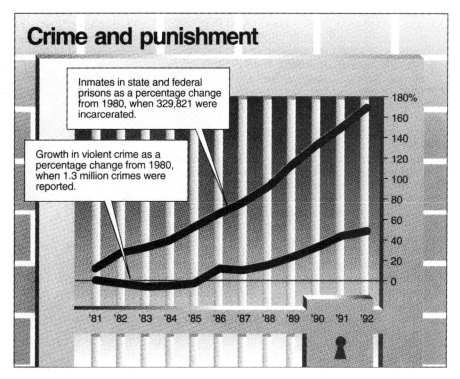

Crime and punishment

Inmates in state and federal prisons as a percentage change from 1980, when 329,821 were incarcerated.

Growth in violent crime as a percentage change from 1980, when 1.3 million crimes were reported.

180%
160
140
120
100
80
60
40
20
0

'81 '82 '83 '84 '85 '86 '87 '88 '89 '90 '91 '92

Source: FBI

201

ers who should be fined and put on probation instead."

But Root challenged that description of Court Employment Project participants. "These aren't people who would be spending 10 or 20 years in prison," he conceded, "but they are felony offenders, and some are second-felony offenders." (Indeed, their offenses are serious enough to keep many CEP participants out of boot camps—ironic, since CEP participants have relative freedom while New York's boot-camp inmates are guarded 24 hours a day.)

The center's good record stems not from Milquetoast, Root said, but from case managers' intensive supervision of only 15 to 20 individuals at a time and their readiness to act swiftly if a participant shows signs of trouble.

"A third of the people fail the [CEP] program," Root pointed out. "In those instances, we tell the judges why, and tell them we're no longer supervising that person. We've worked out an elaborate system not only to get accurate information to judges, but to get it to them very quickly. We help make it possible for judges to take the risk they're taking in sending these people to us."

In Manhattan Supreme Court, Judge Michael Corriero is taking that risk again. A judge since 1980, Corriero spent four years as a prosecutor and another seven as a defense attorney. He also spent his childhood years on some rough Manhattan streets; a black-and-white photo on his desk shows a youthful Corriero sporting a dangling cigarette and a tough-guy attitude.

Last year about 200 defendants—mostly young men with attitudes as well as crimes—stood before Corriero. He sent a tenth of them to CASES. In his recent risk-taking decision, he sent Deshawn M., a 15-year-old who committed armed robbery and who faced one to three years in prison. "The reason I'm prepared to sentence you to youthful-offender treatment and alternative sentencing is that you're in school," Corriero told him, "and there are what may be called mitigating circumstances." (The main one: The gun was unloaded.)

Having leaned thus far in the direction of compassion with Deshawn, Corriero tilted abruptly back toward toughness: "You put a pistol in a man's back and stole his wallet,"

he said with an in-your-face intensity. "Don't think for one minute that just because I'm not putting you in jail, I won't put you in jail. Every week, I'm going to check up on you. If you foul up, I'm going to put you in jail for a minimum of two years and a maximum of six."

As if for emphasis, a half-hour later Corriero confronted Charlene E., a 15-year-old he had sent to CASES' Court Employment Project for beating and robbing a woman. "As far as I can tell, nothing has changed," he snapped. "I warned you. Remanded." Handcuffed and returned to jail, Charlene could face two to six years in prison.

Compassion and consequences—justice and just deserts: Like Corriero, the nation's entire criminal justice system teeters between these polarities daily. With the system running on overload—with more than one million persons already behind bars, tens of thousands more on the way this year, and public fears of crime growing—the balance point has become elusive.

Meanwhile, from courtrooms and classrooms and electronic monitoring centers, a message—sometimes hopeful, sometimes desperate—is emerging: There is an alternative.

Punishment and Prevention

Both are needed if crime in America is to be brought under control.

LAURIN A. WOLLAN, JR.

Laurin A. Wollan, Jr., is associate professor of criminology and criminal justice at Florida State University in Tallahassee.

The hard lesson about crime causation is that we the people have failed to do what most of us know is right. We have failed to parent and school our children effectively and to use punishment along the way. We have allowed delinquency, crime, and even violence to increase. The result has been too many children and adults whose offenses could have been prevented who now must be punished severely. We have failed even to provide the prison space for that. Many of us, and especially our children, have been the victims.

Violence, especially among youngsters, has become so alarming that the whole country has concluded that something must be done. Although crime rates in general have declined, according to statistics kept by the Census Bureau, violent crime has increased. Juvenile crime, especially violent crime, has gone up even more.

Recent polls, such as one by the *New York Times*/CBS News, indicate that the public is now as concerned about crime as it is about the economy. Asked what is the single biggest problem facing the nation, 19 percent said "crime or violence," 15 percent said "health care," 14 percent said "the state of the economy." The number who mentioned crime, violence, or guns was up from 2 percent to 20 percent from January 1992.

Our leaders have been similarly affected by the specter of violence. A strategy of punishment-and-prevention has emerged and enchanted them from the attorney general down; it gets repeated in speeches and newspaper columns like a mantra. And it is high time because it is the right response.

But a fundamental truth about policy is this: Prescription rests on diagnosis. Does this mean that the violence afflicting us stems from the *absence* of punishment and prevention? It does. There has been too little of each—too little punishment, too little prevention. But what that means is complex and controversial.

Criminologists of recent decades have argued (at least implicitly) that violence, like delinquency more generally, is *not* the result of the absence of punishment. Indeed, they contend that there has been altogether too much punishment. The corrections system, they have said, is too punitive: Prison sentences are generally too long and too many offenders receive them.

Criminologists have resisted the idea that punishment deters. Twenty years ago, James Q. Wilson, formerly of Harvard and now of UCLA, observed that the leading criminology textbooks of that day simply dismissed the idea of deterrence. Only gradually, and only by a handful, have some criminologists come to appreciate what common sense tells most of us: that the threat of punishment is an important consideration in the choice of actions, provided that it is a credible threat of swift and certain, though not necessarily severe, punishment.

For the most part, criminologists have argued instead for more prevention, but they mean by that a set of strategies that are not what most ordinary citizens have in mind. The citizen would employ more cops on the beat or

This article first appeared in *The World & I*, April 1994, pp. 36-43. Reprinted by permission of *The World & I*, a publication of the Washington Times Corporation. © 1994.

devices like "the Club" to make crime more dangerous or more difficult for those so inclined. The criminologist, by contrast, would intervene early in the life of "at risk" juveniles to render them disinclined toward delinquency. And so would we all, but not generally in the ways suggested by the theories of criminology.

Modern criminologists have been busy discovering dozens of factors associated with delinquency and inventing at least as many theories to explain the connection. The factors include: age, gender, intelligence, body type, drugs, TV, socioeconomic status, schools, anomie, neighborhood, inequality, housing, peers, mental health, cultural values, discipline, opportunities, self-esteem, employment skills, interpersonal relations, life chances, motivation, family, literacy, class conflict, sexual activity, emotional ties, educational success, role models, to mention only a few—the presence or absence of which (and which?) and the degree (of which?) makes all the difference in the world—or in the science—of delinquency. There are many more factors, of course, and each one—like a carbuncle, a car, or an uncle—has something to do with how we behave, if only on a given occasion.

Theories explaining those connections go by names that only specialists need to know, but the major ones are: the *choice*, *biosocial*, and *psychological* theories, which lodge causation in the individual; the *social disorganization*, *strain*, and *cultural deviance* theories, which lodge it in social structure; *social learning* and *social control* theories, in social process; and *labeling*, *conflict*, and *instrumental theories*, in social reaction. Nearly all theories have subtypes that vary somewhat from each other, such as the theories of differential association, differential rein-

forcement, and neutralization within social learning theory.

Moreover, most of the theories and subtheories have been integrated with others. The permutations and combinations yield dozens of theories. No science has so many theories to explain the same thing. Or as George Homans of Harvard said of sociology, it "sometimes appears to have many theories but no explanations." (For a serious effort to sort it all out, see Larry Siegel and Joseph Senna, *Juvenile Delinquency: Theory, Practice, and Law* 5th ed., West Publishing Company, 1994).

Most criminologists, on the one hand, and the rest of us, on the other hand, could not be much further apart on what to do about crime and, by implication what causes it. (The criminologists are wrong about punishment but right about prevention, at least in citing childhood as the time when preventive measures must begin if they are to work later on in the crime-prone years.) The reason for this division has been suggested by one leading criminologist, Travis Hrischi of the University of Arizona, who has gone against the grain of modern criminology. He says:

The major reason for the neglect of the family is that the explanations of crime that focus on the family are directly contrary to the metaphysics of our age. "Modern" theories of crime accept this metaphysics. They assume that the individual would be noncriminal were it not for the operations of unjust and misguided institutions. "Outdated" theories of crime assume that decent behavior is not part of our native equipment, but is somehow built in by socialization and maintained by the threat of sanctions.

In this welter of theories, few suggest much of a role for punishment, except for the newest one, choice theory, which is also the oldest one. All the others stress prevention, but their prevention strategies involve prolonged and expensive restructuring of society, reallocation of resources, reprocessing of life experience, reshaping of institutions like family and school, and rejiggering of this, that, and many other things as well.

Returning to an older view

The newest theory of crime causation, by contrast, suggests no transformation of society into something new but rather a return to what we seem to have forgotten. Rational-choice theory rests on the idea that people do not merely behave in response to environmental determinants but choose to conduct themselves according to judgments made mindfully that some alternatives are advantageous and others disadvantageous—among which are crime, which brings pleasure, and punishment, which brings pain.

A TWO-TRACK APPROACH TO CONTROL CRIME

Punishment begins with a series of firm measures that parents and teachers must employ so that prisons will be less necessary later on.

Prevention requires more police on patrol and more prison space.

This theory suggests its own strategy. Like the other theories, it calls for a turn from what we have been doing to what we used to do—a return, as it were, to an older view characterized (derisively, one suspects) as classical criminology. Beginning in the eighteenth century, this view held unapologetically that punish-

The Vigilante Society

by Joey Merrill

Society has determined that the government can no longer effectively protect them, and individuals are taking matters into their own hands. The 1993 Gallup Poll on crime indicated this shift to self-protection: 43% had installed special locks, 38% have a guard dog, and for the first time in 35 years, a majority (51%) of households have a gun in the house. A Vermont company that sells Mace reports sales increasing ten-fold in one year. The company that produces a car theft device, the Club, can hardly meet market demand, growing in sales from $22 million to $107 million over two years. Citizens Against Crime reports that each week 15,000 people take their self-protection courses.

People are trying to protect themselves from random violence and from a criminal justice system that often seems to coddle criminals. This move to self-protection was poignantly illustrated during the L.A. riots as Korean business owners held rifles on the roofs of their businesses. Beyond these measures, there is some evidence that a similar backlash to crime is occurring in the judicial system. For example, in 1992 a Bronx jury dismissed attempted murder charges against a man who shot his son's killer on the courthouse steps. The underlying theme of situations such as these is that people are rightly or wrongly taking back control.

Cost of crime

Not only does society now feel the urge to protect itself (apart from dialing 911), we are also literally paying for crime. William Raspberry notes that the threat of becoming a victim to crime has inflicted so much fear that people are increasingly changing the way they live their lives. Working, taking classes, going to school events at night are simply no longer options for many people. These type of changes upset the natural incentives of the American system to improve self and family.

Beyond these indirect costs of crime, there is a very real economic cost of crime. *Business Week* estimates that crime costs America $425 billion every year. The $425 billion in losses are comprised of $90 billion for the criminal justice system, $65 billion for private protection measures, $50 billion in urban decay, $45 billion in property loss, $5 billion in medical care, and $170 billion in indirect costs of crime.

From an economic standpoint, industry must contend with the cost of keeping their businesses safe from crime: a "security tax" is imposed because of crime. The security tax is especially high in inner cities where violent crime rates are from two to seven times higher than in the suburbs—forcing business and jobs out of the inner city. After the killing of the German tourist, some Miami tourism businesses have experienced losses of up to 50%. However, the costs of crime not only have a toll on the inner city, as the manager of a Mobil station which suffered a carjacking in Topanga Canyon, California, explains: "The customers have not come back. Business is down as much as 30%. The people are in shock and they associate what happened with this place. Nothing like this has ever happened here before."

A 1992 Bureau of Alcohol, Tobacco and Firearms study of career criminals found that most commit an average of 160 crimes a year. With an average value of $2,300 per crime (as estimated by the National Institute of Justice), one criminal's habits costs the U.S. about $350,000 a year. A Rand Corporation survey estimated that an average criminal committed even more crimes (187–287 per year)—resulting in even higher costs to society.

Violent crime is especially costly. By using techniques from cost-benefit analysis of safety regulations, economists have determined that a murder costs about $2.4 million. A rape costs approximately $60,000 and assault costs roughly $20,000. *Business Week* reports that violent crime cost the United States $170 billion last year. They note, "The rewards for hard work for the less-educated have fallen, while the payoff for crime has risen." The basic problem is that the incentives have become confused and crime does pay in America.

Reprinted in part from "Personal Security and the Black Community" in Black America 1994: Changing Direction, published by the National Center for Public Policy Research.

Joey Merrill is a research analyst at the Hudson Institute in Indianapolis. She serves on the board of directors of Third Millennium, an organization working to raise pertinent generational public-policy issues.

ment is a deterrent to crime—
and, of course, it is, difficult as it
may be to measure its effects.

But it understood what we
have not, that punishment cannot be held in reserve until a misbehaving youngster turns 18,
only then to be hammered with a
long sentence to a prison cell.
Instead, punishments—for the
most part of a light-handed sort—
must be employed in a sensible
regimen of disciplinary measures

**Polls indicate that
the public is now
as concerned
about crime as
it is about the
economy.**

starting when a child is a toddler.
Rational-choice theory does
not naively suppose that nothing

else matters. Like the other theories, it implicates the family and
the school because both institutions are crucial in the teaching
of values and discipline. And both
have failed, leaving much to be
done remedially. This remedial
work is not so much along innovative as traditional lines.

When this pre-modern, eigh-
teenth-century view is coupled
with the truly ancient view that
justice requires doing right (or at
least avoiding wrong) and that it
can be cultivated by example, the
result is a potent mix of policy
prescriptions that fit the notions
most citizens have of what we
ought to be doing about violence.

None of these preventive
strategies will produce effects for
many years, perhaps a generation. If every parent would begin
to read William Bennett's best-
seller *The Book of Virtues* to every
four-year-old tonight, and if its
moral lessons "took" in every
case, a decade would pass before
any appreciable effects were evident. This does not mean that

any parent should put it off for
even one more night. It means
only that the preventive measures addressed to the deep-seat-
ed wellsprings of human conduct
take time to play out.

But there are preventive
measures that reach less deeply,
that promise some earlier relief,
that are employable by government agencies, and that are of
use to policymakers—though not
to many criminologists because
they do not go to root causes of
crime. Wilson once noted that the
quest for root causes is not helpful to the policymaker, who needs
to know what government can do
about crime. He wrote

Ultimate causes cannot be the
object of policy efforts precisely
because, being ultimate, they
cannot be changed. . . . Social
problems—that is to say, problems occasioned by human
behavior rather than mechanical processes—are almost
invariably "caused" by factors
that cannot be changed easily

An Issue of Character

by Charles W. Colson

What we are witnessing in today's chilling headlines is the loss of a generation—crimi-
nals who kill without rhyme or reason. To stop crime requires us as a culture to once again learn how to inculcate character in young people—to build conscience.

That begins with secure and stable families. Charles Murray describes illegitimacy as "the single most important social problem of our time—more important than crime, drugs, poverty, illiteracy, welfare, or homelessness." Why? Because illegitimacy "drives everything else." President Clinton, with refreshing can-
dor, has joined the chorus saying Dan Quayle was right. Now the president ought to lead the way with policies that support and encourage traditional two-parent families.

We also ought to demand that schools teach real values, real right and wrong: Pressure the networks and entertainment outlets to develop family-friendly programming. Don't wait for Congress to do this. You and I have to.

If we allow ourselves to be deluded that a bill in Congress will lick the crime problem, it will be at our grave peril. The crime plague will continue to spread, bringing fear in its wake, and people will finally turn to the strong arm of the government.

Ominous signs are already everywhere: calls for the National Guard to patrol the streets; cur-

fews for young people in several states, despite their dubious constitutionality. A recent Miami Herald poll found 71 percent sup-
port for police roadblocks to stop drugs, even at the expense of the Fourth Amendment's protection against unreasonable search and seizure.

The dark truth is that people always prefer order to chaos—
even when imposed at the cost of freedom. So there is much more at stake here than building prisons and writing new laws. At stake is nothing less than our lib-
erty.

Reprinted in part from "Neither liberal nor conservative nostrums: Crime is an issue of character first of all," *Washington Times*, 31 Jan. 1994.

*Charles W. Colson is chairman of Prison Fellowship Ministries, a prison outreach and criminal jus-
tice reform organization.*

or at all. This is because human behavior ultimately derives from human volition—tastes, attitudes, values, and so on—and these aspects of volition in turn are either formed entirely by choice or the product of biological or social processes that we cannot or will not change.

Certainly they will not be changed by government bureaucracy, whether lean and mean like a police department or fat and philanthropic like a welfare department.

Incarceration works

There are, however, levers government can manipulate that will alter the rate of violence. But they require a willingness to consider a more modest conception of causation. Willie Sutton said he robbed banks because that's where the money is. Why not separate Sutton from the banks? We did that for many years, and in those years he robbed no banks.

So one cause of crime is allowing criminals to get close to their targets. It follows that prevention is keeping them away from their targets. We can make it difficult for criminals to get close to their targets by putting more police on the streets. Crime rates in Los Angeles plummeted after the riots and earthquake because the police were out in extraordinary numbers. Their visibility was much more plainly established than at normal times.

We can make the proximity of criminal to his target not merely more difficult but impossible. Keep the robber from banks, the cutthroat from throats, the rapist from women, the pedophile from children, the graffiti artist from walls, the thief from cars, the burglar from dwellings, the picker from pockets, the snatcher from purses, the lifter from shops—by locking them up. Incarceration

works not only for punishment but also for incapacitation.

It requires attention by the criminologists to establish how to know who should be locked up and for how long—all in light of the costs of the crimes that would otherwise be committed by one no longer able to do so. Studies indicate that the costs of incarceration are significantly less than the costs of the crimes prevented. Some studies suggest that the benefits of incarceration greatly outweigh the costs.

But who among the unimprisoned should be locked up?

The family and the school are crucial in the teaching of values and discipline.

That is not easy to say, and there is good reason to be wary of locking up someone for offenses not yet committed. (And that, it must be understood, is what incapaci-

■ *L.A. gang:* **To stop crime requires us to once again learn how to inculcate character in young people.**

tation is all about!) But research by the Rand Corporation and others suggests that a policy of selective incapacitation can be carried out on the basis of reasonably accurate predictions (but never completely accurate because the inmates' hypothetical behavior on the outside cannot be observed).

Punishment begins with an array of measures (punitive to be sure, but not brutal) that parents and teachers must be willing to use so that future prisons will be emptier. (But there must be the willingness as well as the capacity to use those prisons later on.) It also means those measures such as more police on patrol and prisons used for incapacitation. This formula is old-fashioned, not easy, and not inexpensive. But when it works, and it usually does, all the guns and drugs and TV violence in the world will have little criminogenic effect.

There are reasons, call them *theory* if theory be necessary, by which we can begin to turn it around. And from it follow these measures:

● Reform the welfare system so that it makes dysfunctional families less likely.
● Empower schools to establish and enforce discipline.
● Remove trouble makers from schools and bus them to special schools (formerly called "reform schools") in Department of Corrections buses, which can be used later in the morning and later in the afternoon to transport prisoners.
● Sentence juveniles over 13 as adults for violent offenses. True enough, we have failed them, but they are too dangerous to be free.
● Develop a range of intermediate sanctions like intensive supervision, electronically monitored "house arrest," and boot camp to punish and somewhat incapacitate those who don't deserve or need prison but do deserve or need more than "walking-around probation."
● Build prisons, as many and as large as necessary to assure that inmates serve 85 percent of their sentence.
● Enact "three strikes and you're in" laws, as New Jersey Gov. Christine Todd Whitman puts it, but not so the inmate is hopeless, therefore dangerous. Better a 70/70 plan so that if a three-time loser goes in at 25, he is eligible for parole 70 percent of the way to age 70, or at age 61 (or 80/80, which would make it 69).
● Put more police on the beat on foot in what is known as community policing, so that small units are responsible for neighborhoods.

Additional Reading

Ronald Akers, *Criminological Theories*, Roxbury Publishing Company, Los Angeles, 1994.

Travis Hirschi and Michael Gottfredson, *A General Theory of Crime*, Stanford University Press, Palo Alto, California, 1990.

James Q. Wilson and Richard Hernnstein, *Crime and Human Nature*, Simon & Schuster, New York, 1985.

James Q. Wilson, *Thinking about Crime*, rev. ed., Basic Books, New York, 1983.

... AND THROW AWAY THE KEY

America's overcrowded prisons have failed as a deterrent.
Building more of them and imposing longer sentences
may only increase the crime rate

Jill Smolowe

For years, Tonya Drake struggled from one welfare check to the next, juggling the cost of diapers, food and housing for her four small children, all under age eight. So when Drake, 30, was handed a $100 bill by a man she barely knew in June 1990 and was told she could keep the change if she posted a package for him, she readily agreed. For her effort, Drake received $47.70 and assumed that would be the end of it. But unknown to Drake, the package contained 232 grams of crack cocaine. Although she had neither a prior criminal record nor any history of drug use, the judge was forced under federal mandatory-sentencing guidelines to impose a 10-year prison term. At the sentencing, District Judge Richard Gadbois Jr. lamented, "That's just crazy, but there's nothing I can do about it."

Now, while Drake serves her time in a federal prison in Dublin, California, at a cost to taxpayers of about $25,000 a year, her children must live with her family 320 miles south in Inglewood. "How are you going to teach her a lesson by sending her to prison for 10 years?" demands her attorney, Robert Campbell III. "What danger is she to society?" Penologists have a ready answer: the danger is that while Drake monopolizes a scarce federal-prison bed, she enables a more dangerous criminal to roam free. To them, Drake's case is a textbook example of the myopia that blinds Americans to the long-term consequences of short-term solutions.

The disturbing truth is that although three decades of lock'em-up fever have made America the world's No. 1 jailer, there still aren't nearly enough cells to go around. The '80s zeal for harsh drug penalties has pushed the U.S. incarceration rate to 455 per 100,000 citizens and has run up an unprecedented annual tab of $21 billion for the construction of prisons and maintenance of inmates. As the nation's inmate population swells toward 1.4 million, prison officials must release career criminals to make room for first-time drug offenders. The growing public outcry against violent crime is

prompting politicians to call for even stiffer, tighter and costlier sanctions. But more prisons and longer sentences likely point in only two directions: larger inmate rosters and a higher crime rate. Robert Gangi, executive director of the Correctional Association of New York, warns, "Building more prisons to address crime is like building more graveyards to address a fatal disease."

Americans' impatience for quick-fix remedies resembles the frustration that drives inner-city youths to seize on illegal get-rich schemes: they want to cut corners, produce high yields and not pay a price. But grim experience indicates that, as with crime, hard time doesn't always pay the anticipated dividends. When money is poured into building another prison cell at the expense of rebuilding a prisoner's self-image, it is often just a prelude to more—and worse—crime. "They start as drug offenders, they eventually become property-crime offenders, and then they commit crimes against people," says Michael Sheahan, the sheriff of Cook County, Illinois. "They learn this trade as they go through the prison system."

America has already been trying to jail its way out of the crime problem—with discouraging results. Over the past two decades, the U.S. has hosted the biggest prison-construction boom in history, laying out $37 billion, with $5 billion more in the pipeline. Yet the pool of street criminals keeps rising. In the past decade, the number of federal and state inmates has doubled, to 925,000, while the local jail population has nearly tripled, to 450,000. State by state, the outlook is bleak. Washington, for instance, has witnessed a 79% increase in its jail population and an 86% increase in prison capacity, though the state population has grown just 18%. "At that rate," says Governor Mike Lowry, "everyone in Washington State will be working in—or in—prison by 2056."

THE PRISON BUILDUP HAS NOT come cheaply. The average annual cost per inmate is now $23,500. The average cost per bed in maximum-security facilities is $74,862. "You don't lock them up and throw away key," says Howard Peters, Illinois' director of corrections. "You lock them up and spend thousands of dollars on them."

But to what end? The politically popular War on Drugs of the '80s has given rise to the far less sexy Cell Crunch of the '90s. Mandatory minimum sentences for minor drug crimes have stuffed the prisons to bursting with nonviolent offenders. By 1990 almost 40 states were under court order to relieve overcrowding by releasing prisoners—even habitual offenders. Today narcotics offenders occupy 61% of the beds in federal prisons. Meanwhile, 1 in 7 state facilities continues to operate beyond capacity. Ohio leads the pack with a stunning 182% of capacity.

Such pressures require creative reshuffling. In North Carolina, where a net gain of 200 new inmates each week has made a mockery of the statutory limit of 21,400, Governor James Hunt Jr. will present a new crime-fighting package to the legislature next week. His proposals include rushing the opening of two of the 12 new prisons currently under construction and leasing space in county jails. Meanwhile, North Carolina is trying to ship 1,000 inmates over state lines. To date, Oklahoma and Rhode Island have contracted to house temporarily a total of 226 inmates. Even so, unless Hunt can persuade legislators to raise the statutory cap by March 15, he will be forced to release 3,400 inmates.

And therein lies the rub. The mandatory sentences that keep drug offenders in push violent criminals out. In Florida drug sentences of, on average, four years have cut time dramatically for other inmates. The average prisoner serves just 41% of his

From *Time*, February 7, 1994, pp. 54-56, 58-59. © 1994 by Time Inc. Magazine Company. Reprinted by permission.

time; serious thugs do half. Although the standard sentence for robbery is 8.6 years and almost 22 years for murder, the average prison stay is just 16 months. Harry Singletary, who heads the state's department of corrections, dryly calls himself the "Secretary of Release." He might just as well call himself the "Secretary of Readmission." Since 1991, some 43,000 convicts who were released early because of overcrowding have been rearrested. That makes for a recidivism rate of 34%, well in line with the national average of 35%.

That disheartening statistic applies only to those who actually go to prison. Overcrowding has enabled countless more repeat offenders to elude incarceration or do snooze time in a county jail. According to Marc Mauer of the Washington-based Sentencing Project, for each crime committed, an offender stands a 1-in-20 chance of serving time. "People ignore the gun laws because there are no stiff penalties," says Antoine McClarn, 22, who sits in the Cook County Jail on charges of armed robbery. "Guys are charged and then released, and it's like a cycle to them, almost fun. People used to be scared to come here, but now it's a game or a joke."

THE UPSHOT IS THAT WHILE JAILS and prisons still incapacitate, incarcerate and punish, they no longer—if they ever did—deter crime. Indeed, in many inner-city neighborhoods, young men regard prison time as more a rite of passage than a deterrent. "Their father's been in prison, their brother's been in prison," says Lieut. Robert Losack, 30, who has served as a Texas prison guard for nine years. "It's socially acceptable; it's part of growing up." Once back on the street, these youths enjoy an enhanced status. They also pose a greater threat. "Prison culture becomes the model for street society," warns Jerome Miller, president of the National Center on Institutions and Alternatives in Washington. "Young black men take onto the streets the ethics, morals and rules of the maximum-security prison."

Or they return with new wiles learned in local cells. Until he turned his life around 18 months ago in a drug-rehabilitation program, Lorenzo Woodley, 35, spent most of his time getting into—and out of—jail. Since age 19, Woodley has been arrested 14 times, all on felonies ranging from burglary to selling cocaine. Yet the longest

stretch he ever spent locked up was six months in Miami's Dade County Jail. He has yet to see the inside of a prison. "I was a very manipulative person," he says with a smile. "You tell a judge you got a drug problem. Judges get soft. They know what drugs do to people. They send you to a drug-rehab program instead of prison." Jail suited Woodley just fine. "You get healthy, you sleep good, you eat good, you get cable TV." Then you get out. "They don't rehab you at all. They don't teach you anything," he says. "So these guys come out and do the same thing all over again."

That revolving door helps explain why 80% of all crimes are committed by about 20% of the criminals. It also helps to make sense of the seeming contradiction that many states with high incarceration rates also have high violent crime rates. Florida has the 12th highest lock-up rate among states, and it ranks first in violent crime. Conversely, 12 of the 15 states with the lowest incarceration rates also score low on violent crime. Minnesota, for instance, has the nation's second lowest incarceration rate, jailing just 90 people per 100,000, and is ranked 37th for violent crime. It is probably no coincidence that Minnesota is one of

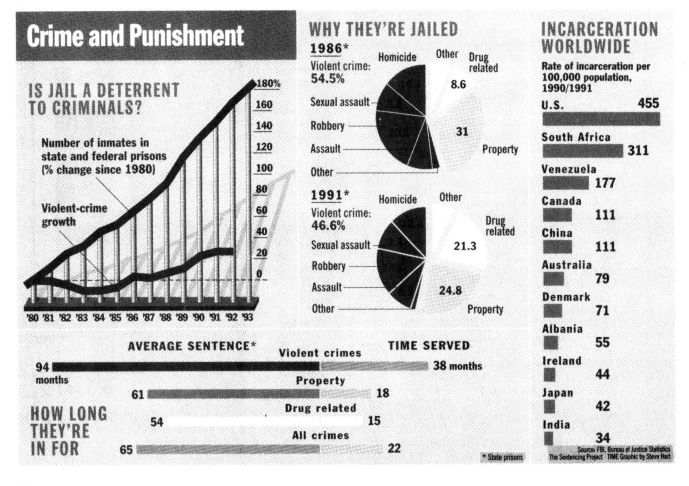

the most progressive states on punishment. Prisoners who are functionally illiterate—35% of the inmates—must take a reading course before they can join other classes. Some 90% of those inmates have enrolled.

Such results have convinced people who spend most of their waking hours in and around prisons—commissioners, wardens, guards, not to mention inmates—that if prisons only punish, and offer no inducements or opportunities for rehabilitation, they simply produce tougher criminals. When prisoners have no constructive way to spend their time, they often fill the hours building a reservoir of resentment, not to mention a grab bag of criminal tricks, that—count on it—they will take back to the streets. "All we do," says Dr. John May, one of the 10 doctors who service the 9,000 inmates at Chicago's Cook County Jail, "is produce someone meaner and angrier and more disillusioned with himself and society."

A MINORITY COUNTERS THAT PRISONS serve a valuable function beyond safeguarding citizens from criminals. "How can you say [prisons] have no impact on crime rates?" challenges Charlie Parsons, who heads the FBI's Los Angeles Regional Office. He points to an FBI effort to curb bank robberies that slashed such incidents in Southern California by 37% in a year. "The bottom line is that if you catch somebody after their first bank robbery or after their tenth, you are going to have an impact," he says. Director Peters of Illinois also sees benefit in stiff time. "For many of the inmates, prison is the first time they have ever had order in their lives," he says. "The average inmate leaves prison either the same or a little better than when he came in."

THE FAR MORE PREVALENT VIEW, though, is that the revolving door puts seasoned criminals back onto the streets to make room for nonviolent offenders, who make up half the prison population. "Prison systems are 'criminogenic': they create criminals," says University of Miami criminologist Paul Cromwell, who served as a commissioner on the Texas Board of Pardons and Paroles. The chronic beatings, stabbings, rapes and isolation ignite fury. "Just about everyone I talk to says

that when they get out they will do something bad," says Larry Jobe, 32, who is imprisoned at a supermax facility in Oak Park Heights, Minnesota. "They are so blind with rage that they can't think about the consequences." Jobe, a former accountant who is serving life for a murder he insists he did not commit, knows the risk of long sentences: "After so many years, they have nothing to lose."

Even the softest inmates can turn into violent thugs. There is no telling yet if Randy Blackburn, 31, will become such a person, but he is worried he might. Blackburn has been in Cook County Jail for the past 13 months, awaiting trial on sexual assault. "I almost felt like a baby," he says of his first days in lockup. "I really didn't know what cocaine was until I got here." Now, Blackburn says, the temptation to become "hard" is constant. "Every night in the dorm, you hear the guys talk about how many people they have shot and how much drugs they've sold and women they've had. It can lead you into that."

Sheer boredom also stokes the rage. Jails, which are designed for short-term incarceration, provide few educational or work opportunities. Prisons do better. Most offer some courses, though tight budgets have forced cutbacks in recent years; 2 out of 3 prison inmates have work assignments. Even so, a quarter of all prisoners have neither jobs nor classes to engage their time and pent-up energies.

Corrections officials know there are no quick fixes. But they—like many inmates—argue that the prison system would function more effectively if justice were served more swiftly, sentences imposed more reliably and space allocated more rationally. The lag of months, sometimes years, between the crime and the punishment is counterproductive. Says Marcus Felson, a sociology professor at the University of Southern California: "[An electric] plug that shocks you a year later or once in a thousand times isn't going to deter you."

Neither are sentences that telescope years into months. "That six months I served, that was a slap on the wrist," says Woodley, who turned himself around without going to prison. "If you get three years, you should do three years." At the same time, the jailers know that prisoners need incentives for good behavior. Florida's Singletary favors 75% sentences for

those of the 53,000 prisoners in his system who "work off" days by doing construction work, cleaning parks and performing other outside tasks. It not only lessens tension within the prison but also addresses the problem of idleness.

Work programs can benefit inmates and taxpayers alike. Minnesota's Sentencing to Service program has been putting nonviolent offenders to work in communities throughout the state since 1986. So far, it has logged 530,000 man-hours, and when program costs are offset against earnings and reductions in prison costs, the effort comes up $6 million in the black. "In work programs, inmates feel like they're paying back society," says Charles Colson, who established the Prison Fellowship after serving seven highly publicized months in prison. "Work restores their sense of dignity—and it's useful to society."

Precious prison space must also be allocated more judiciously. Penologists say that means not only finding alternative penalties for nonviolent offenders, but offering parole to rehabilitated old-timers. Often the hotheads who enter the system while still in their teens and 20s chill out by their 30s and 40s. Life-means-life sentences do a disservice on several fronts. Taxpayers pay ever steeper costs for aging inmates, who require more medical care; wardens are stripped of the ability to motivate these prisoners; and the lifers sink into a hopelessness that can be dangerous.

Most important, the problems connected with crime—inadequate schooling, unemployment, drugs, unstable families—must be addressed as part of America's prison crisis. "Look, I'm not a bleeding-heart liberal; I'm a realist," says Singletary. "But the cure for our crime is *not* prison beds and juvenile boot camps. We need to do something about juveniles at the school level before they get here."

President Clinton sounded the same alarm last week in his State of the Union Address. "I ask you to remember that even as we say no to crime, we must give people, especially our young people, something to say yes to." The question is whether America was listening. —*Reported by Ann Blackman/ Washington, Cathy Booth/Miami, Jon D. Hull/ Chicago, Sylvester Monroe/Los Angeles and Lisa H. Towle/Raleigh*

Privatizing America's Prisons, Slowly

Despite a checkered past, the future is looking brighter for the private prison industry.

Anthony Ramirez

NASHVILLE

Ernest Anderson, his biceps straining his blue prison fatigues, cocks back his shining bald head and smiles his gap-toothed smile as he talks about crime, punishment and private enterprise.

"I am a career criminal," Mr. Anderson said. Then, the 35-year-old convict goes on to describe the last decade of his life, years filled with gunplay, drug dealing and struggling, often unsuccessfully, with what he calls "my anger problem." He has spent most of those years in prison, five different ones.

Mr. Anderson's story is more or less typical of repeat offenders, and seasoned criminals like him account for the majority of the million people locked up in state and Federal prisons today—five times the number two decades ago.

A typical American prisoner perhaps. But Mr. Anderson is one of a growing number of inmates who are being guarded, fed and put through rehabilitation programs run not by government, but by private companies.

So far, less than 2 percent of inmates are in such facilities and only 13 states, including Texas and Florida, allow private prisons. But this veteran consumer of prison services sounds satisfied. "Until this facility,

with this facility's programs, I have not been given the opportunity to turn my life around," Mr. Anderson said.

His current residence, the Metro-Davidson Detention Facility in Nashville, is managed by the Corrections Corporation of America, the largest company in the business of for-profit prisons.

The private-prison industry has no shortage of critics, from public-sector unions out to protect their jobs to civil liberties advocates who warn that company-run prisons are less accountable.

Private prisons are not new; they date back to colonial times. But by the 1950's, prisoner-abuse scandals at private operations led to the public administration of prisons. The private-prison movement revived in the early 1980's, but grew slowly for years.

But while the private-prison business has critics and a checkered past, its future seems bright. True, the $33 billion crime bill that is stalled, for now, in Congress would have accelerated the industry's growth even more with over $10 billion for prison construction, some of which would have gone to private prisons. Still, the industry's optimism remains unshaken, and it is explained mainly by a familiar, if dreary, litany: the unchecked national problems of crime,

and overcrowded state and Federal prisons. The need to control Government spending makes privately managed prisons look increasingly attractive.

A Better Image, Too

The reputation of the $250 million-a-year private prison business has also improved lately. The industry is still small, with nearly a score of little companies in the field. But the two largest companies, Corrections Corporation of America and Wackenhut Corrections Corporation, which went public last month, hold more than half of the private-prison population. Policy experts say these companies manage a wide range of facilities, and are developing innovative drug-rehabilitation, educational and job-training programs.

Leading the industry's surge is the Corrections Corporation of America, based in Nashville. Its 23 prisons under contract in seven states house about a third of the prisoners in the United States who are now held in private prisons. Last year, the company's profits rose 57 percent to $4 million on revenues of $100 million.

This year, Corrections Corporation's income rose 30 percent during the first half, and analysts predict further growth. Over the next two

From the *New York Times*, August 14, 1994. © 1994 by the New York Times Company. Reprinted by permission.

years, the company's 13,000 beds under contract should increase by 85 percent and profits should more than double, said William Oliver, an analyst at Equitable Securities in Nashville. Corrections Corporation's share price more than doubled in the last year, closing Friday at $15.75.

Equally impressive, the company has been able to win over some former critics with its ability to both cut costs and offer ample prison services. Policy analysts and prisoner advocates worry that private contractors like Corrections Corporation will run bare-bones prisons to maximize profits. After all, they reasoned, private operators are paid a per-day fee for each prisoner.

So far, however, these experts say that Corrections Corporation has surprised them and prompted them to rethink at least the Nashville company's version of prison privatization. William C. La Rowe, director of the Texas Center for Correctional Services, a prisoners' rights group, says he was once an opponent of prison privatization and of Corrections Corporation. But Mr. La Rowe, who has made unannounced visits to Texas prisons for years, likes what he has seen.

"At Corrections Corporation prisons you don't have the atmosphere of impending violence that you have in a state prison," Mr. La Rowe said. "If Corrections Corporation ran more prisons, I am sure you'd see an increase in savings and a decrease in violence."

Even prison experts who remain skeptical about privatization in general seem impressed by Corrections Corporation. "Not everybody is Corrections Corporation," said John J. DiIulio Jr., a professor at Princeton University. "I'm worried about the fly-by-night companies."

The praise is welcome indeed to Doctor R. Crants, the 49-year-old, white-haired chairman and chief executive of Corrections Corporation, who led the often difficult struggle to build the business.

A West Point graduate, Mr. Crants founded Corrections Corporation in 1983 along with Thomas W. Beasley, an insurance executive, and T. Don Hutto, a former Virginia corrections commissioner. Mr. Beasley, the former chairman, is now a director of the firm, and Mr. Hutto is international projects manager, including prison ventures in Australia and Britain.

Its founders and financial backers wanted to bring prisons into the wider movement to "privatize" services that were once the exclusive province of government, including public schools, mass transit systems and municipal hospitals. In fact, Corrections Corporation got some of its venture capital from the Massey Burch Investment Group, which also backed HCA Hospital Corporation of America, the nation's largest for-profit operator of hospitals.

But for years, Corrections Corporation seemed to falter. It underestimated the political resistance to the concept of private prisons, and time needed to create a profitable business. Overreaching, it failed in an ambitious bid to persuade the Tennessee legislature to let the company run the entire state prison system in the mid-1980's. The company went public in 1986 with high hopes, but it did not report a yearly profit until 1989. It lost money again in 1991, recovering steadily thereafter.

Today, however, Mr. Crants sounds confident that Corrections Corporation has fine-tuned its private-prison formula. The company's biggest customers are the United States Marshals Service, which is responsible for Federal prisoners up to their sentencing, and the prison systems of Texas, Tennessee and Louisiana. If the door to private prisons should open nationally, Mr. Crants says, his company is ready to expand.

Perhaps, but Corrections Corporation's growth and profits depend on the company being able to run prisons less expensively than states or the Federal Government. In Texas, for example, where it runs four

prisons, the company's contract specifies that it manage prisons for 10 percent less than those of the state.

Corrections Corporation does own 9 of the 25 prisons it manages or is now building, but in each case the company constructed these smaller operations as a condition of its contract. In short, Corrections Corporation does not risk its money in the construction business. Its profit depends on managing its prisons so that its costs are less than the contracted "per diem" fee it receives for each prisoner. Every contract varies, but last year the company collected just under $40 a day on average for each prisoner.

How does Corrections Corporation cut costs? It pays the prevailing wage in the states where it operates, but its prisons are not unionized. The company offers its 2,300 employees a stock-option program, but it does not have a pension plan. According to union officials, pension costs can add up to 15 percent of compensation costs for public-sector prison workers.

The no-pensions approach saves some, but Corrections Corporation executives and wardens insist that the far larger gains come from changing the unhealthy environment found in so many prisons. Part of the formula is to keep potentially quarrelsome prisoners like Mr. Anderson at Metro-Davidson so busy with drug rehabilitation, recreational and educational programs that trouble will not tempt them. These prisoner programs add to costs at the outset, but company officials believe they more than pay for themselves, though the savings are hard to measure.

It is a truism that there are no perfect days in prison. Yet anything that makes prisoners less dissatisfied reduces the tension between the inmates and prison staff, making costly disturbances less likely. That means attention to detail and quality control in basic services like food and mail delivery to inmates, and communicating regularly with prisoners.

6. PUNISHMENT AND CORRECTIONS

"In this environment, little problems become big monsters real fast," said Jimmy Turner, warden of Metro-Davidson.

"In a state prison," Mr. Turner continued, "if a prisoner said, 'I'm going to tear this cell up if you don't talk to me.' Well, the attitude of the state employee was, 'Go ahead and tear it up. We'll repair that $1,000 commode, but you're not going to threaten us to talk to you.'"

Mr. Turner paused. "I can tell you right now, as a shareholder in this company, if an inmate wants to talk to me, he can talk to me."

In the prison environment, small changes can make a big difference. David Myers, who is now the company's president, was warden at Bay County Jail, a Panama City, Fla., operation taken over by Corrections Corporation in 1985 after a series of disturbances. Once there, Mr. Myers found that the prisoners' breakfast consisted of a hard-boiled egg and a stale piece of bread. He ordered the fare changed the next day to scrambled eggs and bacon. The new breakfast menu helped calm the inmates, and disturbances subsided.

The real day-to-day savings from easing the inmate-staff tension in prison life come from reducing labor costs, which represent up to two-thirds of the cost of running a prison. Though salaries vary widely state by state, corrections officers are not highly paid, with a typical salary estimated at $20,000 or less. But it is a high-stress job, with notoriously high levels of absenteeism, or "blue flu."

That adds to overtime costs, swelling the expense of running a prison. If, for example, one corrections officer calls in sick, he is still paid $10 an hour for his day. But his absence may well mean two other officers have to fill in, working eight hours of straight time and four hours each being paid at time and a half. The salary for those three that day becomes $360, or a 50 percent increase because one person called in sick.

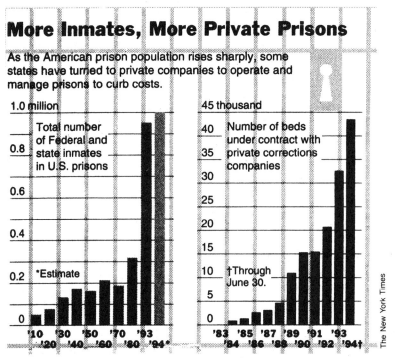

Sources: Corrections Corporation of America, Charles W. Thomas/University of Florida at Gainesville

Stress is hard to measure, but it also leads to costly staff turnover and can lead to prison-yard troubles.

"A better work environment means you are less likely to have tired, short-tempered, confrontational people who become violent," said Mr. Crants, the company chairman. "And I am talking about the guards."

And spending more at the outset might save money in the long run. For example, the company buys costly $40 chairs made from hard-to-destroy plastic. In a state-run prison, wardens might be required to buy cheaper wooden chairs or benches.

Cheaper might even be more dangerous. In Texas, prisoners would shatter wooden benches into four-foot-long planks with rusty nails.

The ideal situation for Corrections Corporation is when it can help design and build a prison from scratch as it did with Metro-Davidson, an $18 million, nearly 900-bed facility that opened in February 1992. The prison holds locally sentenced felons serving one to six years.

The prison employs a "wheel-and-spoke design," where one or two corrections officers in an electronic command post constantly monitor prison cells circled around the post. The arrangement reduces blind spots, company officials say.

"What you want to avoid is the telephone-pole design," said Robert Britton, vice-president for operations. "That's the long, traditional cell block you see in old Jimmy Cagney movies. You can't see. It isn't secure for guards or prisoners."

To keep inmates busy and to prepare them for life after prison, Metro-Davidson has an unusually large number of educational and rehabilitation programs for an operation in which the average stay is 12 months. Inmates not only can get a high-school equivalency degree, but also attend programs that teach marketable skills like computer data processing.

An especially innovative program, called Lifeline, is a six-month drug rehabilitation and psychological counseling program designed to bring brooding loners out of their self-destructive cycle of drug addiction and anger. The program, developed by Corrections Corporation, was not a requirement of the state contract.

Yet the company says there is room for improvement—and cost savings—at state prisons it takes over but had no hand in designing.

The Winn Correctional Center in Winn Parish, La., is an example. It is a classic Jimmy Cagney prison out in the middle of rural nowhere. When Corrections Corporation took over management of the 1,300-bed facility in 1990, it became the first privately operated medium-security prison in the United States.

Small things tell. At the commissary, where prisoners can buy personal items like candy bars, the store once opened onto a long corridor. A guard had to stand there and ob-serve the prisoners. By caging the commissary, a guard could now roam the corridor, enhancing security.

Perhaps the biggest innovation at Winn is the continuing experimentation with programs to try to give prisoners marketable skills. Besides the usual computer and "culinary arts" classes, Corrections Corporation is starting a 60-worker garment factory using standard single- and double-needled tailoring machines to make disposable hazardous waste suits. "These are real skills,' said Michael Phillips, assistant warden.

The prisoners show a qualified enthusiasm for the job training. Ricky Temple, 36, is serving a 40-year sen-tence at Winn for rape and forcible assault. Mr. Temple says he has already learned some things in prison, like "how to be a better burglar, a better bank robber." But, he added, "I want to have a legitimate skill when I get out."

Other inmates, however, are impressed by other advantages that they say the Corrections Corporation prison seems to offer.

"You don't have to sleep with one eye open here," said Jesse Howard, 37, who is serving a 30-year sentence for armed robbery. "You don't have to carry two or three knives with you because the guards are always looking at everybody."

Crime Takes On a Feminine Face

Chi Chi Sileo

Summary: Driven by economic need, self-defense or greed, more women are turning to crime, at a cost beyond the expense of incarceration. Often children are the losers. How should society handle female offenders? Some experts say the solution is in counseling and probation, not jail.

For more and more women, the legend "home sweet home" is being hung on the walls of a prison cell.

The increase in the rate at which women are going to prison has outpaced that of men. Since 1981, the number of men being put behind bars has gone up 112 percent; the number of women, 202 percent. This corresponds neatly with the upward trend in arrest rates; the rate of increase for women is now nearly double that for men.

What's behind these statistics? Are more women being drawn into a life of crime, or is the criminal justice system just getting more adept at catching and sentencing them?

"Both," says Rita Simon, a sociologist at American University in Washington and author of two books on women and crime. "Part of it is that just as women have more opportunities outside the home, they have more opportunities to fall into crime. And it's also true that in the past, judges tended to be more lenient with women, especially when they had children. But now justice is becoming more gender-blind."

The quasi-glamorous phrase "female criminal" conjures up the gun molls, femmes fatales and high-class madams beloved by tabloids and the movies. But the reality of women's criminality has far less to do with these captivating images and far more with the dreary exigencies of petty thievery, low-level drug dealing and small-time grifting. Women's growing presence in jails and prisons is being fueled by changing sentencing laws, a rise in white-collar crime and new legal tactics targeted at prosecuting women (in some cases, for nonexistent crimes).

In actual numbers, men still far outrank women in every type of crime, and even the wildest women don't indulge in the freewheeling activities that some male criminals do. FBI spokesman Kurt Crawford speculates that "there are maybe two" female serial killers at large (compared with estimates of as many as 500 males), and women are barely represented in crimes such as kidnapping, hostage-taking or terrorism. "These are just not female types of crimes," says Harvey Schlossberg, a former police officer and now the chief psychologist for the New York/ New Jersey Port Authority. "Women tend to be motivated by economic concerns, while men are motivated by power and control."

Nancy Hollander, a past president of the National Association of Criminal Defense Lawyers, agrees that economics are at the root of women's fall from legal grace. "Women are going to jail for writing bad checks to get out of abusive homes," she asserts.

That's true of certain crimes, according to Simon, but not all: "Look at white-collar criminals; these are not poor women or abused women.

When I tell radical feminists this, they get furious. They believe that women are inherently more moral, that they only steal to feed their children. Well, the data just don't bear that out."

In fact, white-collar crime is where women seem to be flocking. The primary increase in arrests of women is for property offenses: larceny, fraud, embezzlement and forgery. And it isn't happening only in the United States: Reports are surfacing in Europe of female white-collar criminals, and a few years ago the Egyptian newsweekly *October* reported with alarm a rise in "the feminization of fraud."

When women take the money and run, they do so with much smaller amounts (an average of $50,000 compared with the $150,000 average that men take). Ironically, the barriers that hold women back here are the same ones that stall them in more legitimate professions. But as more women enter top executive circles, many experts predict, more of them will develop both the skills and the opportunity to play for larger criminal stakes. "Just give them time," says Simon.

Women who commit white-collar crime almost always act alone, and in this way such crimes stand out from other women's crimes. When a woman breaks the law it is usually through a personal connection — specifically, involvement with a man.

"Most women who are brought in for drug offenses have gotten there through their connection to a man," says Helen Butler, public affairs specialist at the Federal Bureau of Prisons. "Often their criminal involve-

Reprinted with permission from *Insight*, December 20, 1993, pp. 16-19. © 1993 by the Washington Times Corporation. All rights reserved.

ment is very slight, so in the past judges would look more favorably on giving them things like probation." She adds that recent crime legislation which made drug dealing a federal offense and instituted mandatory minimum sentences has made sentencing stiffer all around, for both men and women. "Judges don't have any choice now. They have to hand down very tough sentences."

The war on drugs is packing prisons and jails with both male and female inmates. In Washington, D.C., for instance, 60 percent of the women held in jail are there for drug-related offenses; in the federal system the percentage is even higher. Most of these women are small-time, low-level accomplices who would have gotten probation or short sentences in the past.

According to Brenda Smith, director of the Women's Prison Project at the National Women's Law Center, women are highly vulnerable to involvement with drugs. "Women historically turn to crime to generate income. And drug dealing is a quick and easy way to do this. Also, because women are more low-level, they're more likely to get caught," says Smith, who has worked with imprisoned women for more than a decade.

In addition to accomplices in drug crimes and theft, there is also what Hollander calls "the most frightening group: women who are accomplices to men who abuse or kill other women or children." Stressing that these are a highly deviant minority of criminal women, Hollander differentiates them from women trapped in abusive relationships who end up abusing their children. In the latter situation, she says, "we have to be careful about assessing blame. . . . After all, these children had two parents. Where was the father? Also, it's possible that in these situations, the women are just so terrorized they can't think straight."

"I have a hard time accepting that," counters Schlossberg. He believes that women might abuse their children as a way of punishing their own abusers. "The child is his, too, and is an easier target. They may not be consciously aware that they're doing it, but at any rate, they still know right from wrong. They know they're harming that child."

Divorced or single mothers may become unwitting accomplices to abuse when they attempt to create a nuclear family. Studies have shown that stepfathers and boyfriends are more likely than natural fathers to abuse and neglect children living in their homes.

Family life in general doesn't seem to keep women out of the law's reach. Violent women rarely attack strangers, usually keeping their violent attacks close to home: Two-thirds of violent female offenders have attacked a family member, compared with 17 percent of violent male inmates. And while fewer than 6 percent of men serving time for homicide have killed a family member, more than 25 percent of women killers turned against what Justice Department statistics call "an intimate" — a lover, spouse, ex-spouse or pimp.

Those numbers have to be taken in context. According to even conservative estimates, about 40 percent of women who are charged with killing an intimate are women who found that deadly force was the only effective counteraction to long-term abuse. "Some of these women truly see no other option," says Smith of the Women's Law Center. "And in a purely technical sense, they are probably right. Think about it this way. A man can overpower a woman without killing her. He can beat her into submission and stop just short of killing her to make her stop doing something. A woman can't usually do that to a man. To stop him, she has to kill him."

Issues about spousal abuse and sticky legalistic questions of self-defense for battered wives are labyrinthine, but here certain facts bear consideration. The majority of women in prison report a history of physical or sexual abuse; almost all crime experts agree that learned violence begets later violence. And while it's true that battered women have more options now, and more awareness of those options, the fact remains that an abused woman's life is most in danger when she decides to leave the relationship.

According to Ann Jones, author of *Women Who Kill*, "There are cases on record of men still harassing and beating their wives twenty-five years after the wives left them and tried to go into hiding. If researchers were not quite so intent upon assigning the pathological behavior to the women, they might see that the more telling question is not 'Why do the women stay?' but 'Why don't the men let them go?' "

For women, if economic necessity, self-defense, punishing their abuser through their children or choosing to become an embezzler doesn't land them in jail, they might try this: getting pregnant.

A new trend in the war on drugs is accusing pregnant drug addicts of fetal abuse, a notion that is legally unclear. Pregnant women who are turned in by doctors when traces of drug use show up in tests are being hit with charges that range from illegal transport of narcotics (through the umbilical cord), child abuse and even assault with a deadly weapon.

"It's an abuse of prosecutorial power, plain and simple," says Lynn Paltrow, director of special litigation for the Center for Reproductive Law and Policy. "A complete misuse of criminal law. There is not one single state in which this law — fetal abuse — is even on the books." In fact, every challenge to these indictments in lower courts has been won, but the indictments keep coming anyway.

Minority women make up more than 70 percent of the 400 or more women charged with these offenses in cases currently before the courts. "These are the women most likely to use public health facilities instead of going to a private doctor who knows you personally," points out Smith. "If you're a middle-class white woman, your doctor would never even ask a question about drug abuse, certainly never administer a test for it."

Adds Paltrow, "These prosecutors claim that they just want the women to be forced into getting treatment. That's nonsense. There are no drug treatment programs for pregnant or parenting women with drug and alcohol problems."

The trend is particularly disturbing in light of new studies which indicate that while alcohol abuse during pregnancy is very dangerous, crack use actually inflicts limited damage on unborn children. And good prenatal care is universally acknowledged as the best way to ensure the birth of healthy children.

But, Paltrow says, "women are being scared away from both prenatal care and drug treatment because they don't want to be turned in. The fact is, if you care about the health of women or babies, you cannot adopt a punitive approach."

Poverty, drugs and physical abuse are the depressing trinity of women behind bars. The majority of them are mothers, and for many their real problems begin when they get out: finding a job and housing and reclaiming children in the care of relatives or foster parents.

Diana Hernandez, the director of counseling for the Fortune Society in

New York, an organization operated by former inmates that helps ex-offenders reintegrate into society, says these are the most difficult problems that many women face when they're released from prison: "Without a job, without a place to live, and a child or two depending on her, what is she supposed to do? Without help and support, chances are she's going to go back."

The impact on society goes beyond the costs of incarceration. The children, raised apart from their mothers and often in unstable conditions, are more likely to grow up with a host of problems—including a higher chance of becoming criminals themselves.

And, Hernandez says, some of the foster families who take care of these children get very attached to them; in some cases, women coming out of jail have lost their children as a result. "In either case, it's traumatic for mother, foster family and child," she says.

Women "getting out," like anyone with a criminal record, have an extremely difficult time finding employment and are more likely to return to crime or end up on welfare. Hernandez notes that just dealing with the bureaucratic red tape of life after imprisonment can be overwhelming.

"These are women whose behavior needs monitoring," Smith says. "But not to be locked up. I mean, they're not killers. What good does prison do them? If they weren't hardcore addicts or criminals when they went in, they sure will be when they get out." Smith, Hollander and other criminologists advocate probation and counseling in place of more-expensive jail terms. Because the majority of nonviolent female offenders (aside from white-collar crooks) do seem driven by economic need, such alternatives would probably be more sensible, they say.

Hollander, who has studied and worked with many child abuse cases, believes that imprisonment is a bad choice, particularly for family abusers — male or female. She cites one of her own cases, in which a year of intensive counseling was offered as an alternative for an abusive family. The family stayed together — without further violence.

"The more people we lock up," she says, "the fewer parents there are. Do we stop caring about 'the family' just because these people are poor and troubled? What's going to happen to those children without their parents? We're going to raise a generation of antisocial outcasts." Counseling does not work in every case, she concedes, but she believes it's worth a try.

"The real truth," Smith says, "is that you can't shut certain things out of your sight. You can't imprison away addiction or poverty or misery."

Psychiatric Gulag or Wise Safekeeping?

Lawmakers use civil commitment to detain sex predators.

Rorie Sherman

National Law Journal *Staff Reporter*

In Washington State, it's called the "Sexual Predator Law." In Minnesota, it's the "Psychopathic Personality Statute." Kansas and Wisconsin have their own versions. But in New Jersey, no matter what formal title the bill receives when enacted, as expected this fall, it will be known as "Megan's Law."

Jesse Timmendequas, previously convicted of sexually assaulting young girls, has admitted he raped, strangled and killed 7-year-old Megan Kanka, his neighbor in Hamilton Township, N.J. Before Mr. Timmendequas, 33, was released from prison in 1988, he told authorities he feared he would strike again. But because he had finished serving six years of his 10-year sentence, authorities say, they were forced to grant him parole.

Outrage at Megan's murder prompted New Jersey legislators to promise a package of legal reforms. A key provision—designed to keep the likes of Mr. Timmedequas off the streets for life—would add New Jersey to a list of at least four other states engaged in a legal experiment so fraught with constitutional questions that it is on appeal to the U.S. Supreme Court in a case from Minnesota. *In Re: Phillip Jay Blodgett, Alleged Psychopathic Personality,* 510 N.W.2d 910 (1994).

These laws target violent rapists and pedophiles who have served their sentences but are deemed by a parole board likely to commit further crimes if released. Under these laws, prosecutors can seek to have them transferred directly from prison to mental institutions, where the odds are they will remain involuntarily committed for the rest of their lives.

Legal observers agree that these measures shakily bridge the criminal justice and mental health systems. "We are pushing the envelope," says James A. Harkness, general counsel to the New Jersey Senate. Says Jim Haney, director of research and information for Wisconsin's attorney general, "It really is on the frontier."

Yet more states are expected to experiment with these laws. Unless appellate courts uniformly strike them down, the Supreme Court, even if it declines to hear *Blodgett,* eventually will have to decide their constitutionality.

The laws pit the public's safety against the liberty interests of individuals deemed likely to strike again. Among the legal objections: The statutes provide for an illegal form of preventive detention, create double jeopardy problems, violate constitutional equal protection and due process rights and operate as ex post facto laws. But two state supreme courts already have rejected these arguments.

CRITICS HORRIFIED

Civil libertarians condemn what they see as the use of the mental health system as a stopgap. According to John Q. La Fond, a professor of both mental health and criminal law at Seattle University School of Law, who has been fighting Washington's sexual predator statute, "We now have a system of lifetime preventive detention in place where we identify in advance who will re-offend and confine them . . . in a psychiatric gulag for what they might do."

Even some prosecutors criticize the civil commitment of dangerous criminals.

Linda Fairstein, chief of the Sex Crimes Prosecution Unit in the Manhattan district attorney's office, says she finds certain aspects of laws like Washington's "attractive" because "we seen an extraordinary amount of recidivist behavior with the stranger rapists and the pedophiles." She suggests that a better answer would be to give these people lengthy criminal sentences and make sure they serve their full term.

Meanwhile, mental health experts who doubt their colleagues' ability to predict dangerousness or cure sexual deviancy say the vast majority of these offenders are simply criminal—not mentally ill. They say only a small subset of sexual offenders actually suffer from an identifiable mental disorder and might benefit from treatment. But many psychiatrists say that they believe even this group can be handled within the criminal justice system, and that treatment must be voluntary to be effective.

HIGH RECIDIVISM

"There are issues of constitutional rights," acknowledges Paul J. Morrison, district attorney of Johnson County, Mo., encompassing Kansas City. "It is hard to make a good argument against doing everything we can to incapacitate violent sex offenders with a high risk of recidivism."

Gregory P. Canova, chief of the criminal division in the Washington attorney general's office, who pushed for the enactment of and helped implement the state's 1990 law, says he's been called for information on it by prosecutors across the United States, as well as from New Zealand and Canada.

Some of the laws have been on the books for years. During the 1960s, Minne-

From *The National Law Journal*, September 5, 1994, pp. A1, A24. © 1994 by the New York Law Publishing Company. Reprinted by permission.

sota prosecutors revived the use of a 1939 law known as the Psychopathic Personality Statute. In a unanimous 1940 opinion authored by then-Chief Justice Charles Evans Hughes, the U.S. Supreme Court found Minnesota's statute not to be unconstitutionally vague. Using a rational basis test, the court also rejected the claim that the statute violated the equal protection clause of the 14th Amendment. *State ex rel Pearson v. Probate Court of Ramsey County,* 287N.W. 297 (1939); 309 U.S. 270 (1940).

By 1959, a total of 26 states and the District of Columbia had sexual psychopath statutes. Half of them have since repealed these laws, however. In 1989, the American Bar Association Standards for Criminal Justice condemned the statutes and recommended that they be eliminated.

Such professional organizations as the Group for the Advancement of Psychiatry and the President's Commission on Mental Health agreed. The remaining states never followed suit, but they didn't apply the laws either. (Those states include New Jersey, Colorado, Connecticut, Illinois, Massachusetts, Minnesota, Nebraska, Oregon, Tennessee, Utah, Virginia, Washington and the District of Columbia.)

Minnesota seems to be alone in continuing to use its old psychopath law, say mental health law experts. And just this January, its supreme court found that the law as now applied does not violate substantive due process or the equal protection clauses of either the state or U.S. constitutions.

Writing for the majority, now-retired Minnesota Justice John E. Simonett summed up the central question posed by these laws: "Is it better for a person with an uncontrollable sex drive to be given an enhanced prison sentence or to be committed civilly?"

Justice Simonett says, "the safety of the public" must be balanced against "the liberty interests of the individual who acts destructively for reasons not fully understood by our medical, biological and social sciences." In the final analysis, he stated, "It is the moral credibility of the criminal justice system that is at stake. In the present imperfect state of scientific knowledge, where there are no definitive answers, it would seem a state legislature should be allowed, constitutionally, to choose either or both alternatives for dealing with the sexual predator. At the very least, we [will allow this] . . .

until the United States Supreme Court says otherwise."

U.S. SUPREME COURT

Unsurprisingly, the *Blodgett* plaintiffs have appealed to the U.S. Supreme Court and asked it to re-examine the Psychopathic Personality Statute using the strict scrutiny standard the high court has come to employ when a liberty interest is at stake. Among many arguments, the plaintiffs point to the high court's 1992 decision in *Foucha v. Louisiana,* 112 S. Ct. 1780. In that case, the justices struck down, as a violation of substantive due process, a Louisiana civil commitment statute that allowed the continued civil commitment of a man who was no longer mentally ill but might still be considered dangerous.

Minnesota Supreme Court Justice Esther M. Tomljanovich, dissenting in *Blodgett,* essentially agreed with the plaintiffs that *Foucha* invalidates the Minnesota statute. Under the Minnesota law, she said, a person "may be involuntarily committed, without the requirement of a finding that the person suffers from a medically diagnosable and treatable mental illness, to a confinement of indefinite duration until the person proves he is no longer dangerous to the public and no longer in need of inpatient treatment." That, added the judge, "in my view, violates the Due Process and Equal Protection Clauses of the Fourteenth Amendment of the United States Constitution."

Also, the dissenting Minnesota justices said, "The rigor and methodical efficiency with which the Psychopathic Personality Statute is presently being enforced is creating a system of wholesale preventive detention, a concept foreign to our jurisprudence."

Minnesota has 68 such criminals in state psychiatric care; one has been held for treatment since 1965.

CONFINED FOR THREE YEARS

On June 30, two decisions were handed down by the state supreme court ordering the release of two such "patients." Peter Rickmyer was released because the state high court found that the spanking and fondling of children for which he was convicted does not rise to the level of dangerousness envisioned by the statute. Mr. Rickmyer had been sentenced to 30 months in prison, which was reduced

to 21; he served six months and then was sent to a mental hospital, where he was confined for three years—a total of about 42 months' confinement.

Dennis D. Linehan was released because the state had failed to show clear and convincing evidence that he could not control his sexual impulses. Mr. Linehan was sentenced to 40 years for kidnapping; he served 14 years in prison and spent two years civilly committed.

Both men were freed from the hospital Aug. 9, according to their attorney, John E. Gryzbek, a St. Paul sole practitioner. *In re Matter of Peter Rickmyer,* C8-93-523; *In re Matter of Dennis D. Linehan,* C3-93-381. In the wake of these decisions, Minnesota lawmakers called a special legislative session for Aug. 31 to codify the court's standards.

NEW GENERATION OF LAWS

While the standard in Minnesota is "clear and convincing," a more stringent standard is being used in the new generation of sex offender civil commitment laws.

These are modeled on Washington's sexual predator law, whose civil commitment procedure is designed to emulate a criminal trial. The statute requires that the criminal justice evidentiary burden of "beyond a reasonable doubt" be met before sexual predators can be civilly committed. It also entitles respondents to appointed counsel, a trial before 12 jurors and a unanimous verdict.

Since July 1990, when Washington's law went into effect, an end-of-sentence review committee has examined the case of every sexual offender in the state who is about to be paroled.

Some 1,600 to 2,000 offenders have been reviewed, according to Mr. Canova. Of those, 130 criminals were referred to the attorney general's office or local prosecutors to consider filing for civil commitment. Eighteen cases are now pending and 17 criminals have been committed, says Mr. Canova, who notes that every respondent who has gone before a jury has been found to be a sexually violent predator.

Of course no one who is put before a jury under such circumstances will go free, says Seattle's Robert Boruchowitz, director of the King County Public Defender's Association and one of the fiercest opponents of sexual predator laws: "It's a kangaroo court. All a prosecutor has to do is stand up and list the

Psychiatrists Object to Predator Laws

The American Psychiatric Association is expected to take a strong stand against using the mental health system to continue the confinement of convicted sex offenders.

Responding to state legislatures' interest in locking convicted sex offenders in mental institutions and the role of psychiatrists in that effort, the APA has created a special task force to develop an official policy on such civil commitment. A preliminary report is due in September; a final statement should be ready by next year.

But already it's clear the APA will reject the wholesale use of civil commitment for convicted sex offenders. The only question is how strongly the APA will word its objections.

Psychiatrists today insist that most sex offenders are criminals—not mentally ill—and therefore belong in prisons, not mental institutions. Mental health experts say that there is no proven therapy for the subgroup that might be mentally ill, and that court orders confining sex offenders in mental institutions until they are rehabilitated are, in effect, life sentences.

Psychiatrists say stranger rapists—a group targeted by Statutes such as Washington's Sexual Predator Law—are not particularly characterized by mental disorder.

"A crime itself is not a syndrome," asserts Dr. Steven Kenny Hoge, chair of the APA Council on Psychiatry and the Law and an associate professor at the University of Virginia School of Law. To qualify as a mental illness, there must be a biological basis or, as with Post Traumatic Stress, a provable set of symptoms that occur with regularity.

Studies demonstrate that stranger rapists have the highest rate of recidivism; pedophiles are next, with incest offenders having the lowest. Among pedophiles, men who molest boys have a higher rate than those who molest girls.

Recidivism rates for all these categories of offenders generally stay below 50 percent with treatment but can run higher than 50 percent without, says Dr. Judith Becker, president of the Oregon-based Association for the Treatment of Sexual Abusers.

Preliminary results from ongoing studies suggest that the most effective form of treatment may be cognitive behavioral therapy conducted in a group setting. Anti-depressants and drugs that curtail the male sex drive also have had some success.

But, since therapeutic work with sex offenders is a relatively new and still developing field, says Prof. Peter Margulies of St. Thomas University School of Law in Miami, reliance on the mental health system is misplaced. "We are putting our faith in a system that can't possibly yet . . . make dangerous people non-dangerous," he says.

Rorie Sherman

---

guy's crimes, and the jury is frightened into putting him away forever."

Despite Mr. Boruchowitz's objections, Washington's sexual predator law recently survived a state constitutional challenge. In a 6–3 decision, the state supreme court in August 1993 ruled that the law was consistent with *Foucha* and passed muster on equal protection grounds. Additionally, the majority found the law did not, as plaintiffs alleged, constitute a form of ex post facto law or violate the double jeopardy prohibition because the court concluded the commitment process is a civil, not a second criminal, action. *In re Young,* 122 Wash. 2d 1.

A federal challenge to the constitutionality of the Washington law is pending. And on June 3, in yet another action, U.S. Judge William Dwyer of Seattle found that the state's current system of civil commitment for sexual predators fails to provide appropriate treatment. *Young v. Weston,* CN480C; *Turay v. Weston,* C91-994.

SPREADING LIKE WILDFIRE

Wisconsin's law went into effect June 2. Already there have been 16 petitions, with two state district court rulings declaring the law unconstitutional. *State v. Carpenter,* 94-CF-1216 (Dane Co.); *State v. Schmidt,* 94-CF-140 (Sauk Co.). The Kansas law went into effect in April, but the first screening of offenders won't occur until the end of August, according to Mr. Morrison, the Johnson County district attorney.

New Jersey's proposal introduced in reaction to Megan Kanka's death calls for increased penalties and mandatory minimum sentencing for violent sexual crimes, including a life sentence for a violent sexual attack on a child. Lawmakers also want lifetime supervision of those defined as "violent sexual predators" and mandatory life sentences if a second offense is committed while under lifetime supervision.

In addition, the bill requires an end-of-sentence review for every convicted sex offender and allows the attorney general to apply for the civil commitment of those who have demonstrated a pattern of compulsive behavior and pose a danger to others. The bill could be up for a vote on the Senate floor as early as Sept. 19.

Why would civil commitment procedures be needed in New Jersey if the state puts in place a system of lifetime mandatory sentences for habitual child molesters?

Because, state Senate counsel Mr. Harkness explains, civil commitment would allow prosecutors to go after those people already in the criminal system "who will max out [of their sentences] in the next couple of years . . . Obviously, we can't change the terms of their [criminal] sentences. And," he says, "it takes care of those who will slip through the cracks."

Manhattan Special Victims Bureau chief Ms. Fairstein says, "I just don't know how it's going to beat the constitutional challenge." But, she adds, "Good luck!"

'THIS MAN HAS EXPIRED'

WITNESS TO AN EXECUTION

ROBERT JOHNSON

ROBERT JOHNSON *is professor of justice, law, and society at The American University, Washington, D.C. This article is drawn from a Distinguished Faculty Lecture, given under the auspices of the university's senate last spring.*

The death penalty has made a comeback in recent years. In the late sixties and through most of the seventies, such a thing seemed impossible. There was a moratorium on executions in the U.S., backed by the authority of the Supreme Court. The hiatus lasted roughly a decade. Coming on the heels of a gradual but persistent decline in the use of the death penalty in the Western world, it appeared to some that executions would pass from the American scene [cf. *Commonweal*, January 15, 1988]. Nothing could have been further from the truth.

Beginning with the execution of Gary Gilmore in 1977, over 100 people have been put to death, most of them in the last few years. Some 2,200 prisoners are presently confined on death rows across the nation. The majority of these prisoners have lived under sentence of death for years, in some cases a decade or more, and are running out of legal appeals. It is fair to say that the death penalty is alive and well in America, and that executions will be with us for the foreseeable future.

Gilmore's execution marked the resurrection of the modern death penalty and was big news. It was commemorated in a best-selling tome by Norman Mailer, *The Executioner's Song*. The title was deceptive. Like others who have examined the death penalty, Mailer told us a great deal about the condemned but very little about the executioners. Indeed, if we dwell on Mailer's account, the executioner's story is not only unsung; it is distorted.

Gilmore's execution was quite atypical. His was an instance of state-assisted suicide accompanied by an element of romance and played out against a backdrop of media fanfare. Unrepentant and unafraid, Gilmore refused to appeal his conviction. He dared the state of Utah to take his life, and the media repeated the challenge until it became a taunt that may well have goaded officials to action. A failed suicide pact with his lover staged only days before the execution, using drugs she delivered to him in a visit marked by unusual intimacy, added a hint of melodrama to the proceedings. Gilmore's final words, "Let's do it," seemed to invite the lethal hail of bullets from the firing squad. The nonchalant phrase, at once fatalistic and brazenly rebellious, became Gilmore's epitaph. It clinched his outlaw-hero image, and found its way onto tee shirts that confirmed his celebrity status.

Befitting a celebrity, Gilmore was treated with unusual leniency by prison officials during his confinement on death row. He was, for example, allowed to hold a party the night before his execution, during which he was free to eat, drink, and make merry with his guests until the early morning hours. This is not entirely unprecedented. Notorious English convicts of centuries past would throw farewell balls in prison on the eve of their executions. News accounts of such affairs sometimes included a commentary on the richness of the table and the quality of the dancing. For the record, Gilmore served Tang, Kool-Aid, cookies, and coffee, later supplemented by contraband pizza and an unidentified liquor. Periodically, he gobbled drugs obligingly provided by the prison pharmacy. He played a modest arrangement of rock music albums but refrained from dancing.

Gilmore's execution generally, like his parting fete, was decidedly out of step with the tenor of the modern death penalty. Most condemned prisoners fight to save their lives, not to have them taken. They do not see their fate in romantic terms; there are no farewell parties. Nor are they given medication to ease their anxiety or win their compliance. The subjects of typical executions remain anonymous to the public and even to their keepers. They are very much alone at the end.

In contrast to Mailer's account, the focus of the research I have conducted is on the executioners themselves as they carry out typical executions. In my experience executioners—not

From *Commonweal*, January 13, 1989, pp. 9-15. © 1989 by Commonweal Foundation. Reprinted by permission.

unlike Mailer himself—can be quite voluble, and sometimes quite moving, in expressing themselves. I shall draw upon their words to describe the death work they carry out in our name.

DEATH WORK AND DEATH WORKERS

Executioners are not a popular subject of social research, let alone conversation at the dinner table or cocktail party. We simply don't give the subject much thought. When we think of executioners at all, the imagery runs to individual men of disreputable, or at least questionable, character who work stealthily behind the scenes to carry out their grim labors. We picture hooded men hiding in the shadow of the gallows, or anonymous figures lurking out of sight behind electric chairs, gas chambers, firing blinds, or, more recently, hospital gurneys. We wonder who would do such grisly work and how they sleep at night.

This image of the executioner as a sinister and often solitary character is today misleading. To be sure, a few states hire free-lance executioners and traffic in macabre theatrics. Executioners may be picked up under cover of darkness and some may still wear black hoods. But today, executions are generally the work of a highly disciplined and efficient team of correctional officers.

Broadly speaking, the execution process as it is now practiced starts with the prisoner's confinement on death row, an oppressive prison-within-a-prison where the condemned are housed, sometimes for years, awaiting execution. Death work gains momentum when an execution date draws near and the prisoner is moved to the death house, a short walk from the death chamber. Finally, the process culminates in the death watch, a twenty-four-hour period that ends when the prisoner has been executed.

This final period, the death watch, is generally undertaken by correctional officers who work as a team and report directly to the prison warden. The warden or his representative, in turn, must by law preside over the execution. In many states, it is a member of the death watch or execution team, acting under the warden's authority, who in fact plays the formal role of executioner. Though this officer may technically work alone, his teammates view the execution as a shared responsibility. As one officer on the death watch told me in no uncertain terms: "We all take part in it; we all play 100 percent in it, too. That takes the load off this one individual [who pulls the switch]." The formal executioner concurred. "Everyone on the team can do it, and nobody will tell you I did it. I know my team." I found nothing in my research to dispute these claims.

The officers of these death watch teams are our modern executioners. As part of a larger study of the death work process, I studied one such group. This team, comprised of nine seasoned officers of varying ranks, had carried out five electrocutions at the time I began my research. I interviewed each officer on the team after the fifth execution, then served as an official witness at a sixth electrocution. Later, I served as a behind-the-scenes observer during their seventh execution.

The results of this phase of my research form the substance of this essay.

THE DEATH WATCH TEAM

The death watch or execution team members refer to themselves, with evident pride, as simply "the team." This pride is shared by other correctional officials. The warden at the institution I was observing praised members of the team as solid citizens—in his words, country boys. These country boys, he assured me, could be counted on to do the job and do it well. As a fellow administrator put it, "an execution is something [that] needs to be done and good people, dedicated people who believe in the American system, should do it. And there's a certain amount of feeling, probably one to another, that they're part of that—that when they have to hang tough, they can do it, and they can do it right. And that it's just the right thing to do."

The official view is that an execution is a job that has to be done, and done right. The death penalty is, after all, the law of the land. In this context, the phrase "done right" means that an execution should be a proper, professional, dignified undertaking. In the words of a prison administrator, "We had to be sure that we did it properly, professionally, and [that] we gave as much dignity to the person as we possibly could in the process….If you've gotta do it, it might just as well be done the way it's supposed to be done—without any sensation."

In the language of the prison officials, "proper" refers to procedures that go off smoothly; "professional" means without personal feelings that intrude on the procedures in any way. The desire for executions that take place "without any sensation" no doubt refers to the absence of media sensationalism, particularly if there should be an embarrassing and undignified hitch in the procedures, for example, a prisoner who breaks down or becomes violent and must be forcibly placed in the electric chair as witnesses, some from the media, look on in horror. Still, I can't help but note that this may be a revealing slip of the tongue. For executions are indeed meant to go off without any human feeling, without any sensation. A profound absence of feeling would seem to capture the bureaucratic ideal embodied in the modern execution.

The view of executions held by the execution team members parallels that of correctional administrators but is somewhat more restrained. The officers of the team are closer to the killing and dying, and are less apt to wax abstract or eloquent in describing the process. Listen to one man's observations:

It's a job. I don't take it personally. You know, I don't take it like I'm having a grudge against this person and this person has done something to me. I'm just carrying out a job, doing what I was asked to do….This man has been sentenced to death in the courts. This is the law and he broke this law, and he has to suffer the consequences. And one of the consequences is to put him to death.

I found that few members of the execution team support the death penalty outright or without reservation. Having seen executions close up, many of them have lingering doubts about the justice or wisdom of this sanction. As one officer put it:

I'm not sure the death penalty is the right way. I don't know if there is a right answer. So I look at it like this: if it's gotta be done, at least it can be done in a humane way, if there is such a word for it. . . . The only way it should be done, I feel, is the way we do it. It's done professionally; it's not no horseplaying. Everything is done by documentation. On time. By the book.

Arranging executions that occur "without any sensation" and that go "by the book" is no mean task, but it is a task that is undertaken in earnest by the execution team. The tone of the enterprise is set by the team leader, a man who takes a hard-boiled, no-nonsense approach to correctional work in general and death work in particular. "My style," he says, "is this: if it's a job to do, get it done. Do it and that's it." He seeks out kindred spirits, men who see killing condemned prisoners as a job—a dirty job one does reluctantly, perhaps, but above all a job one carries out dispassionately and in the line of duty.

To make sure that line of duty is a straight and accurate one, the death watch team has been carefully drilled by the team leader in the mechanics of execution. The process has been broken down into simple, discrete tasks and practiced repeatedly. The team leader describes the division of labor in the following exchange:

the execution team is a nine-officer team and each one has certain things to do. When I would train you, maybe you'd buckle a belt, that might be all you'd have to do. . . . And you'd be expected to do one thing and that's all you'd be expected to do. And if everybody does what they were taught, or what they were trained to do, at the end the man would be put in the chair and everything would be complete. It's all come together now.

So it's broken down into very small steps. . . .

Very small, yes. Each person has *one* thing to do.

I see. What's the purpose of breaking it down into such small steps?

So people won't get confused. I've learned it's kind of a tense time. When you're executin' a person, killing a person—you call it killin', executin', whatever you want—the man dies anyway. I find the less you got on your mind, why, the better you'll carry it out. So it's just very simple things. And so far, you know, it's all come together, we haven't had any problems.

This division of labor allows each man on the execution team to become a specialist, a technician with a sense of pride in his work. Said one man,

My assignment is the leg piece. Right leg. I roll his pants leg up, place a piece [electrode] on his leg, strap his leg in. . . . I've got all the moves down pat. We train from different posts; I can do any of them. But that's my main post.

The implication is not that the officers are incapable of performing multiple or complex tasks, but simply that it is more efficient to focus each officer's efforts on one easy task.

An essential part of the training is practice. Practice is meant to produce a confident group, capable of fast and accurate performance under pressure. The rewards of practice are reaped in improved performance. Executions take place with increasing efficiency, and eventually occur with precision. "The first one was grisly," a team member confided to me. He explained that there was a certain amount of fumbling, which made the execution seem interminable. There were technical problems as well: The generator was set too high so the body was badly burned. But that is the past, the officer assured me. "The ones now, we know what we're doing. It's just like clockwork."

THE DEATH WATCH

The death-watch team is deployed during the last twenty-four hours before an execution. In the state under study, the death watch starts at 11 o'clock the night before the execution and ends at 11 o'clock the next night when the execution takes place. At least two officers would be with the prisoner at any given time during that period. Their objective is to keep the prisoner alive and "on schedule." That is, to move him through a series of critical and cumulatively demoralizing junctures that begin with his last meal and end with his last walk. When the time comes, they must deliver the prisoner up for execution as quickly and unobtrusively as possible.

Broadly speaking, the job of the death watch officer, as one man put it, "is to sit and keep the inmate calm for the last twenty-four hours—and get the man ready to go." Keeping a condemned prisoner calm means, in part, serving his immediate needs. It seems paradoxical to think of the death watch officers as providing services to the condemned, but the logistics of the job make service a central obligation of the officers. Here's how one officer made this point:

Well, you can't help but be involved with many of the things that he's involved with. Because if he wants to make a call to his family, well, you'll have to dial the number. And you keep records of whatever calls he makes. If he wants a cigarette, well he's not allowed to keep matches so you light it for him. You've got to pour his coffee, too. So you're aware what he's doing. It's not like you can just ignore him. You've gotta just be with him whether he wants it or not, and cater to his needs.

Officers cater to the condemned because contented inmates are easier to keep under control. To a man, the officers say this is so. But one can never trust even a contented, condemned prisoner.

The death-watch officers see condemned prisoners as men with explosive personalities. "You don't know what, what a man's gonna do," noted one officer. "He's liable to snap, he's liable to pass out. We watch him all the time to prevent him from committing suicide. You've got to be ready—he's liable to do anything." The prisoner is never out of at least one officer's sight. Thus surveillance is constant, and control, for all intents and purposes, is total.

Relations between the officers and their charges during the death watch can be quite intense. Watching and being watched are central to this enterprise, and these are always engaging activities, particularly when the stakes are life and death. These relations are, nevertheless, utterly impersonal; there are no grudges but neither is there compassion or fellow-feeling. Officers are civil but cool; they keep an emotional distance from the men they are about to kill. To do otherwise, they maintain, would make it harder to execute condemned prisoners. The attitude of the officers is that the prisoners arrive as strangers and are easier to kill if they stay that way.

During the last five or six hours, two specific team officers are assigned to guard the prisoner. Unlike their more taciturn and aloof colleagues on earlier shifts, these officers make a conscious effort to talk with the prisoner. In one officer's words, "We keep them right there and keep talking to them—about anything except the chair." The point of these conversations is not merely to pass time; it is to keep tabs on the prisoner's state of mind, and to steer him away from subjects that might depress, anger, or otherwise upset him. Sociability, in other words, quite explicitly serves as a source of social control. Relationships, such as they are, serve purely manipulative ends. This is impersonality at its worst, masquerading as concern for the strangers one hopes to execute with as little trouble as possible.

Generally speaking, as the execution moves closer, the mood becomes more somber and subdued. There is a last meal. Prisoners can order pretty much what they want, but most eat little or nothing at all. At this point, the prisoners may steadfastly maintain that their executions will be stayed. Such bravado is belied by their loss of appetite. "You can see them going down," said one officer. "Food is the last thing they got on their minds."

Next the prisoners must box their meager worldly goods. These are inventoried by the staff, recorded on a one-page checklist form, and marked for disposition to family or friends. Prisoners are visibly saddened, even moved to tears, by this procedure, which at once summarizes their lives and highlights the imminence of death. At this point, said one of the officers, "I really get into him; I watch him real close." The execution schedule, the officer pointed out, is "picking up momentum, and we don't want to lose control of the situation."

This momentum is not lost on the condemned prisoner. Critical milestones have been passed. The prisoner moves in a limbo existence devoid of food or possessions; he has seen the last of such things, unless he receives a stay of execution and rejoins the living. His identity is expropriated as well. The critical juncture in this regard is the shaving of the man's head (including facial hair) and right leg. Hair is shaved to facilitate the electrocution; it reduces physical resistance to electricity and minimizes singeing and burning. But the process has obvious psychological significance as well, adding greatly to the momentum of the execution.

The shaving procedure is quite public and intimidating. The condemned man is taken from his cell and seated in the middle of the tier. His hands and feet are cuffed, and he is dressed only in undershorts. The entire death watch team is assembled around him. They stay at a discrete distance, but it is obvious that they are there to maintain control should he resist in any way or make any untoward move. As a rule, the man is overwhelmed. As one officer told me in blunt terms, "Come eight o'clock, we've got a dead man. Eight o'clock is when we shave the man. We take his identity; it goes with the hair." This taking of identity is indeed a collective process—the team makes a forceful "we," the prisoner their helpless object. The staff is confident that the prisoner's capacity to resist is now compromised. What is left of the man erodes gradually and, according the officers, perceptibly over the remaining three hours before the execution.

After the prisoner has been shaved, he is then made to shower and don a fresh set of clothes for the execution. The clothes are unremarkable in appearance, except that velcro replaces buttons and zippers, to reduce the chance of burning the body. The main significance of the clothes is symbolic: they mark the prisoner as a man who is ready for execution. Now physically "prepped," to quote one team member, the prisoner is placed in an empty tomblike cell, the death cell. All that is left is the wait. During this fateful period, the prisoner is more like an object "without any sensation" than like a flesh-and-blood person on the threshold of death.

For condemned prisoners, like Gilmore, who come to accept and even to relish their impending deaths, a genuine calm seems to prevail. It is as if they can transcend the dehumanizing forces at work around them and go to their deaths in peace. For most condemned prisoners, however, numb resignation rather than peaceful acceptance is the norm. By the account of the death-watch officers, these more typical prisoners are beaten men. Listen to the officers' accounts:

A lot of 'em die in their minds before they go to that chair. I've never known of one or heard of one putting up a fight. . . . By the time they walk to the chair, they've completely faced it. Such a reality most people can't understand. Cause they don't fight it. They don't seem to have anything to say. It's just something like "Get it over with." They may be numb, sort of in a trance.
They go through stages. And, at this stage, they're real humble. Humblest bunch of people I ever seen. Most all of 'em is real, real weak. Most of the time you'd only need one or two people to carry out an execution, as weak and as humble as they are.

These men seem barely human and alive to their keepers. They wait meekly to be escorted to their deaths. The people who come for them are the warden and the remainder of the death watch team, flanked by high-ranking correctional officials. The warden reads the court order, known popularly as a death warrant. This is, as one officer said, "the real deal," and nobody misses its significance. The condemned prisoners then go to their deaths compliantly, captives of the inexorable, irresistible momentum of the situation. As one officer put it, "There's no struggle. . . . They just walk right on in there." So too, do the staff "just walk right on in there," following a routine they have come to know well. Both the condemned and the executioners, it would seem, find a relief of sorts in mindless mechanical conformity to the modern execution drill.

WITNESS TO AN EXECUTION

As the team and administrators prepare to commence the good fight, as they might say, another group, the official witnesses, are also preparing themselves for their role in the execution. Numbering between six and twelve for any given execution, the official witnesses are disinterested citizens in good standing drawn from a cross-section of the state's population. If you will, they are every good or decent person, called upon to represent the community and use their good offices to testify to the propriety of the execution. I served as an official witness at the execution of an inmate.

At eight in the evening, about the time the prisoner is shaved in preparation for the execution, the witnesses are assembled. Eleven in all, we included three newspaper and two television reporters, a state trooper, two police officers, a magistrate, a businessman, and myself. We were picked up in the parking lot behind the main office of the corrections department. There was nothing unusual or even memorable about any of this. Gothic touches were notable by their absence. It wasn't a dark and stormy night; no one emerged from the shadows to lead us to the prison gates.

Mundane considerations prevailed. The van sent for us was missing a few rows of seats so there wasn't enough room for all of us. Obliging prison officials volunteered their cars. Our rather ordinary cavalcade reached the prison but only after getting lost. Once within the prison's walls, we were sequestered for some two hours in a bare and almost shabby administrative conference room. A public information officer was assigned to accompany us and answer our questions. We grilled this official about the prisoner and the execution procedure he would undergo shortly, but little information was to be had. The man confessed ignorance on the most basic points. Disgruntled at this and increasingly anxious, we made small talk and drank coffee.

At 10:40 P.M., roughly two-and-a-half hours after we were assembled and only twenty minutes before the execution was scheduled to occur, the witnesses were taken to the basement of the prison's administrative building, frisked, then led down an alleyway that ran along the exterior of the building. We entered a neighboring cell block and were admitted to a vestibule adjoining the death chamber. Each of us signed a log, and was then led off to the witness area. To our left, around a corner some thirty feet away, the prisoner sat in the condemned cell. He couldn't see us, but I'm quite certain he could hear us. It occurred to me that our arrival was a fateful reminder for the prisoner. The next group would be led by the warden, and it would be coming for him.

We entered the witness area, a room within the death chamber, and took our seats. A picture window covering the front wall of the witness room offered a clear view of the electric chair, which was about twelve feet away from us and well illuminated. The chair, a large, high-back solid oak structure with imposing black straps, dominated the death chamber. Behind it, on the back wall, was an open panel full of coils and lights. Peeling paint hung from the ceiling and walls; water stains from persistent leaks were everywhere in evidence.

Two officers, one a hulking figure weighing some 400 pounds, stood alongside the electric chair. Each had his hands crossed at the lap and wore a forbidding, blank expression on his face. The witnesses gazed at them and the chair, most of us scribbling notes furiously. We did this, I suppose, as much to record the experience as to have a distraction from the growing tension. A correctional officer entered the witness room and announced that a trial run of the machinery would be undertaken. Seconds later, lights flashed on the control panel behind the chair indicating that the chair was in working order. A white curtain, opened for the test, separated the chair and the witness area. After the test, the curtain was drawn. More tests were performed behind the curtain. Afterwards, the curtain was reopened, and would be left open until the execution was over. Then it would be closed to allow the officers to remove the body.

A handful of high-level correctional officials were present in the death chamber, standing just outside the witness area. There were two regional administrators, the director of the Department of Corrections, and the prison warden. The prisoner's chaplain and lawyer were also present. Other than the chaplain's black religious garb, subdued grey pinstripes and bland correctional uniforms prevailed. All parties were quite solemn.

At 10:58 the prisoner entered the death chamber. He was, I knew from my research, a man with a checkered, tragic past. He had been grossly abused as a child, and went on to become grossly abusive of others. I was told he could not describe his life, from childhood on, without talking about confrontations in defense of a precarious sense of self—at home, in school, on the streets, in the prison yard. Belittled by life and choking with rage, he was hungry to be noticed. Paradoxically, he had found his moment in the spotlight, but it was a dim and unflattering light cast before a small and unappreciative audience. "He'd pose for cameras in the chair—for the attention," his counselor had told me earlier in the day. But the truth was that the prisoner wasn't smiling, and there were no cameras.

The prisoner walked quickly and silently toward the chair, an escort of officers in tow. His eyes were turned downward, his expression a bit glazed. Like many before him, the prisoner had threatened to stage a last stand. But that was lifetimes ago, on death row. In the death house, he joined the humble bunch and kept to the executioner's schedule. He appeared to have given up on life before he died in the chair.

En route to the chair, the prisoner stumbled slightly, as if the momentum of the event had overtaken him. Were he not held securely by two officers, one at each elbow, he might have fallen. Were the routine to be broken in this or indeed any other way, the officers believe, the prisoner might faint or panic or become violent, and have to be forcibly placed in the chair. Perhaps as a precaution, when the prisoner reached the chair he did not turn on his own but rather was turned, firmly but without malice, by the officers in his escort. These included the two men at his elbows, and four others who followed behind him. Once the prisoner was seated, again with help, the officers strapped him into the chair.

The execution team worked with machine precision. Like a disciplined swarm, they enveloped him. Arms, legs, stomach, chest, and head were secured in a matter of seconds. Electrodes were attached to the cap holding his head and to the strap holding his exposed right leg. A leather mask was placed over his face. The last officer mopped the prisoner's brow, then touched his hand in a gesture of farewell.

During the brief procession to the electric chair, the prisoner was attended by a chaplain. As the execution team worked feverishly to secure the condemned man's body, the chaplain, who appeared to be upset, leaned over him and placed his forehead in contact with the prisoner's, whispering urgently. The priest might have been praying, but I had the impression he was consoling the man, perhaps assuring him that a forgiving God awaited him in the next life. If he heard the chaplain, I doubt the man comprehended his message. He didn't seem comforted. Rather, he looked stricken and appeared to be in shock. Perhaps the priest's urgent ministrations betrayed his doubts that the prisoner could hold himself together. The chaplain then withdrew at the warden's request, allowing the officers to affix the death mask.

The strapped and masked figure sat before us, utterly alone, waiting to be killed. The cap and mask dominated his face. The cap was nothing more than a sponge encased in a leather shell with a metal piece at the top to accept an electrode. It looked decrepit and resembled a cheap, ill-fitting toupee. The mask, made entirely of leather, appeared soiled and worn. It had two parts. The bottom part covered the chin and mouth, the top the eyes and lower forehead. Only the nose was exposed. The effect of a rigidly restrained body, together with the bizarre cap and the protruding nose, was nothing short of grotesque. A faceless man breathed before us in a tragicomic trance, waiting for a blast of electricity that would extinguish his life. Endless seconds passed. His last act was to swallow, nervously, pathetically, with his Adam's apple bobbing. I was struck by that simple movement then, and can't forget it even now. It told me, as nothing else did, that in the prisoner's restrained body, behind that mask, lurked a fellow human being who, at some level, however primitive, knew or sensed himself to be moments from death.

The condemned man sat perfectly still for what seemed an eternity but was in fact no more than thirty seconds. Finally the electricity hit him. His body stiffened spasmodically, though only briefly. A thin swirl of smoke trailed away from his head and then dissipated quickly. The body remained taut, with the right foot raised slightly at the heel, seemingly frozen

there. A brief pause, then another minute of shock. When it was over, the body was flaccid and inert.

Three minutes passed while the officials let the body cool. (Immediately after the execution, I'm told, the body would be too hot to touch and would blister anyone who did.) All eyes were riveted to the chair; I felt trapped in my witness seat, at once transfixed and yet eager for release. I can't recall any clear thoughts from that moment. One of the death watch officers later volunteered that he shared this experience of staring blankly at the execution scene. Had the prisoner's mind been mercifully blank before the end? I hoped so.

An officer walked up to the body, opened the shirt at chest level, then continued on to get the physician from an adjoining room. The physician listened for a heartbeat. Hearing none, he turned to the warden and said, "This man has expired." The warden, speaking to the director, solemnly intoned: "Mr. Director, the court order has been fulfilled." The curtain was then drawn and the witnesses filed out.

THE MORNING AFTER

As the team prepared the body for the morgue, the witnesses were led to the front door of the prison. On the way, we passed a number of cell blocks. We could hear the normal sounds of prison life, including the occasional catcall and lewd comment hurled at uninvited guests like ourselves. But no trouble came in the wake of the execution. Small protests were going on outside the walls, we were told, but we could not hear them. Soon the media would be gone; the protestors would disperse and head for their homes. The prisoners, already home, had been indifferent to the proceedings, as they always are unless the condemned prisoner had been a figure of some consequence in the convict community. Then there might be tension and maybe even a modest disturbance on a prison tier or two. But few convict luminaries are executed, and the dead man had not been one of them. Our escort officer offered a sad tribute to the prisoner: "The inmates, they didn't care about this guy."

I couldn't help but think they weren't alone in this. The executioners went home and set about their lives. Having taken life, they would savor a bit of life themselves. They showered, ate, made love, slept, then took a day or two off. For some, the prisoner's image would linger for that night. The men who strapped him in remembered what it was like to touch him; they showered as soon as they got home to wash off the feel and smell of death. One official sat up picturing how the prisoner looked at the end. (I had a few drinks myself that night with that same image for company.) There was some talk about delayed reactions to the stress of carrying out executions. Though such concerns seemed remote that evening, I learned later that problems would surface for some of the officers. But no one on the team, then or later, was haunted by the executed man's memory, nor would anyone grieve for him. "When I go home after one of these things," said one man. "I sleep like a rock." His may or may not be the sleep of the just, but one can only marvel at such a thing, and perhaps envy such a man.

CRIME CLOCK
1993

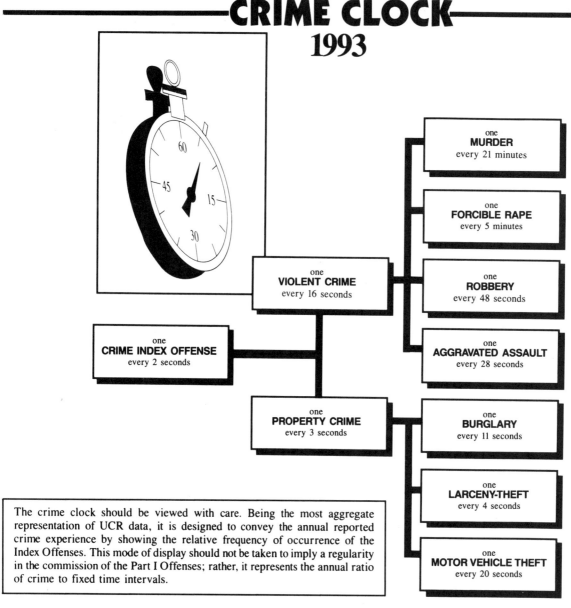

one
MURDER
every 21 minutes

one
FORCIBLE RAPE
every 5 minutes

one
VIOLENT CRIME
every 16 seconds

one
ROBBERY
every 48 seconds

one
CRIME INDEX OFFENSE
every 2 seconds

one
AGGRAVATED ASSAULT
every 28 seconds

one
PROPERTY CRIME
every 3 seconds

one
BURGLARY
every 11 seconds

one
LARCENY-THEFT
every 4 seconds

one
MOTOR VEHICLE THEFT
every 20 seconds

The crime clock should be viewed with care. Being the most aggregate representation of UCR data, it is designed to convey the annual reported crime experience by showing the relative frequency of occurrence of the Index Offenses. This mode of display should not be taken to imply a regularity in the commission of the Part I Offenses; rather, it represents the annual ratio of crime to fixed time intervals.

Crime in the United States 1993

Crime Index Total

The Crime Index total dropped 2 percent to 14.1 million offenses in 1993, the second consecutive year of decline. In the rural and the suburban counties, the Index was also down 2 percent from 1992, while the cities collectively registered a 3-percent decrease. This downward trend was evident in all city population groups, with those having a million or more inhabitants showing the largest decrease, 5 percent. Five- and 10-year percent changes showed the 1993 national experience was 1 percent lower than the 1989 level but 19 percent higher than the 1984 total.

Geographically, the largest volume of Crime Index offenses was reported in the most populous Southern States, which accounted for 38 percent of the total. Following were the Western States with 25 percent, the Mid-western States with 21 percent, and the Northeastern States with 17 percent. The regions showed Crime Index decreases ranging from 1 to 4 percent during 1993 as compared to 1992.

As in previous years, Crime Index offenses occurred most frequently in August and least often in February.

Rate

Crime rates relate the incidence of crime to population. In 1993, there were an estimated 5,483 Crime Index offenses for each 100,000 in United States population. The Crime Index rate was highest in the Nation's metropolitan areas and lowest in the rural counties. The national 1993 Crime Index rate fell 3 percent from 1992 and 4 percent from the 1989 level. It was 9 percent above the 1984 rate.

Regionally, the Crime Index rates ranged from 6,220 in

Table 1. – Index of Crime, United States, 1974-1993

Population[1]	Crime Index total[2]	Modified Crime Index total[3]	Violent crime[4]	Property crime[4]	Murder and non-negligent man-slaughter	Forcible rape	Robbery	Aggravated assault	Burglary	Larceny-theft	Motor vehicle theft	Arson[3]
					Number of Offenses							
Population by year:												
1984-236,158,000	11,881,800		1,273,280	10,608,500	18,690	84,230	485,010	685,350	2,984,400	6,591,900	1,032,200	
1985-238,740,000	12,431,400		1,328,800	11,102,600	18,980	88,670	497,870	723,250	3,073,300	6,926,400	1,102,900	
1986-241,077,000	13,211,900		1,489,170	11,722,700	20,610	91,460	542,780	834,320	3,241,400	7,257,200	1,224,100	
1987-243,400,000	13,508,700		1,484,000	12,024,700	20,100	91,110	517,700	855,090	3,236,200	7,499,900	1,288,700	
1988-245,807,000	13,923,100		1,566,220	12,356,900	20,680	92,490	542,970	910,090	3,218,100	7,705,900	1,432,900	
1989-248,239,000	14,251,400		1,646,040	12,605,400	21,500	94,500	578,330	951,710	3,168,200	7,872,400	1,564,800	
1990-248,709,873	14,475,600		1,820,130	12,655,500	23,440	102,560	639,270	1,054,860	3,073,900	7,945,700	1,635,900	
1991-252,177,000	14,872,900		1,911,770	12,961,100	24,700	106,590	687,730	1,092,740	3,157,200	8,142,200	1,661,700	
1992-255,082,000	14,438,200		1,932,270	12,505,900	23,760	109,060	672,480	1,126,970	2,979,900	7,915,200	1,610,800	
1993-257,908,000	14,141,000		1,924,190	12,216,800	24,530	104,810	659,760	1,135,100	2,834,800	7,820,900	1,561,000	
Percent change: number of offenses:												
1993/1992	-2.1		-.4	-2.3	+3.2	-3.9	-1.9	+.7	-4.9	-1.2	-3.1	
1993/1989	-.8		+16.9	-3.1	+14.1	+10.9	+14.1	+19.3	-10.5	-.7	-.2	
1993/1984	+19.0		+51.1	+15.2	+31.2	+24.4	+36.0	+65.6	-5.0	+18.6	+51.2	
					Rate per 100,000 Inhabitants							
Year:												
1984	5,031.3		539.2	4,492.1	7.9	35.7	205.4	290.2	1,263.7	2,791.3	437.1	
1985	5,207.1		556.6	4,650.5	7.9	37.1	208.5	302.9	1,287.3	2,901.2	462.0	
1986	5,480.4		617.7	4,862.6	8.6	37.9	225.1	346.1	1,344.6	3,010.3	507.8	
1987	5,550.0		609.7	4,940.3	8.3	37.4	212.7	351.3	1,329.6	3,081.3	529.4	
1988	5,664.2		637.2	5,027.1	8.4	37.6	220.9	370.2	1,309.2	3,134.9	582.9	
1989	5,741.0		663.1	5,077.9	8.7	38.1	233.0	383.4	1,276.3	3,171.3	630.4	
1990	5,820.3		731.8	5,088.5	9.4	41.2	257.0	424.1	1,235.9	3,194.8	657.8	
1991	5,897.8		758.1	5,139.7	9.8	42.3	272.7	433.3	1,252.0	3,228.8	659.0	
1992	5,660.2		757.5	4,902.7	9.3	42.8	263.6	441.8	1,168.2	3,103.0	631.5	
1993	5,482.9		746.1	4,736.9	9.5	40.6	255.8	440.1	1,099.2	3,032.4	605.3	
Percent change: rate per 100,000 inhabitants:												
1993/1992	-3.1		-1.5	-3.4	+2.2	-5.1	-3.0	-.4	-5.9	-2.3	-4.1	
1993/1989	-4.5		+12.5	-6.7	+9.2	+6.6	+9.8	+14.8	-13.9	-4.4	-4.0	
1993/1984	+9.0		+38.4	+5.4	+20.3	+13.7	+24.5	+51.7	-13.0	+8.6	+38.5	

[1]Populations are Bureau of the Census provisional estimates as of July 1, except 1980 and 1990 which are the decennial census counts.

[2]Because of rounding, the offenses may not add to totals.

[3]Although arson data are included in the trend and clearance tables, sufficient data are not available to estimate totals for this offense.

[4]Violent crimes are offenses of murder, forcible rape, robbery, and aggravated assault. Property crimes are offenses of burglary, larceny – theft, and motor vehicle theft. Data are not included for the property crime of arson.

Complete data for 1993 were not available for the states of Illinois and Kansas; therefore, it was necessary that their crime counts be estimated.

All rates were calculated on the offenses before rounding.

the West to 4,613 in the Northeast. The 2-year percent changes (1993 versus 1992) showed declines in all regions.

Nature

The Crime Index is composed of violent and property crime categories, and in 1993, 14 percent of the Index offenses reported to law enforcement were violent crimes and 86 percent, property crimes. Larceny-theft was the offense with the highest volume, while murder accounted for the fewest offenses.

Property estimated in value at $15.3 billion was stolen in connection with all Crime Index offenses, with the largest losses due to theft of motor vehicles; jewelry and precious metals; and televisions, radios, stereos, etc. Law enforcement agencies nationwide recorded a 34-percent recovery rate for dollar losses in connection with stolen property. The highest recovery percentages were for stolen motor vehicles, consumable goods, livestock, clothing and furs, and firearms.

Law Enforcement Response

Law enforcement agencies nationwide recorded a 21-percent clearance rate for the collective Crime Index offenses in 1993 and made an estimated 2.8 million arrests for Index crimes. Crimes can be cleared by arrest or by exceptional means when some element beyond law enforcement control precludes the placing of formal charges against the offender. The arrest of one person may clear several crimes, or several persons may be arrested in connection with the clearance of one offense.

The Index clearance rate has remained relatively stable throughout the past 10-year period. As in 1993, the clearance rates in both 1989 and 1984 were 21 percent.

Arrests for Index crimes dropped 2 percent in 1993 when compared to 1992. Adult arrests for Index crimes were down 3 percent, and those of juveniles declined 1 percent. Arrests of males decreased 3 percent for the 2-year period, while those of females increased less than 1 percent.

Considering the individual offenses composing the Index,

CRIME INDEX OFFENSES REPORTED

only murder and aggravated assault showed increases in arrest totals from 1992 to 1993. Decreases for the remaining Index offenses ranged from 1 percent for robbery and arson to 5 percent for burglary.

As in past years, larceny-theft arrests accounted for the highest volume of Crime Index arrests at 1.5 million.

MURDER AND NONNEGLIGENT MANSLAUGHTER

DEFINITION
Murder and nonnegligent manslaughter, as defined in the Uniform Crime Reporting Program, is the willful (non-negligent) killing of one human being by another.

TREND

Year	Number of offenses	Rate per 100,000 inhabitants
1992	23,760	9.3
1993	24,526	9.5
Percent change	+3.2	+2.2

Volume

The total number of murders in the United States during 1993 was estimated at 24,526. Monthly figures show that more persons were murdered in the month of December in 1993, while the fewest were killed in February.

Murder by Month, 1989-1993
[Percent distribution]

Months	1989	1990	1991	1992	1993
January	8.1	7.9	8.0	8.1	8.1
February	7.1	7.0	7.0	7.5	6.7
March	7.8	8.0	7.7	8.2	7.9
April....................	7.9	7.4	7.8	8.0	7.6
May	7.8	8.1	8.1	8.5	7.8
June	8.2	8.4	8.6	7.9	8.6
July.....................	9.1	9.6	9.1	9.1	9.3
August...................	9.0	9.3	9.4	9.1	9.2
September................	8.8	9.2	8.8	8.7	8.3
October..................	8.9	8.8	8.6	8.0	8.4
November	8.5	7.6	7.8	8.1	8.2
December	8.7	8.8	9.0	8.8	9.8

When viewing the regions of the Nation, the Southern States, the most populous region, accounted for 41 percent of the murders. The Western States reported 23 percent; the Midwestern States, 19 percent; and the Northeastern States, 17 percent. Among the regions, the Northeast experienced a 5-percent increase; the South and West each recorded 4-percent increases; and the Midwest registered a less than 1-percent increase.

The murder volume was up 3 percent nationwide in 1993 over 1992. In the Nation's cities overall, murder increased 4 percent, with the greatest increase—10 percent—registered in cities with populations of 100,000 to 249,999. The greatest decrease—6 percent—was recorded in cities with populations of 10,000 to 24,999. The suburban counties recorded a 2-percent rise in the murder volume and the rural counties, a 3-percent increase for the 2-year period.

A 14-percent rise nationally in the murder counts from 1989 to 1993. The 10-year trend showed the 1993 total 31 percent above the 1984 level.

Rate

Up 2 percent over the 1992 rate, the national murder rate in 1993 was 10 per 100,000 inhabitants. Five- and 10-year trends showed the 1993 rate was 9 percent higher than in 1989 and 20 percent above the 1984 rate.

On a regional basis, the South averaged 11 murders per 100,000 people; the West, 10 per 100,000; and the Midwest and Northeast, 8 per 100,000. Compared to 1992, murder rates in 1993 increased in three of the four geographic regions. The Midwest experienced no change.

The Nation's metropolitan areas reported a 1993 murder rate of 11 victims per 100,000 inhabitants. In the rural counties and in cities outside metropolitan areas, the rate was 5 per 100,000.

Nature

Supplemental data provided by contributing agencies recorded information for 23,271 of the estimated 24,526 murders in 1993. Submitted monthly, the data consist of the age, sex, and race of both victims and offenders; the types of weapons used; the relationships of victims to the offenders; and the circumstances surrounding the murders.

Based on this information, 77 percent of the murder victims in 1993 were males; and 87 percent were persons 18 years of age or older. Forty-eight percent were aged 20 through 34 years. Considering victims for whom race was known, an average of 51 of every 100 were black, 46 were white, and the remainder were persons of other races.

Murder Victims by Race and Sex, 1993

Race of Victims	Sex of Victims			
	Total	Male	Female	Unknown
Total White Victims	10,709	7,764	2,945	....
Total Black Victims	11,795	9,642	2,151	2
Total Other Race Victims ...	563	417	146	....
Total Unknown Race	204	126	36	42
Total Victims[1]	23,271	17,949	5,278	44

[1]Total murder victims for whom supplemental data were received.

FORCIBLE RAPE

DEFINITION

Forcible rape, as defined in the Program, is the carnal knowledge of a female forcibly and against her will. Assaults or attempts to commit rape by force or threat of force are also included; however, statutory rape (without force) and other sex offenses are excluded.

TREND

Year	Number of offenses	Rate per 100,000 inhabitants
1992	109,062	42.8
1993	104,806	40.6
Percent change	−3.9	−5.1

Volume

The estimated 104,806 forcible rapes reported to law enforcement agencies across the Nation during 1993 was down 4 percent from the 1992 volume. The 1993 total showed the first decline in forcible rape since 1987 and was the lowest since 1990.

Geographically, 39 percent of the forcible rape total in 1993 was accounted for by the most populous Southern States, 25 percent by the Midwestern States, 23 percent by the Western States, and 14 percent by the Northeastern States. Two-year trends showed that all regions experienced declines ranging from 1 percent in the South to 7 percent in the Midwest and West.

Monthly totals show the greatest numbers of forcible rapes were reported during the summer months.

Forcible Rape by Month, 1989-1993
[Percent distribution]

Months	1989	1990	1991	1992	1993
January	7.4	7.6	7.1	7.0	7.7
February	6.3	6.7	7.0	7.6	6.9
March	7.7	7.9	7.9	8.6	8.5
April	8.3	8.1	8.3	8.5	8.2
May	8.6	9.1	9.2	8.9	8.9
June	8.9	9.0	9.2	8.7	9.2
July	10.0	9.6	9.5	9.4	9.7
August	9.5	9.4	9.7	9.6	9.3
September	8.8	9.1	8.8	8.7	8.3
October	8.9	8.4	8.6	8.4	8.1
November	8.3	7.7	7.8	7.6	7.5
December	7.3	7.4	6.8	7.0	7.7

Rate

By Uniform Crime Reporting definition, the victims of forcible rape are always female. In 1993, an estimated 79 of every 100,000 females in the country were reported rape victims, a rate decrease of 6 percent from 1992. The 1993 female forcible rape rate was, however, 5 percent higher than the 1989 rate.

In 1993, there were 84 victims per 100,000 females in MSAs, 76 per 100,000 females in cities outside metropolitan areas, and 49 per 100,000 females in rural counties. Although MSAs record the highest rape rates, they have shown the smallest change over the past 10 years. During

this time, the greatest rate increase was shown in cities outside metropolitan areas, 90 percent. Rural counties recorded a 44-percent rate rise, while MSAs showed a lesser increase, 6 percent.

Regionally, in 1993, the highest female rape rate was in the Southern States, which recorded 88 victims per 100,000 females. Following were the Western States with a rate of 84, the Midwestern States with 83, and the Northeastern States with 55. Over the last 10 years, regional increases in the female forcible rape rate were 30 percent in the Midwest, 21 percent in the South, and 4 percent in the Northeast. A 3-percent decrease was reported in the West. All regions showed declines, 1992 versus 1993.

Nature

Rapes by force constitute the greatest percentage of total forcible rapes, 87 percent of the 1993 experience. The remainder were attempts or assaults to commit forcible rape. The number of rapes by force decreased 3 percent in 1993 from the 1992 volume, while attempts to rape decreased 12 percent.

As for all other Crime Index offenses, complaints of forcible rape made to law enforcement agencies are sometimes found to be false or baseless. In such cases, law enforcement agencies "unfound" the offenses and exclude them from crime counts. The "unfounded" rate, or percentage of complaints determined through investigation to be false, is higher for forcible rape than for any other Index crime. In 1993, 8 percent of forcible rape complaints were "unfounded," while the average for all Index crimes was 2 percent.

Law Enforcement Response

Nationwide, as well as in the cities, over half of the forcible rapes reported to law enforcement were cleared by arrest or exceptional means in 1993. Rural and suburban county law enforcement agencies cleared a slightly higher percentage of the offenses brought to their attention than did city law enforcement agencies.

Geographically, clearance rates for the regions were lowest in the Western States and highest in the Southern States.

Of the total clearances for forcible rape in the country as a whole, 14 percent involved only persons under 18 years of age. The percentage of juvenile involvement varied by community type, ranging from 13 percent in the Nation's cities to 20 percent in suburban counties.

Law enforcement agencies made an estimated 38,420 arrests for forcible rape in 1993. Of the forcible rape arrestees, about 3 of every 10 were in the 18- to 24-year age group. Over half of those arrested were white.

The number of arrests for forcible rape fell 2 percent nationwide from 1992 to 1993. A decrease of 4 percent was experienced in the Nation's cities, and a 1-percent decline was recorded in the suburban counties. Forcible rape arrests were up 10 percent in the rural counties for the 2-year period.

ROBBERY

DEFINITION

Robbery is the taking or attempting to take anything of value from the care, custody, or control of a person or persons by force or threat of force or violence and/or by putting the victim in fear.

TREND

Year	Number of offenses	Rate per 100,000 inhabitants
1992	672,478	263.6
1993	659,757	255.8
Percent change	−1.9	−3.0

Volume

Reported robberies in 1993 were estimated at 659,757 offenses, accounting for 5 percent of all Index crimes and 34 percent of the violent crimes. During the year, robberies occurred most frequently in December and least often in February.

Robbery by Month, 1989-1993
[Percent distribution]

Months	1989	1990	1991	1992	1993
January	8.8	8.7	8.7	9.0	8.8
February	7.4	7.3	7.5	8.0	7.1
March	8.0	8.1	8.0	8.1	8.3
April	7.3	7.2	7.4	7.8	7.4
May	7.6	7.7	7.8	7.9	7.5
June	7.6	7.8	7.8	7.9	8.1
July	8.4	8.5	8.4	8.4	8.7
August	8.6	8.8	8.8	8.6	8.8
September	8.6	8.6	8.5	8.3	8.4
October	9.2	8.9	9.2	8.7	9.0
November	9,0	8.7	8.7	8.3	8.5
December	9.3	9.6	9.2	9.0	9.4

Compared to 1992 levels, the 1993 robbery volume decreased 2 percent nationally, in the Nation's cities, and in the suburban counties. It declined 1 percent in the rural counties. This downward trend was also evident in most city population groups. The largest decline − 4 percent − was experienced in cities with a million or more inhabitants.

Distribution figures for the regions showed that the most populous region, the Southern States, accounted for 32 percent of all reported robberies. Two-year trends show the number of robberies in 1993 was down in all regions as compared to 1992. The declines were 4 percent in the Northeast, 2 percent in the West, and 1 percent in the Midwest and South.

In 1993, the number of robbery offenses was 14 percent higher than in 1989 and 36 percent above the 1984 total.

Rate

The national robbery rate in 1993 was 256 per 100,000 people, 3 percent lower than in 1992. In metropolitan areas, the 1993 rate was 312; in cities outside metropolitan areas, it

was 71; and in the rural areas, it was 16. With 955 robberies per 100,000 inhabitants, the highest rate was recorded in cities with a million inhabitants. A comparison of 1992 and 1993 regional robbery rates per 100,000 inhabitants showed the Northeastern and Western States' rates of 323 and 283, respectively, down 4 percent; and the rates of 204 in the Midwest and 236 in the South each down 2 percent.

Nature

In 1993, a total estimated national loss of $538 million was attributed to robberies. The value of property stolen during robberies averaged $815 per incident, down from $840 in 1992. Average dollar losses in 1993 ranged from $449 taken during robberies of convenience stores to $3,308 per bank robbery. The impact of this violent crime on its victims cannot be measured in terms of monetary loss alone. While the object of a robbery is to obtain money or property, the crime always involves force or threat of force, and many victims suffer serious personal injury.

As in previous years, robberies on streets or highways accounted for more than half (55 percent) of the offenses in this category. Robberies of commercial and financial establishments accounted for an additional 22 percent, and those occurring at residences, 10 percent. The remainder were miscellaneous types. A comparison of 1992 and 1993 robbery totals by type showed robberies of convenience stores were down 8 percent; gas or service station robberies dropped 6 percent; and street/highway robberies declined 2 percent. Increases of 2 percent or less were recorded for the other categories.

Robbery, Percent Distribution, 1993
[By region]

	United States Total	North-eastern States	Mid-western States	Southern States	Western States
Total[1]	100.0	100.0	100.0	100.0	100.0
Street/highway	54.7	61.2	61.2	50.1	50.8
Commercial house	12.5	10.0	10.3	12.7	15.7
Gas or service station	2.3	2.0	2.9	2.3	2.5
Convenience store	5.3	2.4	4.2	7.7	5.6
Residence	10.3	10.2	8.9	12.6	8.0
Bank	1.8	1.4	1.2	1.4	2.9
Miscellaneous	13.1	12.7	11.3	13.1	14.5

[1]Because of rounding, percentages may not add to totals.

AGGRAVATED ASSAULT

DEFINITION

Aggravated assault is an unlawful attack by one person upon another for the purpose of inflicting severe or aggravated bodily injury. This type of assault is usually accompanied by the use of a weapon or by means likely to produce death or great bodily harm.

<table>
<tr><td colspan="3" align="center">— TREND —</td></tr>
</table>

Year	Number of offenses	Rate per 100,000 inhabitants
1992	1,126,974	441.8
1993	1,135,099	440.1
Percent change	+.7	−.4

Volume

Totaling an estimated 1,135,099 offenses nationally, aggravated assaults in 1993 accounted for 59 percent of the violent crimes. Geographic distribution figures show that 40 percent of the aggravated assault volume was accounted for by the most populous Southern Region. Following were the Western Region with 25 percent, the Midwestern Region with 19 percent, and the Northeastern Region with 16 percent. Among the regions, only the Northeast registered a decline in the number of reported aggravated assaults.

The 1993 monthly figures show that the greatest number of aggravated assaults was recorded during July, while the lowest volume occurred during February.

Aggravated Assault by Month, 1989-1993
[Percent distribution]

Months	1989	1990	1991	1992	1993
January	7.5	7.4	6.9	7.3	7.5
February	6.6	6.7	6.6	7.3	6.5
March	7.9	7.8	7.7	8.0	8.1
April	8.1	8.2	8.1	8.7	8.3
May	8.9	9.0	9.1	9.2	8.9
June	8.9	9.4	9.3	8.9	9.1
July	9.6	10.1	9.7	9.4	9.6
August	9.2	9.3	9.9	9.1	9.2
September	8.8	8.9	9.0	8.6	8.3
October	9.1	8.3	8.6	8.5	8.5
November	7.9	7.4	7.6	7.6	7.4
December	7.5	7.5	7.6	7.4	8.6

In 1993, aggravated assaults were up 1 percent nationwide as compared to 1992. For the same time period, cities collectively experienced an increase of less than 1 percent in the aggravated assault volume. Percent changes among the city population groupings ranged from 4-percent increases in cities with 100,000 to 249,999 inhabitants and in those with 500,000 to 999,999 to a 2-percent decline in cities with 1,000,000 or more inhabitants. The suburban counties registered a 1-percent increase and the rural counties, a 2-percent rise for the 2-year period.

Five- and 10-year trends for the country as a whole showed aggravated assaults up 19 percent over the 1989 level and 66 percent over the 1984 experience.

Rate

Down less than 1 percent from the 1992 rate, there were 440 reported victims of aggravated assault for every 100,000 people nationwide in 1993. The rate was 15 percent higher than in 1989 and 52 percent above the 1984 rate.

Higher than the national average, the rate in metropolitan areas was 486 per 100,000 in 1993. Cities outside metropolitan areas experienced a rate of 389, and rural counties, a rate of 176.

Regionally, the aggravated assault rates ranged from 510 per 100,000 people in the South to 348 per 100,000 in the Midwest. Compared to 1992, 1993 aggravated assault rates were down 1 percent in the Northeast and West and less than 1 percent in the South. Rates in the Midwest showed a less than 1-percent increase.

Nature

In 1993, 31 percent of the aggravated assaults were committed with blunt objects or other dangerous weapons. Of the remaining weapon categories, personal weapons such as hands, fists, and feet were used in 26 percent of the offenses; firearms in 25 percent; and knives or cutting instruments in the remainder.

From 1992 to 1993, assaults with knives or cutting instruments fell 1 percent and those with personal weapons (hands, fists, and feet) declined 3 percent. Those involving blunt objects or other dangerous weapons showed virtually no change. Similar to the murder experience, those with firearms increased 5 percent.

Aggravated Assault, Type of Weapons Used, 1993
[Percent distribution by region]

Region	Total all weapons[1]	Firearms	Knives or cutting instruments	Other weapons (clubs, blunt objects, etc.)	Personal weapons
Total	100.0	25.1	17.6	31.0	26.3
Northeastern States	100.0	17.2	21.1	32.3	29.4
Midwestern States	100.0	28.2	16.8	31.7	23.3
Southern States	100.0	26.8	18.5	31.2	23.5
Western States	100.0	24.7	13.6	27.9	33.8

[1]Because of rounding, percentages may not add to totals.

BURGLARY

DEFINITION

The Uniform Crime Reporting Program defines burglary as the unlawful entry of a structure to commit a felony or theft. The use of force to gain entry is not required to classify an offense as burglary.

<table>
<tr><td colspan="3" align="center">— TREND —</td></tr>
</table>

Year	Number of offenses	Rate per 100,000 inhabitants
1992	2,979,884	1,168.2
1993	2,834,808	1,099.2
Percent change	−4.9	−5.9

Volume

An estimated 2,834,808 burglaries occurred in the United States during 1993. These offenses accounted for 20 percent of the Crime Index total and 23 percent of the property crimes.

233

Distribution figures for the regions showed the highest burglary volume occurred in the most populous Southern States, accounting for 41 percent of the total. The Western States followed with 24 percent, the Midwestern States with 19 percent, and the Northeastern States with 16 percent.

In 1993, the greatest number of burglaries was recorded during December, while the lowest count was reported in February.

Burglary by Month, 1989-1993
[Percent distribution]

Months	1989	1990	1991	1992	1993
January	8.8	8.8	8.1	8.6	8.3
February	7.3	7.5	7.3	7.7	6.9
March	8.2	8.1	8.1	8.2	8.2
April	7.7	7.8	7.9	7.8	7.7
May	8.4	8.1	8.3	8.2	8.0
June	8.3	7.9	8.2	8.1	8.4
July	9.2	8.9	9.2	9.0	9.0
August	9.3	9.0	9.2	9.0	9.1
September	8.6	8.3	8.6	8.4	8.5
October	8.5	8.5	8.6	8.3	8.4
November	8.1	8.3	8.0	8.2	8.1
December	7.8	8.7	8.6	8.3	9.3

Nationwide, the burglary volume dropped 5 percent in 1993 from the 1992 total. By population group, decreases were registered in all city groupings; the largest decrease was in cities with populations of 250,000 and over, which showed a 7-percent decline.

Geographically, all four regions of the United States reported decreases in burglary volumes during 1993 as compared to 1992. Both the Northeastern States and the Midwestern States experienced 6-percent declines. The Southern States showed a 5-percent decrease; and the Western States reported the smallest change, a 2-percent decline.

Longer term national trends show burglary down 11 percent from the 1989 volume and 5 percent below the 1984 level.

Rate

A burglary rate of 1,099 per 100,000 inhabitants was registered nationwide in 1993. The rate was 6 percent lower than in 1992 and 13 percent below the 1984 rate. In 1993, for every 100,000 in population, the rate was 1,182 in the metropolitan areas, 993 in the cities outside metropolitan areas, and 633 in the rural counties.

Regionally, the burglary rate was 1,286 in the Southern States, 1,221 in the Western States, 900 in the Midwestern States, and 878 in the Northeastern States. A comparison of 1992 and 1993 rates showed decreases of 7 percent in the South and Midwest, 6 percent in the Northeast, and 4 percent in the West.

Nature

Two of every 3 burglaries in 1993 were residential in nature. Sixty-eight percent of all burglaries involved forcible entry, 24 percent were unlawful entries (without force), and the remainder were forcible entry attempts. Offenses for which time of occurrence was reported were evenly divided between day and night.

Burglary victims suffered losses estimated at $3.4 billion in 1993, and the average dollar loss per burglary was $1,185. The average loss for residential offenses was $1,189, while for nonresidential property, it was $1,179. Compared to 1992, the 1993 average loss for both residential and nonresidential property declined. Both residential and nonresidential burglary volumes also showed declines from 1992 to 1993, 4 and 6 percent, respectively.

Law Enforcement Response

Nationwide in 1993, a 13-percent clearance rate was recorded for burglaries brought to the attention of law enforcement agencies across the country. Geographically, in the South, the clearance rate was 15 percent; in the Northeast, 13 percent; in the West, 12 percent; and in the Midwest, 11 percent.

Rural county law enforcement agencies cleared 16 percent of the burglaries in their jurisdictions. Agencies in suburban counties cleared 14 percent, and those in cities, 13 percent.

LARCENY-THEFT

DEFINITION

Larceny-theft is the unlawful taking, carrying, leading, or riding away of property from the possession or constructive possession of another. It includes crimes such as shoplifting, pocket-picking, purse-snatching, thefts from motor vehicles, thefts of motor vehicle parts and accessories, bicycle thefts, etc., in which no use of force, violence, or fraud occurs.

TREND

Year	Number of offenses	Rate per 100,000 inhabitants
1992	7,915,199	3,103.0
1993	7,820,909	3,032.4
Percent change	−1.2	−2.3

Volume

Larceny-theft, estimated at 7.8 million offenses during 1993, comprised 55 percent of the Crime Index total and 64 percent of the property crimes. Similar to the experience in previous years, larceny-thefts were recorded most often during August and least frequently in February.

When viewed geographically, the Southern States, the most populous region, recorded 38 percent of the larceny-theft total. The Western States recorded 24 percent; the Midwestern States, 22 percent; and the Northeastern States, 15 percent.

Compared to 1992, the 1993 volume of larceny-thefts decreased 1 percent in the Nation and in rural and suburban counties and 2 percent in all cities collectively. Similar

Larceny-Theft by Month, 1989-1993
[Percent distribution]

Months	1989	1990	1991	1992	1993
January	8.0	8.2	7.8	8.2	7.7
February	7.2	7.4	7.5	7.8	6.8
March	8.2	8.2	8.2	8.3	8.0
April	8.0	7.9	8.1	8.1	8.0
May	8.6	8.3	8.4	8.2	8.2
June	8.7	8.3	8.5	8.5	8.7
July	9.2	8.9	9.2	9.1	9.2
August	9.5	9.1	9.3	9.1	9.3
September	8.3	8.2	8.3	8.4	8.3
October	8.6	8.7	8.7	8.6	8.6
November	8.0	8.1	7.9	7.9	8.0
December	7.7	8.4	8.2	8.0	9.1

to the national experience, city population groups ranging from 50,000 to 999,999 inhabitants experienced l-percent declines in their 1993 larceny volumes; the remaining population groups recorded 2-percent decreases.

Regionally, larceny volumes dropped in the Northeast, 3 percent; in the Midwest, 2 percent; and in the West, 1 percent. The number of larceny-thefts in the South showed no change.

The 5- and 10-year national trends indicated larceny was down 1 percent when compared to the 1989 total but up 19 percent above the 1984 level.

Rate

The 1993 larceny-theft rate was 3,032 per 100,000 U.S. inhabitants. The rate was 2 percent lower than in 1992 and 4 percent under the 1989 level. When compared to 1984, the rate showed an increase of 9 percent. The 1993 rate was 3,289 per 100,000 inhabitants of metropolitan areas; 3,582 per 100,000 population in cities outside metropolitan areas; and 1,006 per 100,000 people in the rural counties.

For all regions, the larceny-theft rate per 100,000 inhabitants declined from 1992 levels. The rate in the Northeast was 2,358, down 4 percent; the rates of 3,360 in the West and 2,850 in the Midwest dropped 3 percent; and the South's rate of 3,339 was down 1 percent.

Nature

During 1993, the average value of property stolen due to larceny-theft was $504, up from $483 in 1992. When the average value was applied to the estimated number of larceny-thefts, the loss to victims nationally was $3.9 billion for the year. This estimated dollar loss is considered conservative since many offenses in the larceny category, particularly if the value of the stolen goods is small, never come to law enforcement attention. Losses in 23 percent of the thefts reported to law enforcement in 1993 ranged from $50 to $200, while in 37 percent, they were over $200.

Losses of goods and property reported stolen as a result of pocket-picking averaged $411; purse-snatching, $341; and shoplifting, $109. Thefts from buildings resulted in an average loss of $831; from motor vehicles, $531; and from coin-operated machines, $208. The average value loss due to

thefts of motor vehicle accessories was $303 and for thefts of bicycles, $241.

Thefts of motor vehicle parts, accessories, and contents made up the largest portion of reported larcenies—37 percent. Also contributing to the high volume of thefts were shoplifting, accounting for 15 percent; thefts from buildings, 13 percent; and bicycle thefts, 6 percent. The remainder was distributed among pocket-picking, purse-snatching, thefts from coin-operated machines, and all other types of larceny-thefts.

Larceny Analysis by Region, 1993
[Percent distribution]

	United States Total	North-eastern States	Mid-western States	Southern States	Western States
Total[1]	100.0	100.0	100.0	100.0	100.0
Pocket-picking	.9	3.3	.4	.5	.5
Purse-snatching	.9	1.7	.9	.7	.6
Shoplifting	15.4	13.5	14.1	15.0	17.8
From motor vehicles (except accessories)	23.4	21.9	20.4	21.0	29.8
Motor vehicle accessories	13.9	13.8	15.3	15.1	11.3
Bicycles	6.1	7.0	6.0	5.2	7.1
From buildings	13.2	18.5	15.5	10.7	12.1
From coin-operated machines	.8	1.1	.7	.7	.7
All others	25.5	19.1	26.7	31.0	20.1

[1]Because of rounding, percentages may not add to totals.

MOTOR VEHICLE THEFT

DEFINITION

Defined as the theft or attempted theft of a motor vehicle, this offense category includes the stealing of automobiles, trucks, buses, motorcycles, motorscooters, snowmobiles, etc.

TREND

Year	Number of offenses	Rate per 100,000 inhabitants
1992	1,610,834	631.5
1993	1,561,047	605.3
Percent change	−3.1	−4.1

Volume

An estimated total of 1,561,047 thefts of motor vehicles occurred in the United States during 1993. These offenses comprised 13 percent of all property crimes. The regional distribution of motor vehicle thefts showed 32 percent of the volume was in the Southern States, 29 percent in the Western States, 22 percent in the Northeastern States, and 18 percent in the Midwestern States.

The 1993 monthly figures show that the greatest numbers of motor vehicle thefts were recorded during the months of July and August, while the lowest count was in February.

235

Motor Vehicle Theft by Month, 1989-1993

[Percent distribution]

Months	1989	1990	1991	1992	1993
January	8.3	8.5	8.3	8.8	8.5
February	7.3	7.6	7.5	7.9	7.3
March	8.1	8.4	8.2	8.2	8.2
April	7.5	7.9	7.8	7.8	7.8
May	8.0	8.1	8.1	8.1	7.9
June	8.2	8.1	8.2	8.2	8.4
July	8.8	8.8	8.7	8.8	8.9
August	9.0	8.8	8.9	8.9	8.9
September	8.5	8.4	8.3	8.2	8.4
October	9.0	8.8	8.7	8.6	8.6
November	8.7	8.3	8.5	8.3	8.3
December	8.5	8.4	8.8	8.2	8.8

The number of motor vehicle thefts nationally fell 3 percent from 1992 to 1993. The largest decline was experienced in cities with populations of 1 million or more, 8 percent. During the same period, increases occurred in the suburban counties, 1 percent, and the rural counties, 2 percent.

Geographically, three regions experienced motor vehicle theft decreases, while the Western Region showed a 1-percent increase.

Rate

The 1993 national motor vehicle theft rate — 605 per 100,000 people — was 4 percent lower than in 1992 and 1989. The 1993 rate was 38 percent above the 1984 rate.

For every 100,000 inhabitants living in MSAs, there were 721 motor vehicle thefts reported in 1993. The rate in cities outside metropolitan areas was 224 and in rural counties, 110. As in previous years, the highest rates were in the Nation's most heavily populated municipalities, indicating that this offense is primarily a large-city problem. For every 100,000 inhabitants in cities with populations over 250,000,

the 1993 motor vehicle theft rate was 1,509. The Nation's smallest cities, those with fewer than 10,000 inhabitants, recorded a rate of 240 per 100,000.

Among the regions, the motor vehicle theft rates ranged from 794 per 100,000 people in the Western States to 454 in the Midwestern States. The Northeastern States' rate was 664 and the Southern States' rate, 556. All regions registered rate decreases from 1992 to 1993.

An estimated average of 1 of every 126 registered motor vehicles was stolen nationwide during 1993. Regionally, this rate was greatest in the Northeast and West where 1 of every 98 motor vehicles registered was stolen. The other two regions reported lesser rates — 1 per 141 in the South and 1 per 178 in the Midwest.

Nature

During 1993, the estimated value of motor vehicles stolen nationwide was nearly $7.5 billion. At the time of theft, the average value per vehicle stolen was $4,808. The recovery percentage for the value of vehicles stolen was higher than for any other property type. Relating the value of vehicles stolen to the value of those recovered resulted in a 62-percent recovery rate for 1993.

Seventy-nine percent of all motor vehicles reported stolen during the year were automobiles, 15 percent were trucks or buses, and the remainder were other types.

Motor Vehicle Theft, 1993

[Percent distribution by region]

Region	Total[1]	Autos	Trucks and buses	Other vehicles
Total[1]	100.0	79.2	15.4	5.5
Northeastern States	100.0	92.3	4.6	3.2
Midwestern States	100.0	82.1	11.8	6.1
Southern States	100.0	75.2	18.0	6.8
Western States	100.0	72.5	22.0	5.5

[1]Because of rounding, percentages may not add to totals.

Glossary

Abet: To encourage another to commit a crime.

Accessory: One who harbors, assists, or protects another person, although he or she knows that person has committed or will commit a crime.

Accomplice: One who knowingly and voluntarily aids another in committing a criminal offense.

Acquit: To free a person legally from an accusation of criminal guilt.

Adjudicatory hearing: The fact-finding process wherein the court determines whether or not there is sufficient evidence to sustain the allegations in a petition.

Admissible: Capable of being admitted; in a trial, such evidence as the judge allows to be introduced into the proceeding.

Affirmance: A pronouncement by a higher court that the case in question was rightly decided by the lower court from which the case was appealed.

Affirmation: Positive declaration or assertion that the witness will tell the truth; not made under oath.

Alias: Any name by which one is known other than his or her true name.

Alibi: A type of defense in a criminal prosecution that proves the accused could not have committed the crime with which he or she is charged, since evidence offered shows the accused was in another place at the time the crime was committed.

Allegation: An assertion of what a party to an action expects to prove.

American Bar Association (ABA): A professional association, comprising attorneys who have been admitted to the bar in any of the 50 states, and a registered lobby.

American Civil Liberties Union (ACLU): Founded in 1920 with the purpose of defending the individual's rights as guaranteed by the U.S. Constitution.

Amnesty: A class or group pardon.

Annulment: The act, by competent authority, of canceling, making void, or depriving of all force.

Appeal: A case carried to a higher court to ask that the decision of the lower court, in which the case originated, be altered or overruled completely.

Appellate court: A court that has jurisdiction to hear cases on appeal; not a trial court.

Arbitrator: The person chosen by parties in a controversy to settle their differences; private judges.

Arraignment: The appearance before the court of a person charged with a crime. He or she is advised of the charges, bail is set, and a plea of "guilty" or "not guilty" is entered.

Arrest: The legal detainment of a person to answer for criminal charges or civil demands.

Autopsy: A postmortem examination of a human body to determine the cause of death.

Bail: Property (usually money) deposited with a court in exchange for the release of a person in custody to assure later appearance.

Bail bond: An obligation signed by the accused and his or her sureties, that ensures his or her presence in court.

Bailiff: An officer of the court who is responsible for keeping order in the court and protecting the security of jury deliberations and court property.

Bench warrant: An order by the court for the apprehension and arrest of a defendant or other person who has failed to appear when so ordered.

Bill of Rights: The first ten amendments to the U.S. Constitution that state certain fundamental rights and privileges that are guaranteed to the people against infringement by the government.

Biocriminology: A relatively new branch of criminology that attempts to explain criminal behavior by referring to biological factors which predispose some individuals to commit criminal acts. *See also* Criminal biology.

Blue laws: Laws in some jurisdictions prohibiting sales or merchandise, athletic contests, and the sale of alcoholic beverages on Sundays.

Booking: A law-enforcement or correctional process officially recording an entry-into-detention after arrest and identifying the person, place, time, reason for the arrest, and the arresting authority.

Breathalizer: A commercial device to test the breath of a suspected drinker and determine that person's blood-alcohol content.

Brief: A summary of the law relating to a case, prepared by the attorneys for both parties and given to the judge.

Bug: To plant a sound sensor or to tap a communication line for the purpose of surreptitious listening or audio monitoring.

Burden of proof: Duty of establishing the existence of fact in a trial.

Calendar: A list of cases to be heard in a trial court, on a specific day, and containing the title of the case, the lawyers involved, and the index number.

Capital crime: Any crime that may be punishable by death or imprisonment for life.

Career criminal: A person having a past record of multiple arrests or convictions for crimes of varying degrees of seriousness. Such criminals are often described as chronic, habitual, repeat, serious, high-rate, or professional offenders.

Case: At the level of police or prosecutorial investigation, a set of circumstances under investigation involving one or more persons.

Case law: Judicial precedent generated as a byproduct of the decisions that courts have made to resolve unique disputes. Case law concerns concrete facts, as distinguished from statutes and constitutions, which are written in the abstract.

Change of venue: The removal of a trial from one jurisdiction to another in order to avoid local prejudice.

Charge: In criminal law, the accusation made against a person. It also refers to the judge's instruction to the jury on legal points.

Circumstantial evidence: Indirect evidence; evidence from which a fact can be reasonably inferred, although not directly proven.

Clemency: The doctrine under which executive or legislative action reduces the severity of or waives legal punishment of one or more individuals, or an individual exempted from prosecution for certain actions.

Code: A compilation, compendium, or revision of laws, arranged into chapters, having a table of contents and index, and promulgated by legislative authority. Criminal code; penal code.

Coercion: The use of force to compel performance of an action; The application of sanctions or the use of force by government to compel observance of law or public policy.

Common law: Judge-made law to assist courts through decision making with traditions, customs, and usage of previous court decisions.

Commutation: A reduction of a sentence originally prescribed by a court.

Complainant: The victim of a crime who brings the facts to the attention of the authorities.

Complaint: Any accusation that a person committed a crime that has originated or been received by a law enforcement agency or court.

Confession: A statement by a person who admits violation of the law.

Confiscation: Government seizure of private property without compensation to the owner.

Conspiracy: An agreement between two or more persons to plan for the purpose of committing a crime or any unlawful act or a lawful act by unlawful or criminal means.

Contempt of court: Intentionally obstructing a court in the administration of justice, acting in a way calculated to lessen its authority or dignity, or failing to obey its lawful order.

Continuance: Postponement or adjournment of a trial granted by the judge, either to a later date or indefinitely.

Contraband: Goods, the possession of which is illegal.

Conviction: A finding by the jury (or by the trial judge in cases tried without a jury) that the accused is guilty of a crime.

Corporal punishment: Physical punishment.

Corpus delicti **(Lat.):** The objective proof that a crime has been committed as distinguished from an accidental death, injury, or loss.

Corrections: Area of criminal justice dealing with convicted offenders in jails, prisons; on probation or parole.

Corroborating evidence: Supplementary evidence that tends to strengthen or confirm other evidence given previously.

Crime: An act injurious to the public, that is prohibited and punishable by law.

Crime Index: A set of numbers indicating the volume, fluctuation, and distribution of crimes reported to local law enforcement agencies for the United States as a whole.

Crime of passion: An unpremeditated murder or assault committed under circumstances of great anger, jealousy, or other emotional stress.

Criminal biology: The scientific study of the relation of hereditary physical traits to criminal character, that is, to innate tendencies to commit crime in general or crimes of any particular type. *See also* Biocriminology.

Criminal insanity: Lack of mental capacity to do or refrain from doing a criminal act; inability to distinguish right from wrong.

Criminal intent: The intent to commit and act, the results of which are a crime or violation of the law.

Criminalistics: Crime laboratory procedures.

Criminology: The scientific study of crime, criminals, corrections, and the operation of the system of criminal justice.

Cross examination: The questioning of a witness by the party who did not produce the witness.

Culpable: At fault or responsible, but not necessarily criminal.

Defamation: Intentional causing, or attempting to cause, damage to the reputation of another by communicating false or distorted information about his or her actions, motives, or character.

Defendant: The person who is being prosecuted.

Deliberation: The action of a jury to determine the guilt or innocence, or the sentence, of a defendant.

Demurrer: Plea for dismissal of a suit on the grounds that, even if true, the statements of the opposition are insufficient to sustain the claim.

Deposition: Sworn testimony obtained outside, rather than in, court.

Deterrence: A theory that swift and sure punishment will discourage others from similar illegal acts.

Dilatory: Law term that describes activity for the purpose of causing a delay or to gain time or postpone a decision.

Direct evidence: Testimony or other proof that expressly or straightforwardly proves the existence of fact.

Direct examination: The first questioning of witnesses by the party who calls them.

Directed verdict: An order or verdict pronounced by a judge during the trial of a criminal case in which the evidence presented by the prosecution clearly fails to show the guilt of the accused.

District attorney: A locally elected state official who represents the state in bringing indictments and prosecuting criminal cases.

Docket: The formal record of court proceedings.

Double jeopardy: To be prosecuted twice for the same offense.

Due process model: A philosophy of criminal justice based on the assumption that an individual is presumed innocent until proven guilty.

Due process of law: A clause in the Fifth and Fourteenth Amendments ensuring that laws are reasonable and that they are applied in a fair and equal manner.

Embracery: An attempt to influence a jury, or a member thereof, in their verdict by any improper means.

Entrapment: Inducing an individual to commit a crime he or she did not contemplate, for the sole purpose of instituting a criminal prosecution against the offender.

Evidence: All the means used to prove or disprove the fact at issue. *See also Corpus delicti.*

Ex post facto **(Lat.):** After the fact. An *ex post facto* law is a criminal law that makes an act unlawful although it was committed prior to the passage of that law. *See also* Grandfather clause.

Exception: A formal objection to the action of the court during a trial. The indication is that the excepting party will seek to reverse the court's actions at some future proceeding.

Exclusionary rule: Legal prohibitions against government prosecution using evidence illegally obtained.

Expert evidence: Testimony by one qualified to speak authoritatively on technical matters because of her or his special training of skill.

Extradition: The surrender by one state to another of an individual accused of a crime.

False arrest: Any unlawful physical restraint of another's freedom of movement; unlawful arrest.

Felony: A criminal offense punishable by death or imprisonment in a penitentiary.

Forensic: Relating to the court. Forensic medicine would refer to legal medicine that applies anatomy, pathology, toxicology, chemistry, and other fields of science in expert testimony in court cases or hearings.

Grandfather clause: A clause attempting to preserve the rights of firms in operation before enactment of a law by exempting these firms from certain provisions of that law. *See also Ex post facto.*

Grand jury: A group of 12 to 23 citizens of a county who examine evidence against the person suspected of a crime and hand down an indictment if there is sufficient evidence. *See also* Petit jury.

Habeas corpus **(Lat.):** A legal device to challenge the detention of a person taken into custody. An individual in custody may demand an evidentiary hearing before a judge to examine the legality of the detention.

Hearsay: Evidence that a witness has learned through others.

Homicide: The killing of a human being; may be murder, negligent or nonnegligent manslaughter, or excusable or justifiable homicide.

Hung jury: A jury which, after long deliberation, is so irreconcilably divided in opinion that it is unable to reach a verdict.

Impanel: The process of selecting the jury that is to try a case.

Imprisonment: A sentence imposed upon the conviction of a crime; the deprivation of liberty in a penal institution; incarceration.

In camera **(Lat.):** A case heard when the doors of the court are closed and only persons concerned in the case are admitted.

Indemnification: Compensation for loss or damage sustained because of improper or illegal action by a public authority.

Indictment: The document prepared by a prosecutor and approved by the grand jury that charges a certain person with a specific crime or crimes for which that person is later to be tried in court.

Injunction: An order by a court prohibiting a defendant from committing an act, or commanding an act be done.

Inquest: A legal inquiry to establish some question of fact; specifically, and inquiry by a coroner and jury into a person's death where accident, foul play, or violence is suspected as the cause.

Instanter: A subpoena issued for the appearance of a hostile witness or person who has failed to appear in answer to a previous subpoena and authorizing a law enforcement officer to bring that person to the court.

Interpol (International Criminal Police Commission): A clearing house for international exchanges of information consisting of a consortium of 126 countries.

Jeopardy: The danger of conviction and punishment that a defendant faces in a criminal trial.

Judge: An officer who presides over and administers the law in a court of justice.

Judicial notice: The rule that a court will accept certain things as common knowledge without proof.

Judicial process: The procedures taken by a court in deciding cases or resolving legal controversies.

Jurisdiction: The territory, subject matter, or persons over which lawful authority may be exercised by a court or other justice agency, as determined by statute or constitution.

Jury: A certain number of persons who are sworn to examine the evidence and determine the truth on the basis of that evidence.

Jury, hung: A trial jury which, after exhaustive deliberations, cannot agree on a unanimous verdict, necessitating an mistrial and a subsequent retrial.

Justice of the peace: A subordinate magistrate, usually without formal legal training, empowered to try petty civil and criminal cases and, in some states, to conduct preliminary hearings for persons accused of a crime, and to fix bail for appearance in court.

Juvenile delinquent: A boy or girl who has not reached the age of criminal liability (varies from state to state) and who commits and act which would be a misdemeanor or felony if he or she were an adult. Delinquents are tried in *Juvenile* Court and confined to separate facilities.

Law Enforcement Agency: A federal, state, or local criminal justice agency or identifiable subunit whose principal functions are the prevention, detection, and investigation of crime and the apprehension of alleged offenders.

Libel and slander: Printed and spoken defamation of character, respectively, or a person or an institution. In a slander action, it is usually necessary to prove specific damages caused by spoken words to recover, but in a case of libel, the damage is assumed to have occurred by publication.

Lie detector: An instrument that measures certain physiological reactions of the human body from which a trained operator may determine whether the subject is telling the truth or lies; polygraph; psychological stress evaluator.

Litigation: A judicial controversy; a contest in a court of justice for the purpose of enforcing a right; any controversy that must be decided upon evidence.

Mala in se **(Lat.):** Evil in itself. Acts that are make crimes because they are, by their nature evil and morally wrong.

Mala fides **(Lat.):** Bad faith, as opposed to *bona fides,* or good faith.

Mala priohibita **(Lat.):** Evil because they are prohibited. Acts that are not wrong in themselves but which, to protect the general welfare, are make crimes by statute.

Malfeasance: The act of a public officer in committing a crime relating to his official duties or powers. Accepting or demanding a bribe.

Malice: An evil intent to vex, annoy, or injure another; intentional evil.

Mandatory sentences: A statutory requirement that a certain penalty shall be set and carried out in all cases upon conviction for a specified offense or series of offenses.

Martial Law: Refers to control of civilian populations by a military commander.

Mediation: Nonbinding third-party intervention in the collective bargaining process.

Mens rea **(Lat.):** Criminal intent.

Miranda Rights: Set of rights that a person accused or suspected of having committed a specific offense has during interrogation and of which he or she must be informed prior to questioning, as stated by the Supreme Court in deciding *Miranda v. Arizona* in 1966 and related cases.

Misdemeanor: Any crime not a felony. Usually, a crime punishable by a fine or imprisonment in the county or other local jail.

Misprison: Failing to reveal a crime.

Mistrial: A trial discontinued before reaching a verdict because of some procedural defect or impediment.

Modus operandi: A characteristic pattern of behavior repeated in a series of offenses that coincides with the pattern evidenced by a particular person or group of persons.

Motion: An oral or written request made to a court at any time before, during, or after court proceedings, asking the court to make a specified finding, decision, or order.

Motive: The reason for committing a crime.

Municipal court: A minor court authorized by municipal charter or state law to enforce local ordinances and exercise the criminal and civil jurisdiction of the peace.

Narc: A widely used slang term for any local or federal law enforcement officer whose duties are focused on preventing or controlling traffic in and the use of illegal drugs.

Negligent: Culpably careless; acting without the due care required by the circumstances.

Neolombrosians: Criminologists who emphasize psychopathological states as causes of crime.

No bill: A phrase used by a Grand jury when they fail to indict.

Nolle prosequi **(Lat.):** A prosecutor's decision not to initiate or continue prosecution.

Nolo contendre **(Lat., lit.):** A pleading, usually used by a defendant in a criminal case, that literally means "I will not contest."

Notary public: A public officer authorized to authenticate and certify documents such as seeds, contracts, and affidavits with his or her signature and seal.

Null: Of no legal or binding force.

Obiter dictum **(Lat.):** A belief or opinion included by a judge in his or her decision in a case.

Objection: The act of taking exception to some statement or procedure in a trial. Used to call the court's attention to some improper evidence or procedure.

Opinion evidence: A witness' belief or opinion about a fact in dispute, as distinguished from personal knowledge of the fact.

Ordinance: A law enacted by the city or municipal government.

Organized crime: An organized, continuing criminal conspiracy that engages in crime as business (e.g., loan sharking, illegal gambling, prostitution, extortion, etc.).

Original jurisdiction: The authority of a court to hear and determine a lawsuit when it is initiated.

Overt act: An open or physical act done to further a plan, conspiracy, or intent, as opposed to a thought or mere intention.

Paralegals: Employees, also know as legal assistants, of law firms, who assist attorneys in the delivery of legal services.

Pardon: There are two kinds of pardons of offenses: the absolute pardon, which fully restores to the individual all rights and privileges of a citizen, setting aside a conviction and penalty, and the conditional pardon, which requires a condition to be met before the pardon is officially granted.

Parole: A conditional, supervised release from prison prior to expiration of sentence.

Penal code: Criminal codes, the purpose of which is to define what acts shall be punished as crimes.

Penology: The study of punishment and corrections.

Peremptory challenge: In the selection of jurors, challenges made by either side to certain jurors without assigning any reason, and which the court must allow.

Perjury: The legal offense of deliberately testifying falsely under oath about a material fact.

Perpetrator: The chief actor in the commission of a crime, that is, the person who directly commits the criminal act.

Petit jury: The ordinary jury composed of 12 persons who hear criminal cases and determines guilt or innocence of the accused. *See also* Grand jury.

Plaintiff: A person who initiates a court action.

Plea-bargaining: A negotiation between the defense attorney and the prosecutor in which the defendant receives a reduced penalty in return for a plea of "guilty."

Police power: The authority to legislate for the protection of the health, morals, safety and welfare of the people.

Postmortem: After death. Commonly applied to an examination of a dead body. *See also* Autopsy.

Precedent: Decision by a court that may serve as an example or authority for similar cases in the future.

Preliminary hearing: The proceeding in front of a lower court to determine if there is sufficient evidence for submitting a felony case to the grand jury.

Premeditation: A design to commit a crime or commit some other act before it is done.

Presumption of fact: An inference as to the truth or falsity of any proposition or fact, make in the absence of actual certainty of its truth or falsity or until such certainty can be attained.

Presumption of innocence: The defendant is presumed to be innocent and the burden is on the state to prove his or her guilt beyond a reasonable doubt.

Presumption of law: A rule of law that courts and judges must draw a particular inference from a particular fact or evidence, unless the inference can be disproved.

Probable cause: A set of facts and circumstances that would induce a reasonably intelligent and prudent person to believe that a particular person had committed a specific crime; reasonable grounds to make or believe an accusation.

Probation: A penalty placing a convicted person under the supervision of a probation officer for a stated time, instead or being confined.

Prosecutor: One who initiates a criminal prosecution against an accused. One who acts as a trial attorney for the governments as the representative of the people.

Public defender: An attorney appointed by a court to represent individuals in criminal proceedings who do not have the resources to hire their own defense council.

Rap sheet: Popularized acronym for record of arrest and prosecution.

Reasonable doubt: That state of mind of jurors when they do not feel a moral certainty about the truth of the charge and when the evidence does no exclude every other reasonable hypothesis except that the defendant is guilty as charged.

Rebutting evidence: When the defense has produced new evidence that the prosecution has not dealt with, the court, at its discretion, may allow the prosecution to give evidence in reply to rebut or contradict it.

Recidivism: The repetition of criminal behavior.

Repeal: The abrogation of a law by the enacting body, either by express declaration or implication by the passage of a later act whose provisions contradict those of the earlier law.

Reprieve: The temporary postponement of the execution of a sentence.

Restitution: A court requirement that an alleged or convicted offender pay money or provide services to the victim of the crime or provide services to the community.

Restraining order: An order, issued by a court of competent jurisdiction, forbidding a named person, or a class of persons, from doing specified acts.

Retribution: A concept that implies that payment of a debt to society and thus the expiation of one's offense. It was codified in the biblical injunction, "and eye for an eye, a tooth for a tooth."

Sanction: A legal penalty assessed for the violation of law. The term also include social methods of obtaining compliance, such as peer pressure and public opinion.

Search warrant: A written order, issued by judicial authority in the name of the state, directing a law enforcement officer to search for personal property and, if found, to bring it before the court.

Selective enforcement: The deploying of police personnel in ways to cope most effectively with existing or anticipated problems.

Self-incrimination: In constitutional terms, the process of becoming involved in or charged with a crime by one's own testimony.

Sentence: The penalty imposed by a court on a person convicted of a crime; the court judgment specifying the penalty; and any disposition of a defendant resulting from a conviction, including the court decision to suspend execution of a sentence.

Small claims court: A special court that provides expeditious, informal, and inexpensive adjudication of small contractual claims. In most jurisdictions, attorneys are not permitted for cases, and claims are limited to a specific amount.

***Stare decisis* (Lat.):** To abide by decided cases. The doctrine that once a court has laid down a principle of laws as applicable to certain facts, it will apply it to all future cases when the facts are substantially the same.

State's attorney: An officer, usually locally elected within a county, who represents the state in securing indictments and in prosecuting criminal cases.

State's evidence: Testimony by a participant in the commission of a crime that incriminates others involved, given under the promise of immunity.

Status offense: An act that is declared by statute to be an offense, but only when committed or engaged in by a juvenile, and that can be adjudicated only by a juvenile court.

Statute: A Law enacted by, or with the authority of, a legislature.

Statute of limitations: A term applied to numerous statutes that set a limit on the length of time that may elapse between an event giving rise to a cause of action and the commencement of a suit to enforce that cause.

Stay: A halting of a judicial proceeding by a court order.

Sting operation: The typical sting involves using various undercover methods to control crime.

Subpoena: A court order requiring a witness to attend and testify as a witness in a court proceeding.

Subpoena *duces tecum:* A court order requiring a witness to bring all books, documents, and papers that might affect the outcome of the proceedings.

Summons: A written order issued by a judicial officer requiring a person accused of a criminal offense to appear in a designated court at a specified time to answer the charge(s).

Superior court: A court of record or general trial court, superior to a justice of the peace or magistrate's court. In some states, an intermediate court between the general trial court and the highest appellate court.

Supreme court, state: Usually the highest court in the state judicial system.

Supreme court, U.S.: Heads the judicial branch of the American government and is the nation's highest law court.

Suspect: An adult or juvenile considered by a criminal agency to be one who may have committed a specific criminal offense but who has not yet been arrested or charged.

Testimony: Evidence given by a competent witness, under oath, as distinguished from evidence from writings and other sources.

Tort: The breach of a duty to an individual that results in damage to him or her, for which one may be sued in civil court for damages. Crime, in contrast may be called the breach of duty to the public. Some actions may constitute both torts and crimes.

Uniform Crime Reports (U.C.R.): Annual statistical tabulation of "crimes known to the police" and "crimes cleared by arrest" published by the Federal Bureau of Investigation.

United States claims court: Established in 1982, it serves as the court of original and exclusive jurisdiction over claims brought against the federal government, except for tort claims, which are heard by district courts.

Untied States district courts: Trial courts with original jurisdiction over diversity-of-citizenship cases and cases arising under U.S. criminal, bankruptcy, admiralty, patent, copyright, and postal laws.

Venue: The locality in which a suit may be tried.

Verdict: The decision of a court.

Vice squad: A special detail of police agents, charged with raiding and closing houses of prostitution and gambling resorts.

Victim and Witness Protection Act of 1984: The federal VWP Act and state laws protect crime victims and witnesses against physical and verbal intimidation where such intimidation is designed to discourage reporting or crimes and participation in criminal trials.

Victimology: The study of the psychological and dynamic interrelationships between victims and offenders, with a view toward crime prevention.

Vigilante: An individual or member of a group who undertakes to enforce the law and/or maintain morals without legal authority.

***Voir dire* (Fr.):** The examination or questioning of prospective jurors in order to determine his or her qualifications to serve as a juror.

Warrant: A court order directing a police officer to arrest a named person or search a specific premise.

White-collar crime: Nonviolent crime for financial gain committed by means of deception by persons who use their special occupational skills and opportunities.

Witness: Anyone called to testify by either side in a trial. More broadly, a witness is anyone who has observed an event.

Work release (furlough programs): Change in prisoners' status to minimum custody with permission to work outside prison.

World court: Formally known as the International Court of Justice, it deals with disputes involving international law.

SOURCES

The Dictionary of Criminal Justice, Fourth edition, © 1994 by George E. Rush. Published by The Dushkin Publishing Group, Inc., Guilford, CT 06437.

Credits/Acknowledgments

Cover design by Charles Vitelli

1. Crime and Justice in America
Facing overview—Photo by Pamela Carley.

2. Victimology
Facing overview—Photo by Pamela Carley.

3. Police
Facing overview—United Nations photo.

4. The Judicial System
Facing overview—Dushkin Publishing Group/Brown & Benchmark Publishers photo.

5. Juvenile Justice
Facing overview—Photo by Dr. Zimbardo.

6. Punishment and Corrections
Facing overview—Dushkin Publishing Group/Brown & Benchmark Publishers photo.

PHOTOCOPY THIS PAGE!!!*

ANNUAL EDITIONS ARTICLE REVIEW FORM

■ NAME: _____ DATE: _____

■ TITLE AND NUMBER OF ARTICLE: _____

■ BRIEFLY STATE THE MAIN IDEA OF THIS ARTICLE: _____

_____

_____

_____

_____

■ LIST THREE IMPORTANT FACTS THAT THE AUTHOR USES TO SUPPORT THE MAIN IDEA:

_____

_____

_____

_____

_____

_____

■ WHAT INFORMATION OR IDEAS DISCUSSED IN THIS ARTICLE ARE ALSO DISCUSSED IN YOUR TEXTBOOK OR OTHER READING YOU HAVE DONE? LIST THE TEXTBOOK CHAPTERS AND PAGE NUMBERS:

_____

_____

_____

_____

_____

_____

■ LIST ANY EXAMPLES OF BIAS OR FAULTY REASONING THAT YOU FOUND IN THE ARTICLE:

_____

_____

_____

_____

■ LIST ANY NEW TERMS/CONCEPTS THAT WERE DISCUSSED IN THE ARTICLE AND WRITE A SHORT DEFINITION:

_____

_____

_____

_____

*Your instructor may require you to use this Annual Editions Article Review Form in any number of ways: for articles that are assigned, for extra credit, as a tool to assist in developing assigned papers, or simply for your own reference. Even if it is not required, we encourage you to photocopy and use this page; you'll find that reflecting on the articles will greatly enhance the information from your text.

ANNUAL EDITIONS: CRIMINAL JUSTICE 95/96

Article Rating Form

We Want Your Advice

Here is an opportunity for you to have direct input into the next revision of this volume. We would like you to rate each of the 42 articles listed below, using the following scale:

1. **Excellent: should definitely be retained**
2. **Above average: should probably be retained**
3. **Below average: should probably be deleted**
4. **Poor: should definitely be deleted**

Your ratings will play a vital part in the next revision. So please mail this prepaid form to us just as soon as you complete it.
Thanks for your help!

Annual Editions revisions depend on two major opinion sources: one is our Advisory Board, listed in the front of this volume, which works with us in scanning the thousands of articles published in the public press each year; the other is you—the person actually using the book. Please help us and the users of the next edition by completing the prepaid article rating form on this page and returning it to us. Thank you.

Rating	Article	Rating	Article
	1. An Overview of the Criminal Justice System		21. The Trials of the Public Defender
	2. What to Do About Crime		22. Why Lawyers Lie
	3. The Economics of Crime		23. Inside the Mind of the Juror
	4. Violence in America		24. Racial, Ethnic, and Gender Bias in the Courts: *What Progress Have We Made, and What Can Be Done?*
	5. Mob Tightens Secretive Style in Retreat from Prosecutors		25. Fault Lines
	6. Russian Gangsters in the United States		26. Jury Consultants: Boon or Bane?
	7. Drugs, Alcohol, and Violence: Joined at the Hip		27. Delinquency Cases in Juvenile Court, 1992
	8. Criminal Victimization in the United States, 1992		28. Their Crimes Don't Make Them Adults
	9. Crime's Toll on the U.S.: Fear, Despair, and Guns		29. A National Agenda for Children: On the Front Lines with Attorney General Janet Reno
	10. 'Til Death Do Us Part		30. Juvenile Judges Say: Time to Get Tough
	11. When Men Hit Women		31. Throw Away the Key
	12. Incest: A Chilling Report		32. Everyday School Violence: How Disorder Fuels It
	13. Murder Next Door		33. On the Front Lines: Interview with Judge David B. Mitchell
	14. Battered Women and the Criminal Justice System		34. American Killers Are Getting Younger
	15. Officers on the Edge		35. Probation's First 100 Years: Growth through Failure
	16. Police Work from a Woman's Perspective		36. Doing Soft Time
	17. Public Safety and Crime: Are Warrantless Searches for Guns in Public Housing Projects Justified?		37. Punishment and Prevention
			38. . . . And Throw Away the Key
	18. A LEN Interview with Professor Carl Klockars of the University of Delaware		39. Privatizing America's Prisons, Slowly
			40. Crime Takes on a Feminine Face
	19. Pepper Spray and In-Custody Deaths		41. Psychiatric Gulag or Wise Safekeeping?
	20. Abuse of Power in the Prosecutor's Office		42. 'This Man Has Expired'

(Continued on next page)

ABOUT YOU

Name_____ Date_____

Are you a teacher? ☐   Or student? ☐

Your School Name _____

Department _____

Address _____

City _____ State _____ Zip _____

School Telephone # _____

YOUR COMMENTS ARE IMPORTANT TO US!

Please fill in the following information:

For which course did you use this book? _____

Did you use a text with this Annual Edition? ☐ yes ☐ no

The title of the text? _____

What are your general reactions to the Annual Editions concept?

Have you read any particular articles recently that you think should be included in the next edition?

Are there any articles you feel should be replaced in the next edition? Why?

Are there other areas that you feel would utilize an Annual Edition?

May we contact you for editorial input?

May we quote you from above?

ANNUAL EDITIONS: CRIMINAL JUSTICE 95/96

BUSINESS REPLY MAIL

First Class   Permit No. 84   Guilford, CT

Postage will be paid by addressee

Dushkin Publishing Group/
Brown & Benchmark Publishers
Sluice Dock
DPG **Guilford, Connecticut 06437**

No Postage
Necessary
if Mailed
in the
United States